1995-96 BIG TEN CENTENNIAL MEN'S BASKETBALL GUIDE

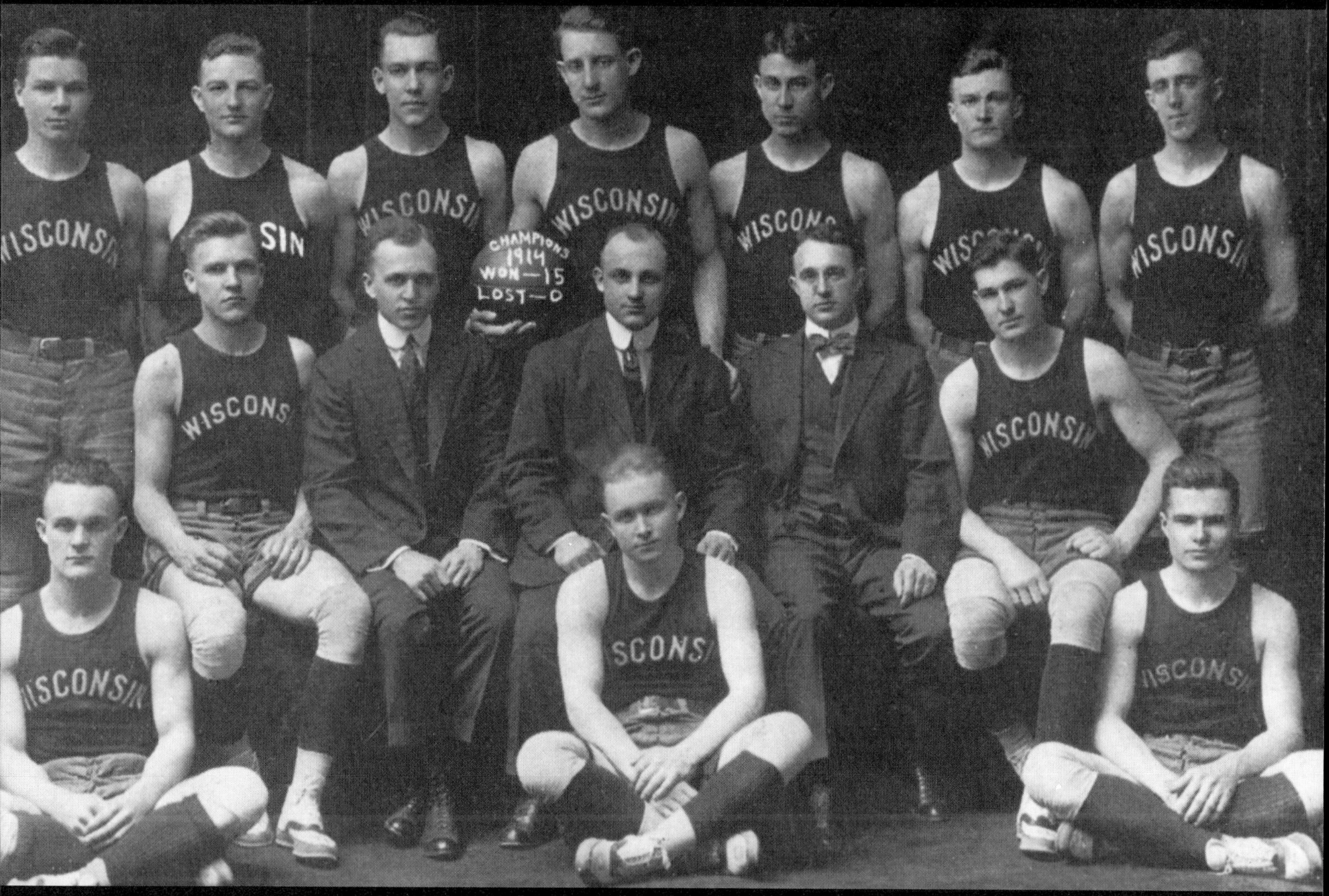

Wisconsin undefeated Big Ten champions, 1913-14

1896-1915

- The first intercollegiate basketball game with five to a side and rules is played on Jan. 18, 1896 as Chicago defeats Iowa 13-12 before 400 spectators at Iowa's Armory.
- Minnesota wins the first Big Ten basketball championship in 1906 with a 6-1 record. Chicago would go on to win or share the next four Big Ten titles, still the second longest championship streak in Conference history.
- Wisconsin's Chris Steinmetz scores an unheard-of 50 points in one game in 1905, while Chicago's John Schommer is the first player to lead the Big Ten in scoring in three straight years (1907-09). They are considered the league's first two stars.
- Using a revolutionary offensive scheme involving speed, weaving and short passing, Wisconsin has the Big Ten's first basketball dynasty, winning seven Conference championships between 1907 and 1918.
- In the first 10 years of play, Big Ten teams post a 323-86 non-conference record. The best single year Big Ten out-of-league mark in history is 21-2, posted during the 1909-10 season.

BASKETBALL '96

BIG TEN CONFERENCE COMMUNICATIONS SERVICES

Big Ten Conference communications services are provided to serve the needs and interests of media, fans and member institution personnel.

The Conference office strives to enhance the ease and accessibility of information about the Big Ten and the accomplishments of the many athletic teams and student-athletes at its member institutions.

Along with this guide, the Conference provides many other services (listed below) in order to help those who write and broadcast about the Big Ten Conference.

Those wishing additional information on Big Ten basketball or any other of its varsity sports are encouraged to contact the Conference at (708) 696-1010.

Mark Rudner
Assistant Commissioner

Mary Masters
Managing Editor and Special Projects Director

Dennis LaBissoniere
Information Services Director

Sue Immekus
Secretary

Marija Neubauer
Jeff Kearney
Print Communications Interns

Big Ten Conference Office Headquarters and Meetings Center

1500 West Higgins Road
Park Ridge, Illinois 60068-6300
(708) 696-1010

Facsimiles:
Communications: (708) 696-1110
Administration: (708) 696-1150

Home Phone Numbers
Dennis LaBissoniere (708) 806-0513
Mary Masters   (312) 728-0206

Press Releases

The most frequently disseminated information from the Big Ten Conference comes through weekly press releases. Each Monday, media releases are issued containing Big Ten standings, results, statistics, notes and Players of the Week. Fans may contact the Conference office for a subscription order form.

Fax on Demand Service

With the fax on demand service, media have 24-hour access to the latest press releases on Big Ten sports from the Conference office **and** from each Big Ten institution.

To utilize this service, the caller must be at the handset of a fax machine. The caller dials the fax on demand phone number (available by contacting the Conference office) and receives a voice message with options. Media can pick and choose which school and/or Conference releases to receive.

Publications

Each year, the Conference publishes a Big Ten Men's Basketball Media Guide which contains rosters, schedules and statistics on each of the 11 teams, in addition to all-time Conference records and results.

Fans wishing to purchase the Big Ten Men's Basketball Media Guide may send $12 to Big Ten Publications at the Conference office's Park Ridge address. Postage and handling is included.

Big Ten Players of the Week

A Big Ten Player of the Week is announced Monday and appears in the weekly release. Players of the Week are chosen from nominations provided by the Big Ten sports information directors.

Other Media Honors and Awards

All-Big Ten teams, Coach of the Year, Player of the Year and Freshman of the Year are selected by a vote of a media panel and by a vote of the coaches. The *Chicago Tribune* Big Ten Most Valuable Player award is chosen from each school's most valuable players. The academic all-Big Ten men's basketball team is comprised of all letterwinners who are starters or important reserves and have an overall career grade-point average of "B" or better. Freshmen and junior college transfers are not eligible.

Electronic Bulletin Board

Information is also available 24-hours-a-day on the Big Ten's electronic bulletin board. This system allows the media to access press releases and other information daily. To obtain results, standings, statistics and other notes, media members simply need to have a computer and a modem. The only cost to the user is a phone call. For more information, contact the Conferenc office.

Credits

The 1995-96 Big Ten Conference Men's Basketball Media Guide was prepared by the Big Ten Conference print communications staff. Managing Editor: Mary Masters. Editor: Dennis LaBissoniere. Assistant editor: Marija Neubauer. Editorial assistance provided by Jeff Kearney. The Conference extends its gratitude to the Conference sports information directors, their assistants and staff for help in preparation of this guide. Big Ten sports information offices are lised on page 108.

Japan Media Representative

Noram International Corporation
Takigen Building
1-24-1 Nishi-Gotanda
Shinagawa-Ku, Tokyo
Japan 141
Phone: (033) 495-4771
Fax: (033) 493-7401
U.S. Phone: (714) 367-8600
U.S. Fax: (714) 367-8602

This book is available in quantity at special discounts for your group or organization. For further information contact:

TRIUMPH

Triumph Books
644 South Clark Street
Suite 2000
Chicago, Illinois 60605
(312) 939-3330

CONTENTS

Big Ten Communications Services 2
Table of Contents 3
Conference Office Staff 3
Commissioner Jim Delany 4
Centennial Feature 5-8
Big Ten Men's Basketball History 9-12
Big Ten Basketball on Television 13
1995-96 Basketball Outlook 14-18
Big Ten Basketball Officials 19
1996 NCAA Championship 20

The Schools 21
Illinois 22-25
Indiana 26-29
Iowa 30-33
Michigan 34-37
Michigan State 38-41
Minnesota 42-45
Northwestern 46-49
Ohio State 50-53
Penn State 54-57
Purdue 58-61
Wisconsin 62-65

1995 Big Ten All-Stars Foreign Tour 66

1994-95 in Review 67
All-Big Ten/Academic
  All-Big Ten Teams 68
Standings/Attendance/Won-Loss
  Breakdown/Players of the Week 69
All Games Statistics 70-71
Conference Games Only Statistics 72-73
Best Performances 74

Records 75
All Game Records 76-77
Single Game Records 78-79
Season Records 80-81
Yearly Statistical Champions 82-85
Point Clubs 86
All-Time Total Standings/Team vs. Team
  Records/Championships 87
Outside the Family/Statistical Trends 88
Postseason History 89-93
National Basketball Rankings 94-95
Attendance Records/Coaches Records 96
Yearly Standings 97-100

Honors 101
Individual Honors/All-Time
  All-Americas 102
All-Time All-Big Ten 103
Most Valuable Players 104-105
All-Time Academic All-Big Ten 106
All-Time Players of the Week 107

Conference Sports Information Offices 108

BIG TEN CONFERENCE OFFICE STAFF

JAMES E. DELANY
Commissioner of Athletics

KEVIN L. WEIBERG
Associate Commissioner

RICHARD FALK
Assistant Commissioner

PHYLLIS L. HOWLETT
Assistant Commissioner

CAROL A. IWAOKA
Assistant Commissioner

MARK D. RUDNER
Assistant Commissioner

ROBERT C. VOWELS, JR.
Assistant Commissioner

JO ANN DIAL
Assistant to the Commissioner

MARY E. MASTERS
Managing Editor/Special Projects Director

DENNIS J. LaBISSONIERE
Director of Information Services

W.T. ROBINSON
Production Coordinator/Building Manager

CAROL WHITESELL
Business Services Manager

LINDA ARNOLD
Secretary

ELAINE CHRISTIANSEN
Secretary

SUE IMMEKUS
Secretary

JERRY LECHOWICZ
Secretary

KATHIE MACKOWIAK
Secretary

KAREN REGAN
Secretary

WENDY WILKINSON
Secretary

ERICKA DOBEK
Receptionist

JEFF KEARNEY
MARIJA NEUBAUER
Print Communications Interns

RYAN McELRATH
Computer Systems Specialist Intern

LAMONT MIMS
C.D. Henry Intern

PATTY BRODERICK
Supervisor of Officials-Women's Basketball

PETER DUNN
Supervisor of Officials-Volleyball

DAVID M. PARRY
Supervisor of Officials-Football

ABOUT THE BACK COVER

The first-ever intercollegiate basketball game using five-player teams took place in 1896 between teams from the Universities of Chicago and Iowa in Iowa City. The Maroons defeated the Hawkeyes 13-12 before 400 spectators on Jan. 18, the same year that the Conference was formed.

In 1896 the first Conference champions were named in baseball and football, but it would not be until the 1905-06 season that the first Conference men's basketball champion would be named. Minnesota claimed the first Big Ten title with a 6-1 Conference record. Since that time, many great players, teams and coaches have contributed to the tradition of Big Ten basketball success. Some of these great players are pictured on the back cover:

Illinois: **Derek Harper**, 1980-83. All-Big Ten selection, team MVP in 1983.

Indiana: **Walt Bellamy**, 1958-61. Two-time all-Big Ten selection, three-time team MVP.

Iowa: **Murray Weir**, 1944-48. Consensus all-America, *Chicago Tribune* Big Ten Most Valuable Player, all-Big Ten selection, two-time team MVP.

Michigan: **Cazzie Russell**, 1963-66. NCAA Division I Player of the Year, two-time consensus all-America, two-time *Chicago Tribune* Big Ten Most Valuable Player, three-time all-Big Ten selection, team MVP.

Michigan State: **Earvin Johnson**, 1977-79. Consensus all-America, *Chicago Tribune* Big Ten Most Valuable Player, two-time all-Big Ten selection, team MVP.

Minnesota: **Kevin McHale**, 1976-80. All-Big Ten selection, team MVP.

Northwestern: **Billy McKinney**, 1974-77. All-Big Ten selection, three-time team MVP.

Ohio State: **Jerry Lucas**, 1959-62. Two-time NCAA Division I Player of the Year, two-time consensus all-America, three-time *Chicago Tribune* Big Ten Most Valuable Player, two-time all-Big Ten honoree, three-time team MVP.

Penn State: **Jesse Arnelle**, 1952-55. First-team all-America and NCAA all-tournament team in 1954. AP all-Pennsylvania team 1952-55.

Purdue: **John Wooden**, 1930-32. Three-time all-America and National Player of the Year in 1932. Later coached UCLA to a record 10 National Championships and 12 Final Four appearances.

Wisconsin: **Harold "Bud" Foster**, player, 1928-30 and coach, 1935-59. All-America center, two-time all-Big Ten selection. As coach, won three Conference titles and the National Championship in 1941.

BASKETBALL '96

James E. Delany

BIG TEN CONFERENCE COMMISSIONER

Entering his seventh year as commissioner of the Big Ten Conference, Jim Delany has been a leader and a visionary in moving the Conference forward to prepare itself for the 21st century.

Since Delany's appointment on April 4, 1989, the Conference has expanded to 11 schools and relocated to its own office building and meeting center in Park Ridge, Ill. Penn State University was accepted as a Conference member in June 1991, and began competing in championships 1991-92. In April 1991, the Conference office headquarters and meetings center opened. Located just 10 minutes from O'Hare International Airport, it effectively serves the needs of over 60 Conference athletic and academic committees and governance groups that meet more than 125 days per year.

This past year, Delany has focused on improving Conference communication systems with the establishment of a student-athlete advisory board and introduction of a Conference orientation videotape for incoming student-athletes. The coaches' council meetings which began last year have continued to be a useful opportunity for communication between coaches and Conference leadership. Delany is also taking advantage of this Centennial year to meet with editorial boards at newspapers throughout the Midwest.

The development of expanded bowl tie-ins for the Conference over the past year will provide five automatic bowl opportunities for Conference teams at the conclusion of this season. While the Big Ten will be celebrating the 50th anniversary of its agreement with the Rose Bowl this year, it also welcomes its association with the CompUSA-Florida Citrus, Outback, Builders Square Alamo and Sun Bowls.

Another hallmark of Delany's tenure with the Conference has been the enhancement of Conference championships and promotional support for Olympic and women's sports. The student-athlete experience at Conference championships has benefitted by the assignment of sport liaisons, funding for signage, programs and participant gifts (made available through a corporate partnership agreement), and television coverage of championships. For each of the past five years, the Conference has provided for the cablecast of seven Conference championships and a women's basketball game of the week series. Also in the area of television, two years ago Delany led the Conference in negotiations with ABC, CBS and ESPN for football and basketball television agreements that will continue through the year 2001.

Promotion of Conference sports initiated during Delany's tenure include a conference women's basketball challenge series, conducted with the SEC and ACC conferences; foreign tours for men's and women's basketball; and promotional luncheons for basketball and volleyball. Last year the Conference successfully launched its first women's basketball tournament since the inaugural women's championship in 1982. Another unique project initiated shortly after Delany came to the Conference is the SCORE (Success Comes Out of Reading Everyday!) program, a community outreach reading program involving close to 600 students at two elementary schools in the city of Chicago.

Only the Big Ten's fifth commissioner since its founding in 1896, Delany is a respected national leader and currently serves as the president of the Collegiate Commissioner's Association (CCA).

Delany, 47, is a native of South Orange, N.J. He received his undergraduate degree in political science from the University of North Carolina in 1970 and juris doctorate degree from the University of North Carolina School of Law in 1973.

At UNC, Delany was a three-year member of the varsity basketball team, serving as tri-captain in 1970. As a Tar Heel, Delany twice participated in NCAA Final Four competition.

After earning his law degree, Delany served as counsel for the North Carolina Senate Judiciary Committee from 1973 to 1974, and was staff attorney for the North Carolina Justice Department from 1974 to 1975.

Delany's distinguished career in administering intercollegiate athletics began at the NCAA where he was employed as an enforcement representative from 1975-79. For the next decade, he served as commissioner of the Ohio Valley Conference, where he oversaw the growth and enhancement of OVC athletic programs for men and women.

Service on numerous NCAA committees and advisory boards for national associations over the years has been another area in which Delany has contributed to intercollegiate athletics.

Active in the community, Delany has held leadership roles in various associations including the Special Olympics, YMCA and other community-related organizations. He is a member of the North Carolina Bar Association.

Delany and his wife, Catherine "Kitty" Fisher Delany, also an attorney, have two sons, Newman, 6 years old and James Chancellor, 3 years old. The Delanys reside in Hinsdale, Illinois.

Jim Delany At A Glance

Personal Information:
- Full Name: James Edward Delany
- Hometown: South Orange, New Jersey
- Wife: Catherine "Kitty" Fisher Delany
- Children: Newman, 6 years, and Chancellor, 3 years

Education:
- High School: St. Benedicts Preparatory, Newark, New Jersey
- College: University of North Carolina, 1970 Political Science major
- Graduate: University of North Carolina, 1973 Juris Doctorate degree

Legal Experience:
- 1973-74 Counsel for the North Carolina Senate Judiciary Committee
- 1974-75 Staff Attorney for the North Carolina Justice Department
- 1973-present Member of the North Carolina Bar Association

Playing Experience:
- Member of the North Carolina varsity basketball team for three years, 1967-70
- Two-time participant in the NCAA Final Four
- Tri-captain of UNC varsity basketball team

Athletic Administration Experience:
- 1975-79 Enforcement Representative, The NCAA
- 1979-89 Commissioner, Ohio Valley Conference
- 1989-present Commissioner, Big Ten Conference

Current Membership on Boards and Committees:
Collegiate Commissioners Association, President

USA Basketball Council, NCAA representative

BIG TEN CENTENNIAL
The Big Ten Celebrates 100 Years

The Big Ten, which is really 11, is into its 100th year. Numbers, all of these - 10, 11, 100.

The Big in Big Ten is genuine because of names, not numbers. It is a century of giants, an uninterrupted stream of them from start to present.

Amos Alonzo Stagg and Fielding Yost and Willie Heston gave it football renown at a time when Mark Twain still was writing, before San Francisco 'quaked. When the first bowl game was played at Pasadena on New Year's Day 1902, Michigan won it —big, 49-0 over Stanford. When Alan Gould invented the national polls for Associated Press in October 1936, Minnesota led the first one — and the last one that year, to be the first poll-declared national champion, though it wasn't the Big Ten champion. Northwestern under Lynn "Pappy" Waldorf won the league title (giving Minnesota its only loss, 6-0) and spent three weeks in No. 1 before losing its season finale to Notre Dame, restoring Minnesota in No. 1.

Before the atom was split under Chicago's Stagg Field, Jay Berwanger had used its surface as a springboard to the first Heisman Trophy (1935). The first, the only man, to win that award twice was Ohio State's Archie Griffin — the 200th, and then a year later the 205th, of the 269 Big Ten players who have been consensus all-Americas.

When basketball discovered the NCAA tournament, its idea man was the Big Ten's Harold Olsen, its first championship game was at Northwestern, and after tourney planner Olsen's own Ohio State team was runnerup in the first tournament, Branch McCracken's 1940 Indiana team won the second and Bud Foster's Wisconsin team the third. When the tournament expanded to include more than one team from major conferences, the first league to show that move's wisdom was the Big Ten, with an all-Conference final in 1976 (Bob Knight's Indiana team - college basketball's last unbeaten champion - over Johnny Orr and Michigan). Four more Big Ten teams have won national championships since then, nine in all now.

By Bob Hammel,
Sports Editor
The Herald-Times
Bloomington, Indiana

Those are the headline sports, the ones of national preoccupation throughout the century. They were not the limits to the Big Ten's scope.

A poll in the 1980s decided that America's best Olympic performance ever was the four-gold track and field sweep by Ohio State's Jesse Owens at Berlin in 1936.

Second in that poll was the seven-gold, seven-world record farewell to swimming by Indiana's Mark Spitz at Munich in 1972.

No poll is needed, just a count of major championships, to list Ohio State's Jack Nicklaus at the top of golf.

Names. Golden names, from one league's first one hundred years.

The Conference was born in an era when the only official sports were football, baseball and track. College football, especially in the East, had more than a 25-year start when seven midwestern university presidents met at the Palmer House in Chicago, upon invitation by Purdue president James Smart. It was the start of the modern conferences, the pattern southern schools, then Pacific Coast, followed years later in broadening the conference concept. "The conference was the crucial collective unit for instilling standards in college sports," author John R. Thelin said in *Games Colleges Play*. "The influential conference to which most colleges and universities looked for advice as a vigilant, organized group was the Big Ten."

The Big Ten was the first conference to select a paid commissioner to oversee enforcement of league regulations. The position's role expanded quickly to national leadership. In 73 years, only five men have been Big Ten Commissioner. The first was Major John L. Griffith (1922-44), a former army officer and athletic director. After him came Kenneth L. "Tug" Wilson (1945-61), a former Stagg lineman at Chicago who also headed the U.S. Olympic Committee; Bill Reed (1961-71), a Wilson aide who in 1939 began the league's "modern era" of record-keeping as the first head of the Big Ten Service Bureau; Wayne Duke (1971-89), a Walter Byers aide in the NCAA office who headed the Big Eight before moving to the Big Ten, and incumbent Jim Delany, a Dean Smith basketball captain at North Carolina and a lawyer who was commissioner of the Ohio Valley Conference when named to the Big Ten role.

Creation of the commissioner's role set a national pattern and carried out a resolve that was clear from the Conference's formation. "Its codes on faculty control, student eligibility and athletic scholarships were emulated by many conferences and eventually by the (NCAA)," Thelin wrote. "Its members were large universities whose athletic programs were well financed, its staff was professionalized and relied on expertise from both its coaches and its athletic directors, its teams were powerful and Conference standards promoted competitive achievement. Most of all, it was highly organized. Universities who belonged to the Conference took sports seriously so that at best its teams were both accomplished and regulated. It stood for an interesting ideal of athletic excellence combined with compliance to the rules that its members themselves had set."

From the beginning, the Conference's underpinning was academics. One of the league's first actions was to insist that each member school put its athletic program under faculty control. Indeed, in its first 90 years of operation - well into the 1980s - the league's formal name was the Intercollegiate Conference of Faculty Representatives. When it changed, it was for a

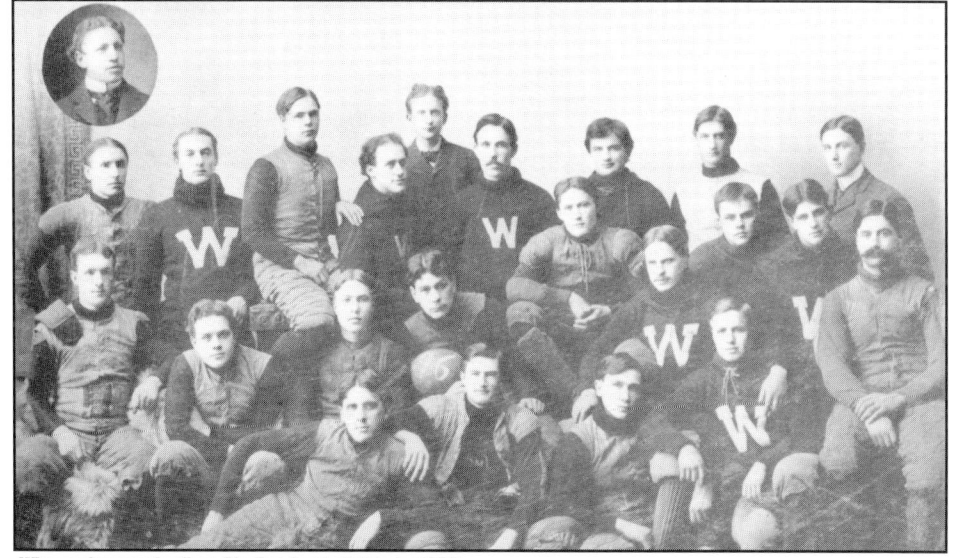
Wisconsin won the first Big Ten football title in 1896.

5

BIG TEN CENTENNIAL

step further into academic responsibility. Incorporation formally put control in the hands of the presidents, a move that was a forerunner of greatly increased national presidential involvement in student-athlete matters. The roots clearly were there all along in the Big Ten. Freshman ineligibility, transfer rules and strict prohibitions against involvement with professional teams all were issues of today dealt with in the Big Ten's formation.

The league's popular title came not from its visionary Founding Fathers. As early as 1899, when Iowa and Indiana were added to charter members Chicago, Illinois, Michigan, Minnesota, Northwestern, Purdue and Wisconsin, newspapers first began referring to the young league as the Big Nine.

In those opening years, the league didn't officially recognize team champions. Newspapers kept track of the results and declared the champions, till the league took that over.

The league's first recognized champion was Chicago in baseball in the spring of 1896. Wisconsin won the Conference's first football championship the following fall. Michigan won the first Conference track and field championship in spring 1901. Gymnastics became a Big Ten sport (1901-02) before basketball did (in 1905-06) — this despite the fact that one of the league's early giants, multi-sports coach Amos Alonzo Stagg of Chicago, had played in the first basketball game, when James Naismith brought out the peach baskets and tried something new at a Springfield, Mass., YMCA Dec. 21, 1891.

Stagg, who also was an end (from Yale) on the first all-America team selected by Walter Camp in 1889, represented Chicago in the first Conference faculty representatives' meetings because he was the first coach who had been given faculty status.

Football was the glamour sport in the Big Ten's infancy, so much so that the innovative confederation of major state universities broke into, then ultimately took the spotlight away from Yale, Harvard and Princeton, the "Ivy League" that had been dominant in the late 1890s when college football became prominent. Those three schools, plus Pennsylvania, had every all-America on the first nine teams selected by Camp. In 1898, the breakthrough athletes for the outside world were center William Cunningham of Michigan and back Clarence Herschberger, one of Stagg's players at Chicago.

By then, Stagg was in his seventh season at Chicago and he already had taken football teams to California for games, as well as back to his native East. In 1900, Dr. Henry Williams began coaching football at Minnesota; in 1901, Fielding H. Yost at Michigan. Yost's first Michigan team went 11-0 and outscored its opponents 550-0, including the 49-0 victory over Stanford in the first Rose Bowl. His 1903 team played a 6-6 tie against Williams' team at Minnesota, and 20,000 watched that game that launched the "Little Brown Jug" rivalry. Yost's "Point-a-Minute" teams were 55-0-1, ahead of opponents 2,821 points to 40 over that stretch, when in the final game of the 1905 season, Stagg's Chicago team beat the Wolverines, 2-0.

The league's legends had begun.

A 28-year-old Purdue graduate, Ray Ewry, gave the Big Ten its first Olympic champion with gold medals at Paris in 1900 in the standing high jump (5-5), long jump (10-6 1/4) and triple jump (34-8 1/2). He won the same events at 32 in St. Louis in 1904 and the standing high jump and long jump golds in 1906 and 1908.

In the 1904 St. Louis Olympics, the new Conference made enormous impact. Michigan sprinter Archie Hahn won gold medals at 60 and 100 meters and finished second in the 200, in which he was the world recordholder. As fast as Hahn was, back on campus in Ann Arbor football star Willie Heston was "a 190-pounder who could beat Archie Hahn at 50 yards," Yost said. Records were not so precise in those days, but Heston was credited with 93 touchdowns — 28 more than the official NCAA record Anthony Thompson set at Indiana in the 1980s. Nearly 40 years after Heston, sports writer Grantland Rice was pondering the relative greatness of Army backs Glenn Davis and Doc Blanchard and skipped over them and all who had come before to offer Heston as "probably the greatest ball-carrier ever."

Another Wolverine, Ralph Rose, won his first of two Olympic shot put golds at St. Louis, and James Lightbody of Chicago

Minnesota's Bronko Nagurski epitomized the rough and tumble play of Big Ten football in the 1920s.

Purdue's John Wooden, best known for coaching 10 national championship teams at UCLA, was also the Big Ten's first three-time all-America basketball player (1930-32).

won the 800 and 1,500 - Lightbody (1904 and 1906) and New York policeman Mel Sheppard (1908) are the only Americans ever to win the prestigious "metric mile" at the Olympics.

By 1911, the first great college basketball coach, Dr. Walter Meanwell, a practicing physician, already had his Wisconsin program in place. It clicked instantly: 44-1 in league play over his first three seasons for the first of what would be seven Conference championships in his first 10 seasons. The coaching lineage that sprang from him reads like the Bible's begats; the man even helped design the valve-free, hidden-lace basketball.

Michigan, though out of the Conference temporarily, had Branch Rickey as its baseball coach from 1910-13, two generations before he invented farm systems and changed society by giving Jackie Robinson a big league chance — and Wolverine coach Rickey had as a first baseman George Sisler, the first future Hall of Famer from the league family.

America roared through its '20s, the roars no louder for Babe Ruth or Bobby Jones than for Red Grange, the Galloping Ghost from Illinois. The day that Illinois dedicated huge new Memorial Stadium — Oct. 18, 1924, when Grange ran for four touchdowns in the first 12 minutes, five all-told, against a Michigan team that gave up just two other touchdowns all year and six in a 37-game span covering six seasons - that day college football exploded in popularity. The very same day Notre Dame went to New York and beat Army, its backfield coming home with Grantland Rice's "Four Horsemen" tag that it rode forever. But on their historic day, the Horsemen were in the shadow of Grange, so universally popular from that day forward that professional football became a feasibility.

The stories that came out of Minnesota in that same decade of the '20s gave Bronko Nagurski the same legendary status as Grange. Notre Dame coach Knute Rockne called him "the only football player I ever saw who could have played every position." One all-America ballot his senior year carried just 10 names; Nagurski got the vote as a tackle and as a fullback. On the final day of the 1928 season against rival Wisconsin, Nagurski played wearing a steel corset to protect a vertebra cracked four weeks earlier. Tackle Nagurski recovered a Wisconsin fumble at the Badgers 17, and fullback Nagurski carried six straight times to bang home the touchdown. Then he caught a Wisconsin receiver from behind to protect the 6-0 lead that became a victory with his late-game interception.

In the same '20s, Purdue uncovered a three-year all-America basketball player named Johnny Wooden.

In the '30s, there was the Big Ten outdoor track championship at Ferry Field in Ann Arbor when in one afternoon Jesse Owens of Ohio State set or tied world records in the 100, 220, low hurdles and long jump. His 26-8 1/4 long jump stayed a world record for 25 years. None of his records from that day ever was broken in a subsequent Big Ten meet, and not until 1994 did the league even see another 26-foot jump in its outdoor championship. That performance and the one over a longer period with not quite so eternal numbers in winning four gold medals at the Hitler Olympics in 1936 are why the Big Ten's best male athlete each year wins the Jesse Owens Award.

Bernie Bierman's Golden Gophers were the Big Ten's dominant football team of the '30s, and Ward "Piggy" Lambert's Pur-

The Big Ten men's Athlete of the Year award is named for Ohio State's Jesse Owens who once set four world track and field records at a Big Ten championship in 1935.

Quinn Buckner (21) and Scott May (42) were members of Indiana's 1976 national champions, the last undefeated team in Division I men's college basketball.

due Boilermakers were in basketball as the sport picked up speed. The young NCAA introduced the swimming national championships in the '30s and Matt Mann's Michigan teams won the first five titles. Wrestling flourished, and Ed Belshaw of 1932 champion Indiana became the first to win the NCAA's Outstanding Wrestler Award. Chicago beat out Illinois for the first NCAA gymnastics championship (1938), and Indiana won the first NCAA cross country title (1938).

In the '40s, Michigan won the first NCAA hockey tournament (1948). The league collected Heisman Trophies (four in a six-year period from 1939 through '44: Nile Kinnick of Iowa, Tom Harmon of Michigan, Bruce Smith of Minnesota and Les Horvath of Ohio State) and national football championships (five in the decade: Minnesota in '40 and '41, Ohio State under Paul Brown in '42, Michigan under Fritz Crisler in '47 and under Bennie Oosterbaan in '48). The Indiana-Wisconsin back-to-back basketball championships launched that sport's decade, and Illinois's "Whiz Kids" may have been denied their own titles by World War II. The '40s also brought the first membership change in decades: Chicago dropped out and Michigan State, already a national football power, was voted in.

Woody Hayes arrived at the start of the '50s and reshaped Ohio State and Big Ten football in his ball-control image. Ohio State and Michigan combined for seven of the 1950s' NCAA swimming championships, and McCracken got Indiana its second basketball title in 1953. In 1956, Dick Siebert began an Olympic-year pattern: NCAA baseball championships for his Minnesota teams in '56, '60 and '64. A third baseman of his, Jack McCartan, was the goalie for the gold-medal U.S. hockey team at Squaw Valley.

Ohio State coach Fred Taylor dynamically changed Big Ten basketball opening the '60s (five straight Big Ten titles, the '60 NCAA championship, NCAA runnerup finishes in '61 and '62 — Taylor, plus stars Jerry Lucas and John Havlicek and astute reserve Bob Knight from his first recruiting class, all in the Basketball Hall of Fame now). Cazzie Russell gave basketball new zest at Michigan, and before the decade was out, Rick Mount reset league scoring records at Purdue.

Parity became a buzzword in college football decades later, but in the '60s, Big Ten football achieved it to an astonishing degree. Every team in the league won at least a share of the championship (Illinois, Indiana, Iowa, Michigan, Michigan State, Minnesota, Ohio State, Purdue and Wisconsin), played in the Rose Bowl (all of those but Iowa, which had played in the 1959 game) or was ranked for at least a week or two No. 1 in the land (Iowa, Michigan State, Minnesota, Northwestern, Ohio State and Purdue). As the decade closed, that changed. Hayes put together as good a team as the league ever had (the '68 national-championship team launching a three-year era of excellence) just as Michigan brought in Bo Schembechler to meet the Hayes teachings head-on.

While the Bo and Woody Show was dominating the league's football '70s, including the unmatched Archie Griffin set of Heismans, Taylor pupil Knight came on at Indiana and set defensive and performance standards so high the whole league was lifted. Knight's 32-0 national-championship team of 1976 always gets consideration with the sport's all-time best as the era of UCLA dominance ended and the spotlight swung to the Midwest. The all-Big Ten final game of 1976 between Indiana and Michigan paid off in such a recruiting harvest for the Big Ten over the next few years that for four straight seasons ('77 through '80) the league had the first player taken in the NBA draft. One of those was Michigan

BIG TEN CENTENNIAL

State's Magic Johnson, who led Jud Heathcote's Spartans over Larry Bird and unbeaten Indiana State in the 1979 title game, still the most-watched game ever.

Big Ten football made a radical switch from ground to air in the '80s, and the "Big Two and Little Eight" epithet was shoved aside by Iowa under Hayden Fry, then Illinois and others in a suddenly opened up league. The decade was just days old when Wisconsin's Mark Johnson was the leading scorer of the "Do you believe in miracles" 1980 U.S. Olympic team, which had nine players from Minnesota and was coached to gold at Lake Placid by the Gophers' Herb Brooks. Indiana won two more national basketball championships in the decade ('81 and '87, Isiah Thomas and Steve Alford the all-Americas) and Michigan, third in the league, rode Glen Rice past Illinois in the semifinals on the way to its first basketball title in '89.

It was in the '80s, too, that other doors opened. The first year of official Big Ten women's competition was 1981-82. The league's first NCAA team champion was Wisconsin's 1984 cross country, and Peter Tegen's Badgers repeated in '85. Iowa won in field hockey in 1986, and the Hawkeyes and Northwestern became virtually annual national tournament qualifiers. Penn State preceded its 1989 entry into the Big Ten by winning NCAA lacrosse championships in 1987 and '89.

The league's first woman to win an NCAA individual championship was Diane Dixon, 1983 indoor champion at 400 meters for Ohio State - just ahead of Michigan State's Judi Brown, who won the NCAA 400-meter hurdles title outdoors the same year (the first Big Ten women's Athlete of the Year, Judi now coaches the Spartans). Swimming and diving breakthroughs were by three Buckeyes in 1987: Janelle Bosse in the 400-yard individual medley and Karen LaFace and Kim Fugett in the two dives.

No other Big Ten woman was as dominant in NCAA competition as Wisconsin's Suzy Favor, who won four straight outdoor 1,500-meter titles and three at the distance indoors, plus championships at a couple of other distances from 1987 through '90. And that's why the top Big Ten female athlete each year wins the Suzy Favor Award.

The Big Ten's impact event of the '90s was the arrival of Penn State. In the Nittany Lions' second Big Ten football season, coach Joe Paterno unleashed on the league perhaps the most dominant offensive attack it has seen. Big Ten MVP Kerry Collins at quarterback and Heisman Trophy runnerup Ki-Jana Carter at tailback were the leaders, the nation's first consensus all-America passer-runner combination in nearly 50 years. The Lions specialized in striking quickly, a two-minute TD drive almost tarrying for them as they averaged 47 points and 512 yards in their 12-0 season.

The league also added soccer, both men's and women's, during the '90s, accommodating an Indiana men's program that had already won three NCAA championships under Jerry Yeagley.

In '93, Ohio State just missed giving the league its first NCAA women's basketball champion. The Buckeyes' season and strong, national-contender level seasons by Penn State, Purdue and Iowa in the same stretch showed why the Big Ten was the national attendance leader, in totals and average per game, in the fast-rising women's college game - and in volleyball as well. The league had its powers in other women's sports, too - Indiana, in tennis under Lin Loring, and Michigan, in swimming and diving under Jim Richardson, put together dynasties, each winning nine straight Big Ten titles. Loring's Hoosiers have won 12 league titles in 14 years and in 1982, won the AIAW team championship and had the national singles champion, in Heather Crowe.

In the '90s, Michigan went to the men's basketball championship game with an all-freshman lineup and went back with all-sophomores (1992 and '93). Indiana had the No. 1-ranked team and the Player of the Year in Big Ten record-breaking scorer Calbert Cheaney in 1992-93, Purdue the Player of the Year in Glenn Robinson in '93-94, the first of back-to-back Big Ten title seasons for Gene Keady.

At the '93 NCAA men's outdoor track championships, the Big Ten did what it hadn't since the '40s, winning seven events - five different schools chipping in.

And what Indiana swimming had been through the '60s and '70s under Doc Counsilman (20 straight Big Ten championships, a record six straight NCAA titles), Iowa wrestling was under Dan Gable as the '80s rolled through the '90s (19 straight Big Ten championships, a record nine NCAA titles in a row through to '86).

The Big Ten, which is really 11, is 100 years old and golden as ever.

Michigan's Lara Hooiveld, the Big Ten's 1993 women's Athlete of the Year, was a member of the Wolverines' swimming dynasty that has won nine straight Conference titles dating back to 1987.

Wisconsin's Suzy Favor won the Big Ten women's Athlete of the Year honor an unprecedented three times, an award that now carries her name.

Dan Gable has coached Iowa to 19 consecutive Big Ten wrestling championships (since 1977) and tied a record with nine straight NCAA titles from 1978-86.

Big Ten Basketball Legends and Lore

The 1995-96 academic year marks the 100th anniversary of the Big Ten Conference and for almost all of that time, men's basketball has played a big part in the Conference's success story. Since 1905, Big Ten basketball has steadily escalated in popularity. Increased crowd sizes almost every season justify this assertion. The Big Ten owns NCAA single-season attendance records in both total and average per game tallies and has led the nation in attendance every year since 1977. More evidence of Big Ten basketball's popularity is found in consistently high television ratings.

The Game That Developed

Big Ten men's basketball popularity and quality is not a late-arriving fad. Conference attendance has led the nation through the years with good reason. League basketball action has provided many thrills, with great teams, players and coaches. And even as it is favored by basketball fans everywhere this century, the Big Ten has also been a leader in the game's advancement.

Since James Naismith invented the game in Springfield, Mass. with his 13 rules and the use of the two peach baskets, the Big Ten has been at the forefront of college basketball's development. Even prior to basketball becoming a Big Ten-sponsored sport, Conference teams were to be leaders in the collegiate basketball movement. It was University of Chicago Athletic Director Amos Alonzo Stagg, more renown as the Maroons' football coach, who actually introduced the game to the Big Ten. A fellow instructor and friend of Dr. Naismith at Springfield College, Stagg initiated basketball as a varsity sport at Chicago in 1894.

Just a month before the Intercollegiate Conference of Faculty Representatives (the Big Ten's actual name until 1986) was founded, the first college basketball game with five players to a side was played as Iowa hosted Chicago on Jan. 18, 1896. Previously, games featured seven to nine players on the floor at once, but that made competition rather crowded, so Iowa physical education professor H.F. Callenberg scaled down the size of the two competing teams to five apiece. Chicago won in the new format, 13-12 at the Iowa Armory before about 400 spectators.

In 1906, the NCAA was founded in Chicago and the previous fall, the Big Ten's inaugural season of basketball got underway.

The Teams That Stood Out

Many outstanding Big Ten hoops juggernauts have come and gone since Minnesota won the first Conference championship with a 6-1 record in 1906. The University of Chicago was the first dominating team, taking the next four Big Ten crowns, tying for the title in 1907 and '08.

In its infancy, college basketball developed into a rough and tumble competition with many elbows and even fists thrown about. The game featured two types of shots, the underhand shot and the push shot from the chest. Players were mostly stationary, with long and looping passes. Contact was inevitable and even Dr. Naismith probably didn't expect to see some of the violence that resulted from this style of play.

In 1911, along came a Wisconsin team which pioneered a quick, finesse-oriented offensive game featuring short passes, weaving player movement and the use of pivots and screens. This new format dubbed "The Wisconsin System" earned the Badgers Big Ten championships from 1912 through 1914. In that stretch, UW lost only one game in 1913 and amassed a 35-1 record. Wisconsin would eventually win five Conference titles during the decade and four more in the next.

A number of teams shared the spotlight in the 1920s. In 1926, the only four-way tie

The Big Ten's first three-time all-America, Purdue guard John Wooden led the powerful Boilermakers in the early 1930's.

for the Big Ten championship took place between Indiana, Michigan, Purdue and Iowa. It epitomized play during the decade. But by the end of the '20s, Wisconsin's dominance gave way to Purdue as the Boilermakers became one of the nation's most powerful teams and eventually had a hand in at least six championships during the next decade.

In the 1930s, the Boilermakers succeeded Wisconsin as the league's second real powerhouse, winning Big Ten titles every other year from 1926 to 1940. Northwestern interrupted Purdue's dynasty, winning Conference titles in 1931 and '33.

The Big Ten was responsible for another milestone in college basketball in 1939 as Northwestern's Patten Gym hosted the first NCAA championship. Ohio State was a finalist, losing to the "Tall Firs" of Oregon before 5,500 (which included numerous fraternity and sorority club members, many of which were let in free to beef up attendance) for the title. In 1940, Indiana became the first Big Ten national titlist, winning the second NCAA championship. After finishing ninth in the Big Ten the year before, Conference champion Wisconsin followed up with a national crown in 1941.

The early 1940s saw the era of the "Whiz Kids," Illinois' high-scoring, fast-breaking squad. In 1942, the team won a Big Ten title with a squad of four sophomores and a junior. Beating teams by an average margin of 24 points, the Fighting Illini would win the Conference championship again in 1943, losing only a nonconference game, but the kids were not able to finish out their college careers as all were called to service in the armed forces immediately prior to the 1943 NCAA tournament.

Ohio State, which was to taste greater success 20 years later, also put together some fine teams in the '40s.

Enter the post-war years and it was Indiana and Illinois that became the prominent Big Ten basketball programs.

The University of Iowa, birthplace of the modern collegiate game, hosts a contest around 1920.

BIG TEN CENTENNIAL

The Hoosiers won their second national title in 1953. With the advent of the one-and-one free throw situation, scoring totals jumped up by more than 13 points per game. As a result, IU was responsible for 12 Big Ten records that year. The Illini also were a Big Ten and national force as they made it to the Final Four in 1949, '51 and '52, each time finishing third.

Come the mid-50s and it was Iowa's turn. The Hawkeyes made it to the 1955 Final Four and further, to the 1956 championship game, losing to the Bill Russell-led San Francisco squad. Michigan State's 1957 Conference co-championship team (with Indiana) gave the Big Ten its sixth appearance in the NCAA round of four in the '50s.

In the next decade, the Big Ten was represented seven more times in the Final Four. Star-studded Ohio State put together a run of five Big Ten championship or co-championship teams starting with the NCAA champion 1960 squad and national runnerup units of 1961 and '62. Ohio State's Big Ten dynasty was the longest-running ever, as the Bucks won or shared Conference crowns from 1960 to '64. Michigan made it to two Final Fours in 1964 and '65, while the Buckeyes and Purdue also had their moments near the end of the '60s. Iowa's 1970 Big Ten championship juggernaut was the highest scoring Conference team ever, averaging almost 103 points a game in league play.

In the 1970s, defense came back into style thanks to the play of Ohio State, Minnesota and especially Indiana. The Hoosiers put together two of the finest college basketball teams ever seen in 1975 and 1976. In those two years, IU became the only school ever to finish two consecutive Conference seasons undefeated and was 63-1 overall. The 1976 team finished its season at 32-0, as the first unbeaten Big Ten team in 57 years. Since then, no team in Division I has gone undefeated. In the bicentennial year, the Big Ten became the first conference to send two teams to the NCAA finals, as the Hoosiers prevailed over Michigan in the national championship game.

It was the two schools from the state of Michigan that won national crowns a decade apart, with Michigan State winning it all in 1979 and Michigan 10 years later. With the Spartans' championship, a Big Ten team was yet again part of a watershed moment in college basketball. MSU, led by Earvin "Magic" Johnson, defeated Larry Bird's Indiana State team in a game which vaulted the NCAA tournament into the big time. The '89 Michigan team, which took third place in the Big Ten, won the national crown under then-interim and current head coach Steve Fisher.

The Wolverines, Indiana, Purdue, and Illinois held much of the spotlight during the 1980s with the Hoosiers winning two more NCAA championships in 1981 and '87. A Big Ten Final Four double took place at the decade's beginning and end as Purdue and Iowa both made it to the 1980

One of the finest college basketball teams in the sport's history, the 1976 NCAA champion Indiana Hoosiers, were Division I's last undefeated squad at 32-0.

Final Four while in 1989, eventual champion Michigan defeated Illinois in the NCAA semifinals.

Big Ten teams have continued to earn national prominence into the 1990s as for the fourth time two Conference teams, Indiana and Michigan, made it into the 1992 NCAA Final Four. The Wolverines repeated the feat in 1993, and for the second consecutive time, finished as national runnerup. The 1992 U-M team created a stir by making it all the way to the national finals on the wings of five freshmen, otherwise known as the "Fab Five". Ohio State took its first Big Ten title in 20 years, sharing it in 1991 with Indiana and repeating in 1992, while Purdue won its Conference-leading 20th league crown in 1995, becoming the first team to win two in a row outright since Michigan in 1985 and '86.

The Players That Starred

Although a team game, there is plenty of opportunity in basketball for individuals to stand out. This is no different in the Big Ten. From the league's very beginning, some of the nation's top basketball stars emerged at Conference universities. Early players that captured Big Ten fans' imagination include Chicago center John Schommer, who was probably the league's first great player. Schommer, later the inventor of the modern backboard, became the first and only one of four players to capture Big Ten scoring titles three times from 1907 to '09.

In an era in which teams usually scored 50 points combined, Wisconsin's Chris Steinmetz shocked the college basketball world by scoring 50 in a 1905 game. He added a 44-point effort one month later. Steinmetz would eventually score almost 500 points that season, unheard of in the game's early days. Along with Minnesota's George Tuck, Steinmetz was the Conference's first all-America. Steinmetz's feats were to portend future success for the Badgers. In the teens, the early Wisconsin powers featured all-Americas in forward George Levis and guard Harold Olsen, who went on to coach at Indiana and Ohio State, respectively.

Minnesota center Arnie Oss and Purdue forward George Spradling were outstanding

Two important leaders of their respective teams, Cazzie Russell (left) led Michigan to Big Ten championships from 1964 to 1966 and an NCAA runnerup finish in '65, while Earvin "Magic" Johnson paced Michigan State to the 1979 NCAA title.

Big Ten players in the 1920s. Illinois' Chuck Carney became the first Big Ten athlete to be named football (in 1920) and basketball (1922) all-America. Following Carney was Michigan's Bennie Oosterbaan who was named all-America as the Conference's leading scorer in 1928 after he won all-America honors on the football field the previous fall.

The best was yet to come for Purdue in the 1930s. Center Stretch Murphy and guard John Wooden led the powerful Boilermakers. Wooden was the first of two three-time Big Ten all-Americas and of course, went on to coaching fame at UCLA. In 1932, he was also the first guard to lead the Big Ten in scoring and helped increase national emphasis on backcourt play. As a two-time leading Big Ten scorer in the late '30s, Boiler forward Jewell Young kept the Purdue dynasty going.

Illinois forward Andy Phillip, an all-America in 1942 and '43, was the Illini war-time "Whiz Kids" standard-bearer. Phillip set numerous Conference scoring records. Other league performers of note during the decade include Iowa forward Murray Weir and two-time Big Ten scoring champ, Northwestern forward Max Morris, who was the first winner of the Big Ten *Chicago Tribune* Most Valuable Player award for basketball in 1946.

The early 1950s saw a great influx of talent, for as in the mid-40s, freshmen briefly became eligible. The yearling invasion was led by Indiana center Don Schlundt, a three- time all-Conference pick and longtime IU scoring leader. In fact, Schlundt was such a prolific point-maker, he became the new Big Ten career scoring leader as a sophomore and held the league top spot for 15 years. Other fine players worthy of mention during the early '50s are Ohio State center Paul Ebert, a three-time all-Big Ten selection and three-time team MVP, along with Illinois center Johnny "Red" Kerr and guards Bob "Slick" Leonard of Indiana and Chuck Mencel of Minnesota. Later in the decade, Ohio State guard Robin Freeman, Indiana center Archie Dees, Illinois guard Don Ohl and Michigan State center Johnny Green were standouts.

The marquee names of Jerry Lucas, the only other Big Ten three-time all-America (besides Purdue's Wooden), John Havlicek and Larry Siegfried dominated the scene as Ohio State went on to great success in the early 1960s. Later, Buckeye center Gary Bradds averaged over 33 points a game as a senior as did Michigan guard Cazzie Russell, who led the Wolverines to Final Four appearances in 1964 and '65. As a sophomore in '64, Russell and teammate Bill Buntin became the highest scoring duo until that time in Big Ten history.

The decade ended with a bang with the record-breaking scoring of Purdue guard Rick Mount, who set a Big Ten single game record of 61 points in a 1970 game vs. Iowa. The contest featured the Big Ten's highest scoring player in a season (Mount averaged 39.4 points a game that year)

against the highest scoring Conference team ever. The Hawkeyes eventually won the epic, 108-107.

Not to be overlooked in the 1960s was Purdue center Terry Dischinger, the third player to lead the Conference in scoring in three consecutive years from 1960 to '62. Dischinger, fellow Boilermaker Dave Schellhase and Michigan's Buntin were all three- time all-league picks. Other stars included Wolverine forward Rudy Tomjanovich and Indiana center Walt Bellamy, whose 33 rebounds in a game against Michigan in 1961 remains a Big Ten record.

In the 1970s, Indiana players were responsible for many postseason honors. Standouts included forward Scott May, center Kent Benson and guard Quinn Buckner, all important members of IU's amazing teams of the mid-70s. May was named 1976 NCAA Division I player of the year. Michigan players worth mentioning during that period are forwards Henry Wilmore and Campy Russell. Michigan State guard Mike Robinson earned all-Big Ten honors three times as did Ohio State guards, Allan Hornyak in the early '70s and Kelvin Ransey at the end of the decade. Minnesota center Mychal Thompson was a part of Minnesota's basketball resurgence in the 1970s, while Michigan State closed out the decade with an NCAA title on the shoulders of Earvin "Magic" Johnson and Greg Kelser.

In the 1980s, there were many talented athletes to be found including brilliant Indiana guards Isiah Thomas and Steve Alford, leaders of IU national championship teams in 1981 and '87. Alford, a two-time consensus all-America, is the only four-time Hoosier most valuable player and became the first men's basketball player to be named Big Ten-Jesse Owens Men's Athlete of the Year. Joe Barry Carroll was a Purdue standout at the

The most decorated Conference player ever, Ohio State's Jerry Lucas was named Big Ten Chicago Tribune MVP from 1960 to '62 and national player of the year in 1961 and '62.

beginning of the decade, and led the Boilers to the 1980 Final Four while guard Troy Lewis and forward Todd Mitchell paced Purdue to two consecutive Conference crowns at the end of the '80s.

Michigan also put together back-to-back championship teams in 1985 and '86 with the help of center Roy Tarpley and guard Gary Grant. Some of the decade's finest performers were from Illinois in guard and defensive whiz Bruce Douglas and forward Nick Anderson. Michigan State guard Scott Skiles was a top scorer and team leader, while Minnesota center Randy Breuer was an intimidating shot-blocker. Wolverine swingman Glen Rice became the leading scorer in an NCAA tournament, pacing U-M to its 1989 national title. That same year, Rice was named the Big Ten-Jesse Owens Men's Athlete of the Year.

Two-time consensus all-America Andy Phillip (left) led the Illinois' "Whiz Kids" (Ken Menke, Art Mathisen, Jack Smiley and Gene Vance) to Big Ten titles in 1942 and '43.

BIG TEN CENTENNIAL

Big Ten players have shown to be among the nation's best in the present decade. The 1993 and '94 national players of the year (Indiana's Calbert Cheaney and Purdue's Glenn Robinson) came from the Conference. Cheaney is the Big Ten's all-time leading scorer with 2,613 points, while in 1994 the Boilermakers' "Big Dog" became the first player to lead the Big Ten in scoring and rebounding in 23 years.

Ohio State all-America forward Jim Jackson led the Buckeyes to success in the early '90s while Michigan State guard Steve Smith and Iowa center Acie Earl also were players of note. All-America forward Chris Webber, center Juwan Howard and guard Jalen Rose were members of Michigan's heralded "Fab Five" which visited the NCAA championship game twice. In 1995, Michigan State all-America guard Shawn Respert became the Big Ten's most prolific three-point shooter of all-time and is the league's leading scorer in Conference games only.

The Coaches That Led

In the Big Ten coaching ranks, many illustrious names can be found. Indiana's Bob Knight, the Hoosiers' coach since 1971, owns the Big Ten record for Conference victories and overall winning percentage. His teams have always featured a suffocating defense and an offense that features precise screening. Knight has led IU to three national titles and is a six-time Big Ten Coach of the Year, an honor he's won more than any other coach.

Ward "Piggy" Lambert was Purdue's mentor from 1917 to 1945 and is second in Big Ten winning percentage and league wins to Knight. He holds the Conference record for longevity, with 28 years as the Boilermakers' coach, and with Knight shares the most Big Ten titles with 11.

Lambert's teams may not have all been tall (not one player on his 1934 Big Ten championship team was over 6-feet), but were quick and one of the first programs to emphasize backcourt play.

Walter Meanwell was probably the first great Conference coach. His Wisconsin teams revolutionized college basketball in the "teens" emphasizing finesse rather than rough play, winning nine Big Ten titles. Meanwell's weaving, short-passing Badger offense confused opponents from 1911 to 1934. Another long-time Conference coach was Minnesota's L.J. Cook, who from 1897 to 1924, led the Golden Gophers with a .660 winning percentage.

Indiana has had a history of fine coaches, including Everett Dean and his successor Branch McCracken, a former Hoosier standout and early practitioner of the one-handed push shot. Dean led IU to the first Big Ten NCAA title in 1940, while McCracken introduced a gameplan that favored defense, rebounding and especially, the fast break. He coached the Hoosiers to a national crown in 1953.

Also during that time, Illinois' Doug Mills was the architect of the high-scoring Illini offensive machines throughout the 1940s. Mills's successor was Harry Combes, who in 20 years, led Illinois to four Big Ten titles and three NCAA Final Four appearances.

Fred Taylor coached the great Ohio State teams of the early '60s, winning an NCAA title and coming in second, nationally, twice. Taylor coached the Buckeyes to at least a share of nine Big Ten titles and an unprecedented five in a row from 1960 to '64.

Lou Henson is in his 21st year as Illinois' head coach, and is climbing the Conference win charts, currently fourth in Conference games only victories with 207. Another outstanding Big Ten coach still in

In 1911, Walter "Doc" Meanwell introduced "The Wisconsin System" of short passing, weaving and screening to Badger teams, eventually winning nine Big Ten titles.

service today is Purdue's Gene Keady, who has kept the Boilermakers' basketball tradition alive since 1981 and current winning mark of 69 percent is the fifth best among all Conference mentors. After 20 years at Michigan State, Jud Heathcote recently retired as the Spartans' most successful head coach ever, with the 1979 NCAA championship to his credit.

The Growth of a Game and a Conference

The addition of Penn State in 1992 was a positive step for Conference schools and its fans. Penn State has appeared in the NCAA championship six times. All-America center Jesse Arnelle led the Lions to the 1954 and '55 tournaments, including a Final Four appearance in '54. Arnelle is the school's all-time scorer and rebounder. Other Penn State players of note include DeRon Hayes (1989-93) and Tom Hovasse (1985-89), the program's No. 2 and No. 3 career scorers and most recently, center John Amaechi, twice the Conference's top shot-blocker and the Big Ten's most recent first team academic all-America. In 1995, Amaechi became Penn State's initial first-team all-Big Ten selection.

So there you have it. The Big Ten's history of men's basketball, which spans all but nine years of the Conference's 100 years of existence, has consistently shown the league to be a leader in the game's advancement in skills and play, and in its growth in popularity. No conference can match the Big Ten's longevity and success both regionally and nationally. While at the same time it is good to reflect on this rich past, it is essential to focus on what Big Ten basketball can be in the future. The Big Ten intends to stay a leader in the sport as the Conference continues into its next 100 years.

Jesse Arnelle, who led Penn State to a 1954 NCAA Final Four appearance, is the all-time Nittany Lion scorer and rebounder.

TELEVISION
Big Ten Men's Basketball on Television in 1995-96

A new multimedia national cable and syndication agreement that extends and expands Big Ten sporting events through 2001 has begun with the 1995-96 academic year. The agreement between the Big Ten and ESPN began this fall and features over-the-air, regional and local syndication by Creative Sports, a Charlotte, N.C.-based sports marketing and production company owned by ESPN.

The agreement extends a 1989 accord with ESPN, which nationally cablecasts Conference men's basketball games by ESPN, ESPN2 and regional and local syndication by Creative Sports, a Charlotte, N.C.-based sports marketing and production company acquired by ESPN in May, 1994.

"The Big Ten is a national conference, and the depth and breadth of this landmark agreement places Big Ten universities in a favorable position to take advantage of new and emerging technologies in national and international markets," Jim Delany, Big Ten commissioner said. "ESPN and Creative Sports have a superior tradition of exemplary broadcast standards. We're confident Big Ten fans will be pleased with the quality and caliber of the ESPN and Creative Sports telecasts."

The agreement supplements the Conference's pact with CBS, which was extended last year to provide exclusive national broadcast exposure beginning with the 1995-96 academic year. Under the extension, CBS will nationally televise a minimum of 126 Big Ten men's basketball appearances through the 2000-01 season, with no fewer than 18 and no more than 24 appearances each year.

The ESPN agreement provides that the cable sports network will cablecast a minimum of 18 men's basketball games each season, with 16 intraconference matchups on Tuesday, Wednesday and/or Thursday nights in January, February and March.

Creative Sports assumes the Big Ten's syndicator's role beginning with this season. Creative will market and produce Big Ten local institutional basketball packages in addition to the Conference's 23-game regional weekend series.

1995-96 Men's Basketball Television Schedule

November
WED	15	De Paul at Michigan*	ESPN	9:30 EST
FRI	17	Quarterfinal (Michigan)*	ESPN2	7:30 EST
TUE	21	Semifinal (Michigan State)^	ESPN	7 EST
		Semifinal (Wisconsin)^	ESPN	9 EST
WED	22	Semifinal (Michigan)*	ESPN	8 EST
		Finals (Michigan State, Wisconsin)^	ESPN	10:30 EST
THU	23	Indiana vs. Alaska-Anchorage!	ESPN2	10 EST
FRI	24	Finals (Michigan)*	ESPN	9:30 EST
		Semifinal (Iowa)!	ESPN2	8 CST
		Semifinals (Indiana)!	ESPN	12 a.m. EST
SAT	25	Purdue vs. Memphis#	ESPN	1:30 EST
		Final (Indiana, Iowa)!	ESPN	11 CST
TUE	28	Michigan State vs. Arkansas+	ESPN	7 EST
		Notre Dame at Indiana	ESPN2	7:30 EST

December
SAT	2	Kentucky vs. Indiana<	CBS	3 EST
		Illinois at Duke	ESPN	6 CST
TUE	5	Michigan at Louisiana State	ESPN	7:30 EST
WED	6	Oklahoma at Purdue	ESPN	7:30 EST
SAT	9	Duke at Michigan	CBS	3 EST
WED	13	Minnesota at Cincinnati	ESPN	7:30 EST
SAT	16	Seton Hall at Ohio State	ESPN	4 EST
		Indiana vs. Kansas#	CBS	4 EST
		California at Minnesota%	ESPN	8:30 CST
WED	20	Illinois vs. Missouri=	ESPN	8:30 CST
SAT	23	California vs. Illinois>	CBS	Noon CST
WED	27	Illinois vs. Syracuse$	ESPN2	9 CST
THU	28	Michigan at UNLV	ESPN2	12 a.m. EST
FRI	29	Semifinal (Illinois)$	ESPN2	9 CST
SUN	31	Third place (Illinois)$	ESPN2	9:30 CST
		Final (Illinois)$	ESPN2	12 a.m. CST

January
WED	3	Iowa at Purdue	ESPN	7 CST
SAT	6	Northwestern at Michigan	CS	Noon EST
		Michigan State at Illinois	CS	1:15 CST
TUE	9	Illinois at Michigan	ESPN	7:30 EST
WED	10	Purdue at Northwestern	ESPN2	6:30 CST
THU	11	Minnesota at Penn State	ESPN	7:30 EST
SAT	13	Michigan at Michigan State	CS	Noon EST
		Purdue at Minnesota	CS	1:15 CST
		Penn State at Northwestern	CS	3:15 CST
TUE	16	Indiana at Purdue	ESPN	7:30 EST
THU	18	Illinois at Iowa	ESPN	6:30 CST
SAT	20	Iowa at Michigan State	CS	Noon EST
		Wisconsin at Northwestern	CS	1:15 CST
SUN	21	Penn State at Michigan	CBS	Noon EST
TUE	23	Michigan at Indiana	ESPN	7:30 EST
SAT	27	Indiana at Penn State	CS	Noon EST
		Illinois at Northwestern	CS	1:15 CST
		Michigan State at Minnesota	CS	3:15 CST
SUN	28	Michigan at Iowa	CBS	Noon CST
TUE	30	Iowa at Indiana	ESPN	7:30 EST
WED	31	Purdue at Michigan	ESPN	7 EST
		Wisconsin at Ohio State	ESPN2	7:30 EST

February
SAT	3	Michigan State at Purdue	CBS	1 EST
		Penn State at Iowa	CS	2 CST
SUN	4	Northwestern at Indiana	CS	Noon EST
TUE	6	Indiana at Minnesota	ESPN	6:30 CST
THU	8	Illinois at Penn State	ESPN	7:30 EST
SAT	10	Michigan at Purdue	CS	Noon EST
		Ohio State at Wisconsin	CS	1:15 CST
SUN	11	Indiana at Iowa	CBS	Noon CST
TUE	13	Iowa at Michigan	ESPN	7:30 EST
THU	15	Purdue at Ohio State	ESPN	7:30 EST
SAT	17	Illinois at Ohio State	CS	Noon EST
		Wisconsin at Minnesota	CS	1:15 CST
SUN	18	Indiana at Michigan	CBS	4 EST
TUE	20	Purdue at Illinois	ESPN	6:30 CST
WED	21	Northwestern at Wisconsin	ESPN	6 CST
SAT	24	Wisconsin at Michigan State	CS	Noon EST
		Iowa at Illinois	CS	1:15 CST
SUN	25	Purdue at Indiana	CBS	2 EST
TUE	27	Michigan State at Michigan	ESPN	7:30 EST

March
SAT	2	Michigan at Illinois or Iowa at Ohio State	CS	1 EST
		Penn State at Minnesota	CS	2:15 CST
SUN	3	Michigan at Illinois or Iowa at Ohio State	CBS	2 EST
WED	6	Illinois at Michigan State	ESPN	7:30 EST
SAT	9	Ohio State at Penn State	CS	Noon EST
		Minnesota at Illinois	CS	1:15 CST
		Michigan State at Indiana or Purdue at Iowa	CBS	4 EST
SUN	10	Michigan State at Indiana or Purdue at Iowa	ESPN	3 EST

CS=Creative Sports regional weekend series

* Preseason NIT
\# Kemper Arena, Kansas City, MO
\+ The Great Eight, Auburn Hills, MI
^ Maui Invitational, Maui, HI
! Great Alaska Shootout, Anchorage, AK
< Indianapolis, IN
> Chicago, IL
$ Rainbow Classic, Honolulu, HI
% Metrodome, Minneapolis, MN
= St. Louis, MO

SUBJECT TO CHANGE

BIG TEN MEN'S BASKETBALL ON TELEVISION

Sunday	Monday	Tuesday	Wednesday	Thursday	Friday	Saturday
*CBS national		*ESPN national (8 to 9 games at 7:30 EDT)	*CSM local (prime time)	→	→	*Pregame show *CBS national or *CSM regional afternoon doubleheader *CSM local (prime time)
*CSM regional	←	*ESPN national (7 to 8 games at various times)				

CSM - Creative Sports Marketing

OUTLOOK '96
Big Ten Men's Basketball Teams Continue Their Star Search

Illinois forward Jerry Hester

Indiana center Todd Lindeman

Iowa guard Chris Kingsbury

Year in and year out Big Ten's basketball teams rank among the nation's best with Conference players lighting up arenas from coast to coast. The Big Ten boasts a total of 50 consensus all-Americas, the most recent being 1995 Big Ten Player of the Year Shawn Respert from Michigan State. Although the league has lost numerous headliners to graduation and the pro ranks, including Respert, Wisconsin's Michael Finley and Indiana's Alan Henderson, a talented group of underclassmen appear ready for the spotlight. Leading the young guns are Indiana's **Brian Evans**, Iowa's **Jess Settles** and **Chris Kingsbury**, Illinios' **Kiwane Garris** and Michigan's **Maurice Taylor**. Although time will only tell if any of these players achieve all-America status, they will certainly make the 1995-96 season as exciting as ever.

A Glance at the Teams

Illinois junior guard **Kiwane Garris**, the Big Ten's third leading returning scorer with 15.9 ppg, and **Richard Keene**, Illinois' all-time three-point field goal leader with 168 treys, combine to form one of the Conference's top backcourts. With the graduation of forward Robert Bennett and center Shelly Clark, forward **Jerry Hester** is the Illini's only returning starter on the front line. Head Coach Lou Henson expects Hester to improve on his 10.8 ppg and 4.8 rpg as he will be expected to carry more of the scoring and rebounding load...despite the loss of all-America Alan Henderson, preseason expectations have **Indiana** as one of the teams to beat in the Big Ten. **Brian Evans** is the Big Ten's leading returning scorer with 17.4 ppg and will be counted on for leadership as one of only two seniors on the Hoosier squad. The Hoosiers are a fairly young group, as the roster lists six sophomores and a total of eight second-year players. Three of these sophomores — **Andrae Patterson**, **Neil Reed** and **Charlie Miller** — combined to average 18.8 points, 8.4 rebounds and 4.1 assists per game last season...at the top of many Big Ten preseason polls is **Iowa**, due in part to the fact that the Hawkeyes return three all-Big Ten selections, 79 percent of their scoring and 69 percent of their rebounding, and three of the Conference's top five returning scorers. Second-team all-Big Ten (media) selection **Chris Kingsbury** is the Conference's second leading returning scorer (16.8 ppg) and top returning three-point shooter (3.55 per game). Forward **Jess Settles**, a third-team all-Big Ten selection (media and coaches), averaged 15.6 ppg while guard **Andre Woolridge**, who was voted second-team all-Big Ten by the league's coaches, added 14.0 ppg and dished out 5.8 apg...at **Michigan**, **Dugan Fife** is the Wolverines' only upperclassman and a two-year starter at point guard. Joining Fife are a group of freshmen and sophomores that many consider one of the nation's top recruiting classes in recent years. A unanimous pick as the 1995 Big Ten Freshman of the Year, forward **Maurice Taylor** added 15 pounds of muscle in the offseason in an effort to improve on his 12.4 ppg and 5.1 rpg. Michigan once again landed one of the nation's best in **Robert Traylor**, a 6-8, 300-pound center who was a McDonald's and *Parade* all-American as a senior at Murray-Wright High School in Detroit... although **Michigan State's** premier "Fire and Ice" guard tandem of Shawn Respert and Eric Snow has graduated to the professional ranks, the Spartans will field an experienced team as three starters and nine upperclassmen return. Although the guard spots are up for grabs, **Ray Weathers** appears to be an early frontrunner for the position. Weathers gained valuable experience touring Japan as a member of the Big Ten All-Star team this past summer. The 6-3 junior averaged 12.9 points and 4.9 rebounds per game. MSU's strength will lie in its frontcourt as all three starters return from last year. Senior center **Jamie Feick** was named third-team all-Big Ten by the coaches after leading the league with 10.0 rpg. Forwards **Jon Garavaglia** and **Quinton Brooks** bring 7.6 ppg and 11.3 ppg, respectively, to the table...**Minnesota** enters its second century of

basketball with a lot of potential and talent, but little experience. The Golden Gophers lost five senior letterwinners, including starters Voshon Lenard, Townsend Orr, Jayson Walton and Chad Kolander, a group that accounted for 49 of the team's 76.1 points per game last season. One starter, **John Thomas**, returns as one of the Conference's top young centers after averaging 7.3 ppg and 4.6 rpg last season. The Gophers will look to sophomore **Sam Jacobson** for points as he is the team's top returning scorer with 7.7 ppg. With the departure of Lenard and Orr, Jacobson will return to his natural shooting guard spot after spending his freshman campaign at small forward. Six new recruits will have an immediate impact as they are Minnesota's highest rated class since 1978. The group is highlighted by 6-9 forward **Courtney James**, a consensus top-25 recruit who averaged 19.2 points and 12.3 rebounds at Ben Davis High School in Indianapolis... **Northwestern** struggled to an 11th-place Big Ten finish last year, but aims to rebound with the determined play of seven returning letterwinners and a talented group of newcomers. Although the squad will be inexperienced, head coach Ricky Byrdsong feels his team's strength will lie in its depth. Sophomore point guard **Geno Carlisle** will quarterback the Wildcat offense as the team's top returning scorer with 11.7 ppg. Carlisle also handed out 101 assists, the most for a NU freshman since Patrick Baldwin had 106 in 1991. Senior forward **Brian Chamberlain** was the team's top rebounder with 5.7 boards per outing... **Ohio State** is in a situation similar to the Gophers as its roster features 12 underclassmen and only three upperclassmen. **Rick Yudt**, a 6-7 senior forward, is the lone returning starter. He averaged 12.8 points and 4.3 rebounds last year and is Ohio State's leading returner in both categories. 6-4 guard **Carlos Davis** and 6-9 center **John Lumpkin**, who also plays football for the Buckeyes, both figure prominently in the mix. The rookie class, which many consider tops in the Conference, will get an opportunity early on to strut their stuff. **Damon Stringer**, last year's Ohio Mr. Basketball, leads the eight-member class... **Penn State** underwent a coaching change with first-year head coach Jerry Dunn taking over the reigns following the departure of Bruce Parkhill. The Nittany Lions lost big man John Amaechi, but do return eight letterwinners, including four of the team's top five scorers. **Dan Earl** could evolve into one of the Conference's top point-guards after a sophomore campaign that saw the 6-4 junior lead the team in three-point percentage (.407) and steals (39) and rank second in minutes played (1,050) and free-throw percentage (83.5). Senior forward **Glenn Sekunda**, an honorable mention all-Big Ten selection by the media, is the team's leading

Michigan forward Maceo Baston

Michigan State forward Quinton Brooks

ASSETS AND LIABILITIES

	Roster Size	FR	SO	JR	SR	Letterwinners Returning	Lost	Starters Returning	Lost
Illinois	11	1	6	3	1	10	4	3	2
Indiana	12	1	8	1	2	8	4	3	2
Iowa	13	5	2	3	3	8	1	4	1
Michigan	10	3	5	0	2	7	4	2	3
Michigan State	13	3	1	4	5	10	4	3	2
Minnesota	15	6	3	4	2	5	5	1	4
Northwestern	13	5	3	2	3	7	4	2	3
Ohio State	15	8	3	2	2	6	4	1	4
Penn State	16	4	3	4	5	8	5	3	2
Purdue	14	3	4	1	6	11	3	3	2
Wisconsin	14	6	5	2	1	8	6	1	4
Totals	146	45	43	26	32	88	44	26	29
Percentage	100	30.8	29.5	17.8	21.9				

Minnesota guard Sam Jacobson

OUTLOOK '96

Northwestern forward Brian Chamberlain

Ohio State guard Carlos Davis

Penn State guard Dan Earl

returning scorer and rebounder with 12.8 ppg and 6.3 rpg...after claiming the last two Big Ten titles, **Purdue** will strive for an unprecedented third consecutive league title. The Boilermakers must replace all-Big Ten first-team forward Cuonzo Martin and guard Matt Waddell. Honorable mention all-Big Ten point guard **Porter Roberts** could be the man for the Boilermakers as he started 31 of 32 games last season and dished out a team-high 3.8 apg. Purdue's front court should be solid as center **Brad Miller** and forward **Justin Jennings** return. At 6-11, Miller is an excellent ballhander who is a threat both near the basket and from the perimeter, while Jennings is an offensive threat... **Wisconsin** is one of three Conference schools to introduce a new head coach this season. Dick Bennett led Wisconsin-Green Bay to five postseason appearances, including three trips to the NCAA tournament during his decade with the Phoenix. Bennett will ask a lot of point guard **Darnell Hoskins**, the Badgers' sole player with more than one year of Big Ten experience. Wisconsin must replace Michael Finley and Rashard Griffith, both of whom are now playing professionally. The Badgers are strongest at the guard positions, and will likely feature a three-man backcourt consisting of Hoskins (6.8 ppg, 3.4 apg) and sophomores **Sean Mason** (5.0 ppg) and **Mosezell Peterson** (3.7 ppg). Sophomore forward **Sean Daugherty** will carry much of the frontcourt load, but will receive help from freshman forward **Sam Okey**, one of Wisconsin's most highly-touted recruits.

Big Ten Rests Atop 1994-95 NCAA Attendance Figures

According to NCAA figures, Division I men's basketball enjoyed a banner year as attendance was higher than the previous year for the first time in three years. The 23,560,495 people who attended games last season bested the 1993-94 mark by 285,337 fans and represents the fourth-highest turnout since record-keeping began in 1976. For the 19th consecutive year, the Big Ten has led all conferences in attendance with an average of 12,708 fans per game. Two years ago, the Conference established the national conference record of 2,163,693 total fans.

1994-95 NCAA Division I Attendance Figures

Conferences	Games	Att.	Avg.
1. Big Ten	162	2,058,763	12,708
2. SEC	174	2,002,761	11,510
3. Great Midwest	110	1,239,060	11,264
4. Big East	150	1,679,312	11,195
5. ACC	142	1,548,589	10,906
6. Big Eight	121	1,267,183	10,473
7. WAC	163	1,443,150	8,854
8. Pac-10	147	1,147,671	7,807
9. Metro	104	736,686	7,084
10. MVC	151	924,269	6,121

Big Ten Teams in the Top 25

	Games	Att.	Avg.
8. Indiana	13	220,382	16,952
10. Illinois	14	221,772	15,841
12. Iowa	18	272,847	15,158
14. Michigan State	15	221,127	14,742
16. Purdue	13	183,599	14,123
18. Minnesota	16	224,744	14,047
20. Michigan	13	176,306	13,562

Boilermakers Strive for "Three-peat"

After winning the last two Big Ten Championships outright, Purdue aims to become the first team since Ohio State (1960-62) to win three consecutive uncontested league titles. In 1993, the Boilermakers claimed the top spot with a 29-5 overall and 14-4 Big Ten record and reached the "Great Eight" of the NCAA Tournament before losing. Last year, Purdue finished with a 25-7 overall and 15-3 Big Ten record, but were upset by Memphis in the second round of the NCAA Tournament.

Shooting the Long Bomb

In league games last year, Conference players blew away Big Ten records for three-point shooting as nine different individual and team records were set. Northwestern's **Dion Lee** set the mark for most three-point field goals in a single game with 10 vs. Minnesota and, along with Michigan State's Shawn

Respert, tossed up 17 attempts. As a team, Iowa hit 14 field goals from beyond the stripe against the Spartans. As for season records, Respert etched his name atop several categories. Respert connected on 80 from behind the arc, beating his own record of 58, set the previous year while averaging 4.44 three-pointers per game. He attempted 173 three-point field goals for an average of 9.6 per game. Led by sharp shooter **Chris Kingsbury**, Iowa holds the top spot for three-pointers made (158) and attempted (413).

Tappin' the Local Well

Head coach Lou Henson likes what he sees in the Land of Lincoln as ten of his eleven players hail from Illinois. In addition, four of those players list their hometown as Chicago: junior **Kiwane Garris** (Westinghouse HS) and sophomores **Jerry Gee** (St. Martin De Porres), **Bryant Notree** (Simeon) and **Kevin Turner** (Simeon). Illinois' lone out-of-state player is newcomer **Ryan Blackwell**, a *Parade* all-America from Pittsford, N.Y. And even Blackwell has ties to the state of Illinois. Blackwell grew up in Champaign until eighth grade when his father took a job in New York. Blackwell, who lived just a few blocks from Lou Henson's home, was a ballboy at Illini home games during the late 1980s when Illinois advanced to the Final Four in 1989.

'A' is For Amaechi

Penn State senior **John Amaechi** was honored as an academic all-America last year, notching the Conference's 35th academic all-America citation. Amaechi, who has been a member of the league's academic all-Big Ten team since the Nittany Lions joined the Conference in 1993, holds a 3.33 GPA in psychology. In addition, seventeen men's basketball players were named academic all-Big Ten, a result of achieving a career "B" average or better. Penn State has a Conference-leading four all-Big Ten selections, followed by Michigan State's three. Iowa junior **Jess Settles**, an English major, boasts the Conference's highest GPA at 3.72.

Young Guns Set to Unload

For the first time in 22 years, the Big Ten lost more starters than it returns. In the 1973-74 season, the Conference welcomed back 24 starters and said good-bye to 26. This year, 26 are back in action as compared to the 29 who have departed. In addition, 60.3 percent of the Conference's returning letter-winners are underclassmen. The Big Ten's 45-member freshman class is the league's largest since 1992 when 48 newcomers made their debut in the Conference.

Returning Starters

By class:
Sophomores 4
Juniors 11
Seniors 11
TOTAL 26

By position:
Guards 9
Forwards 14
Centers 3
TOTAL 26

Twin Towers in the Twin Cities

Milwaukee natives **Jayson** and **Jermaine Stanford**, newcomers to the Minnesota roster, may make Golden Gopher opponents feel like they are seeing double. The twin brothers are both listed at 6-6 and 180 pounds and occupy the forward position. Jayson will wear No. 30 while Jermaine will sport No. 31.

Sizin' Them Up

Most players will literally be looking up to five Conference players this season as the Big Ten boasts five seven-footers. The league's tallest player is Purdue's **Matt ten Dam**, a 7-2 center from Holland. Indiana leads the count with two players listed on its roster at 7-0, senior center **Todd Lindeman** and center **Richard Mandeville**. The two other seven-footers are Minnesota's **Trevor Winter** and Northwestern's **Dan Kreft**. On the other end of the spectrum, only five players are listed at under six-feet on their respective school rosters. The leagues's shortest player is Golden Gopher **Hosea Crittenden**, a 5-9 senior

Purdue center Brad Miller

Wisconsin guard Darnell Hoskins

OUTLOOK '96

guard. The others — MSU's **Mike Respert**, OSU's **Damon Stringer**, PSU's **Chris Rogers** and UW's **Jeremy Hall** — are listed at 5-11.

Tallest player:
7-2   Matt ten Dam, PUR
Shortest player:
5-9   Hosea Crittenden, MINN
Heaviest player:
300   Robert Traylor, MICH
Lightest player:
162   Kevin Turner, ILL

Big Ten Welcomes New Mentors

Although some new faces will be directing the action this year, the Big Ten's three new head coaches are not all that unfamiliar to the Conference, as two were longtime assistants prior to being elevated to the top spot. At Michigan State, **Tom Izzo** replaces the legendary Jud Heathcote who retired after 24 years of coaching, 19 of which were at MSU. Izzo, who played guard at Northern Michigan, was Heathcote's assistant coach from 1985-95. **Jerry Dunn** replaces Bruce Parkhill at Penn State after 12 years as Parkhill's assistant and brings 18 years of coaching experience to University Park. Basketball fans in Wisconsin couldn't be happier to have **Dick Bennett** guiding the Badgers. Bennett has spent the last 30 years coaching throughout the state, most recently at Wisconsin-Green Bay.

'Four'eign Link

Over the last few years, the Boilermakers and the Badgers have extended their recruiting turf to foreign soils, each grabbing two players from oversees. Although Purdue's **Matt ten Dam** and **David Lesmond** attended high school in the United States, they call Holland and France, respectively, home. A 7-2 sophomore, ten Dam saw action in nine games last season while Lesmond, a 6-8 forward, played in 15 contests. Senior forward **Osita Nwachukwu** came to Madison from Nigeria via Kilgore, TX, Junior College. Joining Nwachukwu in the Dairyland state is **Hennssy Auriantal**, a 6-1 freshman guard out of Montreal, Quebec.

Where They Come From

26	Michigan	4	Florida	2	N. Carolina	1	S. Carolina
20	Illinois	4	Kentucky	1	Arkansas	1	Tennessee
20	Ohio	4	Texas	1	Georgia	1	West Virginia
13	Indiana	3	New Jersey	1	Kansas	1	France
10	Wisconsin	3	New York	1	Louisiana	1	Holland
7	Pennsylvania	2	California	1	Missouri	1	Nigeria
5	Iowa	2	Maryland	1	Nebraska	1	Canada
5	Minnesota	2	Mississippi	1	Oklahoma		

Returning Statistical Leaders
(NCAA Ranking)

SCORING	GP	PTS	AVG	
5. Brian Evans, IND	31	538	17.4	
8. Chris Kingsbury, IOWA	33	553	16.8	
11. Kiwane Garris, ILL	31	494	15.9	
13. Jess Settles, IOWA	26	405	15.6	
16. Andre Woolridge, IOWA	33	461	14.0	
19. Glenn Sekunda, PSU	32	411	12.8	
Rick Yudt, OSU	25	319	12.8	

FIELD GOAL PERCENTAGE	GP	FGM	FGA	PCT
7. Maurice Taylor, MICH	31	161	342	.471
8. Jess Settles, IOWA	26	138	294	.469
9. Brian Evans, IND	31	177	383	.462

3-POINT FIELD GOAL PCT.	GP	3PM	3PA	PCT
4. Brian Evans, IND	31	58	139	.417
6. Dan Earl, PSU	32	50	123	.407
8. Chris Kingsbury, IOWA	33	117	297	.394
9. Pete Lisicky, PSU	32	68	173	.393

FREE THROW PERCENTAGE	GP	FTM	FTA	PCT
2. Glenn Sekunda, PSU (25)	32	91	107	.850
3. Kiwane Garris, ILL	31	148	178	.831
4. Brandon Brantley, PUR	32	93	114	.816
5. Chris Kingsbury, IOWA	33	98	122	.803
6. Jess Settles, IOWA	26	97	121	.802
8. Brian Evans, IND	31	126	161	.783

REBOUNDS	GP	NO	AVG	
2. Jamie Feick, MSU	28	281	10.0	
8. Brian Evans, IND	31	208	6.7	
9. Glenn Sekunda, PSU	32	202	6.3	
10. Jess Settles, IOWA	26	162	6.2	

ASSISTS	GP	NO	AVG	
2. Andre Woolridge, IOWA	33	190	5.8	
3. Dan Earl, PSU	32	181	5.7	
6. Geno Carlisle, NU	26	101	3.9	
8. Porter Roberts, PUR	32	123	3.8	
Kiwane Garris, ILL	31	117	3.8	
10. Richard Keene, ILL	31	111	3.6	

STEALS	GP	NO	AVG	
6. Kenyon Murray, IOWA	33	58	1.76	
9. Andre Woolridge, IOWA	33	42	1.27	
10. Michael Hermon, IND	28	35	1.25	

BLOCKED SHOTS	GP	NO	AVG	
4. Maurice Taylor, MICH	31	34	1.10	
5. Brandon Brantley, PUR	32	35	1.09	
6. Brad Miller, PUR	32	34	1.06	
Ryan Bowen, IOWA	33	34	1.06	
8. Todd Lindeman, IND	30	31	1.03	
9. Maceo Baston, MICH	30	30	1.00	

Officiating

BASKETBALL OFFICIATING AND RULE CHANGES

by Rich Falk, assistant commissioner

The 1995-96 Big Ten men's basketball season shapes up as another exciting and successful year. There should be once again, a very competitive race. There are several teams who feel they have a legitimate chance for the Big Ten championship—and as in the past, many teams will have a great chance to advance into the NCAA Tournament and the National Invitation Tournament (NIT).

The Big Ten men's basketball officiating staff consists of 40 outstanding men from the eight-state Big Ten area. In addition, we do have a select few from outside the area. This brings tremendous balance and national respect to our staff, and we are extremely proud of the overall quality of work and achievements each year by our officials from Big Ten competition through all postseason games. For the record and for which the Big Ten is very proud, 25 officials were selected last season for the NCAA Tournament first round; 18 advanced in the Regionals; and three advanced to the Final Four in Seattle. Additionally, there were 33 officials selected to work the NIT in 1994-95.

Ed Hightower was honored as the "Gold Whistle" award-winner which recognizes outstanding officiating, citizenship, integrity and service to the community.

Our Big Ten office structure begins with Commissioner Jim Delany; to myself, the assistant commissioner/supervisor of men's basketball officials; to assistant, Kathie Mackowiak; to our many highly qualified and experienced officials; to the Big Ten office-appointed observers who help evaluate and rate our officials at each game throughout the season.

We also work closely with university-appointed game management people, directors of athletics, SIDs, coaches, television liaison people, and all the other responsible and dedicated people in each university's athletic department to make certain Big Ten basketball games are well-staffed, managed, administered, and played in the best interest of everyone involved, including of course, our great fans.

Every Big Ten season becomes a tremendous challenge and opportunity for everyone involved to help promote a positive image and gather respect for Big Ten basketball and our 11 universities.

With six Big Ten teams invited to the NCAA championship last season, this will bring added recognition and high expectations to the upcoming season. The Big Ten in 1994-95 was again ranked as one of the top Conferences in the land by power rating services. In order to maintain a high level of excellence and respect, we must strive for continued quality of player performance, coaching, officiating, sportslike behavior, and fan spirit and support. The Big Ten needs and expects everyone's cooperation in promoting superior performance and in stressing good sportslike conduct in every contest.

1995-96 OFFICIATING STAFF

Terry Anderson, began officiating 1972, started Big Ten 1995
David Bair, began officiating 1979; started Big Ten 1989.
John Bonder, began officiating 1969, started Big Ten 1995
Phil Bova, began officiating 1969; started Big Ten 1977.
Jim Burr, began officiating 1966; started Big Ten 1986.
Dan Chrisman, began officiating 1967; started Big Ten 1989.
Tom Clark, began officiating 1974; started Big Ten 1990.
J.D. Collins, began officiating 1989, started Big Ten 1995
Randy Drury, began officiating 1969; started Big Ten 1982.
Mark Gelle, began officiating 1977, started Big Ten 1995
Donnee Gray, began officiating 1983, started Big Ten 1995
Ron Grissom, began officiating 1962; started Big Ten 1989.
Eric Harmon, began officiating 1966; started Big Ten 1976.
Rick Hartzell, began officiating 1979; started Big Ten 1991.
Tim Higgins, began officiating 1970; started Big Ten 1990.
Ed Hightower, began officiating 1972; started Big Ten 1982.
Ted Hillary, began officiating 1970; started Big Ten 1982.
Tim Hutchinson, began officiating 1982, started Big Ten 1995
Paul Janssen, began officiating 1980; started Big Ten 1991.
James Jenkins, began officiating 1991, started Big Ten 1995
Sam Lickliter, began officiating 1969; started Big Ten 1984.
Mark Masariu, began officiating 1967; started Big Ten 1995
Glenn Mayborg, began officiating 1974, started Big Ten 1995
Art McDonald, began officiating 1969; started Big Ten 1991.
Lenny Memminger, began officiating 1979, started Big Ten 1995
Eugene Monje, began officiating 1966; started Big Ten 1991.
Steve Olson, began officiating 1985; started Big Ten 1991.
Tom O'Neill, began officiating 1970; started Big Ten 1990.
Jerry Petro, began officiating 1971; started Big Ten 1991.
Sid Rodeheffer, began officiating 1967; started Big Ten 1985.
Tom Rucker, began officiating 1966; started Big Ten 1972.
Mike Sanzere, began officiating 1968; started Big Ten 1991.
Verl Sell, began officiating 1961; started Big Ten 1974.
Steve Skiles, began officiating 1972; started Big Ten 1995
Joseph Silvester, began officiating 1960; started Big Ten 1986.
Mike Spanier, began officiating 1975; started Big Ten 1991.
Ted Valentine, began officiating 1975; started Big Ten 1986.
Steve Welmer, began officiating 1974; started Big Ten 1988.
Rick Wulkow, began officiating 1971; started Big Ten 1991.
Ron Zetcher, began officiating 1968; started Big Ten 1991.

RULE CHANGES

MEN'S MAJOR RULE CHANGES REGARDING PLAY FOR 1995-96
- The requirement for an official to signal the point value of a free throw by raising one finger to face level is deleted.
- All unsporting technical fouls charged to anyone on the bench count toward the team foul total.
- The reference to "striking with the fist" will be removed from the definition of a flagrant foul.
- A request for a timeout can be either visual or oral.
- Teams are allowed one 20-second timeout per half. If a team has not used its 20-second timeout in the second half and the game goes into overtime, that 20-second timeout carries over to the extra period.
- The free thrower shall not purposely fake a try, nor shall the free thrower's teammate or opponents fake a violation.
- A player is ejected when he receives any combination of three technical fouls.
- The penalty for a foul on a tap is the same as the penalty for a foul on a try.

MEN'S APPROVED EXPERIMENTATION
In 1995-96, teams may experiment with a three-point line distance of 20 feet, 6 inches. The experiment will not be used in NCAA championship play. The Big Ten will not use the experiment.

MEN'S POINT OF EMPHASIS (from the NCAA Rulebook)
In each edition of the NCAA Men's and Women's Basketball Rules and Interpretations, there are several areas that are given special attention. These are identified as Points of Emphasis. While they may not represent any rule changes as such, their importance must not be overlooked. In fact, in some cases, the points of emphasis probably are more important than some of the rules changes. When a topic is included in the Points of Emphasis, there has been evidence during the previous year that there has been inconsistency in administering this area.

Sporting Behavior
In intercollegiate basketball sporting behavior must become the norm, lest fair play, respect for others and the very essence of competition become secondary to self-aggrandizement and the exhibitionism which, in the long run, diminish the participants and make the game meaningless.

During the past several seasons, the men's and women's basketball rules committee have made a concerted effort to curb a growing trend toward unsporting actions by many players and verbal misbehavior by some coaches. The committees are adamant that misconduct by players, coaches and other team personnel will not be tolerated. In addition, the committees are concerned with unsporting behavior demonstrated by band members, mascots and cheerleaders.

The use of profanity or vulgarity, ridiculing, pointing a finger, making obscene gestures or any other manner of taunting or baiting an opponent has no place in a game played by student-athletes who represent institutions of higher learning. Similarly, coaches who purposely and repeatedly violate bench decorum do not reflect the ideals of higher education nor do they reflect the values of the individual schools they represent.

Unsporting behavior must be penalized by game officials but, more importantly, players, coaches, officials and administrators must work together to create an atmosphere that enhances the opportunities for players to use their skills within a team framework and at the same time foster mutual respect among opponents.

BASKETBALL '96

1996 National Collegiate Division I Men's
BASKETBALL CHAMPIONSHIP

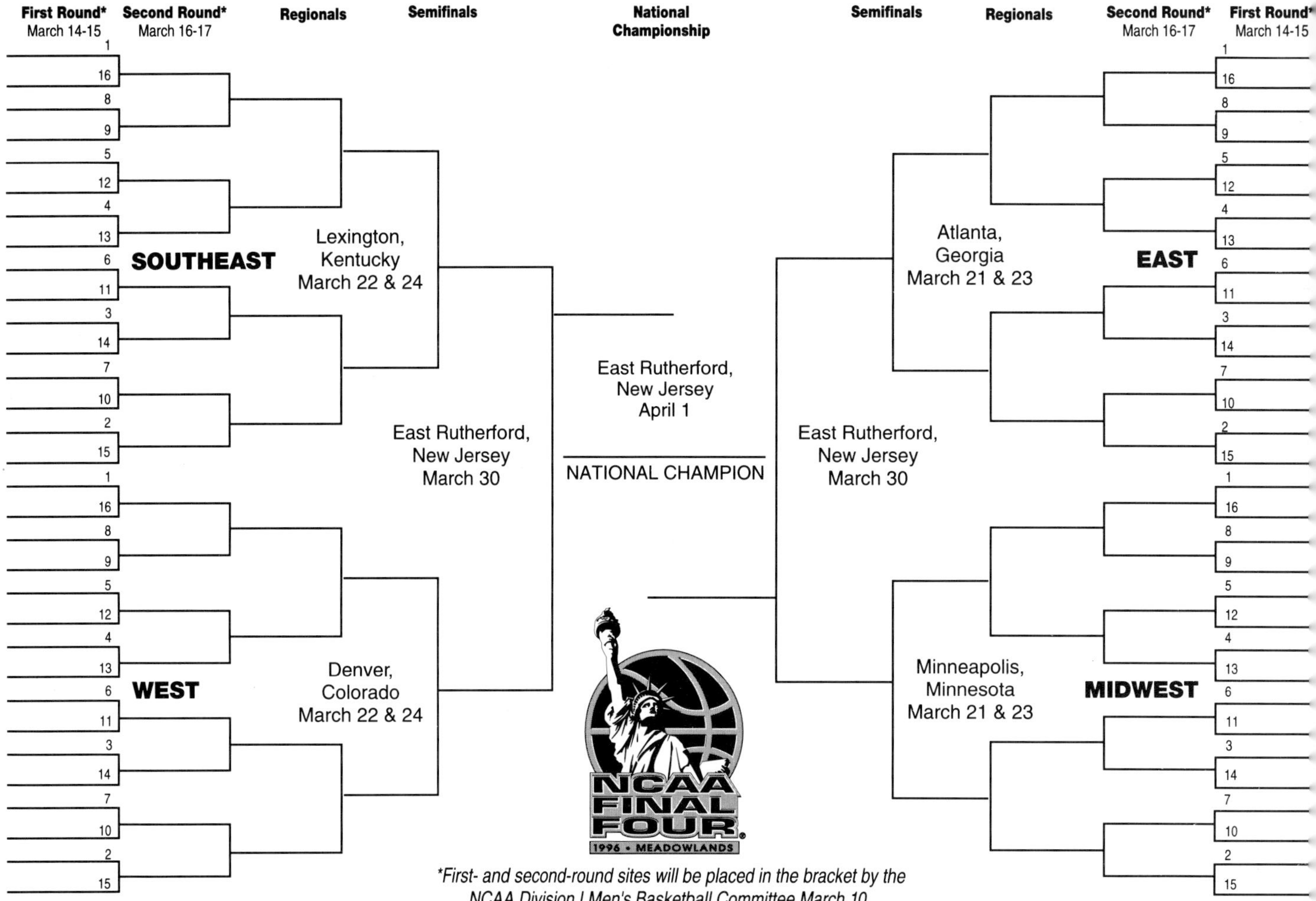

First Round* — March 14-15
Second Round* — March 16-17
Regionals
Semifinals
National Championship

SOUTHEAST — Lexington, Kentucky — March 22 & 24
WEST — Denver, Colorado — March 22 & 24
EAST — Atlanta, Georgia — March 21 & 23
MIDWEST — Minneapolis, Minnesota — March 21 & 23

East Rutherford, New Jersey — March 30 (Semifinals, both sides)

East Rutherford, New Jersey — April 1
NATIONAL CHAMPION

*First- and second-round sites will be placed in the bracket by the NCAA Division I Men's Basketball Committee March 10.

NCAA 10571-9/95

© 1985, 1996 National Collegiate Athletic Association
No commercial use without the NCAA's written permiss

GENERAL INFORMATION
(All Times Subject to Change)

Important Dates
Sunday, March 10, 1996 – Complete bracket and seeding announced at 5 p.m. Central time at the Hyatt Regency, Kansas City, Missouri.

First/Second-Round Sites (March 14 & 16)
- East — Providence Civic Center (Providence College, host) Providence, Rhode Island.
- Southeast — RCA Dome (Butler University and the Midwestern Collegiate Conference, cohosts) Indianapolis, Indiana.
- Midwest — Reunion Arena (Southwest Conference, host) Dallas, Texas.
- West — University Arena (University of New Mexico, host) Albuquerque, New Mexico.

First/Second-Round Sites (March 15 & 17)
- East — Richmond Coliseum (Virginia Commonwealth University, host) Richmond, Virginia.
- Southeast — Orlando Arena (Stetson University, host). Orlando, Florida
- Midwest — Bradley Center (Marquette University, host) Milwaukee, Wisconsin.
- West — University Activity Center (Arizona State University, host) Tempe, Arizona.

Regional Sites (March 21 & 23)
- East — Georgia Dome (Metropolitan Collegiate Athletic Conference, host), Atlanta, Georgia.
- Midwest — Hubert H. Humphrey Metrodome (University of Minnesota, Twin Cities, host), Minneapolis, Minnesota

Regional Sites (March 22 & 24)
- Southeast — Rupp Arena (University of Kentucky, host) Lexington, Kentucky.
- West — McNichols Arena (University of Colorado, Boulder, host) Denver, Colordo.

Championship Site (March 30 & April 1)
Meadowlands Arena, East Rutherford, New Jersey (Rutgers University, New Brunswick, host).
- March 30 — National Semifinals, East vs. Midwest, Southeast vs. West; sequence has not been determined.
- April 1 — National Collegiate Championship.

FUTURE FINAL FOURS
- 1997 RCA Dome, Indianapolis, Indiana (Butler University and Midwestern Collegiate Conference, cohosts)
- 1998 Alamodome, San Antonio, Texas (Southwest Conference, host)
- 1999 Thunderdome, St. Petersburg, Florida (University of South Florida, host)
- 2000 Hoosier Dome, Indianapolis, Indiana (Butler University and Midwestern Collegiate Conference, cohosts)
- 2001 Metrodome, Minneapolis, Minnesota (University of Minnesota, Twin Cities, host)
- 2002 Georgia Dome, Atlanta, Georgia (Georgia Institute of Technology and Metropolitan Collegiate Athletic Conference, cohosts)

OUTLOOK

Michigan vs. Illinois, 1924

1916-1935

- In 1919, Minnesota is 10-0 in Conference play, 13-0 overall, and generally considered the nation's best basketball team. No other Big Ten team would finish the season undefeated until Indiana 57 years later in 1976.
- By winning or sharing 10 Big Ten championships in the 1920s and 30s, Purdue becomes the second great Conference power. From 1920 to 1944, the Boilermakers enjoy winning seasons and capture a Big Ten title every other year from 1926 to 1940.
- Indiana, Iowa, Michigan and Purdue share the Big Ten crown in 1926 with 8-4 records, the only quadruple basketball title in Conference history.
- From 1929 to 1933, nine Big Ten players are named all-America, three of them coming from the Conference in 1930 and '31. Purdue's John Wooden becomes the first of two Big Ten players to win three all-America honors from 1930 to 1932.
- Three coaching legends are at different stages in their careers during this era. Wisconsin's Walter Meanwell retires in 1934, Purdue's Ward Lambert is in the middle of his 28-year run and Branch McCracken is just getting started at Indiana.

ILLINOIS

Fighting Illini

QUICK FACTS

Location: Champaign-Urbana, IL
Population: 110,000
Founded: 1867
Enrollment: 35,000
Nickname: Fighting Illini
Colors: Orange and Blue
Arena: Assembly Hall (1963, 16,450)
President: James Stukel
Chancellor: Michael T. Aiken
Faculty Representatives: Mildred Griggs, David Chicione
Athletic Director: Ron Guenther
Head Coach: Lou Henson (New Mexico State '55), 21st year
Assistant Coaches: Dick Nagy, Jimmy Collins, Mark Bial
Sports Information Director: Mike Pearson
Basketball Contact: Kent Brown (Asst. SID)
SID Phone: (217) 333-1391
SID Fax Phone: (217) 333-5540
Press Row Phone: (217) 333-1227
1994-95 Record: 19-12, 10-8 Big Ten (5th-tie)
Starters Returning/Lost: 3/2
Letterwinners Returning/Lost: 10/4
Best time to contact coach: Anytime through SID Office

Assembly Hall (1963)
Capacity 16,450

After setting a school record for three-point field goals and attempts in 1994-95, Lou Henson's Fighting Illini will once again depend on strong perimeter play in the 21st season at the Illini helm.

Expect Henson to build a large portion of his offense around junior guard Kiwane Garris, who led the Fighting Illini in scoring (15.9 ppg), assists (3.8 apg), steals (1.2 spg), free-throw shooting (.831) and minutes played (33.5 mpg) in 1995. He earned first-team all-Big Ten honors from *Basketball Weekly*, second-team all-Big Ten mention from the league's coaches and third-team recognition from the media.

Senior Richard Keene returns as Illinois' all-time three-point field goal leader with 168 treys, 10th all-time in the Big Ten, and most among returning players for the 1995-96 season. He was Illinois' third-leading scorer in 1995 (10.9 ppg), fourth-leading rebounder (3.8 rpg) and second in assists (3.6 apg). Keene topped 100 assists for the second consecutive year and stands ninth on the Illinois career assists list with 297. Sophomores Kevin Turner and Matt Heldman should provide good depth off the bench.

Jerry Hester is Henson's only returning starter on the front line with the graduation of forward Robert Bennett and center Shelly Clark. Hester was Illinois' fourth-leading scorer (10.8 ppg) and third-leading rebounder (4.8 rpg) in 1995, while shooting a team-high 40 percent from three-point range, and 46 percent on all shots.

Sophomore Jerry Gee was Illinois' first front court player off the bench in 1995, and should now replace Bennett at power forward while alternating with Robisch in the post. Gee averaged 6.0 points and 3.4 rebounds for the season, but nearly 9.0 points off the bench over the final eight games of the season. He gives the Illini more scoring range from the power forward slot.

Redshirt sophomore Brett Robisch showed improvement in the final weeks of the 1995 season and is expected to battle for the starting center spot in the coming season. Sophomore Bryant Notree can play shooting guard, small forward, and may also take his powerful body down low to the power forward slot when Henson wants to use a "fast" team.

Redshirt junior Chris Gandy started seven games for the Illini early in the 1994-95 season, but saw limited action as the season progressed. An excellent shooter, Gandy needs to improve his rebounding and defense to work his way back into the lineup.

Freshman Ryan Blackwell could also be a force on Henson's front line. A *Parade Magazine* all-American as a senior, Blackwell has the shooting range and ball-handling ability to play small forward or shooting guard, and the size (6-8, 215) to play inside.

LOU HENSON
Head Coach

James Stukel
President

Michael T. Aiken
Chancellor

Mildred Griggs
Faculty Representative

David Chicoine
Faculty Representative

Ron Guenther
Athletic Director

Mike Pearson
Sports Information Director

ROSTER

No.	Name	POS	HT	WT	Year	Hometown (High School)
44	Ryan Blackwell	F	6-8	207	FR	Pittsford, NY (Pittsford-Sutherland)
45**	Chris Gandy	F	6-9	207	JR	Kankakee, IL (Bradley-Bourbonnais)
22**	Kiwane Garris	G	6-2	183	JR	Chicago, IL (Westinghouse)
32*	Jerry Gee	F	6-8	239	SO	Chicago, IL (St. Martin De Porres)
21*	Matt Heldman	G	6-0	162	SO	Libertyville, IL
40**	Jerry Hester	F	6-6	194	JR	Peoria, IL (Manual)
34*	Brian Johnson	F	6-6	196	SO	Des Plaines, IL (Maine West)
24***	Richard Keene	G	6-6	205	SR	Collinsville, IL
25*	Bryant Notree	G	6-5	205	SO	Chicago, IL (Simeon)
31*	Brett Robisch	C	6-11	239	SO	Springfield, IL (Calvary)
33*	Kevin Turner	G	6-2	162	SO	Chicago, IL (Simeon)

*letters earned

RETURNING/LOST

Letterwinners Returning	YR	POS	FG%	FT%	PPG	RPG	APG
Chris Gandy	JR	F	.552	.750	3.1	2.2	0.0
*Kiwane Garris	JR	G	.439	.831	15.9	2.8	3.8
Jerry Gee	SO	F	.456	.639	6.0	3.4	0.2
Matt Heldman	SO	G	.300	.857	0.9	0.6	0.2
*Jerry Hester	JR	F	.458	.534	10.8	4.8	1.9
Brian Johnson	SO	F	.548	.714	2.1	1.0	0.4
*Richard Keene	SR	G	.380	.659	10.9	3.8	3.6
Bryant Notree	SO	G/F	.356	.296	2.6	2.1	0.5
Brett Robisch	SO	F/C	.588	.250	1.3	0.7	0.0
Kevin Turner	SO	G	.333	.412	2.7	0.7	0.6
Letterwinners Lost		POS	FG%	FT%	PPG	RPG	APG
*Robert Bennett		F	.551	.606	8.5	6.2	0.5
*Shelly Clark		C	.500	.620	11.8	8.3	1.5
Steve Roth		C	.286	.333	0.6	1.0	0.0
Derrick Thomas		G	.167	.625	0.5	0.3	0.0

* - starter in 1994-95

1995-96 SCHEDULE

Tue., Nov. 14	Australian Select Team (exh.) (7 CST)
Tue., Nov. 21	Converse All Stars (exh.) (7 CST)
Sat., Nov. 25	Texas-San Antonio (8 CST)
Tue., Nov. 28	Eastern Illinois (7 CST)
Sat., Dec. 2	@ Duke (ESPN) (6 CST)
Mon., Dec. 4	Kansas State (CS) (7 CST)
Fri., Dec. 8	vs. SE Missouri (CS) (7 CST)*
Sat., Dec. 9	vs. San Jose St. or Ball St. (CS) (6/8 CST)*
Sat., Dec. 16	Illinois-Chicago (7 CST)
Wed., Dec. 20	vs. Missouri (Kiel Center, St. Louis) (ESPN) (8:30 CST)
Sat., Dec. 23	vs. California (United Center, Chicago) (CBS) (Noon CST)
Wed., Dec. 27	vs. Syracuse (ESPN2) (9 CST)#
Fri., Dec. 29	vs. Rhode Island or Hawaii (Time TBA)#
Sat., Dec. 30	vs. TBA (Time TBA)#
Wed., Jan. 3	@ Minnesota (CS) (7 CST)
Sat., Jan. 6	Michigan State (CS Regional) (1:15 CST)
Tue., Jan. 9	@ Michigan (ESPN) (6:30 CST)
Sat., Jan. 13	Indiana (CS) (7 CST)
Thu., Jan. 18	@ Iowa (ESPN) (6:30 CST)
Sat., Jan. 20	@ Purdue (CS) (7 CST)
Wed., Jan. 24	Ohio State (CS) (7 CST)
Sat., Jan. 27	@ Northwestern (CS Regional) (1:15 CST)
Sat., Feb. 3	Wisconsin (CS) (7 CST)
Thu., Feb. 8	@ Penn State (ESPN) (6:30 CST)
Wed., Feb. 14	Northwestern (CS) (7 CST)
Sat., Feb. 17	@ Ohio State (CS Regional) (11 a.m. CST)
Tue., Feb. 20	Purdue (ESPN) (6:30 CST)
Sat., Feb. 24	Iowa (CS Regional) (1:15 CST)
Wed., Feb. 28	@ Indiana (CS) (7 CST)
Sat., March 2	Michigan (CS Regional) (Noon CST) **or**
Sun., March 3	Michigan (CBS) (1 CST)
Wed., March 6	@ Michigan State (ESPN) (6:30 CST)
Sat., March 9	Minnesota (CS Regional) (1:15 CST)

CS – Creative Sports Local Package
CS Regional – Creative Sports Regional Weekend Series

* – Illini/Pepsi Classic, Champaign, IL
# – Rainbow Classic, Honolulu, HI

SUBJECT TO CHANGE

Kiwane Garris led the Illini in scoring (15.9 ppg), assists (3.8 apg), steals (1.2 spg) and free-throw shooting (.831) last season.

ILLINOIS

Fighting Illini

Head Coach
LOU HENSON

Birth Date: January 10, 1932
Hometown: Okay, OK
Education:
Okay High School ... Connors (OK) Junior College ... B.S Secondary Education, New Mexico State, 1955 ... M.A. Educational Administration, New Mexico State, 1956
Playing Experience:
Guard, Connors Junior College, 1952-53 ... guard, New Mexico State, 1954-55
Coaching Experience:
Junior varsity coach, Las Cruces (NM) High School, 1956-58
Head Coach, Las Cruces High School, 1958-62
Head Coach, Hardin-Simmons, 1962-66
Head Coach, New Mexico State, 1966-75
Head Coach, Illinois, 1975-present
Honors and achievements:
Team captain, sophomore and senior years in college ... won three consecutive state high school championships at Las Cruces ... took New Mexico State to six NCAA Championships ... national semifinalists at 1970 NCAA Tournament ... eight consecutive NCAA Tournament appearances at Illinois ... Final Four semifinalist in 1989 ... only four losing seasons in coaching career ... seventh winningest active NCAA Division I men's basketball coach ... 1984 ESPN national coach of the year ... guided his Illinois teams to nine straight upper-division Big Ten finishes ... has eleven 20-plus victory seasons at Illinois ... has led the Illini to 12 NCAA tournaments.
Personal Data:
Full name Louis R. Henson ... wife Mary ... son Lou Jr., daughters Lori, Lisa and Leigh Ann ... resides in Champaign.

Henson's Record:

Year	School	Overall		Big Ten	
1962-63	Hardin-Simmons	10-16	.385		
1963-64	Hardin-Simmons	20-6	.769		
1964-65	Hardin-Simmons	17-8	.680		
1965-66	Hardin-Simmons	20-6	.769		
1966-67	New Mexico St.	15-11	.577		
1967-68	New Mexico St.	23-6	.793		
1968-69	New Mexico St.	24-5	.828		
1969-70	New Mexico St.	27-3	.900		
1970-71	New Mexico St.	19-8	.667		
1971-72	New Mexico St.	19-6	.760		
1972-73	New Mexico St.	12-14	.462		
1973-74	New Mexico St.	14-11	.560		
1974-75	New Mexico St.	20-7	.741		
1975-76	Illinois	14-13	.519	7-11	.389
1976-77	Illinois	16-14	.533	8-10	.444
1977-78	Illinois	13-14	.481	7-11	.389
1978-79	Illinois	19-11	.633	7-11	.389
1979-80	Illinois	22-13	.629	8-10	.444
1980-81	Illinois	21-8	.724	12-6	.667
1981-82	Illinois	18-11	.621	10-8	.556
1982-83	Illinois	21-11	.656	11-7	.611
1983-84	Illinois	26-5	.839	15-3	.833
1984-85	Illinois	26-9	.743	12-6	.667
1985-86	Illinois	22-10	.688	11-7	.611
1986-87	Illinois	23-8	.742	13-5	.722
1987-88	Illinois	23-10	.674	12-6	.667
1988-89	Illinois	31-5	.861	14-4	.778
1989-90	Illinois	21-8	.724	11-7	.611
1990-91	Illinois	21-10	.667	11-7	.611
1991-92	Illinois	13-15	.464	7-11	.389
1992-93	Illinois	19-13	.594	11-7	.611
1993-94	Illinois	17-11	.607	10-8	.556
1994-95	Illinois	19-12	.613	10-8	.556
School Total		405-211	.658	207-153	.575
Career Total		645-318	.670		

Big Ten Championship: (1) 1984(co)
NCAA Appearances: (16) 1967-68-69-70-75-81-83-84-85-86-87-88-89-90-93-94-95
NIT Appearances: (1) 1982

Lou Henson

FIGHTING ILLINI TO WATCH

KIWANE GARRIS, G, 6-2, 183, JR, Chicago, IL
Led the Fighting Illini in scoring (15.9 ppg), assists (3.8 apg), steals (1.2 spg), minutes 33.5 mpg) and free-throw shooting (.831) ... earned second-team all-Big Ten honors from Big Ten coaches and third team honors from the media... one of just two Big Ten players selected for the 25-man preseason Wooden Award Watch List... made a school-record 39 consecutive free throws during the 1994-95 season, the third-longest streak in Big Ten history.

JERRY HESTER, F, 6-6, 194, JR, Peoria, IL
Fighting Illini's fourth leading scorer (10.8) and third-leading rebounder (4.8) in 1995... started 27 of 30 games... increased his field-goal shooting from .407 as a freshman to .458 as a sophomore, including an increase from .323 to .418 from three-point range... scored career-high 29 points in Illini win over Memphis Dec. 29, 1994... made school record for one half with six three pointers in Illini win over Indiana Jan. 14, 1995.

RICHARD KEENE, G, 6-6, 205, Collinsville, IL
Illinois' all-time three-point field-goal leader with 168 treys, 10th all-time in the Big Ten... Fighting Illini's third-leading scorer (10.9 ppg), fourth-leading rebounder (3.8 rpg) and second in assists (3.6 apg) in 1995... topped 100 assists for the second consecutive year in 1995 and stands ninth on the UI career assists list with 297 ... enters the 1995-96 season with a streak of 54 consecutive starts.

1994-95 RESULTS
(19-12/10-8)

November
25	W	89-77	American University**
26	W	65-57	College of Charleston**
27	W	85-75	Virginia Tech**

December
3	L	65-70	DUKE (at Chicago, IL)
5	W	76-69	Kansas State
9	W	71-53	NORTHEASTERN ILLINOIS#
10	W	59-37	PRINCETON#
17	W	75-60	ILLINOIS-CHICAGO
19	W	90-66	MERCER
22	L	58-76	Missouri (at St. Louis, MO)
27	L	56-71	Connecticut
29	W	86-76	MEMPHIS STATE

January
4	W	79-70	OHIO STATE
7	W	82-55	Northwestern
10	W	62-58	Purdue
14	W	78-67	INDIANA
17	L	59-69	MICHIGAN
21	L	66-77	Minnesota
28	L	67-75	MICHIGAN STATE

February
1	W	79-74	Iowa
4	L	60-73	Wisconsin
8	W	67-58	PENN STATE
11	W	104-97	IOWA (OT)
15	L	58-68	Michigan State
22	W	94-88	MINNESOTA (OT)
26	L	51-63	Michigan

March
2	L	85-89	Indiana
4	L	56-69	PURDUE
8	W	99-57	NORTHWESTERN
11	W	82-63	Ohio State
17	L	62-68	Tulsa*

* NCAA first round, Albany, NY
** San Juan Shootout, San Juan, PR (1st)
\# Illini Classic, Champaign, IL (1st)

1994-95 STATISTICS *(1995-96 returnees in ALL CAPS)*
Record: 19-12   Home: 11-3   Road: 6-6   Neutral: 2-3

Player	G-GS	Min-Avg	FG-FGA	Pct	3P-3PA	Pct	FT-FTA	Pct	Off-Def	Tot-Avg	PF-FD	AT	TO	BS	ST	Pts-Avg
KIWANE GARRIS	31-30	1038-33.5	150-342	.439	46-119	.387	148-178	.831	17-71	88-2.8	74-0	117	75	0	36	494-15.9
Shelly Clark	28-25	775-27.7	131-262	.500	0-0	.000	67-108	.620	114-119	233-8.3	87-2	43	68	11	28	329-11.8
RICHARD KEENE	31-31	939-30.3	123-324	.380	63-173	.364	29-44	.659	20-99	119-3.8	72-1	111	63	4	30	338-10.9
JERRY HESTER	30-27	906-30.2	119-260	.458	38-94	.404	47-88	.534	60-85	145-4.8	83-2	57	50	10	23	323-10.8
Robert Bennett	31-24	820-26.5	98-178	.551	0-2	.000	66-109	.606	66-125	191-6.2	88-2	15	58	13	22	262-8.5
JERRY GEE	31-6	598-19.3	73-160	.456	0-0	.000	39-61	.639	47-59	106-3.4	58-0	7	26	7	12	185-6.0
CHRIS GANDY	23-7	186-8.1	32-58	.552	2-6	.333	6-8	.750	24-27	51-2.2	29-0	1	15	3	2	72-3.1
KEVIN TURNER	27-0	264-9.8	26-78	.333	14-38	.368	7-17	.412	3-17	20-0.7	19-0	17	18	0	2	73-2.7
BRYANT NOTREE	31-4	358-11.5	36-101	.356	2-12	.167	8-27	.296	35-31	66-2.1	43-0	15	22	2	7	82-2.6
BRIAN JOHNSON	24-0	181-7.5	17-31	.548	1-5	.200	15-21	.714	7-16	23-1.0	11-0	10	13	3	7	50-2.1
BRETT ROBISCH	18-0	42-2.3	10-17	.588	1-5	.200	2-8	.250	7-5	12-0.7	4-0	0	1	0	1	23-1.3
MATT HELDMAN	21-1	68-3.2	3-10	.300	0-2	.000	12-14	.857	1-11	12-0.6	8-0	4	11	0	3	18-0.9
Steve Roth	15-0	36-2.4	4-14	.286	0-0	.000	1-3	.333	10-5	15-1.0	10-0	0	2	0	0	9-0.6
Derrick Thomas	14-0	14-1.0	1-6	.167	0-1	.000	5-8	.625	1-3	4-0.3	1-0	0	1	0	1	7-0.5
Robert Rodgers	1-0	1-1.0	0-0	.000	0-0	.000	0-0	.000	0-0	0-0.0	0-0	0	0	0	0	0-0.0
Bob Edgerton	1-0	1-1.0	0-1	.000	0-1	.000	0-0	.000	0-1	1-1.0	0-0	0	0	0	0	0-0.0
Karl Schulz	1-0	1-1.0	0-0	.000	0-0	.000	0-0	.000	0-0	0-0.0	0-0	0	0	0	0	0-0.0
John Larson	1-0	1-1.0	0-0	.000	0-0	.000	0-0	.000	0-0	0-0.0	0-0	0	0	0	0	0-0.0
John Steele	1-0	1-1.0	0-0	.000	0-0	.000	0-0	.000	0-0	0-0.0	1-0	0	0	0	0	0-0.0
Team										87			2			
Illinois	31	6230	823-1842	.447	167-458	.365	452-694	.651	412-674	1173-37.8	588	397	425	53	174	2265-73.1
Opponents	31	6230	780-1728	.451	190-508	.374	375-597	.628	331-657	988-31.9	620	411	447	102	166	2125-68.5

SCHOOL RECORDS

Individual

SCORING
Game: 53   Dave Downey at Indiana 2/16/63
Season: 688   Don Freeman   1965-66
Career: 2129 Deon Thomas   1990-94

REBOUNDING
Game: 24   Skip Thoren at UCLA 12/28/63
Season: 349   Skip Thoren   1964-65
Career: 853   Efrem Winters 1982-86

ASSISTS
Game: 16   Tony Wysinger at Pittsburgh 12/6/86
Season: 200   Bruce Douglas 1984-85
Career: 765   Bruce Douglas 1982-86

STEALS
Game: 8   Bruce Douglas vs. Purdue 2/25/84
Season: 89   Kenny Battle 1988-89
Career: 324   Bruce Douglas 1982-86

BLOCKED SHOTS
Game: 11   Derek Holcomb vs. South Carolina 12/8/78
Season: 86   Derek Holcomb 1978-79
Career: 174   Derek Holcomb 1978-81

Team

SCORING
Game: 127   12/22/88 (Louisiana State)
Season: 3110 1988-89

REBOUNDING
Game: 79   2/16/59 (Wisconsin)
Season: 1349 1962-63

ASSISTS
Game: 35   3/10/82 (Long Island)
               12/7/85 (Utah State)
Season: 639   1988-89

STEALS
Game: 20   11/24/78 (Texas-Arlington)
               2/23/87 (Purdue)
Season: 341   1988-89

BLOCKED SHOTS
Game: 14   11/28/78 (Denver)
Season: 162   1978-79

Big Ten record in **bold**

TOP TEN SCORERS

1. Deon Thomas (1990-94)   2,129
2. Eddie Johnson (1979-81)   1,692
3. Mark Smith (1978-81)   1,653
4. Andy Kaufmann (1988-93)   1,533
5. Efrem Winters (1983-86)   1,487
6. Nick Weatherspoon (1971-73) 1,481
7. Dave Scholz (1967-69)   1,459
8. Don Freeman (1964-66)   1,449
9. Kendall Gill (1987-90)   1,409
10. Ken Norman (1985-87)   1,393

Senior guard Richard Keene is Illinois' all-time three-point field goal leader with 168 treys, which ranks 10th on the all-time Big Ten chart.

INDIANA

 **Hoosiers**

QUICK FACTS

Location: Bloomington, IN
Population: 60,000
Founded: 1820
Enrollment: 36,000
Nickname: Hoosiers
Colors: Cream & Crimson
Arena: Assembly Hall (1971, 17,357)
President: Myles Brand
Faculty Representative: William Perkins
Athletic Director: Clarence Doninger
Head Coach: Bob Knight (Ohio State '62), 25th year
Assistant Coaches: Ron Felling, Dan Dakich, Craig Hartman
Sports Information Director: Kit Klingelhoffer
Basketball Contact: Gregg Elkin (Asst. SID)
SID Phone: (812) 855-9399
SID Fax Phone: (812) 855-9401
Media Hotline: (812) 855-0835
Press Row Phone: (812) 855-2754
1994-95 Record: 19-12, 11-7 Big Ten (3rd-tie)
Starters Returning/Lost: 3/2
Letterwinners Returning/Lost: 8/4
Best time to contact coach: Contact SID Office

Assembly Hall (1971)
Capacity 17,357

Three starters return for the Indiana Hoosiers in 1995-96 and despite the loss of all-America Alan Henderson, preseason expectations have the Hoosiers as one of the teams to beat in the Big Ten.

The Hoosiers were 19-12 last season and managed an 11-7 Big Ten record, which placed IU third in the Conference standings. A loss in the first round of the NCAA Tournament to Missouri ended the Hoosiers streak of four consecutive trips to the Sweet Sixteen.

This season, the Hoosiers have to do without all-America Alan Henderson who took his 23.5 points and 9.7 rebounds per game to the NBA.

Three starters – Brian Evans, Andrae Patterson and Neil Reed – will be counted on to help offset the loss of Henderson. Knight, who begins his 25th season at the helm of the Hoosiers, will use these three to go along with seven other returnees and four newcomers, three of whom are junior college players, to compose his 1995-96 squad.

A quick look at the Indiana roster shows six returning sophomores and a total of eight second-year players. This group forms the nucleus of the team. Three of these sophomores – Andrae Patterson, Neil Reed and Charlie Miller – combined to average 18.8 points, 8.4 rebounds and 4.1 assists per game while starting 50 times between them.

For the first time in a number of years, a majority of Indiana's newcomers are not right out of high school. Three of these four players come to Bloomington via the junior college route.

The front line is where the Hoosiers return most of their experience. The only two seniors on the roster reside there in forward Brian Evans and center Todd Lindeman. Sophomore Andrae Patterson was the third leading scorer for the Hoosiers at 7.3 ppg while grabbing 3.9 rpg.

Richard Mandeville returns after sitting out last season as a redshirt, and Robbie Eggers also returns. Two of the three newcomers on the frontline are junior college transfers. Haris Mujezinovic is a 6-9, 250-pound forward who adds size and toughness to the frontcourt. Lou Moore is one of two JC newcomers who has three years of eligibility remaining at IU. The third newcomer is 6-9, 220-pound freshman Larry Richardson.

The main backcourt players are three who have all played only one season of college basketball apiece. Neil Reed and Charlie Miller saw a considerable amount of playing time as freshmen last year while Sherron Wilkerson saw the same amount of action two years ago before sitting out last season with an injury.

Chris Rowles signed with the Hoosiers in May after spending last season at Carl Sandburg Community College in Galesburg, Ill.

BOB KNIGHT
Head Coach

Myles Brand
President

William Perkins
Faculty Representative

Clarence Doninger
Athletic Director

Kit Klingelhoffer
Sports Information Director

ROSTER

No.	Name	POS	HT	WT	Year	Hometown (High School)
32*	Robbie Eggers	F	6-10	245	SO	Cuyahoga Falls, OH
34***	Brian Evans	F	6-8	220	SR	Terre Haute, IN (South)
50***	Todd Lindeman	C	7-0	265	SR	Channing, MI (North Dickinson)
21*	Richard Mandeville	C	7-0	250	SO	Pasadena, CA (La Canada)
3*	Charlie Miller	G	6-7	205	SO	Miami, FL (South Miami)
42	Lou Moore	F/G	6-7	205	SO	Rock Hill, SC (Southern Union St., AL JC)
55	Haris Mujezinovic	C	6-9	260	JR	Chicago, IL (Amundsen HS/Joliet, IL JC)
45*	Andrae Patterson	F	6-8	230	SO	Abilene, TX (Cooper)
5*	Neil Reed	G	6-2	185	SO	Metairie, LA (East Jefferson)
33	Larry Richardson	F	6-8	210	FR	Orange Park, FL
4	Chris Rowles	G	6-1	180	SO	Kansas City, MO (Raytown South/Carl Sandburg, IL JC)
20*	Sherron Wilkerson	G	6-4	185	SO	Jeffersonville, IN

*letters earned

RETURNING/LOST

Letterwinners Returning	YR	POS	FG%	FT%	PPG	RPG	APG
*Brian Evans	SR	F	.462	.783	17.4	6.7	3.3
*Andrae Patterson	SO	F	.494	.689	7.3	3.9	0.8
*Neil Reed	SO	G	.383	.667	5.9	1.7	2.8
Todd Lindeman	SR	C	.492	.569	4.9	3.1	0.4
Charlie Miller	SO	F/G	.467	.621	5.6	2.8	0.8
Richard Mandeville	SO	C	Redshirted in 94-95				
Sherron Wilkerson	SO	G	Redshirted in 94-95				
Robbie Eggers	SO	F	.316	.214	0.6	1.1	0.1

Letterwinners Lost		POS	FG%	FT%	PPG	RPG	APG
*Alan Henderson		F	.597	.633	23.5	9.7	1.7
Pat Knight		G	.268	.750	1.5	1.2	1.9
*Michael Hermon		G	.418	.659	6.0	3.1	3.4
Steve Hart		G	.460	.694	4.7	2.3	1.4

*starters

1995-96 SCHEDULE

Fri., Nov. 10	Russia Aquarius (exh.) (CS) (8 EST)
Tue., Nov. 14	Athletes in Action (exh.) (CS) (8 EST)
Thu., Nov. 23	vs. Alaska-Anchorage (ESPN2) (10 EST)*
Fri., Nov. 24	vs. Old Dominion or Duke (Time TBA)*
Sat., Nov. 25	vs. TBA*
Tue., Nov. 28	Notre Dame (Creative Sports/ESPN2) (7:30 EST)
Sat., Dec. 2	vs. Kentucky (RCA Dome, Indianapolis) (CBS) (3 EST)
Fri., Dec. 8	vs. Delaware (CS) (7 EST)#
Sat., Dec. 9	vs. Bowling Green/Citadel (CS) (7/9 EST)#
Sat., Dec. 16	vs. Kansas (Kemper Arena) (CBS) (4 EST)
Wed., Dec. 20	@ Evansville (CS) (7:30 EST)
Sat., Dec. 23	De Paul (CS) (3 EST)
Fri., Dec. 29	vs. Appalachian State (CS) (6:30 EST)+
Sat., Dec. 30	vs. Kent/Weber State (CS) (7/9 EST)+
Thu., Jan. 4	@ Michigan State (CS) (8 EST)
Sat., Jan. 6	Ohio State (CS) (4:30 EST)
Wed., Jan. 10	Wisconsin (CS) (8 EST)
Sat., Jan. 13	@ Illinois (CS) (8 EST)
Tue., Jan. 16	@ Purdue (ESPN) (7:30 EST)
Tue., Jan. 23	Michigan (ESPN) (7:30 EST)
Sat., Jan. 27	@ Penn State (CS Regional) (Noon EST)
Tue., Jan. 30	Iowa (ESPN) (7:30 EST)
Sun., Feb. 4	Northwestern (CS Regional) (Noon EST)
Tue., Feb. 6	@ Minnesota (ESPN) (7:30 EST)
Sun., Feb. 11	@ Iowa (CBS) (1 EST)
Wed., Feb. 14	Penn State (CS) (8 EST)
Sun., Feb. 18	@ Michigan (CBS) (4 EST)
Sun., Feb. 25	Purdue (CBS) (2 EST)
Wed., Feb. 28	Illinois (CS) (8 EST)
Sat., Mar. 2	@ Wisconsin (CS) (5:30 EST)
Wed., Mar. 6	@ Ohio State (CS) (8 EST)
Sat., Mar. 9 or	Michigan State (CBS) (4 EST) or
Sun., Mar. 10	Michigan State (ESPN) (3 EST)

* – Great Alaska Shootout, Anchorage, AK
\# – Indiana Classic, Bloomington, IN
\+ – Hoosier Classic, Indianapolis, IN

CS – Creative Sports Local Package
CS Regional – Creative Sports Regional Weekend Series

SUBJECT TO CHANGE

Senior forward Brian Evans, a third team all-Big Ten selection last season, is the Hoosiers' leading returning scorer (17.4 ppg) and rebounder (6.70 rpg).

INDIANA

Hoosiers

Head Coach
BOB KNIGHT

Birth Date: Oct. 25, 1940
Hometown: Orrville, OH
Education:
Orrville H.S., 1958, bachelors degree, History and Government, Ohio State, 1962
Playing Experience:
Orrville, H.S., 1955-58, Ohio State, 1960-62
Coaching Experience:
Assistant Coach, Cuyahoga Falls (OH) H.S., 1962-63
Assistant Coach, Army, 1963-65
Head Coach, Army, 1965-71
Head Coach, Indiana, 1971-present
Honors and achievements:
Member of three-time Big Ten championship Buckeye teams of 1960-62 ... team won NCAA championship in 1960 ... named head coach at Army at age of 24 ... 19 NCAA championship appearances ... coach of three national championship teams at Indiana (1976, '81, '87) ... winningest coach in Big Ten history in all games (659) and Conference games only (304) ... winning percentage of .724 is also best among Conference coaches ... coached 11 Big Ten championship teams ... 19 different players have been named both all-Big Ten and all-America ... coached 1979 U.S. Basketball team to gold medal in Pan American Games ... 1984 Olympic team which he coached also won gold ... six-time Big Ten Coach of the Year.
Personal Data:
Full name Robert Montgomery Knight ... wife Karen ... two sons, Tim (1986 Stanford graduate) and Pat (1995 Indiana graduate)... trustee of Naismith Memorial Basketball Hall of Fame ... honorary member of Beta Gamma Sigma business honor society.

Knight's Record:

Year	School	Overall		Big Ten	
1965-66	Army	18-8	.692		
1966-67	Army	13-8	.619		
1967-68	Army	20-5	.800		
1968-69	Army	18-10	.643		
1969-70	Army	22-6	.786		
1970-71	Army	11-13	.458		
1971-72	Indiana	17-8	.680	9-5	.643
1972-73	Indiana	22-6	.786	11-3	.786
1973-74	Indiana	23-5	.821	12-2	.857
1974-75	Indiana	31-1	.969	18-0	1.000
1975-76	Indiana	32-0	1.000	18-0	1.000
1976-77	Indiana	16-11	.953	11-7	.611
1977-78	Indiana	21-8	.724	12-6	.667
1978-79	Indiana	22-12	.647	10-8	.556
1979-80	Indiana	21-8	.724	13-5	.722
1980-81	Indiana	26-9	.743	14-4	.778
1981-82	Indiana	19-10	.655	12-6	.667
1982-83	Indiana	24-6	.800	13-5	.722
1983-84	Indiana	22-9	.710	13-5	.722
1984-85	Indiana	19-14	.576	7-11	.389
1985-86	Indiana	21-8	.724	13-5	.556
1986-87	Indiana	30-4	.882	15-3	.833
1987-88	Indiana	19-10	.655	11-7	.611
1988-89	Indiana	27-8	.771	15-3	.833
1989-90	Indiana	18-11	.621	8-10	.444
1990-91	Indiana	29-5	.853	15-3	.833
1991-92	Indiana	27-7	.794	14-4	.778
1992-93	Indiana	31-4	.886	17-1	.944
1993-94	Indiana	21-9	.700	12-6	.667
1994-95	Indiana	19-12	.613	11-7	.611
School Total		557-185	.751	304-116	.724
Career Total		659-235	.737		

Big Ten Championship: (11) 1973-74(co)-75-76-80-81-83-87(co)-89-91(co)-93
NCAA Appearances: (20) 1973-75-76(Champion)-78-80-81(Champion)-82-83-84-85-86-87(Champion)-88-89-90-91-92-93-94-95
NIT Appearances: (7) 1966-68-69-70-72-79(Champion)-85

Bob Knight

HOOSIERS TO WATCH

BRIAN EVANS, F, 6-8, 220, SR, Terre Haute, IN
Indiana's leading returning scorer (17.4 ppg) and rebounder (6.70) from last year... third team all-Big Ten selection last season... named to the NABC/Sears District 10 second team... posted career-highs in every offensive category last season... had six "double-double" performances in '94-95... enters the season No. 30 on IU's all-time scoring list... fourth on IU's all-time three-point shooting list... member of USA Basketball's gold medal-winning World University Games team over the summer.

TODD LINDEMAN, C, 7-0, 265, SR, Channing, MI
Played in 30 games last season and averaged 4.9 points and 3.1 rebounds per game... set career bests in blocks (31) and assists (11)... scored a career-high 18 points vs. Butler and set a Conference career-high with 16 points at Northwestern... tallied a career-high 13 rebounds vs. Arkansas-Little Rock.

ANDRAE PATTERSON, F, 6-8, 230, SO, Abilene, TX
Appeared in 28 games a year ago and averaged 7.3 points and 3.9 rebounds per game... both of those totals were the third best marks on the team ... scored a career-high 19 points vs. Tulane in the third game of his career... Big Ten career best of 18 points (including 4-4 3-pointers) at Wisconsin... missed three games after spraining his knee in the Kansas game... in just nine minutes vs. the Jayhawks had eight rebounds.

1994-95 RESULTS

(19-12/11-7)

November
21	L	72-77	Utah**
22	W	92-79	Chaminade**
23	L	68-86	Tulane**
29	L	79-80	Notre Dame (OT)

December
3	W	84-63	Evansville (at Indianapolis, IN)
7	L	70-73	Kentucky (at Louisville, KY)
9	W	79-62	MOREHEAD STATE#
10	W	92-77	MIAMI OHIO#
17	W	80-61	KANSAS
21	W	89-66	BUTLER
28	W	92-49	Eastern Kentucky+
29	W	77-53	Arkansas-Little Rock+

January
4	L	55-74	Iowa
7	W	73-70	WISCONSIN
11	W	89-82	MICHIGAN STATE
14	L	67-78	Illinois
18	W	71-69	Penn State
24	L	62-65	MICHIGAN
28	W	90-75	OHIO STATE
31	L	66-76	Purdue

February
4	W	88-67	Northwestern
8	L	54-64	MINNESOTA
12	W	82-73	PURDUE
14	W	69-52	Ohio State
19	L	61-50	Michigan
25	W	73-60	PENN STATE

March
2	W	89-85	ILLINOIS
5	L	61-67	Michigan State
8	W	72-70	Wisconsin
12	W	110-79	IOWA
17	L	60-65	Missouri*

*NCAA first round, Boise, ID
**Maui Classic, Maui, HI (6th)
#Indiana Classic, Bloomington, IN (1st)
+Hoosier Classic, Indianapolis, IN (1st)

1994-95 STATISTICS *(1995-96 returnees in ALL CAPS)*
Record: 19-12   Home: 11-2   Road: 4-6   Neutral: 4-4

Player	G-GS	Min-Avg	FG-FGA	Pct	3P-3PA	Pct	FT-FTA	Pct	Rebounds Off-Def	Tot-Avg	PF-FD	AT	TO	BS	ST	Pts-Avg
Alan Henderson	31-31	1093-35.3	284-476	.597	2-10	.200	159-251	.633	106-196	302-9.7	97-5	54	89	64	42	729-23.5
BRIAN EVANS	31-30	1051-33.9	177-383	.462	58-139	.417	126-161	.783	53-155	208-6.7	77-2	101	72	17	25	538-17.4
ANDRAE PATTERSON	28-20	540-19.3	84-170	.494	4-8	.500	31-45	.689	39-69	108-3.9	80-5	21	49	16	16	203-7.3
Michael Hermon	28-17	598-21.4	66-158	.418	6-26	.231	29-44	.659	20-68	88-3.1	73-1	94	69	1	35	167-6.0
NEIL REED	30-18	706-23.5	57-149	.383	22-71	.310	40-60	.667	5-45	50-1.7	49-0	76	36	1	18	176-5.9
CHARLIE MILLER	31-12	581-18.7	63-135	.467	8-15	.533	41-66	.621	28-59	87-2.8	36-0	25	42	5	9	175-5.6
TODD LINDEMAN	30-10	489-16.3	59-120	.492	0-0	.000	29-51	.569	37-57	94-3.1	74-3	11	35	31	10	147-4.9
Steve Hart	30-14	612-20.4	57-124	.460	3-13	.231	25-36	.694	17-52	69-2.3	48-1	43	38	10	16	142-4.7
Pat Knight	31-3	424-13.7	15-56	.268	3-12	.250	12-16	.750	5-32	37-1.2	19-0	60	37	0	10	45-1.5
Jean Paul	10-0	23-2.3	2-6	.333	1-3	.333	3-4	.750	0-1	1-0.1	5-0	0	1	0	1	8-0.8
ROBBIE EGGERS	24-0	113-4.7	6-19	.316	0-0	.000	3-14	.214	10-17	27-1.1	13-0	2	4	1	2	16-0.6
Team										101				5		
Indiana	31	6225	870-1796	.484	107-297	.360	498-748	.666	320-751	1172-37.8	571	487	477	146	184	2345-75.6
Opponents	31	6225	771-1881	.410	186-555	.335	430-632	.680	405-684	1089-35.1	665	387	482	71	198	2158-69.6

SCHOOL RECORDS

Individual

SCORING
Game: 56   Jimmy Rayl vs. Minnesota 1/27/62
               Jimmy Rayl vs. Michigan State 2/23/63
Season: 785   Calbert Cheaney 1992-93
Career: **2,613** **Calbert Cheaney 1989-93**

REBOUNDING
Game: 33   **Walt Bellamy vs. Michigan 3/11/61**
Season: 428   Walt Bellamy   1960-61
Career: 1,091 Alan Henderson   1992-95

ASSISTS
Game: 15   Keith Smart vs. Auburn 3/14/87
Season: 197   Isiah Thomas   1980-81
Career: 542   Quinn Buckner   1972-76

STEALS
Game: 9   Scott May vs. Michigan, 1976
Season: 74   Isiah Thomas   1980-81
Career: 178   Steve Alford   1984-87

BLOCKED SHOTS
Game: 8   Dean Garrett vs. Montana State, 1987
               Dean Garrett vs. Iowa, 1988
Season: 99   Dean Garrett   1987-88
Career: 213   Alan Henderson   1992-95

Team

SCORING
Game: 122   2/2/59 (Ohio State)
               1962 (Notre Dame)
Season: 2817 1974-75

REBOUNDING
Game: 95   3/11/61 (Michigan)
Season: 1433 1974-75

ASSISTS
Game: 30   1981 (Northwestern)
Season: 655   1975-76

STEALS
Game: 19   1987 (Northwestern)
Season: 250   1991-92

BLOCKED SHOTS
Game: 11   1988 (Iowa)
Season: 135   1986-87

Big Ten record in **bold**

TOP TEN SCORERS

1. Calbert Cheaney (1989-93)   2,613
2. Steve Alford (1984-87)   2,438
3. Don Schlundt (1952-55)   2,192
4. Mike Woodson (1977-80)   2,061
5. Alan Henderson (1992-95)   1,979
6. Damon Bailey (1990-94)   1,741
7. Kent Benson (1974-77)   1,640
8. Eric Anderson (1988-92)   1,715
9. Scott May (1974-76)   1,593
10. Greg Graham (1990-93)   1,590

Sophomore forward Andrae Patterson was a member of the 1995 Big Ten All-Star team which toured Japan, averaging 14.4 ppg and 8.3 rpg.

IOWA

Hawkeyes

QUICK FACTS

Location: Iowa City, IA
Population: 60,000
Founded: 1847
Enrollment: 28,000
Nickname: Hawkeyes
Colors: Old Gold and Black
Arena: Carver-Hawkeye Arena (1983, 15,500)
President: Mary Sue Coleman
Faculty Representative: Bonnie Slatton
Men's Athletic Director: Robert Bowlsby
Head Coach: Tom Davis (Wisconsin-Platteville, 1960) 10th year
Assistant Coaches: Gary Close, Rich Walker, Frank DiLeo
Sports Information Director: Phil Haddy
Asst. SID: Steve Roe
SID Emeritus: George Wine
SID Phone: (319) 335-9411
SID Fax Phone: (319) 335-9417
Media Hotline: (319) 335-1100
Press Row Phone: (319) 335-7284
1994-95 Record: 21-12, 9-9 Big Ten (7th-tie)
Starters Returning/Lost: 4/1
Letterwinners Returning/Lost: 8/3
Best time to contact coach: Tuesday mornings

It's hard to paint Iowa's basketball 1995-96 prospectus with anything but an optimistic brush. From a team that finished 21-12 in all games and 9-9 in the Big Ten, the Hawkeyes return: 79 percent of their scoring and 69 percent of their rebounding, three of the Big Ten's top five returning scorers in juniors Chris Kingsbury, Jess Settles and Andre Woolridge (the other two are Brian Evans of Indiana and Kiwane Garris of Illinois), a fourth starter, senior Kenyon Murray, who led the Big Ten in steals (2.2 per game) and averaged 11.5 points and most of the players from a team that led the Big Ten in five categories (scoring, 3-point field goals, free throw percentage, steals and turnover margin).

Some unforeseen circumstances occurred last season, most notably Settles' back problems that kept him out of seven games and prevented him from starting seven others. Ineligibility and illness restricted Russ Millard to only 12 games.

It's reasonable to assume Iowa will contend in the Big Ten this season if it improves its record in close games. The Hawkeyes lost six contests last season that were decided in the final seconds or overtime. Five were in the Big Ten, one in the NIT.

The biggest loss for the Hawkeyes was the versatile Jim Bartels, who led the team in rebounding, was the most accurate 3-point shooter, finished second in steals and averaged 11.2 points.

Iowa's 1995-96 schedule is another strong one. Iowa opens the season at the Great Alaska Shootout, meeting Ohio University in the first round. Other teams in the field include Connecticut, Duke, Indiana, Texas Christian, Old Dominion and Alaska-Anchorage.

Iowa's Super Chevy Shootout field includes Mississippi, East Tennessee State and Colgate, with Iowa meeting East Tennessee State in the first round. Iowa opens the home season against Drake and will host Texas Southern, an NCAA tournament participant last season.

Non-conference road games, in addition to the Alaska tournament, are at Northern Iowa, Iowa State and Colorado. In Big Ten play, Iowa meets Penn State (home) and Northwestern (away) just once.

As many as 20 of Iowa's 30 games could be against teams that were invited to post-season play a year ago, including 17 against teams that were in the NCAA tournament.

TOM DAVIS
Head Coach

Mary Sue Coleman
President

Bonnie Slatton
Faculty Representative

Robert Bowlsby
Men's Athletic Director

Phil Haddy
Men's Sports Information Director

Carver-Hawkeye Arena (1983)
Capacity 15,500

ROSTER

No.	Name	POS	HT	WT	Year	Hometown (High School)
42*	Ryan Bowen	F	6-9	215	SO	Ft. Madison, IA
23	Trey Bullet	G	6-5	195	FR	Jackson, MS (St. Andrew's)
13***	Mon'ter Glasper	G	6-2	175	SR	Albion, MI
55*	Greg Helmers	C	6-10	230	SO	Palmer, IA (Pomeroy-Palmer)
14**	Chris Kingsbury	G	6-5	215	JR	Hamilton, OH
44	J.R. Koch	F	6-10	210	FR	Morton, IL
32	Kent McCausland	G	6-3	180	FR	Waterloo, IA (West)
52***	Russ Millard	F/C	6-8	240	SR	Cedar Rapids, IA (Washington)
3***	Kenyon Murray	F	6-5	190	SR	Battle Creek, MI (Central)
50	Alvin Robinson	F	6-9	225	FR	Chicago, IL (Carver)
54	Guy Rucker	C	6-11	235	FR	Inkster, MI (John Glenn)
4**	Jess Settles	F	6-7	220	JR	Winfield, IA (Winfield-Mt. Union)
5*	Andre Woolridge	G	6-1	190	JR	Omaha, NE (Benson)

*letters earned

RETURNING/LOST

Letterwinners Returning	YR	POS	FG%	FT%	PPG	RPG	APG
Ryan Bowen	SO	F	.527	.593	4.6	4.5	0.5
Mon'ter Glasper	SR	G	.435	.511	3.9	1.7	2.4
Greg Helmers	SO	C	.692	.813	1.1	2.1	2.0
*Chris Kingsbury	JR	G	.400	.803	16.8	2.7	1.7
Russ Millard	SR	F/C	.511	.588	5.2	3.3	0.9
*Kenyon Murray	SR	F	.459	.592	11.5	4.2	1.2
*Jess Settles	JR	F	.469	.802	15.6	6.2	2.0
*Andre Woolridge	JR	G	.478	.766	14.0	2.5	5.8
Letterwinners Lost		POS	FG%	FT%	PPG	RPG	APG
*Jim Bartels		F	.504	.740	11.2	6.2	1.7
John Carter		C	.435	.559	3.2	3.5	0.4
Kevin Skillett		G	.491	.889	2.8	1.8	1.2

*starters

1995-96 SCHEDULE

Sun., Nov. 12	Republic of Georgia (exh.) (CS) (2 CST)
Wed., Nov. 15	Marathon Oil (exh.) (CS) (7 CST)
Wed., Nov. 22	vs. Ohio (CS) (8:15 CST)*
Fri., Nov. 24	vs. Texas Christian or Connecticut (Time TBA)*
Sat., Nov. 25	vs. TBA*
Tue., Nov. 28	Drake (CS) (7 CST)
Fri., Dec. 1	vs. East Tennessee State (CS) (8 CST)#
Sat., Dec. 2	vs. Colgate/Mississippi (CS) (6/8 CST)#
Tue., Dec. 5	@ Northern Iowa (CS) (7 CST)
Sat., Dec. 9	@ Iowa State (8 CST)
Sat., Dec. 16	Texas Southern (CS) (7 CST)
Wed., Dec. 20	Western Illinois (CS) (7 CST)
Sat., Dec. 23	Morehead State (CS) (3 CST)
Thu., Dec. 28	@ Colorado (CS) (8 CST)
Wed., Jan. 3	@ Purdue (ESPN) (6 CST)
Sat., Jan. 6	Minnesota (CS) (7 CST)
Wed., Jan. 10	Ohio State (CS) (7 CST)
Sat., Jan. 13	@ Wisconsin (CS) (3:30 CST)
Thu., Jan. 18	Illinois (ESPN) (6:30 CST)
Sat., Jan. 20	@ Michigan State (CS Regional) (11 a.m. CST)
Sun., Jan. 28	Michigan (CBS) (Noon CST)
Tue., Jan. 30	@ Indiana (ESPN) (6:30 CST)
Sat., Feb. 3	Penn State (CS Regional) (2 CST)
Wed., Feb. 7	@ Northwestern (CS) (7 CST)
Sun., Feb. 11	Indiana (CBS) (Noon CST)
Tue., Feb. 13	@ Michigan (ESPN) (6:30 CST)
Wed., Feb. 21	Michigan State (CS) (7 CST)
Sat., Feb. 24	@ Illinois (CS Regional) (1:15 CST)
Wed., Feb. 28	Wisconsin (CS) (7 CST)
Sat., Mar. 2 or	@ Ohio State (CS Regional) (Noon CST) or
Sun., Mar. 3	@ Ohio State (CBS) (1 CST)
Wed., Mar. 6	@ Minnesota (CS) (7 CST)
Sat., Mar. 9 or	Purdue (CBS) (3 CST) or
Sun., Mar. 10	Purdue (ESPN) (2 CST)

* – Great Alaska Shootout, Anchorage, AK
\# – Super Chevy Shootout, Iowa City, IA

CS – Creative Sports Local Package
CS Regional – Creative Sports Regional Weekend Series

SUBJECT TO CHANGE

Junior forward Jess Settles was honored as an all-Big Ten third team selection after averaging 15.6 points and 6.2 rebounds per game last year.

IOWA
Hawkeyes

Head Coach
TOM DAVIS

Birth Date: December 3, 1938
Hometown: Ridgeway, WI
Education:
Ridgeway High School, 1955 ... B.A., Wisconsin-Platteville, 1960 ... M.A., Wisconsin, 1964 ... Ph.D., History, Maryland, 1970.
Playing Experience:
Ridgeway H.S., 1952-55 ... UW-Platteville, 1956-59.
Coaching Experience:
Head coach, Midgewille (IL) High School, 1960-61
Assistant coach, Maryland, 1967-69
Assistant coach, American, 1970-71
Head coach, Lafayette, 1971-77
Head coach, Boston College, 1977-82
Head coach, Stanford, 1982-86
Head coach, Iowa, 1986-present
Honors and achievements:
Four-time letterwinner at UW-Platteville ... team made NAIA championship twice ... captain as senior ... Widemer's Eastern, Eastern Basketball Magazine and Boston Herald New England Coach of the Year in 1977-78 ... Widemer's, Big East, District I coach of the year in 1980-81 ... AP national and Big Ten Coach of the Year in 1986-87 as Iowa won a school-record 30 games and No. 1 ranking during season ... first three seasons at Iowa were school's winningest seasons ... eight NCAA and four NIT appearances in his career ... coached U.S. team to gold medal at 1981 World University Games.
Personal Data:
Wife Shari ... son Keno ... resides in Iowa City.

Davis's Record:

1971-72	Lafayette	21-6	.778		
1972-73	Lafayette	16-19	.457		
1973-74	Lafayette	17-9	.654		
1974-75	Lafayette	22-6	.786		
1975-76	Lafayette	19-7	.731		
1976-77	Lafayette	21-6	.778		
1977-78	Boston College	15-11	.577		
1978-79	Boston College	21-9	.700		
1979-80	Boston College	19-10	.655		
1980-81	Boston College	23-7	.767		
1981-82	Stanford	22-10	.688		
1982-83	Stanford	14-14	.500		
1983-84	Stanford	19-12	.613		
1984-85	Stanford	11-17	.393		
1985-86	Stanford	14-16	.467		
1986-87	Iowa	30-5	.857	14-4	.778
1987-88	Iowa	24-10	.706	12-6	.667
1988-89	Iowa	23-10	.697	10-8	.556
1989-90	Iowa	12-16	.429	4-14	.222
1990-91	Iowa	21-11	.656	9-9	.500
1991-92	Iowa	19-11	.633	10-8	.556
1992-93	Iowa	23-9	.719	11-7	.611
1993-94	Iowa	11-16	.407	5-13	.278
1994-95	Iowa	21-12	.636	9-9	.500
School Total		184-100	.648	84-78	.519
Career Total		458-250	.647		

NCAA Appearances: (8) 1981-82-87-88-89-91-92-93
NIT Appearances: (4) 1972-75-80-95

Tom Davis

HAWKEYES TO WATCH

JESS SETTLES, F, 6-7, 220, JR, Winfield, IA

One of 25 players named to pre-season list for the 1996 John R. Wooden All-American Team and Player of the Year award... all-Big Ten third team selection by both coaches and media... academic all-Big Ten team...missed seven games and did not start seven others due to back injury...averaged 15.6 points and 6.2 rebounds, shooting .469 from the field and .802 from free throw line in 26 games...scored in double figures in 19 of 26 games.

ANDRE WOOLRIDGE, G, 6-1, 190, JR, Omaha, NE

Selected third team all-Big Ten by league media and honorable mention by Big Ten coaches... in Big Ten stats, ranked second in assists (5.7), seventh in field goal percentage (.487), 11th in steals (1.2) and 12th in scoring (15.3) and free throw percentage (7.25)... 190 assists is second-best in a single season at Iowa, one shy of school record... averaged 15.3 points in Big Ten games.

CHRIS KINGSBURY, G, 6-5, 215, JR, Hamilton, OH

Second team all-Big Ten as selected by the media... selected to USBWA all-District Five team... Big Ten Player of the Week, Feb. 20... 553 points in 33 games is the most ever by an Iowa sophomore... holds Iowa records for three-point field goals and three-point attempts in a game (9, 19), season (117, 297) and career (161, 434)... averaged 21 points in five games for People to People all-star team over the summer... begins season with 773 career points.

1994-95 RESULTS
(21-12/9-9)

November
25	W	126-79	MORGAN STATE
29	W	103-68	Drake

December
2	W	99-63	Pepperdine**
3	W	91-75	Ohio**
7	W	80-48	NORTHERN IOWA
10	L	63-76	IOWA STATE
17	W	102-72	LONG ISLAND
20	W	85-60	WESTERN CAROLINA
23	W	61-57	BYU-Hawaii
27	W	81-71	Duke##
29	W	84-82	Hawaii##
30	L	91-101	Arkansas##

January
4	W	74-55	INDIANA
7	L	68-69	Michigan State
11	L	82-83	Michigan (2OT)
14	L	83-84	PURDUE
21	W	96-84	WISCONSIN
25	W	81-66	Ohio State
28	L	54-55	MINNESOTA

February
1	L	74-79	ILLINOIS
4	L	64-74	Penn State
9	W	116-77	NORTHWESTERN
11	L	97-104	Illinois (OT)
15	W	74-70	Minnesota
18	W	85-66	OHIO STATE
22	W	84-77	Wisconsin

March
1	L	85-92	Purdue
5	W	89-69	MICHIGAN
8	W	79-78	MICHIGAN STATE
12	W	79-110	Indiana
15	W	96-87	DePaul*
21	W	66-62	OHIO (ESPN)#
23	L	64-67	PENN STATE+

* NIT first round, Moline, IL
\# NIT second round
\+ NIT quarterfinals
** Hawkeye Invitational, Iowa City, IA (1st)
\#\# Kraft Rainbow Classic, Honolulu, HI (2nd)

1994-95 STATISTICS *(1995-96 returnees in ALL CAPS)*
Record: 21-12   Home: 13-5   Road: 6-6   Neutral: 2-1

Player	G-GS	Min-Avg	FG-FGA	Pct	3P-3PA	Pct	FT-FTA	Pct	Rebounds Off-Def	Tot-Avg	PF-FD	AT	TO	BS	ST	Pts-Avg
CHRIS KINGSBURY	33-25	929-28.2	169-423	.400	117-297	.394	98-122	.803	27-61	88-2.7	94-2	55	58	5	41	553-16.8
JESS SETTLES	26-19	634-24.4	138-294	.469	32-91	.352	97-121	.802	62-100	162-6.2	73-1	53	86	4	31	405-15.6
ANDRE WOOLRIDGE	33-32	961-29.1	153-320	.478	24-62	.387	131-171	.766	17-65	82-2.5	57-1	190	87	5	42	461-14.0
KENYON MURRAY	33-31	929-28.2	141-307	.459	26-80	.325	71-120	.592	74-65	139-4.2	80-0	39	61	14	58	379-11.5
Jim Bartels	33-30	929-28.2	128-254	.504	59-143	.413	54-73	.740	65-139	204-6.2	58-0	55	41	9	70	369-11.2
RUSS MILLARD	12-2	168-14.0	24-47	.511	4-13	.308	10-17	.588	16-23	39-3.3	20-0	11	12	2	9	62-5.2
RYAN BOWEN	33-19	647-19.6	58-110	.527	0-1	.000	35-59	593	71-77	148-4.5	65-0	16	32	34	38	151-4.6
MON'TER GLASPER	32-2	515-16.1	47-108	.435	8-34	.235	24-47	.511	15-39	54-1.7	39-0	76	40	0	37	126-3.9
John Carter	29-3	307-10.6	30-69	.435	0-0	.000	33-59	.559	48-53	101-3.5	35-0	10	31	15	9	93-3.2
Kevin Skillett	31-2	385-12.4	26-53	.491	2-12	.167	32-36	.889	22-35	57-1.8	37-0	36	19	1	22	86-2.8
GREG HELMERS	15-0	130-8.7	9-13	.692	0-0	.000	13-16	.813	11-19	30-2.0	19-0	7	7	5	2	31-2.1
Nathan Koch	15-0	56-3.7	9-16	.563	0-0	.000	3-8	.375	2-11	13-0.9	4-0	2	12	1	3	21-1.4
John Fritzel	8-0	24-3.0	2-8	.250	2-7	.286	3-4	.750	1-3	4-0.5	1-0	2	1	0	0	9-1.1
Jason Shay	5-0	19-3.8	0-2	.000	0-1	.000	5-6	.833	1-4	5-1.0	1-0	2	1	0	0	5-1.0
DARRYL MOORE	5-0	14-2.8	1-8	.125	0-2	.000	1-2	.500	1-1	2-0.4	3-0	0	1	0	1	3-0.6
Michael White	9-0	25-2.8	0-2	.000	0-0	.000	3-4	.750	2-4	6-0.7	1-0	1	0	0	2	3-0.3
BRIAN HABERER	1-0	3-3.0	0-0	.000	0-0	.000	0-0	.000	1-0	1-1.0	0-0	0	0	0	0	0-0.0
Team										78						
Iowa	33	6675	935-2034	.460	274-743	.369	613-865	.709	436-699	1213-36.8	587	555	489	96	365	2757-83.5
Opponents	33	6675	936-1961	.477	203-595	.341	385-571	.674	393-755	1148-34.8	707	571	653	129	233	2460-74.5

SCHOOL RECORDS

Individual

SCORING
Game: 49 John Johnson vs. Northwestern 2/24/70
Season: 699 John Johnson 1969-70
Career: 2116 Roy Marble 1985-89

REBOUNDING
Game: 30 Charles Darling vs. Wisconsin 3/3/52
Season: 387 Charles Darling 1950-51
Career: 914 Kevin Kunnert 1970-73

ASSISTS
Game: 16 Cal Wulfsberg vs. Ohio State 1/24/76
Season: 191 Cal Wulfsberg 1975-76
Career: 517 B.J. Armstrong 1985-89

STEALS
Game: 9 Acie Earl vs. Texas Southern 12/28/92
Kenyon Murray vs. Ohio State 21/18/95
Season: 72 Bill Jones 1987-88
Career: 183 Roy Marble 1985-89

BLOCKED SHOTS
Game: 9 Acie Earl vs. Wisconsin 1/29/92
Season: 121 Acie Earl 1991-92
Career: 365 **Acie Earl** **1990-93**

Team

SCORING
Game: 126 12/30/87 (Oral Roberts)
          11/25/94 (Morgan State)
Season: 3181 1987-88

REBOUNDING
Game: 77 12/30/72 (Minnesota-Duluth)
Season: 1508 1986-87

ASSISTS
Game: 34 12/1/84 (George Mason)
Season: 600 1984-85 and 1987-88

STEALS
Game: 23 **2/22/86 (Northwestern)**
          12/7/94 (Northern Iowa)
Season: 365 1994-95

BLOCKED SHOTS
Game: 11 1/4/93 (Drake)
Season: 165 1992-93

TOP TEN SCORERS

1. Roy Marble (1985-89)   2,116
2. Acie Earl (1990-93)   1,779
3. Greg Stokes (1981-85)   1,768
4. B.J. Armstrong (1985-89) 1,705
5. Ronnie Lester (1976-80) 1,675
6. Don Nelson (1959-62)   1,522
7. Ed Horton (1985-89)   1,372
8. Bruce King (1974-77)   1,361
9. James Moses (1989-92)   1,343
10. Jeff Moe (1984-88)   1,248

Andre Woolridge's 190 assists last year ranks second on Iowa's season assist list, one shy of the school record.

MICHIGAN Wolverines

QUICK FACTS

Location: Ann Arbor, MI
Population: 115,000
Founded: 1817
Enrollment: 36,468
Nickname: Wolverines
Colors: Maize and Blue
Arena: Crisler Arena (1967, 13,562)
President: James J. Duderstadt
Faculty Representative: Percy Bates
Athletic Director: Joe Roberson
Head Coach: Steve Fisher (Illinois State, 1967) 7th year
Assistant Coaches: Brian Dutcher, Scott Perry, Jay Smith
Sports Information Director: Bruce Madej
Basketball Contact: B.J. Sohn (Asst. SID)
SID Phone: (313) 763-4423
SID Fax Phone: (313) 747-1188
Press Row Phone: (313) 998-7188
1994-95 Record: 17-14, 11-7 Big Ten (3rd-tie)
Starters Returning/Lost: 2/3
Letterwinners Returning/Lost: 7/4
Best time to contact coach: Contact SID

STEVE FISHER
Head Coach

Although the last of the Fab Five may be gone, the Michigan Wolverines boast a pile of young, versatile talent for 1995-96 and look to return to national prominence following a 17-14 season that included Michigan's earliest exit from the NCAA Tournament under head coach Steve Fisher.

"I am very excited about this year's team," said Fisher. "I'm convinced we will have a better season. On paper, it may be pointed out that eight of our 10 players are freshmen or sophomores and that doesn't bode well. However, six of those players are experienced and I anticipate marked improvement in all of them. Traditionally, you make a big step between your freshman and sophomore season, and I hope that happens with this group."

Senior Dugan Fife is Michigan's only upperclassman and a two-year starter at point guard. He is the team's captain and follows in the footsteps of his father, Dan, who captained Michigan's 1971 team coached by Johnny Orr. Fife is joined by a group of freshmen and sophomores that have comprised one of the nation's top recruiting classes the past two seasons. Sophomore Maurice Taylor, the Big Ten's Freshman of the Year last season, is a returning starter at power forward and looks to expand his perimeter game while fellow sophomore Maceo Baston is expected to add some offensive punch to his rebounding and shot blocking skills and can play any of three positions along the frontcourt.

Another pair of athletic sophomores will also battle for starting positions. Jerod Ward and Willie Mitchell each provided stretches of impressive play last season, and Fisher, who enters his seventh full season at Michigan with a 140-59 record, is counting on and needs improved play from each in 1995-96. Sophomore point guard Travis Conlan came on strong during the Big Ten season last year and is the team's best passer and ball handler.

Robert Traylor leads a class of impressive newcomers and is expected to make an immediate contribution to the Wolverine frontline. Albert White is another solid freshman who can play a number of positions and combines with sharpshooter Louis Bullock to potentially give Michigan a lethal blend of inside and outside weapons.

Overall, the frontline is big, versatile, and can smother opponents inside. However, much of the team's success will depend on improved perimeter shooting and molding a defense that lost standouts Ray Jackson and Jimmy King who helped Michigan set a Big Ten record (Conference games only) for opponent field goal percentage defense.

"I like our players," said Fisher. "I believe with the combination of attitude, athleticism and togetherness this team brings, we are going to have a basketball team that will be fun to coach, exciting, and extremely enjoyable to watch."

James Duderstadt
President

Percy Bates
Faculty Representative

Joe Roberson
Athletic Director

Bruce Madej
Athletic Public Relations Director

Crisler Arena (1967)
Capacity 13,562

ROSTER

No	Name	POS	HT	WT	Year	Hometown (High School)
30 *	Maceo Baston	F/C	6-9	210	SO	Dallas, TX (H.G. Spruce)
22	Louis Bullock	G	6-2	165	FR	Temple Hills, MD (Laurel Baptist Academy)
21 *	Travis Conlan	G	6-5	190	SO	St. Clair Shores, MI (Lake Shore)
11***	Dugan Fife	G	6-3	185	SR	Clarkston, MI
13 *	Willie Mitchell	F/G	6-8	217	SO	Detroit, MI
20 *	Neal Morton	G/F	6-5	200	SR	Ann Arbor, MI (Gabriel Richard/Aquinas College)
23 *	Maurice Taylor	F/C	6-9	250	SO	Detroit, MI (Henry Ford)
54	Robert Traylor	C	6-8	300	FR	Detroit, MI (Murray-Wright)
32 *	Jerod Ward	F/G	6-9	215	SO	Clinton, MI
44	Albert White	F/G	6-6	230	FR	Inkster, MI

*letters earned

RETURNING/LOST

Letterwinners Returning	YR	POS	FG%	FT%	PPG	RPG	APG
*Maurice Taylor	SO	F	.471	.602	12.4	5.1	1.2
Maceo Baston	SO	F	.674	.547	7.7	5.5	0.2
Jerod Ward	SO	F	.364	.676	6.0	3.7	0.6
Willie Mitchell	SO	F	.360	.580	5.3	2.8	0.6
*Dugan Fife	SR	G	.377	.619	3.8	1.8	1.9
Travis Conlan	SO	G	.351	.313	1.4	1.2	1.4
Neal Morton	SR	G	.000	1.000	0.3	0.3	0.0

Letterwinners Lost		POS	FG%	FT%	PPG	RPG	APG
*Ray Jackson		F	.478	.774	15.8	5.3	3.0
*Jimmy King		G	.433	.679	14.7	5.0	2.9
*Makhtar Ndiaye		C	.489	.543	5.0	5.2	0.6
Bobby Crawford		G	.208	.500	1.9	0.9	0.9

*starters

1995-96 SCHEDULE

Wed., Nov. 1	Athletes in Action (exh.) (7:30 EST)
Thu., Nov. 9	Russian Select Team (exh.) (7:30 EST)
Wed., Nov. 15	De Paul (ESPN) (9:30 EST)
Fri., Nov. 17	Preseason NIT
Wed., Nov. 22	Preseason NIT Semifinal
Fri., Nov. 24	Preseason NIT Final
Mon., Nov. 27	St. Francis (7:30 EST)
Wed., Nov. 29	at Ball State (CS) (7 EST)
Sat., Dec. 2	at Detroit-Mercy (7:30 EST)
Tue., Dec. 5	at Louisiana State (ESPN) (7:30 EST)
Sat., Dec. 9	Duke (CBS) (3 EST)
Sat., Dec. 16	Washington (CS) (1 EST)
Mon., Dec. 18	Cleveland State (7:30 EST)
Thu., Dec. 30	at UNLV (ESPN2) (11:59 p.m. EST)
Sat., Dec. 30	vs. Davidson (at Las Vegas) (8:30 p.m. EST)
Wed., Jan. 3	at Wisconsin (CS) (8 EST)
Sat., Jan. 6	Northwestern (CS Regional) (Noon EST)
Tue., Jan. 9	Illinois (ESPN) (7:30 EST)
Sat., Jan. 13	at Michigan State (CS Regional) (Noon EST)
Sun., Jan. 21	Penn State (CBS) (Noon EST)
Tue., Jan. 23	at Indiana (ESPN) (7:30 EST)
Sun., Jan. 28	at Iowa (CBS) (1 EST)
Wed., Jan. 31	Purdue (ESPN) (7 EST)
Sat., Feb. 3	at Ohio State (CS) (8 EST)
Sat., Feb. 10	at Purdue (CS Regional) (Noon EST)
Tue., Feb. 13	Iowa (ESPN) (7:30 EST)
Sun., Feb. 18	Indiana (CBS) (4 EST)
Thu., Feb. 22	at Penn State (CS) (8 EST)
Sat., Feb. 24	Minnesota (CS) (8 EST)
Tue., Feb. 27	Michigan State (ESPN) (7:30 EST)
Sat., March 2 or	at Illinois (CS Regional) (1 EST)
Sun., March 3	or at Illinois (CBS) (2 EST)
Wed., March 6	at Northwestern (CS) (8 EST)
Sat., March 9	Wisconsin (CS) (4:30 EST)

CS - Creative Sports Local Package
CS Regional - Creative Sports Regional Weekend Series

SUBJECT TO CHANGE

A 6-9 center/forward, Maurice Taylor was a consensus selection as 1995 Big Ten Freshman of the Year by league coaches and the media.

MICHIGAN Wolverines

Head Coach
STEVE FISHER

Birth Date: March 24, 1945
Hometown: Herrin, IL
Education:
Herrin High School, 1963 ... B.S., Math/Physical Education, Illinois State, 1967 ... M.S., Physical Education, Illinois State, 1968.
Playing Experience:
Guard, Herrin H.S., 1960-63 ... guard, Illinois State, 1964-67.
Coaching Experience:
Graduate assistant, Illinois State, 1968-70
Head coach, Park Forest, IL Rich East, 1971-79
Assistant coach, Western Michigan, 1979-82
Assistant coach, Michigan, 1982-89
Head coach, Michigan, 1989-present
Honors and achievements:
Earned three varsity letters at Herrin H.S. and at Illinois State...won four conference championships at Rich East H.S. and is school's winningest coach...has guided Michigan to three NCAA Final Fours, winning the national championship in 1989 and finishing as runnerup in 1992 and '93... served as interim head coach in 1989 and is the only interim coach and only first-year coach to win an NCAA title...has compiled a 20-5 NCAA tournament record, the best mark of any active coach and third-best all-time...had three players drafted in 1990 NBA first round; only three other college coaches have had as many players chosen in round one.
Personal Data:
Full name Stephen Louis Fisher... wife Angie, sons Mark, 17 and Jonathan, 9 ... resides in Ann Arbor.

Fisher's Record:

Year	School	Overall		Big Ten	
1988-89	Michigan	6-0	1.000	0-0	.000
1989-90	Michigan	23-8	.742	12-6	.667
1990-91	Michigan	14-15	.483	7-11	.389
1991-92	Michigan	25-9	.735	11-7	.611
1992-93	Michigan	31-5	.861	15-3	.833
1993-94	Michigan	24-8	.750	13-5	.722
1994-95	Michigan	17-14	.548	11-7	.611
School Total		140-59	.704	69-39	.639
Career Total		140-59	.704		

NCAA Appearances: (6) 1989 (Champions)-90-92-93-94-95
NIT Appearances: (1) 1991

Steve Fisher

WOLVERINES TO WATCH

DUGAN FIFE, G, 6-3, 185, SR, Clarkston, MI
Experienced floor leader who provides non-stop hustle at both ends of the court ... team captain... son of Dan Fife, team captain of Johnny Orr's 1971 Wolverine team and a former U-M assistant coach ... only player to start all 63 games the past two seasons.. enters his senior season ranked ninth on Michigan's all-time three-point field goals list... needs 34 treys this year to become just the fourth player in Michigan's history to make at least 100 career three-pointers.

MAURICE TAYLOR, F, 6-9, 250, SO, Detroit, MI
Consensus pick by league coaches and the media as Big Ten Freshman of the Year... added nearly 15 pounds of muscle to his frame... Michigan's top returning scorer at 12.4 ppg... has good post-up moves and runs the floor well for a player his size... led the team in scoring eight times and in rebounding six times... began Big Ten career with 18 points and six rebounds in win over Purdue... tallied 14 points and nine rebounds with one steal at Iowa.... recorded 11 points, eight rebounds and two blocks in home win over Illinois.

MACEO BASTON, F, 6-9, 210, SO, Dallas, TX
Michigan's most improved player in 1994-95... outstanding rebounder who is especially adept on the offensive glass... finished the season strong, averaging 10 points and 7.8 rebounds over the last 14 games... he hit double digit scoring in 11 of the last 18 games... posted three "double-doubles" for the season... finished the season with the highest rebounding average on the team (5.5) and fourth-best scoring average (7.7)... has a wingspan the equivalent of six inches above his height, or comparable to that of a person 7'3" tall.

1994-95 RESULTS
(17-14/11-7)

November
21	W	75-73	Tulane**
22	L	62-79	Arizona State**
23	W	73-69	Utah**
30	L	57-78	Arizona (at Auburn Hills, MI)

December
3	W	83-71	Tennessee-Chattanooga
5	W	87-76	DETROIT-MERCY
10	L	59-69	Duke
13	L	60-62	PENNSYLVANIA
22	W	87-81	JACKSON STATE
29	W	88-84	Idaho (OT)#
30	L	61-65	Washington#

January
3	W	71-61	PURDUE
8	L	63-73	Penn State
11	W	83-82	IOWA (2OT)
14	W	92-70	Northwestern
17	W	69-59	Illinois
22	L	71-73	MICHIGAN STATE
24	W	65-62	Indiana
29	L	77-82	ST. JOHN'S

February
1	W	62-58	WISCONSIN
4	L	58-80	Minnesota
8	W	72-58	OHIO STATE
11	L	65-70	Wisconsin
19	W	61-50	INDIANA
21	L	64-67	Michigan State
26	W	63-51	ILLINOIS

March
1	W	81-64	NORTHWESTERN
5	L	69-89	Iowa
8	W	67-60	PENN STATE
12	L	67-73	Purdue
16	L	76-82	Western Kentucky (OT)*

* NCAA first round, Dayton, OH
** Maui Classic, Maui, HI (5th)
\# Washington Tournament, Seattle, WA (2nd)

1994-95 STATISTICS *(1995-96 returnees in ALL CAPS)*
Record: 17-14   Home: 10-3   Road: 4-8   Neutral: 3-3

Player	G-GS	Min-Avg	FG-FGA	Pct	3P-3PA	Pct	FT-FTA	Pct	Rebounds Off-Def	Tot-Avg	PF-FD	AT	TO	BS	ST	Pts-Avg
Ray Jackson	31-31	1040-33.5	177-370	.478	24-78	.308	113-146	.774	64-99	163-5.3	89-2	93	115	10	33	491-15.8
Jimmy King	31-31	1012-32.6	168-388	.433	28-109	.257	93-137	.679	48-107	155-5.0	72-0	90	94	5	58	457-14.7
MAURICE TAYLOR	31-29	830-26.6	161-342	.471	3-7	.429	59-98	.602	65-93	158-5.1	102-4	36	64	34	14	384-12.4
MACEO BASTON	30-2	549-18.3	89-132	.647	0-0	.000	52-95	.547	72-93	165-5.5	98-6	6	55	30	22	230-7.7
JEROD WARD	20-4	313-15.7	43-118	.364	10-31	.323	23-34	.676	38-36	74-3.7	27-0	11	22	5	10	119-6.0
WILLIE MITCHELL	31-4	505-16.3	62-172	.360	11-42	.262	29-50	.580	40-46	86-2.8	49-1	18	28	11	25	164-5.3
Makhtar Ndiaye	30-23	623-20.8	65-133	.489	1-2	.500	19-35	.543	57-99	156-5.2	101-7	18	52	29	13	150-5.0
Olivier Saint-Jean	4-0	51-12.8	8-16	.500	1-2	.500	2-2	1.000	7-6	13-3.3	11-0	0	6	1	1	19-4.8
DUGAN FIFE	31-31	773-24.9	32-100	.320	23-84	.274	19-28	.679	13-44	57-1.8	89-4	60	45	1	36	106-3.4
BOBBY CRAWFORD	15-0	180-12.0	10-48	.208	7-35	.200	2-4	.500	4-10	14-0.9	19-0	13	9	0	6	29-1.9
Travis Conlan	27-0	360-13.3	13-37	.351	6-21	.286	5-16	.313	5-28	33-1.2	32-1	37	29	4	17	37-1.4
Neal Morton	7-0	9-1.3	0-4	.000	0-0	.000	2-2	1.000	0-2	2-0.3	0-0	0	0	0	0	2-0.3
Chris Fields	2-0	2-1.0	0-1	.000	0-1	.000	0-0	.000	0-1	1-0.5	0-0	0	0	0	0	0-0.0
Alex Lengemann	4-0	4-1.0	0-2	.000	0-0	.000	0-0	.000	1-0	1-0.3	1-0	0	0	0	0	0-0.0
Micky Zitzmann	2-0	2-1.0	0-2	.000	0-2	.000	0-0	.000	0-2	2-1.0	0-0	0	0	0	0	0-0.0
Team										95			3			
Michigan	31	6253	828-1865	.444	114-414	.275	418-647	.646	465-710	1175-37.9	690	382	522	130	235	2188-70.6
Opponents	31	6253	724-1707	.424	181-525	.345	532-788	.675	407-680	1087-35.1	603	403	541	69	167	2161-69.7

SCHOOL RECORDS

Individual

SCORING
- Game: 48 — Cazzie Russell vs. Northwestern 3/5/66; Rudy Tomjanovich vs. Indiana 1/7/69
- Season: 949 — Glen Rice 1988-89
- Career: 2442 — Glen Rice 1985-89

REBOUNDING
- Game: 30 — Rudy Tomjanovich vs. Loyola (IL) 2/1/69
- Season: 389 — Phil Hubbard 1976-77
- Career: 1039 — Rudy Tomjanovich 1967-70

ASSISTS
- Game: 14 — Gary Grant vs. Western Michigan 12/7/87
- Season: 234 — Gary Grant 1987-88
- Career: 731 — Gary Grant 1984-88

STEALS
- Game: 7 — Gary Grant vs. Iowa 1/19/85; Eric Turner vs. Michigan 12/12/81
- Season: 86 — Gary Grant 1986-87
- Career: 300 — Gary Grant 1984-88

BLOCKED SHOTS
- Game: 10 — Roy Tarpley vs. Florida Southern 12/7/85
- Season: 97 — Roy Tarpley 1985-86
- Career: 251 — Roy Tarpley 1982-86

Team

SCORING
- Game: 128 — 2/19/66 (Purdue)
- Season: 3393 — 1988-89

REBOUNDING
- Game: 77 — 2/2/63 (Michigan State)
- Season: **1521** — 1964-65

ASSISTS
- Game: 37 — 12/7/87 (W. Michigan); 12/12/87 (E. Michigan)
- Season: 745 — 1988-89

STEALS
- Game: 18 — 12/3/94 (UT-Chattanooga)
- Season: 267 — 1993-94

BLOCKED SHOTS
- Game: 18 — 12/7/85 (Florida Southern)
- Season: 191 — 1992-93

Big Ten record in **bold**

TOP TEN SCORERS

1. Glen Rice (1985-89) — 2,442
2. Mike McGee (1977-81) — 2,439
3. Gary Grant (1984-88) — 2,222
4. Cazzie Russell (1963-66) — 2,164
5. Rudy Tomjanovich (1967-70) — 1,808
6. Jalen Rose (1992-94) — 1,788
7. Bill Buntin (1962-65) — 1,725
8. Henry Wilmore (1970-73) — 1,652
9. Roy Tarpley (1982-86) — 1,601
10. Antoine Joubert (1983-87) — 1,594

Senior captain Dugan Fife is the son of Dan Fife, captain of Johnny Orr's 1971 Wolverine team and a former U-M assistant coach.

MICHIGAN STATE

Spartans

QUICK FACTS

Location: East Lansing, MI
Population: 51,392
Founded: 1855
Enrollment: 39,743
Nickname: Spartans
Colors: Green and White
Arena: Jack Breslin Student Events Center (1989, 15,138)
President: M. Peter McPherson
Faculty Representative: Michael Kasavana
Athletic Director: Merritt J. Norvell
Head Coach: Tom Izzo (Northern Michigan '77), 1st year
Assistant Coaches: Tom Crean, Stan Joplin, Brian Gregory
Sports Information Director: Ken Hoffman
Basketball Contact: John Farina (Asst. SID)
SID Phone: (517) 355-2271
SID Fax Phone: (517) 353-9636
Media Hotline: (517) 353-7990
Press Row Phone: (517) 353-1626
1994-95 Record: 22-6, 14-4 Big Ten (2nd)
Starters Returning/Lost: 3/2
Letterwinners Returning/Lost: 10/4
Best time to contact coach: Weekday mornings

Jack Breslin Student Events Center (1989)
Capacity 15,138

The Michigan State basketball program starts a new era this year with head coach Tom Izzo beginning his first season at the helm of the Spartan program replacing the legendary Jud Heathcote who retired after 19 campaigns at MSU and 24 as a college coach.

Izzo and his '95-96 Spartan cagers will be looking to notch the program's eighth consecutive winning season and post-season berth.

The rookie head coach will have his work cut out for him as last year's premier "Fire & Ice" guard tandem of Shawn Respert (25.6 ppg), the Big Ten's leading scorer and MVP, and Eric Snow, the Conference's top assists man (7.8 apg) in '94-95, both having graduated and moving on to the professional ranks.

Returning is Ray Weathers, a quick and intense 6-foot-3 performer, who appeared in 27 games last year and averaged 3.5 points and 2.0 rebounds per outing. Weathers distinguished himself as a member of the Big Ten All-Star Team that toured Japan over the summer, averaging 12.9 points and 4.9 rebounds per contest.

Thomas Kelley, an excellent penetrator, saw his freshman season cut short when he suffered a stress fracture in his foot late in the year. He appeared in 16 contests in '94-95 and a healthy return would certainly boost the team's prospects at the position.

Look for a host of other players to contribute in the backcourt including seniors Steve Nicodemus and David Hart along with juniors Mike Respert and Anthony Mull.

While there are questions marks at the guards, the Spartans own a talented and experienced front court that could rank as the Big Ten's finest. Leading the group is senior center Jamie Feick who averaged 9.9 points and 10.0 rebounds per game, good for third place in the league last year. Senior Quinton Brooks is an extremely talented offensive player and hopes to increase his 11.3 points per game average (second on the team in '94-95) from last year. Junior forward Jon Garavaglia is another potentially explosive offensive player who averaged 7.6 points per game last season. Senior Daimon Beathea (5.0 ppg, 3.5 rpg) gives MSU some versatility and is the Spartans' top defensive forward. Junior Steve Polonowski, who played in 27 games last season, will be another contributor up front with his outside shooting ability his greatest asset.

Three incoming freshmen, forward Antonio Smith along with swing players Jason Klein and Morris Peterson, all will get the chance to make an impact in their first years.

TOM IZZO
Head Coach

M. Peter McPherson
President

Michael Kasavana
Faculty Representative

Merritt J. Norvell, Jr.
Athletic Director

Ken Hoffman
Sports Information Director

ROSTER

No.	Name	POS	HT	WT	Year	Hometown (High School)
23***	Daimon Beathea	F	6-7	220	SR	Elkhart, IN (Memorial)
40***	Quinton Brooks	F	6-7	225	SR	Akron, OH (Firestone)
30***	Jamie Feick	C	6-9	250	SR	Lexington, OH
25**	Jon Garavaglia	F	6-9	230	JR	Allen Park, MI (Aquinas)
44***	David Hart	C	6-4	170	SR	Battle Creek, MI (Central)
3	Thomas Kelley	G	6-2	185	SO	Grand Rapids, MI (Union)
11	Jason Klein	G/F	6-7	190	FR	Grosse Isle, MI
22***	Steve Nicodemus	G	6-4	187	SR	S. Whitley, IN (Whitko)
42	Morris Peterson	F	6-6	190	FR	Flint, MI (Northwestern)
35**	Steve Polonowski	F	6-9	220	JR	Rockford, MI
15*	Mike Respert	G	5-11	170	JR	Detroit, MI (Bishop Borgess)
13	Antonio Smith	F	6-8	235	FR	Flint, MI (Northern)
5 *	Ray Weathers	G	6-3	180	JR	Jackson, MI
14	Jason Webber	G/F	6-5	190	FR	Farmington, MI (Country Day)

*letters earned

RETURNING/LOST

Letterwinners Returning	YR	POS	FG%	FT%	PPG	RPG	APG
Daimon Beathea	SR	F	.481	.345	5.0	3.5	1.0
*Quinton Brooks	SR	F	.532	.613	11.3	5.2	0.9
*Jamie Feick	SR	C	.617	.581	9.9	10.0	1.0
*Jon Garavaglia	JR	F	.484	.595	7.6	5.1	0.6
David Hart	SR	G	.000	1.000	0.5	0.8	0.3
Thomas Kelley	SO	G	.000	.000	1.4	0.5	0.5
Steve Nicodemus	SR	G	.400	1.000	1.2	0.5	0.2
Steve Polonowski	JR	F	.478	.700	2.2	1.4	0.6
Mike Respert	JR	G	.429	.750	1.3	0.1	0.3
Ray Weathers	JR	G	.414	.625	3.5	2.0	0.7
Letterwinners Lost		POS	FG%	FT%	PPG	RPG	APG
Andy Penick		G	.412	1.000	1.6	0.2	0.5
Mark Prylow		G	.154	.750	0.8	0.5	0.3
*Shawn Respert		G	.473	.869	25.6	4.0	3.0
*Eric Snow		G	.520	.608	10.8	3.3	7.8

*starters

Senior center Jamie Feick was named to the coaches' all-Big Ten third team last year after averaging 9.9 ppg and 10.0 rpg.

1995-96 SCHEDULE

Tue., Nov. 7	Russia Aquarius - Volgogard (exh.) (7:30 EST)
Tue., Nov. 14	Marathon Oil (exh.) (7:30 EST)
Mon., Nov. 20	vs. Chaminade (9 a.m. HST)*
Tue., Nov. 21	vs. North Carolina or Vanderbilt (Time TBA)*
Wed., Nov. 22	vs. TBA*
Tue., Nov. 28	vs. Arkansas in "Great Eight" (ESPN) (7 EST)
Sat., Dec. 2	@ Louisville (CS) (7:30 EST)
Wed., Dec. 6	Evansville (8 EST)
Sun., Dec. 10	Detroit Mercy (CS) (2 EST)
Sat., Dec. 16	@ Kansas State (CS) (4 EST)
Mon., Dec. 18	@ Oklahoma State (8 EST)
Thu., Dec. 21	East Tennessee State (7:30 EST)
Fri., Dec. 29	vs. Central Michigan (8 EST)#
Sat., Dec. 30	vs. Idaho or Rice (6/8 EST)#
Thu., Jan. 4	Indiana (CS) (8 EST)
Sat., Jan. 6	@ Illinois (CS Regional) (2:15 EST)
Sat., Jan. 13	Michigan (CS Regional) (Noon EST)
Wed., Jan. 17	@ Wisconsin (CS) (8 EST)
Sat., Jan. 20	Iowa (CS Regional) (Noon EST)
Wed., Jan. 24	Northwestern (CS) (8 EST)
Sat., Jan. 27	@ Minnesota (CS Regional) (4:15 EST)
Wed., Jan. 31	Penn State (CS) (8 EST)
Sat., Feb. 3	@ Purdue (CBS) (1 EST)
Wed., Feb. 7	Ohio State (CS) (8 EST)
Sat., Feb. 10	@ Penn State (CS) (8 EST)
Wed., Feb. 14	Minnesota (CS) (8 EST)
Sat., Feb. 17	@ Northwestern (CS) (8 EST)
Wed., Feb. 21	@ Iowa (CS) (8 EST)
Sat., Feb. 24	Wisconsin (CS Regional) (Noon EST)
Tue., Feb. 27	@ Michigan (ESPN) (7:30 EST)
Wed., Mar. 6	Illinois (ESPN) (7:30 EST)
Sat., Mar. 9 **or**	@ Indiana (CBS) (4 EST) **or**
Sun., Mar. 10	@ Indiana (ESPN) (3 EST)

* – Maui Invitational, Maui, HI
# – Oldsmobile Spartan Classic, Lansing, MI

CS – Creative Sports Local Package
CS Regional – Creative Sports Regional Weekend Series

SUBJECT TO CHANGE

MICHIGAN STATE Spartans

Head Coach
TOM IZZO

Birth Date: January 30, 1955
Hometown: Iron Mountain, MI
Education:
Iron Mountain, MI High School... Health & Physical Education, Northern Michigan, 1977

Playing Experience:
Guard, basketball, Iron Mountain H.S., 1971-73... guard, basketball, Northern Michigan, 1973-77

Coaching Experience:
Head coach, Ishpeming, MI H.S., 1977-78
Assistant coach, Northern Michigan, 1979-83
Assistant coach, Michigan State, 1983-95
Head coach, Michigan State, 1995-present

Honors and achievements:
In high school, earned all-state recognition as a junior and senior, earning three letters... played football at Northern Michigan his junior year (1976)... Northern Michigan team MVP as senior... third team Division II all-America... established NMU record for most minutes played in a season... member of Northern Michigan University Hall of Fame.

Personal Data:
Full name Thomas Michael Izzo... wife Lupe, daughter Raquel... resides in Haslett, MI

Izzo's Record

First year as a head coach

Tom Izzo

SPARTANS TO WATCH

JAMIE FEICK, C, 6-9, 250, SR, Lexington, OH

Named to *The Sporting News* 1995-96 Preseason all-Big Ten second team... earned third-team all-Big Ten honors in 1994-95 as picked by the coaches while grabbing an honorable-mention spot on the media's team... fourth on the team in scoring (9.9 ppg) and first in rebounding with a 10.0 per-game effort, good for third place among Big Ten performers... is the Conference's leading returning rebounder in 1995-96... shot a team-high 61.7 percent (111 of 180) from the floor... selected as MSU's Most Improved Player in 1994-95.

QUINTON BROOKS, F, 6-7, 225, SR, Akron, OH

Ranked second on the the club in scoring (11.3 ppg) and rebounding (5.2 rpg)... shot 53.2 percent (134-252) from the floor which placed him second on the team... shot 50 percent or better from the field in 16 games... posted four double-doubles last season... scored in double figures in 16 games... hit 12 of 16 field goals en route to a season-high 24 points in an 82-62 home win over Penn State... second on the team in offensive rebounds with 57.

JON GARAVAGLIA, F, 6-9, 230, JR, Allen Park, MI
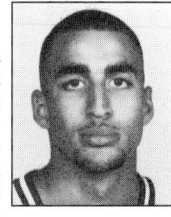
Finished fifth on the squad in scoring (7.6 ppg) and third in rebounding (5.1 rpg)... scored in double figures on 11 occasions in 1994-95... shot 50 percent or better from the field in 17 performances... connected on eight of 15 field goal tries en route to a career-high 18 points, while grabbing a team-best eight boards, at Indiana (1/11)... hit a game-winning 18 foot jumper with seven seconds remaining that gave the Spartans a 54-53 home win over Minnesota.

1994-95 RESULTS
(22-6/14-4)

November
| 30 | W | 92-78 | Illinois-Chicago |

December
3	W	85-71	LOUISVILLE
10	L	91-96	Nebraska
12	W	111-68	CLEVELAND STATE
17	W	80-63	Detroit-Mercy
20	W	79-68	TENNESSEE
29	W	117-95	BALL STATE**
30	W	70-60	LONG BEACH ST.**

January
4	W	78-64	Wisconsin
7	W	69-68	IOWA
11	L	82-89	Indiana
14	W	70-69	OKLAHOMA STATE
18	W	93-56	NORTHWESTERN
22	W	73-71	Michigan
25	W	54-53	MINNESOTA
28	W	75-67	Illinois

February
2	W	82-62	PENN STATE
4	W	67-58	Ohio State
7	L	69-78	PURDUE
11	W	68-53	Penn State
15	W	68-58	ILLINOIS
18	L	57-66	Minnesota
21	W	67-64	MICHIGAN
25	W	83-60	Northwestern

March
5	W	67-61	INDIANA
8	L	78-79	Iowa
11	W	97-72	WISCONSIN
17	L	72-79	Weber State*

*NCAA first round, Tallahassee, FL
**Spartan Classic, East Lansing, MI (1st)

1994-95 STATISTICS *(1995-96 returnees in ALL CAPS)*
Record: 22-6   Home: 14-1   Road: 8-4   Neutral: 0-1

Player	G-GS	Min-Avg	FG-FGA	Pct	3P-3PA	Pct	FT-FTA	Pct	Rebounds Off-Def	Tot-Avg	PF-FD	AT	TO	BS	ST	Pts-Avg
Shawn Respert	28-28	940-33.6	229-484	.473	119-251	.474	139-160	.869	26-85	111-4.0	71-0	85	81	1	38	716-25.6
QUINTON BROOKS	28-26	672-24.0	134-252	.532	1-10	.100	46-75	.613	57-88	145-5.2	72-1	25	54	16	11	315-11.3
Eric Snow	28-28	916-32.7	117-225	.520	7-24	.292	62-102	.608	15-77	92-3.3	77-3	217	86	4	52	303-10.8
JAMIE FEICK	28-28	875-31.3	111-180	.617	0-0	.000	54-93	.581	76-205	281-10.0	62-1	29	45	12	26	276-9.9
JON GARAVAGLIA	28-23	694-24.8	91-188	.484	10-31	.323	22-37	.595	42-101	143-5.1	68-1	17	34	8	10	214-7.6
DAIMON BEATHEA	28-6	649-23.2	64-133	.481	1-1	.200	10-29	.345	45-54	99-3.5	38-0	29	23	2	16	139-5.0
RAY WEATHERS	27-0	415-15.4	36-87	.414	7-19	.368	15-24	.625	21-34	55-2.0	43-1	20	23	0	17	94-3.5
STEVE POLONOWSKI	27-1	207-7.7	22-46	.478	2-9	.222	14-20	.700	20-18	38-1.4	38-1	17	22	2	6	60-2.2
Andy Penick	14-0	73-5.2	7-17	.412	6-15	.400	2-2	1.000	0-3	3-0.2	7-0	7	5	0	0	22-1.6
THOMAS KELLEY	16-0	88-5.5	9-20	.450	0-1	.000	4-8	.500	0-8	8-0.5	13-0	8	10	1	0	22-1.4
MIKE RESPERT	7-0	12-1.7	3-7	.429	0-2	.000	3-4	.750	0-1	1-0.1	2-0	2	3	0	2	9-1.3
STEVE NICODEMUS	11-0	30-2.7	4-10	.400	3-8	.375	2-2	1.000	3-2	5-0.5	2-0	2	1	0	0	13-1.2
Mark Prylow	12-0	39-3.3	2-13	.154	2-12	.167	3-4	.750	2-4	6-0.5	0-0	3	1	0	2	9-0.8
DAVID HART	4-0	12-3.0	0-2	.000	0-0	.000	2-2	1.000	0-3	3-0.8	2-0	1	1	0	0	2-0.5
Team										84			6			
Michigan State	28	5622	829-1664	.498	158-387	.408	378-562	.673	307-683	1074-38.4	495	462	395	46	180	2194-78.4
Opponents	28	5622	720-1660	.434	177-520	.340	309-487	.634	300-587	887-31.7	528	362	406	76	150	1926-68.8

SCHOOL RECORDS

Individual

SCORING
- Game: 50, Terry Furlow vs. Iowa 1/5/76
- Season: 850, Scott Skiles 1985-86
- Career: 2531, Shawn Respert 1990-95

REBOUNDING
- Game: 28, Horace Walker vs. Iowa 1/23/60
- Season: 392, Johnny Green 1957-58
- Career: 1092, Gregory Kelser 1975-79

ASSISTS
- Game: 14, Earvin Johnson vs. Wisconsin 1/4/79
- Season: **269**, **Earvin Johnson 1978-79**
- Career: 645, Scott Skiles 1982-86

STEALS
- Game: 8, Greg Kelser vs. Northwestern 2/2/76
- Darryl Johnson vs. Ohio State 1/10/87
- Season: 75, Earvin Johnson 1978-79
- Career: 175, Scott Skiles 1982-86

BLOCKED SHOTS
- Game: 8, Ken Johnson vs. San Diego State 12/29/84
- Season: 72, Ken Johnson 1984-85

Team

SCORING
- Game: 121, 12/1/92 (Morehead State)
- Season: 2592, 1989-90

REBOUNDING
- Game: 84, 1/19/59 (Ohio State)
- Season: 1508, 1958-59

ASSISTS
- Game: 30, 12/21/85 (Illinois-Chicago)
- Season: 576, 1989-90

Big Ten records in **bold**

TOP TEN SCORERS

1. Shawn Respert (1991-95) — 2,531
2. Steve Smith (1987-91) — 2,263
3. Scott Skiles (1982-86) — 2,145
4. Greg Kelser (1975-79) — 2,014
5. Jay Vincent (1977-81) — 1,914
6. Sam Vincent (1981-85) — 1,851
7. Terry Furlow (1972-76) — 1,777
8. Mike Robinson (1971-74) — 1,717
9. Darryl Johnson (1983-87) — 1,383
10. Robert Chapman (1974-78) — 1,382

Jon Garavaglia finished fifth on the squad in scoring (7.6 ppg) and third in rebounding (5.1 rpg) in 1994-95.

MINNESOTA

Golden Gophers

QUICK FACTS

Location: Minneapolis, MN
Population: 370,000
Founded: 1851
Enrollment: 39,000
Nickname: Golden Gophers
Colors: Maroon and Gold
Arena: Williams Arena (1928, 14,300)
President: Nils Hasselmo
Faculty Representatives: Norman Chervany, Mariah Snyder
Vice President for Student Development and Athletics: McKinley Boston
Athletic Director: Mark Dienhart
Head Coach: Clem Haskins (Western Kentucky, 1967), 10th year
Assistant Coaches: Milton Barnes, Bill Brown, Larry Davis
Director of Men's Media Relations: Marc Ryan
Basketball Contact: Bill Crumley (Asst. Dir.)
SID Phone: (612) 625-4090
SID Fax Phone: (612) 625-0359
Hotline: (612) 625-7887
Press Row Phone: (612) 626-1308
1994-95 Record: 19-12, 10-8 Big Ten (5th-tie)
Starters Returning/Lost: 1/4
Letterwinners Returning/Lost: 5/5
Best time to contact coach: Mornings

Williams Arena (1928)
Capacity 14,300

This is the dawn of a new era in Golden Gopher basketball. The Maroon and Gold will begin the school's second century of basketball with a new look that is young, fresh, exciting and very athletic.

The departure of five senior letterwinners (Chad Kolander, Voshon Lenard, Townsend Orr, Jayson Walton and Ryan Wolf) created a huge hole in the Golden Gopher roster. Those five players accounted for 106 out of 155 starts, and 49 of the team's 76.1 points per game last season.

But the well is not completely dry. One of the top young centers in the Big Ten returns in junior John Thomas. He will be the man in the middle for the Golden Gophers and is looking to make his mark this season. Senior forward and team captain David Grim returns for his final campaign. A relentless competitor who will do anything to help the team win, he is a dangerous threat from behind the three-point arc.

The top returning scorer is sophomore Sam Jacobson who came in as a freshman with great credentials and lived up to all of them. Last year Jacobson saw most of his action at the small forward spot but this year he will be looking to see extended action at his natural shooting guard position.

Another veteran guard returning is sophomore Eric Harris who saw action last year as a defensive stopper and point guard substitution for Orr. Seven-foot junior center Trevor Winter returns to back-up Thomas and could start at center, sliding Thomas to the power forward spot.

Rounding out the returners are senior point guard Hosea Crittenden, sophomore guard Micah Watkins and identical twin forwards Jason and Jermaine Stanford.

The new recruits will have a big impact this year as Minnesota landed its highest rated class since 1978. The group is highlighted by 6-9, 255-pound forward Courtney James of Ben Davis High School in Indianapolis, Ind. Junior Bobby Jackson was a second-team all-America selection and has the skills to help fill the void at the guard position.

To go with that duo the Golden Gophers added a "Gatorade Player of the Year" from Arkansas (Quincy Lewis) and "Mr. Basketball" from Kentucky (Charles Thomas) as well as a promising forward from Oakland, Calif. in Miles Tarver. To finish off the class, the Golden Gophers added 6-6 sharp-shooting swing man Mark Jones from Anderson JC.

CLEM HASKINS
Head Coach

Nils Hasselmo
President

Norman Chervany
Faculty Representative

Mariah Snyder
Faculty Representative

Mark Dienhart
Men's Athletic Director

Marc Ryan
Director of Men's Media Relations

ROSTER

No.	Name	POS	HT	WT	Year	Hometown (High School)
11	Hosea Crittenden	G	5-9	175	SR	Rosemount, MN
22***	David Grim	F	6-7	220	SR	Massillon, OH (Washington)
33*	Eric Harris	G	6-3	200	SO	New York, NY (St. Raymond)
24	Bobby Jackson	G	6-1	185	JR	Salisbury, NC (Western Nebraska CC)
5*	Sam Jacobson	G/F	6-6	205	SO	Cottage Grove, MN (Park)
4	Courtney James	F	6-8	260	FR	Indianapolis, IN (Ben Davis)
25	Mark Jones	G	6-6	205	JR	Milwaukee, WI (Tech/Anderson JC)
20	Quincy Lewis	G/F	6-7	210	FR	Little Rock, AK (Parkview)
42	Miles Tarver	F	6-8	215	FR	Oakland, CA (St. Joseph's/Maine Central Prep)
34	Charles Thomas	G	6-4	190	FR	Harlan, KY
12**	John Thomas	C	6-9	265	JR	Minneapolis, MN (Roosevelt)
30	Jason Stanford	F	6-6	180	FR	Milwaukee, WI (Nicolet)
31	Jermaine Stanford	F	6-6	180	FR	Milwaukee, WI (Nicolet)
23	Micah Watkins	G	6-5	225	SO	Minneapolis, MN (Minnehaha Academy)
50*	Trevor Winter	C	7-0	260	JR	Slayton, MN

*letters earned

RETURNING/LOST

Letterwinners Returning	YR	POS	FG%	FT%	PPG	RPG	APG
David Grim	SR	F	38.8	71.0	5.2	3.3	1.2
Eric Harris	SO	G	35.9	67.6	2.3	1.0	1.5
Sam Jacobson	SO	G/F	46.5	66.7	7.7	4.8	1.2
*John Thomas	JR	C	46.7	53.6	7.3	4.6	0.7
Trevor Winter	JR	C	53.7	69.7	3.5	3.1	0.6
Letterwinners Lost		POS	FG%	FT%	PPG	RPG	APG
*Voshon Lenard		G	41.2	75.9	17.3	4.3	2.6
*Townsend Orr		G	41.4	73.5	13.0	4.6	4.7
*Jayson Walton		F	42.2	74.1	10.9	7.1	1.7
*Chad Kolander		F/C	52.1	61.0	6.0	3.6	1.1
Ryan Wolf		G	29.3	82.4	2.1	0.8	0.9

*starters

1995-96 SCHEDULE

Thu., Nov. 9	Republic of Georgia (CS) (exh.) (7 CST)
Thu., Nov. 16	Marathon Oil (exh.) (CS) (7 CST)
Fri., Nov. 24	vs. Valparaiso (9:30 CST)*
Sat., Nov. 25	vs. Utah State or Wichita State (4/6:15 CST)*
Sun., Nov. 26	vs. TBA (TBA)*
Tue., Nov. 28	Charleston Southern (CS) (7 CST)
Thu., Nov. 30	Bethune Cookman (CS) (7 CST)
Sat., Dec. 9	Nebraska (CS) (6 CST)
Wed., Dec. 13	@ Cincinnati (ESPN) (6:30 CST)
Sat., Dec. 16	California (Metrodome) (ESPN) (8:30 CST)
Tue., Dec. 19	@ Clemson (CS) (6:30 CST)
Sat., Dec. 23	@ Sacramento State (CS) (4 CST)
Thu., Dec. 28	Mt. St. Mary's (CS) (7 CST)
Sun., Dec. 31	Mercer (CS) (3 CST)
Wed., Jan. 3	Illinois (CS) (7 CST)
Sat., Jan. 6	@ Iowa (CS) (7 CST)
Thu., Jan. 11	@ Penn State (ESPN) (6:30 CST)
Sat., Jan. 13	Purdue (CS Regional) (1:15 CST)
Sat., Jan. 20	@ Ohio State (CS) (7 CST)
Wed., Jan. 24	@ Wisconsin (CS) (7 CST)
Sat., Jan. 27	Michigan State (CS Regional) (3:15 CST)
Wed., Jan. 31	Northwestern (CS) (7 CST)
Tue., Feb. 6	Indiana (ESPN) (6:30 CST)
Sat., Feb. 10	@ Northwestern (CS) (7 CST)
Wed., Feb. 14	@ Michigan State (CS) (7 CST)
Sat., Feb. 17	Wisconsin (CS Regional) (1:15 CST)
Wed., Feb. 21	Ohio State (CS) (7 CST)
Sat., Feb. 24	@ Michigan (CS) (8 EST)
Thu., Feb. 29	@ Purdue (CS) (7 CST)
Sat., Mar. 2	Penn State (CS Regional) (2:15 CST)
Wed., Mar. 6	Iowa (CS) (7 CST)
Sat., Mar. 9	@ Illinois (CS Regional) (1:15 CST)

* – Big Island Invitational, Hilo, HI

CS – Creative Sports Local Package
CS Regional – Creative Sports Regional Weekend Series

SUBJECT TO CHANGE

Minnesota's captain is senior forward David Grim, a three-time letterwinner and academic all-Big Ten honoree.

MINNESOTA
Golden Gophers

Head Coach
CLEM HASKINS

Birth Date: August 11, 1943
Hometown: Campbellsville, KY
Education:
Taylor County, Ky. H.S., 1963 ... B.S. Sociology/Physical Education, Western Kentucky, 1967 ... M.A. Secondary Education, Western Kentucky, 1971.
Playing Experience:
Forward-center-guard, basketball 1959-63; first base, baseball 1961-63; sprints, track and field, 1959-63; cross country, 1961-63; Taylor County H.S. ... forward-center-guard, Western Kentucky, 1965-67 ... guard, Chicago Bulls, 1967-70; Phoenix Suns, 1970-74; Washington Bullets, 1974-76.
Coaching Experience:
Part-time assistant coach, Western Kentucky 1977-78
Assistant coach, Western Kentucky, 1978-80
Head coach, Western Kentucky, 1980-86
Head coach, Minnesota, 1986-present
Honors and achievements:
At Taylor County H.S., all-America and all-state in basketball ... led team to state tournament ... all-conference, all-district in baseball ... member, WKU Hall of Fame ... all-America and all-Ohio Valley, 1965-67 ... OVC player of the year in 1965-67... two-time OVC scoring leader ... member of two OVC championship squads ... third player selected in 1967 NBA draft ... made an NCAA tournament appearance in first year as head coach ... NBC-TV Rookie Coach of the Year in 1981 ... named to the National Association of Basketball Coaches Balfour Silver Anniversary All-America Team ... member of Kentucky Athletic and Kentucky High School Athletic Association Halls of Fame ... coached North squad to gold medal at '91 U.S. Olympic Festival ... directed Minnesota to 10-4 post-season record including the 1993 NIT title...led U.S. Junior National team to the gold medal in this past summer's World Games qualifier in Argentina ... 1996 U.S. Olympic assistant coach.
Personal Data:
Full name Clem Smith Haskins ... wife Yevette ... daughters Clemette and Lori and son Brent.

Haskins record:

Year	School	Overall		Big Ten	
1980-81	Western Kentucky	21-8	.724		
1981-82	Western Kentucky	19-10	.655		
1982-83	Western Kentucky	12-16	.429		
1983-84	Western Kentucky	12-17	.414		
1984-85	Western Kentucky	14-14	.500		
1985-86	Western Kentucky	23-8	.742		
1986-87	Minnesota	9-19	.321	2-16	.111
1987-88	Minnesota	10-18	.357	4-14	.222
1988-89	Minnesota	19-12	.613	9-9	.500
1989-90	Minnesota	23-9	.719	11-7	.611
1990-91	Minnesota	12-16	.429	5-13	.278
1991-92	Minnesota	16-16	.500	8-10	.444
1992-93	Minnesota	22-10	.688	9-9	.500
1993-94	Minnesota	21-12	.636	10-8	.556
1994-95	Minnesota	19-12	.613	10-8	.556
School Total		151-124	.550	68-94	.420
Career Total		252-197	.561		

NCAA Appearances: (6) 1981-86-89-90-94-95
NIT Appearances: (3) 1982-92-93 (Champion)

Clem Haskins

GOLDEN GOPHERS TO WATCH

DAVID GRIM, F, 6-7, 220, SR, Massillon, OH

Team captain and a three year letterwinner... played in 28 games last year and averaged 5.2 points and 3.3 rebounds... a three-time academic all-Big Ten selection... has played in 77 career games and has a career scoring average of 5.0 per game... has 215 career rebounds for a 2.8 average... will help the team in any way he can... can be very dangerous from behind the three-point arc.

SAM JACOBSON, G/F, 6-6, 205, SO, Cottage Grove, MN

One of the top freshmen in the Big Ten last year... has tremendous explosion to the basket... rated one of the best leapers in the Conference... is the leading returning scorer and rebounder for the Golden Gophers... has the ability to hit the outside shot or go in and jam over the big guys... is also an excellent passer and playmaker... played at small forward last year but will see most of his action at his natural shooting guard position this year.

JOHN THOMAS, C, 6-9, 265, SO, Minneapolis, MN

A prototype low post player with great strength and strong rebounding skills... will be one of the top centers in the Big Ten this season... started all 31 games for the Golden Gophers last year averaging 7.3 points and 4.6 rebounds per contest... will be the focal point of Minnesota's inside game this year... has nice hands and good shooting touch to 15 feet... a horse defensively, he wears his opponents down with his size and strength.

1994-95 RESULTS
(19-12/10-8)

November
24	W	72-70	Arizona**
25	W	85-64	Villanova**
26	W	79-74	Brigham Young**
29	W	102-84	SACRAMENTO STATE

December
1	W	92-56	CENTRAL CONNECTICUT
11	W	90-65	RHODE ISLAND
13	L	88-91	CINCINNATI
17	L	75-82	California
21	L	71-50	TEXAS SOUTHERN
23	W	115-68	SAN JOSE STATE
28	W	74-68	James Madison
31	W	98-57	MIDDLE TENNESSEE STATE

January
4	W	69-67	PENN STATE
7	L	60-68	Purdue
11	W	105-74	NORTHWESTERN
14	L	67-74	Wisconsin
18	W	81-61	OHIO STATE
21	W	77-66	ILLINOIS
25	L	53-54	Michigan State
28	W	55-54	Iowa

February
4	W	80-58	MICHIGAN
8	W	64-54	Indiana
15	L	70-74	IOWA
18	W	66-57	MICHIGAN STATE
22	L	88-94	Illinois (OT)
25	L	65-73	Ohio State
28	W	78-70	WISCONSIN

March
4	W	82-70	Northwestern
9	L	59-72	PURDUE
11	L	60-69	Penn State
16	L	61-64	Saint Louis (OT)*

*NCAA first and second round, Baltimore, MD
**Great Alaska Shootout, Anchorage, AK (1st)

1994-95 STATISTICS *(1995-96 returnees in ALL CAPS)*

Record: 19-12　Home: 12-4　Road: 4-7　Neutral: 3-1

Player	G-GS	Min-Avg	FG-FGA	Pct	3P-3PA	Pct	FT-FTA	Pct	Rebounds Off-Def	Tot-Avg	PF-FD	AT	TO	BS	ST	Pts-Avg
Voshon Lenard	31-31	997-32.2	174-422	.412	81-244	.332	107-141	.759	44-90	134-4.3	71-0	80	49	10	30	536-17.3
Townsend Orr	31-31	953-30.7	130-314	.414	67-176	.381	75-102	.735	27-116	143-46	72-1	146	60	1	55	402-13.0
Jayson Walton	31-24	710-22.9	125-296	.422	1-3	.333	86-116	.741	78-142	220-7.1	72-3	53	49	8	21	337-10.9
SAM JACOBSON	31-12	608-19.6	92-198	.465	17-53	.321	38-57	.667	72-77	149-4.8	85-5	37	44	3	20	239-7.7
JOHN THOMAS	31-30	649-20.9	91-195	.467	0-0	.000	45-84	.536	68-76	144-4.6	81-3	23	62	11	19	227-7.3
Chad Kolander	31-20	653-21.1	75-144	.521	0-0	.000	36-59	.610	51-60	111-3.6	76-3	35	43	17	21	186-6.0
DAVID GRIM	28-6	537-19.2	52-134	.388	19-61	.311	22-31	.710	26-66	92-3.3	43-1	34	41	11	28	145-5.2
TREVOR WINTER	31-1	445-14.4	43-80	.538	0-0	.000	23-33	.697	36-59	95-3.1	78-2	20	28	18	11	109-3.5
ERIC HARRIS	30-0	343-11.4	23-64	.359	1-8	.125	23-34	.676	10-19	29-1.0	46-0	45	20	0	19	70-2.3
Ryan Wolf	28-1	198-7.1	17-58	.293	12-44	.273	14-17	.824	3-18	21-0.8	33-0	26	23	1	10	60-2.1
Darrell Whaley	20-0	124-6.2	16-35	.457	4-10	.400	3-10	.300	4-14	18-0.9	18-0	11	13	5	4	39-2.0
MICAH WATKINS	13-0	33-2.5	2-3	.667	0-1	.000	1-3	.333	2-5	7-0.5	8-0	2	1	1	2	5-0.4
HOSEA CRITTENDEN	13-0	17-1.3	1-3	.333	0-1	.000	3-4	.750	1-3	4-0.3	0-0	4	4	0	1	5-0.4
Aaron Osterman	8-0	8-1.0	0-0	.000	0-0	.000	0-0	.000	0-3	3-0.4	1-0	0	0	0	2	0-0.0
Team										98			5			
Minnesota	31	6275	841-1946	.432	202-601	.336	476-691	.689	422-748	1268-40.9	.684	516	442	86	243	2360-76.1
Opponents	31	6275	713-1734	.411	195-565	.345	502-750	.669	377-745	1122-36.2	622	412	511	87	177	2123-68.5

SCHOOL RECORDS

Individual

SCORING
- Game: 42　Eric Magdanz vs. Michigan 3/5/62
- 　　　　　Ollie Shannon vs. Wisconsin 3/6/71
- Season: 647　Mychal Thompson 1975-76
- Career: 2103　Voshon Lenard 1991-95

REBOUNDING
- Game: 28　Larry Mikan vs. Michigan 3/3/70
- Season: 349　Larry Mikan 1969-70
- Career: 956　Mychal Thompson 1974-78

ASSISTS
- Game: 16　Arriel McDonald vs. Wisconsin 1/12/94
- Season: 179　Arriel McDonald 1993-94
- Career: 547　Arriel McDonald 1990-94

STEALS
- Game: 9　Melvin Newbern vs. Rider 1/3/90
- Season: 101　Melvin Newbern 1988-89
- Career: 215　Melvin Newbern 1987-90

BLOCKED SHOTS
- Game: 12　Mychal Thompson vs. Ohio State 1/26/76
- Season: 87　Randy Breuer 1982-83
- Career: 235　Kevin McHale 1976-80

Team

SCORING
- Game: 120　12/29/82 (Indiana State)
- Season: 2666　1989-90

REBOUNDING
- Game: 69　1/9/56 (Indiana)
- Season: 1287　1993-94

ASSISTS
- Game: 32　2/27/94 (Indiana)
- Season: 607　1993-94

STEALS
- Game: 21　1/3/90 (Rider)
- Season: 276　1989-90

BLOCKED SHOTS
- Game: 13　3/5/83 (Michigan)
- 　　　　　1/26/76 (Ohio State)
- Season: 129　1991-92

TOP TEN SCORERS

1. Voshon Lenard (1991-95)　2,103
2. Mychal Thompson (1974-78)　1,992
3. Willie Burton (1986-90)　1,800
4. Randy Breuer (1979-83)　1,755
5. Kevin McHale (1976-80)　1,704
6. Tommy Davis (1981-85)　1,481
7. Trent Tucker (1978-82)　1,443
8. Chuck Mencel (1951-55)　1,391
9. Marc Wilson (1983-86)　1,386
10. Kevin Lynch (1987-91)　1,355

A strong player with good rebounding skills, sophomore center John Thomas started all 31 Minnesota games last year and averaged 7.3 ppg.

NORTHWESTERN Wildcats

QUICK FACTS

Location: Evanston, IL
Population: 73,750
Founded: 1851
Enrollment: 7,400 (undergraduate)
Nickname: Wildcats
Colors: Purple and White
Arena: Welsh-Ryan Arena (1951, 8,117)
President: Henry S. Bienen
Faculty Representative: Fred Hemke
Athletic Director: Rick Taylor
Head Coach: Ricky Byrdsong (Iowa State, 1978) 3rd year
Assistant Coaches: Paul Swanson, Shawn Parrish, Jamal Meeks
Director of Media Services: Brad Hurlbut
Asst. Directors: Lisa Juscik, Mark Simpson
SID Phone: (708) 491-7503
SID Fax Phone: (708) 491-8818
Media Hotline: (708) 491-2287
Press Row Phone: (708) 491-8852
1994-95 Record: 5-22, 1-17 Big Ten (11th)
Starters Returning/Lost: 2/3
Letterwinners Returning/Lost: 7/4
Best time to contact coach: contact Brad Hurlbut

Welsh-Ryan Arena (1951)
Capacity 8,117

Head coach Ricky Byrdsong enters his third season at the helm of the Northwestern basketball program armed with a wealth of new talent to compliment the determined play of the veterans that return from the 1994-95 squad.

Gone from last year's 5-22 squad are seniors Dion Lee, Cedric Neloms, Matt Purdy and Dewey Williams. They combined for 53 percent of the Wildcat offense in 1994-95.

The strengths of this year's squad will be depth. If the upperclassmen return healthy, coupled with the addition of some top-notch recruits, Northwestern's inside game should be stronger and its outside shooting should be much improved. The weakness of the team is its youth as NU will be counting on players who haven't played in Big Ten games.

The guard spots should be in competent hands as four experienced ball handlers return. Leading the pack is sophomore Geno Carlisle. The point guard started in 20 games last season as a freshman and is the team's leading returning scorer, averaging 11.7 ppg. Carlisle, who played on the Big Ten's All-Star Team in Japan last summer, also led the Wildcats in assists (101, 3.9 apg) and minutes played (29.6 mpg) and was second in steals.

Also returning are senior Craig Duerksen, junior Jevon Johnson and sophomore Joe Branch. Johnson started the first seven games at point last year before being sidelined with a season-ending knee injury. Duerksen started in 10 games for the Wildcats and was replaced in January when Dion Lee returned to the lineup. Branch garnered his five starts toward the end of the season and averaged 7.6 ppg in those contests.

Three of Byrdsong's recruits for the upcoming season are guards. Julian Bonner, an all-state point guard from Detroit, will provide depth at the position. Nick Knapp and Nate Pomeday are both long-range shooters who have the ability to be impact players for the Wildcats.

Although the frontcourt lacks the depth of the backcourt, it will be in capable hands this season and could finally get its chance to shine if Evan Eschmeyer is ready to return to the lineup at center. He has entirely missed the last two seasons due to a stress fracture in his right foot. Until Eschmeyer gets his game legs back, the spot will be in the capable hands of senior Dan Kreft who continues to make tremendous progress in his game.

Back at small forward is sophomore Darreion Dean who played in 24 contests as a freshman and worked his way into the starting lineup on two occasions. Junior Brian Chamberlain who started at power forward in 26 of Northwestern's 27 games last season, will most likely hold down that spot again. However, if Eschmeyer is ready to start, Chamberlain could take over at small forward. He averaged a team-high 5.7 rpg, while chipping in 5.9 ppg.

Also pushing for time will be freshmen Matt Moran and Joe Harmsen. Moran, a 6-7 forward, was an Illinois all-starter at Pekin High School where he averaged 26.1 ppg and 11.5 rpg. The 6-10 Harmsen was accorded first-team all-state honors as a junior and a senior while averaging 20 ppg and 11 rpg.

RICKY BYRDSONG
Head Coach

Henry S. Bienen
President

Fred Hemke
Faculty Representative

Rick Taylor
Athletic Director

Brad Hurlbut
Director of Media Services

ROSTER

No.	Name	POS	HT	WT	Year	Hometown (High School)
4	Julian Bonner	G	6-1	185	FR	Detroit, MI (University of Detroit H.S.)
13*	Joe Branch	G	6-4	196	SO	Houston, Texas (Kincaid)
25*	Geno Carlisle	G	6-2	182	SO	Grand Rapids, MI (Ottawa Hills)
51*	Brian Chamberlain	F	6-7	235	SR	O'Fallon, IL
23*	Darreion Dean	F	6-5	185	SO	Houston, TX (Kincaid)
22*	Craig Duerksen	G	6-4	180	SR	Hillsboro, KS
42	Evan Eschmeyer	C	6-11	240	JR	New Knoxville, OH
00	Joe Harmsen	C	6-10	240	FR	Fond du Lac, WI (Goodrich)
12**	Jevon Johnson	G	6-3	180	JR	Savannah, GA
3	Nick Knapp	G	6-5	195	FR	Peoria, IL (Woodruff)
55**	Dan Kreft	C	7-0	238	SR	Coral Springs, FL
34	Matt Moran	F	6-7	220	FR	Pekin, IL
31	Nate Pomeday	G	6-3	180	FR	Cedar Grove, WI

*letters earned

RETURNING/LOST

Letterwinners Returning	YR	POS	FG%	FT%	PPG	RPG	APG
Joe Branch	SO	G	.372	.625	3.3	1.7	0.4
*Geno Carlisle	SO	G	.389	.756	11.7	2.8	3.9
*Brian Chamberlain	SR	F	.434	.696	5.9	5.7	0.9
Craig Duerksen	SR	G	.367	.682	5.6	2.1	1.4
Jevon Johnson	JR	G	.250	.750	4.6	2.6	2.4
Letterwinners Lost		POS	FG%	FT%	PPG	RPG	APG
*Dion Lee		G	.379	.807	12.0	3.7	2.0
Matt Purdy		F	.298	.641	4.2	2.3	0.7
*Cedric Neloms		F	.426	.727	13.7	5.2	1.2
*Dewey Williams		F	.531	.667	8.1	4.8	1.0

*starters

1995-96 SCHEDULE

Tue., Nov. 7	Foreign Team TBA (exh.) (7 CST)
Sat., Nov. 18	AAU (exh.) (7 CST)
Fri., Nov. 24	@ San Diego State (Time TBA)
Tue., Nov. 28	Youngstown State (7 CST)
Sat., Dec. 2	Robert Morris (7 CST)
Sat., Dec. 9	@ Seton Hall (Time TBA)
Tue., Dec. 12	Army (7 CST)
Sat., Dec. 16	De Paul (CS) (7 CST)
Tue., Dec. 19	@ Central Michigan (Time TBA)
Sat., Dec. 30	@ Loyola, IL (Time TBA)
Tue., Jan. 2	Brown (7 CST)
Sat., Jan. 6	@ Michigan (CS Regional) (11 a.m. CST)
Wed., Jan. 10	Purdue (ESPN2) (6:30 CST)
Sat., Jan. 13	Penn State (CS Regional) (3:15 CST)
Wed., Jan. 17	@ Ohio State (CS) (7 CST)
Sat., Jan. 20	Wisconsin (CS Regional) (1:15 CST)
Wed., Jan. 24	@ Michigan State (CS) (7 CST)
Sat., Jan. 27	Illinois (CS Regional) (1:15 CST)
Wed., Jan. 31	@ Minnesota (CS) (7 CST)
Sun., Feb. 4	@ Indiana (CS Regional) (11 a.m. CST)
Wed., Feb. 7	Iowa (CS) (7 CST)
Sat., Feb. 10	Minnesota (CS) (7 CST)
Wed., Feb. 14	@ Illinois (CS) (7 CST)
Sat., Feb. 17	Michigan State (CS) (7 CST)
Wed., Feb. 21	@ Wisconsin (ESPN) (6 CST)
Sat., Feb. 24	Ohio State (CS) (7 CST)
Wed., Feb. 28	@ Penn State (7 CST)
Sat., March 2	@ Purdue (CS) (7 CST)
Wed., March 6	Michigan (CS) (7 CST)

CS – Creative Sports Local Package
CS Regional – Creative Sports Regional Weekend Series

SUBJECT TO CHANGE

Point guard Geno Carlisle started 20 games last season, averaging 11.7 ppg and 3.9 apg in his first campaign as a Wildcat.

NORTHWESTERN Wildcats

Head Coach
RICKY BYRDSONG

Birth Date: June 24, 1956
Hometown: Atlanta, GA
Education:
Douglas High School, 1974...B.S. Communications, Iowa State, 1978
Playing Experience:
Guard, basketball, 1972-74, Douglas H.S. ... guard, basketball, Pratt, KS Junior College, 1975-76 ... guard, basketball, Iowa State
Coaching Experience:
Assistant coach, Iowa State, 1978-79
Assistant coach, Western Michigan, 1979-80
Assistant coach, Eastern Illinois, 1980-82
Assistant coach, Arizona, 1982-88
Head coach, Detroit Mercy, 1989-93
Head coach, Northwestern, 1993-present
Honors and achievements:
Lettered three times in basketball at Douglas H.S. ... led team to 90-4 overall record and to Georgia State semifinals on two occasions ... selected all-state three years ... two-time all-conference in junior college ... captained Iowa State team as a senior ... at Arizona, helped team improve record from 4-24 in 1983 to 35-3 in 1988 ... led Detroit Mercy to 15-12 record in 1992, the first winning mark for the school since 1984 and most wins since 1982...led Northwestern to second post-season tournament in school history with 1994 N.I.T. bid.
Personal Data:
Wife Sherialyn ... daughters Sabrina (8) and Kelley (6) and son Ricky Jr. (5).

Byrdsong's Record:

Year	School	Overall		Big Ten	
1988-89	Detroit Mercy	12-17	.414		
1989-90	Detroit Mercy	9-19	.321		
1990-91	Detroit Mercy	10-18	.357		
1991-92	Detroit Mercy	7-21	.250		
1992-93	Detroit Mercy	15-12	.556		
1993-94	Northwestern	15-14	.517	5-13	.278
1994-95	Northwestern	5-24	.172	1-17	.056
School Total		20-38	.345	6-30	.167
Career Total		73-125	.369		

Ricky Byrdsong

WILDCATS TO WATCH

GENO CARLISLE, G, 6-2, 182, SO, Grand Rapids, MI

Very exciting player to watch ... has great shot-making ability... good passer, with a lot of "flash"... thrown into fire last season as NU's starting point guard with injury to Jevon Johnson... third on team in scoring (11.7)... averaged 13.1 ppg in Conference games... scored in double figures on 17 occasions... led team in scoring a team-high 11 times... notched 101 assists, most for an NU freshman since Patrick Baldwin had 106 in 1990-91.

JOE BRANCH, G, 6-4, 196, SO, Houston, TX

Strong, aggressive athlete... has nose for the ball... came on strong towards end of last year ... will be counted on to become a tough defender... garnered his five starts at season's end, averaging 7.6 ppg in those contests... during that span, he scored in double figures twice and led the team with 16 points versus then No. 24 Purdue on Feb. 18, while adding four rebounds... grabbed a career high seven rebounds against Penn State on Feb. 22.

BRIAN CHAMBERLAIN, F, 6-7, 235, SR, O'Fallon, IL

Rugged, warrior mentality... great leadership qualities... good defender... can score inside or hit perimeter shot from 19 feet... needs to cut down on fouls and become more consistent on outside shot... started in all but one contest... top rebounder (5.7 rpg)... led team in boards in 13 contests... scored 15 points and collected nine rebounds in win over Ohio State on Feb. 1.

1994-95 RESULTS

(5-22/1-17)

November
| 26 | W | 77-66 | ALCORN STATE |
| 29 | L | 69-70 | LOYOLA (IL) |

December
2	W	79-70	Sienna*
3	L	60-94	Marquette*
10	W	73-68	CENTRAL MICHIGAN
13	W	71-62	YOUNGSTOWN STATE
17	L	49-84	DePaul
21	L	48-80	Western Illinois
31	L	68-86	Illinois State

January
7	L	55-82	ILLINOIS
11	L	74-105	Minnesota
14	L	70-92	MICHIGAN
18	L	56-93	Michigan State
21	L	51-79	Penn State
25	L	84-96	PURDUE
28	L	73-97	Wisconsin

February
1	W	76-71	OHIO STATE
4	L	67-88	INDIANA
9	L	77-116	Iowa
11	L	66-70	Ohio State
15	L	56-70	WISCONSIN
18	L	57-94	Purdue
22	L	59-89	PENN STATE
25	L	60-83	MICHIGAN STATE

March
1	L	64-81	Michigan
4	L	70-82	MINNESOTA
8	L	57-99	Illinois

*First Bank Classic, Milwaukee, WI (2nd)

1994-95 STATISTICS *(1995-96 returnees in ALL CAPS)*
Record: 5-22   Home: 4-9   Road: 0-13   Neutral: 1-0

Player	G-GS	Min-Avg	FG-FGA	Pct	3P-3PA	Pct	FT-FTA	Pct	Rebounds Off-Def	Tot-Avg	PF-FD	AT	TO	BS	ST	Pts-Avg
Cedric Neloms	26-24	693-26.7	113-265	.426	4-26	.154	125-172	.727	56-80	136-5.2	67-1	30	65	0	9	355-13.7
Deon Lee	21-10	550-26.2	83-219	.379	39-108	.361	46-57	.807	13-64	77-3.7	34-0	41	49	7	13	251-12.0
GENO CARLISLE	26-20	770-29.6	103-265	.389	30-84	.357	68-90	.756	9-65	74-2.8	48-3	101	74	7	15	304-11.7
Dewey Williams	27-27	792-29.3	93-175	.531	0-2	.000	34-51	.667	42-87	129-4.8	81-6	28	42	22	7	220-8.1
BRIAN CHAMBERLAIN	27-27	737-27.3	63-145	.434	1-2	.500	32-46	.696	57-97	154-5.7	79-3	23	54	5	19	159-5.9
CRAIG DUERKSEN	27-10	529-19.6	55-150	.367	11-43	.256	30-44	.682	7-49	56-2.1	35-0	39	55	1	8	151-5.6
JEVON JOHNSON	7-7	149-21.3	5-20	.250	1-4	.250	21-28	.750	3-15	18-2.6	12-0	17	19	1	8	32-4.6
Matt Purdy	25-4	399-16.0	28-94	.298	23-73	.315	25-39	.641	8-49	57-2.3	48-2	17	28	0	8	104-4.2
JOE BRANCH	24-5	265-11.0	29-78	.372	6-15	.400	15-24	.625	21-20	41-1.7	20-0	10	13	6	5	79-3.3
DAN KREFT	26-0	289-11.1	18-47	.383	0-0	.000	16-32	.500	23-29	52-2.0	49-0	6	34	21	1	52-2.0
T.J. Rayford	12-0	61-5.1	6-20	.300	0-0	.000	9-19	.474	7-10	17-1.4	5-0	0	8	2	1	21-1.8
DARREION DEAN	24-2	168-7.0	12-47	.255	4-13	.308	10-17	.588	4-0	13-0.5	7-0	2	14	2	0	38-1.6
Team										107			3			
Northwestern	27	5402	608-1525	.399	119-370	.322	431-619	.696	250-574	931-34.5	485	314	460	74	95	1766-65.4
Opponents	27	5402	852-1816	.469	185-486	.381	378-562	.673	411-720	1131-41.9	564	467	328	100	216	2267-84.0

SCHOOL RECORDS

Individual

SCORING
Game: 49   Rich Falk vs. Iowa 2/24/64
Season: 582   Dale Kelley   1969-70
Career: 1900 Billy McKinney   1973-77

REBOUNDING
Game: 31   Joe Ruklick vs. Kansas 12/7/58
Season: 321   Jim Pitts   1965-66
Career: 885   Kevin Rankin   1990-94

ASSISTS
Game: 14   Patrick Baldwin vs. Youngstown State 12/5/92
Season: 154   Patrick Baldwin   1993-94
Career: 452   Patrick Baldwin   1990-94

STEALS
Game: 9   Pat Baldwin vs. Oakland 11/27/90
Season: 90   Pat Baldwin   1990-91
Career: 272   Patrick Baldwin   1990-94

BLOCKED SHOTS
Game: 10   Jim Pitts vs. Purdue 1/8/66
Season: 123   Jim Pitts   1965-66
Career: 133   Kevin Rankin   1990-94

Team

SCORING
Game: 121   12/19/66 (Tulane)
Season: 2189   1989-90

REBOUNDING
Game: 72   12/18/72 (Western Illinois)
                12/5/66 (Ball State)
Season: 1398   1964-65

ASSISTS
Game: 27   2/19/77 (Wisconsin)
                1/26/80 (Michigan)
Season: 516   1993-94

STEALS
Game: 22   12/1/92 (Chicago)
Season: 225   1989-90

BLOCKED SHOTS
Game: 11   12/26/84 (Loras)
Season: 123   1965-66

TOP TEN SCORERS

1. Billy McKinney (1973-77)   1,900
2. Jim Stack (1978-83)   1,583
3. Kevin Rankin (1990-94)   1,575
4. Cedric Neloms (1991-95)   1,533
5. Shon Morris (1984-88)   1,407
6. Jim Burns (1964-67)   1,368
7. Rod Roberson (1977-81)   1,347
8. Joe Ruklick (1956-59)   1,315
9. Dale Kelley (1967-70)   1,310
10. Art Aaron (1980-84)   1,200

After finishing last year strong, Joe Branch will be counted on to become one of Northwestern's defensive leaders.

OHIO STATE

Buckeyes

QUICK FACTS

Location: Columbus, OH
Population: 615,000
Founded: 1870
Enrollment: 49,542
Nickname: Buckeyes
Colors: Scarlet and Gray
Arena: St. John Arena (1957, 13,276)
President: E. Gordon Gee
Faculty Representative: Susan Hartmann
Athletic Director: Andy Geiger
Head Coach: Randy Ayers (Miami, OH '78), 7th year
Assistant Coaches: Randy Roth, Jerry Francis, Jene Davis
Director of Athletic Communications: Steve Snapp
Assistant SIDs: D.C. Koehl, Liz Cook, Dianna Heimiller
SID Phone: (614) 292-6861
SID Fax Phone: (614) 292-8547
Press Row Phone: (614) 292-1813
1994-95 Record: 6-22, 2-16 Big Ten (10th)
Starters Returning/Lost: 1/4
Letterwinners Returning/Lost: 6/4
Best time to contact coach:
  2:30-3.30 p.m. EST

This year's Ohio State basketball team will be young. Very young! Eight true freshmen, a redshirt freshman and three sophomores dominate the Buckeyes' 1995-96 preseason roster, a list that also includes two juniors and one senior.

"We are young and inexperienced," says Randy Ayers, who is beginning his seventh season as head coach of the Buckeyes. "We have a lot of work to do and a lot to learn.

"But we do have better depth than we did a year ago and we are more athletic, so we have a starting point."

There are six letterwinners returning from last year's team – two of which are walk-ons and another, John Lumpkin, who is on a football scholarship and will rejoin the basketball team in January as he did a year ago.

Rick Yudt, a 6-7 senior forward, is the lone returning starter. He averaged 12.8 points and 4.3 rebounds last year and is OSU's leading returnee in both categories.

Six-four guard Carlos Davis, who started 15 times and played in all 28 games last year, returns for his sophomore season. He averaged 5.3 points and 2.8 rebounds as a rookie, and had the second highest assist total on the team with 88.

Marlon Minifee, a 6-6 junior, returns at forward. Bothered by a knee injury, he saw limited action in 11 games last year and is somewhat of an unknown.

Walk-ons Don Jantonio, a 6-2 junior, and Kevin Martin, a 6-5 sophomore, are both expected to make the squad again this year. Jantonio, a defensive specialist, was voted OSU's most inspirational player last year, while Martin played in 27 games and started four times.

Lumpkin, a 6-9, 250-pounder, averaged 2.8 points and 3.2 rebounds in 18 games after football season last year. He figures prominently when he returns.

The freshman class, rated by many as one of the best in the Big Ten, will get a chance early on to show what it can do.

The newcomers include 5-11 point guard Damon Stringer, last year's Ohio Mr. Basketball, plus All-Ohio performers Shaun Stonerook, a 6-7 forward, Neshaun Coleman, a 6-3 guard, and Jami Bosley, a 6-1 guard.

"Our young players will get tested in a hurry," says Ayers, who enters the season with a career record of 104-74, all with the Buckeyes.

RANDY AYERS
Head Coach

E. Gordon Gee
President

Susan Hartmann
Faculty Representative

Andy Geiger
Athletic Director

Steve Snapp
Director of Athletic Communications

St. John Arena (1957)
Capacity 13,276

ROSTER

No.	Name	POS	HT	WT	Year	Hometown (High School)
54	Steve Belter	C	6-8	215	SR	West Chester, OH (Lakota)
44	Jami Bosley	G	6-1	205	FR	Massillon, OH (Jackson)
3	Neshaun Coleman	G	6-3	180	FR	Toledo, OH (St. John's)
21*	Carlos Davis	G	6-4	200	SO	Columbus, OH (Eastmoor)
55	Scott Gradney	F	6-9	200	FR	Louisville, KY (Ballard)
52	Mark Howard	C	6-10	230	FR	East Canton, OH
35*	Don Jantonio	G	6-2	205	JR	Mentor, OH
50*	John Lumpkin	C	6-9	250	SO	Dayton, OH (Trotwood-Madison)
12*	Kevin Martin	F	6-5	190	SO	Westerville, OH (North)
13*	Marlon Minifee	F	6-6	200	JR	Chicago, IL (Near North)
23	Jason Singleton	F	6-6	190	FR	Detroit, MI (Southgate Aquinas)
40	Shaun Stonerook	F	6-7	205	FR	Westerville, OH (North)
4	Damon Stringer	G	5-11	165	FR	University Hts., OH (Cleveland Hts.)
30	Jermaine Tate	F	6-8	200	FR	Toledo, OH (Central Catholic)
24*	Rick Yudt	F	6-7	210	SR	Portage, IN

*letters earned

RETURNING/LOST

Letterwinners Returning	YR	POS	FG%	FT%	PPG	RPG	APG
*Rick Yudt	SR	F	.446	.736	12.8	4.3	1.1
Carlos Davis	SO	G	.371	.729	5.3	2.8	3.1
John Lumpkin	SO	C	.474	.483	2.8	3.1	0.2
Don Jantonio	JR	G	.417	.550	2.3	1.3	1.1
Kevin Martin	SO	F	.293	.629	3.4	2.4	1.7
Marlon Manifee	JR	F	.636	.400	2.0	1.2	0.3

Letterwinners Lost		POS	FG%	FT%	PPG	RPG	APG
*Rickey Dudley		F	.458	.630	13.3	7.5	2.2
*Antonio Watson		C	.544	.643	14.8	7.1	1.1
*Doug Etzler		G	.453	.895	16.3	2.7	3.9
*Otis Winston		G	.406	.571	4.5	2.9	1.1

*starters

1995-96 SCHEDULE

Thu., Nov. 16	Athletes in Action (exh.) (CS) (8 EST)
Tue., Nov. 21	Foreign Team TBA (exh.) (CS) (8 EST)
Sun., Nov. 26	Central Connecticut State (CS) (2 EST)
Tue., Nov. 28	West Virginia (CS) (8 EST)
Sat., Dec. 2	Cleveland State (CS) (8 EST)
Sat., Dec. 9	@ George Mason (CS) (4:30 EST)
Sat., Dec. 16	Seton Hall (ESPN) (4 EST)
Tue., Dec. 19	@ Tennessee-Chattanooga (CS) (7:30 EST)
Fri., Dec. 22	San Diego State (CS) (8 EST)
Thu., Dec. 28	vs. Eastern Kentucky (CS) (11 EST)*
Fri., Dec. 29	vs. Wyoming or Alcorn State (CS) (9/11 EST)*
Wed., Jan. 3	Penn State (CS) (8 EST)
Sat., Jan. 6	@ Indiana (CS) (4:30 EST)
Wed., Jan. 10	@ Iowa (CS) (8 EST)
Wed., Jan. 17	Northwestern (CS) (8 EST)
Sat., Jan. 20	Minnesota (CS) (8 EST)
Wed., Jan. 24	@ Illinois (CS) (8 EST)
Sat., Jan. 27	@ Purdue (CS) (8 EST)
Wed., Jan. 31	Wisconsin (ESPN2) (7:30 EST)
Sat., Feb. 3	Michigan (CS) (8 EST)
Wed., Feb. 7	@ Michigan State (CS) (8 EST)
Sat., Feb. 10	@ Wisconsin (CS Regional) (2:15 EST)
Thu., Feb. 15	Purdue (ESPN) (7:30 EST)
Sat., Feb. 17	Illinois (CS Regional) (Noon EST)
Wed., Feb. 21	@ Minnesota (CS) (8 EST)
Sat., Feb. 24	@ Northwestern (CS) (8 EST)
Sat., Mar. 2 **or**	Iowa (CS Regional) (1 EST) **or**
Sun., Mar. 3	Iowa (CBS) (2 EST)
Wed., Mar. 6	Indiana (CS) (8 EST)
Sat., Mar. 9	@ Penn State (CS Regional) (Noon EST)

* – Cowboy Shootout, Casper, WY

CS – Creative Sports Local Package
CS Regional – Creative Sports Regional Weekend Series

SUBJECT TO CHANGE

Ohio State's lone senior and only returning starter from last year, Rick Yudt is the Buckeyes' top returning scorer (12.8 ppg) and rebounder (4.3 rpg).

OHIO STATE Buckeyes

Head Coach
RANDY AYERS

Hometown: Springfield (OH)
Education:
Springfield North High School ... B.A. Education, Miami (OH), 1978 ... masters, Miami, 1981
Playing Experience:
Springfield North H.S. ... Miami (OH).
Coaching Experience:
Graduate assistant coach, Miami (OH)
Assistant coach, Army, 1981-83
Assistant coach, Ohio State, 1983-89
Head coach, Ohio State, 1989-present
Honors and achievements:
Ohio state high school player of the year ... two-time all-conference at Miami ... four-year starter and team captain ... recorded school's first-ever triple-double ... third round pick of the Chicago Bulls in 1978 draft ... two-time Big Ten Coach of the Year with back-to-back Conference championships ... postseason appearances in first four years as a head coach, three of which were in the NCAA Tournament.
Personal Data:
Wife Carol ... sons Ryan, 8 and Cameron, 4.

Ayers's Record:

Year	School	Overall		Big Ten	
1989-90	Ohio State	17-13	.567	10-8	.556
1990-91	Ohio State	27-4	.871	15-3	.833
1991-92	Ohio State	26-6	.813	15-3	.833
1992-93	Ohio State	15-13	.536	8-10	.444
1993-94	Ohio State	13-16	.448	6-12	.333
1994-95	Ohio State	6-22	.214	2-16	.111
School Total		104-74	.584	56-52	.519
Career Total		104-74	.584		

Big Ten championships: (2) 1991co-92
NCAA Appearances: (3) 1990-91-92
NIT Appearances: (1) 1993

Randy Ayers

BUCKEYES TO WATCH

RICK YUDT, F, 6-7, 210, SR, Portage, IN
Only returning starter from last year and OSU's lone senior... excellent outside shooter who can also put the ball on the floor... will be looked at to provide leadership... played in 25 of 28 games, starting 24... was fourth on the team in scoring at 12.8 points and third in rebounding at 4.3, the top returnee in both categories... second on team with 38 three-pointers... scored over 20 points five times, including career-high 33 vs. Morgan State.

CARLOS DAVIS, G, 6-4, 200, SO, Columbus, OH
A good, strong athlete who can play both the point and off guard positions... has improved ballhandling... played in all 28 games last year, starting 15... averaged 5.3 points and 2.8 rebounds per game... second on team with 3.1 assists and led team 23 steals... had career-high 22 points vs. George Mason and a double-double against Cleveland State (15 points, 10 rebounds).

JOHN LUMPKIN, C, 6-9, 260, SO, Dayton, OH
On football scholarship at Ohio State, but will join the team once that season is over just as he did in 1994-95... big, strong athlete who is a presence down low... had career-best game of nine points and 12 rebounds vs. Indiana... averaged 2.8 points and 3.1 rebounds... gained additional basketball experience over the summer as a member of the Big Ten All-Star team, which toured Japan and was coached by Randy Ayers.

1994-95 RESULTS
(6-22/2-16)

November
16	L	67-76	OHIO*
28	W	81-74	DREXEL
30	L	70-82	MARQUETTE

December
3	L	71-91	Pennsylvania
15	W	84-83	TENN-CHATTANOOGA
17	L	73-75	Cleveland State
22	L	50-59	BOWLING GREEN
27	W	95-74	MORGAN STATE
30	L	69-79	West Virginia

January
4	L	70-79	Illinois
8	W	121-96	GEORGE MASON
11	L	59-81	WISCONSIN
14	L	64-78	PENN STATE
18	L	61-81	Minnesota
21	L	66-92	Purdue
25	L	66-81	IOWA
28	L	75-90	Indiana

February
1	L	71-76	Northwestern
4	L	58-67	MICHIGAN STATE
8	L	58-72	Michigan
11	W	70-66	NORTHWESTERN
14	L	52-69	INDIANA
18	L	66-85	Iowa
22	L	55-64	PURDUE
25	W	73-65	MINNESOTA

March
1	L	68-75	Penn State
4	L	69-80	Wisconsin
11	L	63-82	ILLINOIS

*Preseason NIT

1994-95 STATISTICS *(1995-96 returnees in ALL CAPS)*

Record: 6-22   Home: 10-5   Road: 0-11   Neutral: 0-1

Player	G-GS	Min-Avg	FG-FGA	Pct	3P-3PA	Pct	FT-FTA	Pct	Off-Def	Tot-Avg	PF-FD	AT	TO	BS	ST	Pts-Avg
Doug Etzler	28-28	983-35.1	163-360	.453	78-178	.438	51-57	.895	19-57	76-2.7	58-2	109	55	1	21	455-16.3
Antonio Watson	28-27	927-33.1	166-305	.544	1-5	.200	81-126	.643	76-124	200-7.1	79-3	32	109	28	13	414-14.8
Rickey Dudley	19-17	655-34.5	81-177	.458	4-13	.308	87-138	.630	49-94	143-7.5	55-1	42	72	3	17	253-13.3
RICK YUDT	25-24	765-30.6	121-271	.446	38-100	.380	39-53	.736	35-72	107-4.3	76-2	28	50	4	16	319-12.8
Robert Shelton	4-0	57-14.3	8-20	.400	7-13	.538	0-1	.000	2-2	4-1.0	2-0	2	5	0	1	23-5.8
CARLOS DAVIS	28-15	576-20.6	52-140	.371	9-30	.300	35-48	.729	27-51	78-2.8	54-1	88	73	0	23	148-5.3
Otis Winston	21-19	454-21.6	43-106	.406	0-1	.000	8-14	.571	17-44	61-2.9	63-5	23	28	4	19	94-4.5
KEVIN MARTIN	27-4	435-16.1	29-99	.293	13-42	.310	22-35	.629	26-40	66-2.4	53-2	45	28	1	7	93-3.4
JOHN LUMPKIN	18-6	270-15.0	18-38	.474	0-0	.000	14-29	.483	19-37	56-3.1	49-2	4	13	4	3	50-2.8
DON JANTONIO	26-0	340-13.1	20-48	.417	10-22	.455	11-20	.550	8-26	34-1.3	50-1	29	15	0	9	61-2.3
MARLON MINIFEE	11-0	85-7.7	7-11	.636	0-0	.000	8-20	.400	7-6	13-1.2	16-0	3	3	1	3	22-2.0
Scott Zack	11-0	72-6.5	4-9	.444	0-0	.000	3-4	.750	7-7	14-1.3	15-0	3	7	5	0	11-1.0
Jerry White	5-0	5-1.0	0-1	.000	0-0	.000	2-4	.500	0-0	0-0.0	1-0	0	0	0	0	2-0.4
Eric Hanna	1-0	1-1.0	0-0	.000	0-0	.000	0-0	.000	0-0	0-0.0	0-0	0	0	0	0	0-0.0
Team										79			7			
Ohio State	28	5625	712-1585	.449	160-404	.396	361-549	.658	292-560	931-33.3	571	408	465	51	132	1945-69.5
Opponents	28	5625	767-1635	.469	182-468	.389	458-655	.699	364-616	980-35.0	525	446	384	66	216	2174-77.6

SCHOOL RECORDS

Individual

SCORING
- Game: 49 — Gary Bradds vs. Illinois 2/10/64
- Season: 958 — Dennis Hopson 1986-87
- Career: 2,096 — Dennis Hopson 1983-87

REBOUNDING
- Game: 32 — Frank Howard vs. Brigham Young 1/29/56
- Season: **496** — **Jerry Lucas** 1961-62
- Career: **1,411** — **Jerry Lucas** 1959-62

ASSISTS
- Game: 14 — Curtis Wilson vs. Purdue 1/7/88
- Season: 188 — Curtis Wilson 1987-88
- Career: 516 — Kelvin Ransey 1976-80

STEALS
- Game: 8 — Troy Taylor vs. St. Joseph's 12/29/83
- Season: 188 — Curtis Wilson 1987-88
- Career: 204 — Jay Burson 1985-89

BLOCKED SHOTS
- Game: 9 — Herb Williams vs. Iowa 2/23/80; Brad Sellers vs. Louisiana Tech 3/24/86
- Season: 97 — Brad Sellers 1985-86
- Career: 328 — Herb Williams 1977-81

Team

SCORING
- Game: 116 — 11/25/90 (Delaware State)

REBOUNDING
- Game: 75 — 12/27/60 (Seton Hall)

ASSISTS
- Game: 31 — 12/28/74 (Indiana)

STEALS
- Game: 20 — 12/4/86 (Siena)

BLOCKED SHOTS
- Game: 15 — 2/23/80 (Iowa)

Big Ten records in **bold**

TOP TEN SCORERS

1. Dennis Hopson (1983-87) — 2,096
2. Herb Williams (1977-81) — 2,011
3. Jerry Lucas (1959-62) — 1,990
4. Kelvin Ransey (1976-80) — 1,934
5. Jim Jackson (1990-92) — 1,785
6. Jay Burson (1985-89) — 1,756
7. Dave Sorenson (1967-70) — 1,622
8. Perry Carter (1987-91) — 1,613
9. Robin Freeman (1953-56) — 1,597
10. Allan Hornyak (1970-73) — 1,572

Center John Lumpkin, who also plays football for OSU, tallied a career-best nine points and 12 rebounds vs. Indiana last year.

PENN STATE

Nittany Lions

QUICK FACTS

Location: State College, PA
Population: 41,317
Founded: 1855
Enrollment: 31,400
Nickname: Nittany Lions
Colors: Blue and White
Arena: Rec Hall (1928, 6,846) and Bryce Jordan Center (1995, 15,000)
President: Graham Spanier
Faculty Representative: John Coyle
Athletic Director: Tim Curley
Head Coach: Jerry Dunn (George Mason, 1980), 1st year
Assistant Coaches: Ed DeChellis, Monroe Brown
Associate Athletic Director for Communications: L. Budd Thalman
Sports Information Director: Jeff Nelson
Basketball Contact: Jeff Brewer (Asst. SID)
SID Phone: (814) 865-1757
SID Fax Phone: (814) 863-3165
Press Row Phone: (814) 863-3516
1994-95 Record: 21-11, 9-9 Big Ten (7th-tie)
Starters Returning/Lost: 3/2
Letterwinners Returning/Lost: 8/5
Best time to contact coach: Contact Sports Information

Bryce Jordan Center (1995)
Capacity 15,000

In 1991, Penn State followed an National Invitation Tournament semifinal appearance with a trip to the NCAA Tournament. First-year head coach Jerry Dunn is hoping the Nittany Lions can duplicate that feat in 1996.

"Our goal is to get back to the NCAA Tournament," stated Dunn, who after serving 12 seasons as Bruce Parkhill's assistant, was elevated to head coach on Sept. 6 when Parkhill resigned.

Gone is cornerstone John Amaechi, but eight lettermen do return, including four of the team's top five scorers and senior forward Matt Gaudio, who has missed two of the last three seasons and underwent back surgery in May, 1994.

Junior point guard Dan Earl is primed to establish himself as one of the best playmakers in the Big Ten. An NIT All-Tournament selection, Earl shot a team-high 40.7 percent on three-point attempts (50-for-123) and doled out a school record 181 assists last winter.

Sophomore guard Pete Lisicky, whose game-winner at Iowa lifted the Lions into the NIT semi, would appear to be a starter this season after sinking 68 three-pointers (39.3 percent) a year ago and being named the *Daily Collegian*'s Freshman Athlete-of-the-Year.

Seniors Rahsaan Carlton and Glenn Sekunda give the Lions a great 1-2 punch at small forward. Carlton had a solid NIT despite an up-and-down regular season in which he averaged 8.2 points per game. He racked up a game-high 19 points at Nebraska and has five career 20-point games.

Sekunda, the team's top returning scorer (12.8 ppg) and rebounder (6.3 rpg), moves from power forward back to small forward. An honorable-mention all-Big Ten pick by the media, he had 26 points against Vanderbilt.

At power forward, the Lions will look much like they did in '93-94. Burly junior Phil Williams (a.k.a. Big House) is a prolific offensive rebounder and will once again team with Gaudio. Gaudio, a student assistant coach last season, averaged 9.4 points and 4.7 rebounds two seasons ago.

The Nittany Lions hope to have a tag-team arrangement at center. Junior transfer Jeremy Metzger (6-10, 250), who averaged 9.3 points per game as a sophomore for Richmond, and redshirt freshman Calvin Booth (6-11, 205), with his 88-inch wingspan, might surprise people with their aggregate numbers.

Scheduled to open in January on the east side of campus is the state-of-the-art Bryce Jordan Center. Built at a cost of $55 million, the Jordan Center features a state-of-the-art sound system, a scoreboard with video capability, one of the largest portable basketball floors in the world, and 15,000 seats with full back and arm rests.

The 1995-96 season also marks the centennial year of basketball at Penn State. The Nittany Lions first competed in 1897 – six years after Dr. James Naismith invented the game in Springfield, Mass.

JERRY DUNN
Head Coach

Graham Spanier
President

John Coyle
Faculty Representative

Tim Curley
Athletic Director

Jeff Nelson
Sports Information Director

ROSTER

No.	Name	POS	HT	WT	Year	Hometown (High School)
52	Calvin Booth	C	6-11	205	FR	Reynoldsburg, OH (Groveport-Madison)
15***	Rahsaan Carlton	F	6-6	220	SR	Harrisburg, PA (Susquehanna Twp.)
10**	Dan Earl	G	6-4	180	JR	Medford Lakes, NJ (Shawnee)
21	Dana Fritz	G	6-2	200	SR	St. Mary's, PA (Elk County Christian)
24**	Matt Gaudio	F	6-8	240	SR	Follansbee, WV (Brooke)
23	Aaron Jack	F	6-8	215	FR	Tulsa, OK (Jenks)
20	Carlton Langley	G	6-0	165	SO	Mt. Vernon, NY
32*	Pete Lisicky	G	6-4	190	SO	Whitehall, PA
14*	Damien McKnight	G	6-2	170	SO	Miami, FL (Edison)
00	Bryan Machamer	F	6-5	205	JR	Schuylkill Haven, PA
4	Jeremy Metzger	C/F	6-10	250	JR	Erie, PA (McDowell)
3	Joseph Pryor	G	6-4	175	FR	Pikeville, NC (Charles B. Aycock)
11***	Chris Rogers	G	5-11	170	SR	Bellefonte, PA
33*	Glenn Sekunda	F	6-8	225	SR	Morris Plains, NJ (Parsippany Hills)
31	Jarrett Stephens	F	6-6½	245	FR	Ferndale, MI
45**	Phil Williams	F/C	6-8	265	JR	Frederick, MD (Thomas Johnson)

*letters earned

RETURNING/LOST

Letterwinners Returning	YR	POS	FG%	FT%	PPG	RPG	APG
*Glenn Sekunda	SR	F	46.4	85.0	12.8	6.3	1.6
Pete Lisicky	SO	G	39.9	83.1	9.7	2.0	1.6
*Dan Earl	JR	G	42.4	83.5	9.3	2.3	5.7
*Rahsaan Carlton	SR	F	40.3	64.7	8.6	3.1	0.9
Phil Williams	JR	F	50.0	54.4	3.5	4.0	0.3
Damien McKnight	SO	G	37.5	45.5	2.8	0.6	1.2
Chris Rogers	SR	G	00.0	00.0	0.0	0.0	0.1
Matt Gaudio#	SR	F	54.3	78.2	9.4	4.7	0.8

#(1993-94 stats)

Letterwinners Lost		POS	FG%	FT%	PPG	RPG	APG
*John Amaechi		C	56.0	67.7	16.1	9.9	1.7
*Donovan Williams		G	41.3	60.7	4.6	1.8	2.2
Greg Bartram		F/G	39.0	60.5	4.2	2.8	1.6
Michael Joseph		C	48.6	60.0	1.2	1.5	0.3
Nate Althouse		G	38.5	30.0	1.0	0.2	0.1

*starters

1995-96 SCHEDULE

Sun., Nov. 12	Marathon Oil (exh.) (2 EST)
Fri., Nov. 17	Russian Aquarius Team (exh.) 7:30 EST)
Sat., Nov. 25	Morgan State (Noon EST)
Mon., Nov. 27	Vermont (7:30 EST)
Thu., Nov. 30	Virginia Military (7:30 EST)
Sat., Dec. 2	@ Tennessee (2 EST)
Sat., Dec. 9	vs. Pennsylvania (@ Atlantic City, NJ) (6:30 EST)
Sun., Dec. 17	Tennessee-Chattanooga (Creative Sports) (3 EST)
Fri., Dec. 22	Bucknell (7:30 EST)
Fri., Dec. 29	vs. Santa Clara (11 EST)*
Sat., Dec. 30	vs. Bradley or Georgia Tech (9/11 p.m. EST)*
Wed., Jan. 3	@ Ohio State (CS) (8 EST)
Sun., Jan. 7	Wisconsin (2 EST)
Thu., Jan. 11	Minnesota (ESPN) (7:30 EST)
Sat., Jan. 13	@ Northwestern (CS Regional) (4:15 EST)
Sun., Jan. 21	@ Michigan (CBS) (Noon EST)
Wed., Jan. 24	Purdue (CS) (8 EST)
Sat., Jan. 27	Indiana (CS Regional) (Noon EST)
Wed., Jan. 31	@ Michigan State (CS) (8 EST)
Sat., Feb. 3	@ Iowa (CS Regional) (3 EST)
Thu., Feb. 8	Illinois (ESPN) (7:30 EST)
Sat., Feb. 10	Michigan State (CS) (8 EST)
Wed., Feb. 14	@ Indiana (CS) (8 EST)
Sat., Feb. 17	@ Purdue (CS) (8 EST)
Thu., Feb. 22	Michigan (CS) (8 EST)
Wed., Feb. 28	Northwestern (8 EST)
Sat., Mar. 2	@ Minnesota (CS Regional) (3:15 EST)
Wed., Mar. 6	@ Wisconsin (CS) (8 EST)
Sat., Mar. 9	Ohio State (CS Regional) (Noon EST)

* – Cable Car Classic, San Jose, CA

CS – Creative Sports Local Package
CS Regional – Creative Sports Regional Weekend Series

SUBJECT TO CHANGE

Rahsaan Carlton, Penn's State first scholarship player to play his entire career in the Big Ten, needs just 276 points to reach 1,000 career points.

PENN STATE

Nittany Lions

Head Coach
JERRY DUNN

Birth Date: May 6, 1953
Hometown: Washington, DC
Education:
Pemberton (N.J.) Township High School, 1971 ... bachelors, George Mason, 1980.
Playing Experience:
At Casper (Wyo.) College: Basketball, 1973-74
Coaching Experience:
Assistant coach, George Mason, 1977-83
Assistant coach, Penn State, 1983-95
Head coach, Penn State, 1995-present
Honors and achievements:
All-conference football and basketball player at Pemberton (N.J.) Township High School ... played basketball for Swede Erickson at Casper (Wyo.) College in 1973-74 ... enrolled at George Mason, serving as a volunteer coach, then part-time, finally being elevated to full-time assistant under head coaches John Linn and Joe Harrington ... joined Bruce Parkhill at Penn State in 1983 ... top assistant as the Lions won 20 or more games five of the last seven seasons, reached NIT Final Four twice, won Atlantic 10 Conference title in 1991 and defeated UCLA in the first round of the '91 NCAA Tournament... played key role in Penn State's Big Ten Conference transition ... volunteer for several Centre Region charities.

Dunn's Record:

First year as head coach

Jerry Dunn

NITTANY LIONS TO WATCH

RAHSAAN CARLTON, F, 6-6, 220, SR, Harrisburg, PA
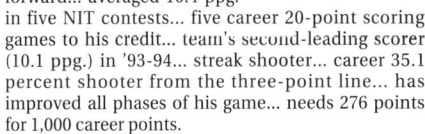
Pronounced ruh-SHAWN... will become the first scholarship player at Penn State to have played his entire career in the Big Ten... started 29 of 32 games last season at small forward... averaged 10.4 ppg. in five NIT contests... five career 20-point scoring games to his credit... team's second-leading scorer (10.1 ppg.) in '93-94... streak shooter... career 35.1 percent shooter from the three-point line... has improved all phases of his game... needs 276 points for 1,000 career points.

DAN EARL, G, 6-4, 180, JR, Medford Lakes, NJ

One of the Big Ten's top returning point guards... 1995 NIT All-Tournament Team... broke the Penn State season assist mark last winter with 181 in 32 games (5.7 per game)... led the team in three-point percentage (40.7, 50-for-123) and steals (39) and ranked second in minutes played (1,050) and free-throw percentage (83.5)... member of the Big Ten foreign all-star team which played eight games in Argentina in June, 1994.

GLENN SEKUNDA, F, 6-8, 225, SR, Morris Plains, NJ

Team's leading returning scorer (12.8 ppg.) and rebounder (6.3 rpg.)... honorable mention all-Big Ten selection by the media... had three 20-point scoring games ... ranked second in the Big Ten in free-throw percentage (85.0)... should return to his natural small forward position this season, after playing at power forward last winter... Syracuse transfer.

1994-95 RESULTS
(21-11/9-9)

November
25	W	90-60	MOUNT ST. MARY'S
30	W	70-69	Duquesne

December
3	W	95-73	VANDERBILT
6	W	86-55	MARYLAND-EASTERN SHORE
8	W	78-55	BUCKNELL
10	W	85-62	CENTRAL CONNECTICUT ST.
22	W	80-45	AKRON
28	L	61-67	Texas Tech**
30	W	66-53	Richmond**

January
4	L	67-69	Minnesota
8	W	73-63	MICHIGAN
14	W	78-64	Ohio State
18	L	69-71	INDIANA
21	W	79-51	NORTHWESTERN
26	W	78-67	Wisconsin
28	L	62-65	PURDUE

February
2	L	62-82	Michigan State
4	W	74-64	IOWA
8	L	58-67	Illinois
11	L	53-68	MICHIGAN STATE
15	L	51-71	Purdue
18	W	74-67	WISCONSIN
22	W	89-59	Northwestern
25	L	60-73	Indiana

March
1	W	75-68	OHIO STATE
8	L	60-67	Michigan
11	W	69-60	MINNESOTA
15	W	62-56	MIAMI (FL)*
21	W	65-59	Nebraska#
23	W	67-64	Iowa+
27	L	79-87	Marquette$
29	W	66-62	Canisius$$

*NIT first round
#NIT second round
+NIT quarterfinals
$ NIT Semifinal, New York, NY
$$ NIT Consolation, New York, NY
**Fiesta Bowl Classic, Tucson, AZ (3rd)

1994-95 STATISTICS *(1995-96 returnees in ALL CAPS)*
Record: 21-11   Home: 13-3   Road: 6-6   Neutral: 2-2

Player	G-GS	Min-Avg	FG-FGA	Pct	3P-3PA	Pct	FT-FTA	Pct	Reb Off-Def	Tot-Avg	PF-FD	AT	TO	BS	ST	Pts-Avg
John Amaechi	32-32	1108-34.6	168-300	.560	2-6	.333	176-260	.677	87-229	316-9.9	67-0	55	100	68	21	514-16.1
GLENN SEKUNDA	32-31	794-24.8	147-317	.464	26-84	.310	91-107	.850	69-133	202-6.3	80-3	51	68	9	28	411-12.8
PETE LISICKY	32-2	709-22.2	96-244	.393	68-173	.393	49-59	.831	9-54	63-2.0	51-2	51	29	3	17	309-9.7
DAN EARL	32-31	1050-32.8	86-203	.424	50-123	.407	76-91	.835	5-68	73-2.3	49-0	181	78	0	39	298-9.3
RASHAAN CARLTON	32-29	783-24.5	106-263	.403	29-95	.305	33-51	.647	37-61	98-3.1	64-0	29	45	12	18	274-8.6
Donovan Williams	31-30	606-19.5	62-150	.413	1-9	.111	17-28	.607	4-53	57-1.8	65-2	69	59	0	35	142-4.6
Greg Bartram	32-3	505-15.8	46-118	.390	19-56	.339	23-38	.605	27-63	90-2.8	36-0	50	28	6	24	134-4.2
PHIL WILLIAMS	31-0	490-15.8	38-76	.500	0-0	.000	31-57	.544	52-73	125-4.0	65-0	8	26	8	10	107-3.5
DAMIEN McKNIGHT	12-0	108-9.0	12-32	.375	4-16	.250	5-11	.455	2-5	7-0.6	9-0	14	10	0	4	33-2.8
Michael Joseph	31-1	181-5.7	17-35	.486	0-1	.000	3-5	.600	14-34	48-1.5	38-0	10	9	4	7	37-1.2
Nate Althouse	14-1	25-1.8	5-13	.385	1-5	.200	3-10	.300	2-1	3-0.2	5-0	1	4	0	3	14-1.0
DANA FRITZ	4-0	5-1.3	1-1	1.000	1-1	1.000	1-2	.500	0-0	0-0.0	1-0	0	0	0	0	4-1.0
BRYAN MACHAMER	8-0	12-1.5	2-3	.667	0-0	.000	0-2	.000	4-0	4-0.5	1-0	0	2	0	0	4-0.5
CHRIS ROGERS	10-0	15-1.5	0-5	.000	0-5	.000	0-0	.000	0-0	0-0.0	0-0	1	1	0	1	0-0.0
CARLTON LANGLEY	1-0	1-1.0	0-0	.000	0-0	.000	0-0	.000	0-0	0-0.0	0-0	0	0	0	0	0-0.0
Brad Kopcha	6-0	7-1.2	0-1	.000	0-1	.000	0-0	.000	0-0	0-0.0	0-0	0	0	0	0	0-0.0
Team										102						
Penn State	32	6400	786-1761	.446	201-575	.350	508-721	.705	312-774	1188-37.1	531	520	468	110	207	2281-71.3
Opponents	32	6400	785-1936	.405	165-530	.311	28-518	.633	413-743	1156-36.1	625	437	449	101	215	2063-64.5

SCHOOL RECORDS

Individual

SCORING
- Game: 46 — Gene Harris vs. Holy Cross 12/28/61
- Season: 731 — Jesse Arnelle 1954-55
- Career: 2138 — Jesse Arnelle 1951-55

REBOUNDING
- Game: 27 — Jesse Arnelle vs. Temple 1/29/55
- Season: 428 — Jesse Arnelle 1954-55
- Career: 1238 — Jesse Arnelle 1951-55

ASSISTS
- Game: 15 — Tom Doaty vs. Syracuse 1/29/75
- Season: 181 — Dan Earl 1994-95
- Career: 600 — Freddie Barnes 1988-92

STEALS
- Game: 8 — Tom Doaty vs. West Virginia 2/18/70; Monroe Brown vs. Rhode Island 1/5/91
- Season: 97 — Ron Brown 1973-74
- Career: 252 — Ron Brown 1971-74

BLOCKED SHOTS
- Game: 6 — John Amaechi, twice
- Season: 68 — John Amaechi 1994-95
- Career: 191 — John Amaechi 1992-95

Team

SCORING
- Game: 110 — 12/15/54 (Colgate)
- Season: 2466 — 1988-89

REBOUNDING
- Game: 71 — 12/4/71 (Cornell)
- Season: 1200 — 1966-67

ASSISTS
- Game: 33 — 1/28/81 (Colgate)
- Season: 533 — 1988-89

STEALS
- Game: 15 — 12/22/89 (Southwest Texas State)
- Season: 250 — 1990-91

BLOCKED SHOTS
- Game: 10 — 3/5/89 (Rhode Island)
- Season: 110 — 1994-95

TOP TEN SCORERS

1. Jesse Arnelle (1951-55) — 2,138
2. DeRon Hayes (1989-93) — 1,570
3. Tom Hovasse (1985-89) — 1,459
4. Freddie Barnes (1988-92) — 1,342
5. Ed Fogell (1985-90) — 1,329
6. John Amaechi (1992-95) — 1,310
7. Monroe Brown (1988-92) — 1,244
8. Ron Brown (1971-74) — 1,184
9. Carver Clinton (1963-66) — 1,165
10. Mark DuMars (1958-61) — 1,139

Senior forward Glenn Sekunda is the Nittany Lions' top returning scorer (12.8 ppg) and rebounder (6.3 rpg).

PURDUE

Boilermakers

QUICK FACTS

Location: West Lafayette, IN
Population: 25,907
Founded: 1869
Enrollment: 34,685
Nickname: Boilermakers
Colors: Old Gold and Black
Arena: Mackey Arena (1967, 14,123)
President: Steven C. Beering
Faculty Representatives: Philip E. Nelson, Martha O. Chiscon
Athletic Director: Morgan Burke
Head Coach: Gene Keady (Kansas State, 1958), 16th year
Assistant Coaches: Bruce Weber, Frank Kendrick, Jay Price
Athletic Public Relations Director: Jim Vruggink
Sports Information Director: Mark Adams
Sports Information Contact: Steve Allen
SID Phone: (317) 494-3202
SID Fax Phone: (317) 494-5447
Media Hotline: (317) 496-1111
Press Row Phone: (317) 494-6364
1994-95 Record: 25-7, 15-3, Big Ten (1st)
Starters Returning/Lost: 3/2
Letterwinners Returning/Lost: 11/3
Best time to contact coach: Monday noon teleconference or contact SID

With eight of its top 10 players returning, Purdue will aim for an unprecedented "three-peat" in 1995-96. The Boilermakers won the last two Big Ten championships outright (first time in school history), and earned a 25-7 overall record last season. Eleven lettermen and three starters return from that squad which won 15 of its last 17 games to finish 12th in the Associated Press national rankings.

Purdue's challenge will be to replace forward Cuonzo Martin and guard Matt Waddell.

Eight veterans who have starting experience will blend with a highly-regarded recruiting class.

Point guard Porter Roberts, an honorable mention all-Big Ten pick last year, led his teammates in assists (3.8) and starts (31) while averaging 4.9 points. Roberts, an effective penetrator and defender, had a nearly 3-to-1 ratio of assists to turnovers as a sophomore.

Purdue was 15-2 after senior forward Justin Jennings and sophomore center Brad Miller entered the lineup early in the Big Ten season. Jennings paced the squad in field goal percentage (.600), was second in dunks (21), and averaged 7.0 points and 3.6 rebounds in Conference action. Miller, an excellent ballhandler at 6-11, 235 pounds, made an impact both near the basket and from the perimeter.

Seniors Roy Hairston and Brandon Brantley were early season starters who provided unique talents off the bench in Purdue's late season success last year. Hairston, a talented and versatile threat, was Purdue's No. 3 scorer (9.6), rebounder (4.5) and shot blocker (27 total) while shooting with 50.7 percent accuracy from the floor. Brantley was fifth in the Big Ten in both blocked shots (1.1, tops on the team) and free throw percentage (.831), averaged 10.0 points, a team-leading 6.1 rebounds and 56.2 percent field goal shooting last year.

Sophomore guard Chad Austin was one of the league's top freshmen a year ago. He shot with 40.7 percent accuracy from three-point range and added 5.7 points, 2.0 rebounds, 2.0 assists and 23 steals (third-best) in only 14 minutes per appearance.

Senior Herb Dove is a 6-5 jumping jack with a vertical leap of 39 inches. He is a stingy defender who became an offensive threat this past summer, leading the Big Ten All-Star Team in scoring (14.7) on its undefeated (7-0) tour of Japan.

Guard Todd Foster is a hard-nosed player who has won the team's Mr. Hustle Award the past three years. He averaged 2.0 points as a junior.

The three other returning lettermen all saw limited action last year: 7-2 sophomore center Matt ten Dam, 6-8 sophomore forward David Lesmond and 6-9 junior walk-on forward Paul Gilvydis. The recruiting class features three exciting freshmen: forwards Luther Clay and Brian Cardinal, and guard Alan Eldridge.

GENE KEADY
Head Coach

Steven Beering
President

Philip Nelson
Faculty Representative

Martha Chiscon
Faculty Representative

Morgan Burke
Athletic Director

Mark Adams
Sports Information Director

Mackey Arena (1967)
Capacity 14,123

ROSTER

No.	Name	POS	HT	WT	Year	Hometown (High School)
3*	Chad Austin	G	6-2	200	SO	Richmond, IN
42***	Brandon Brantley	F/C	6-8	205	SR	East Chicago, IN (Andrean)
35	Brian Cardinal	F	6-8	220	FR	Tolono, IL (Unity)
34	Luther Clay	F	6-8	210	FR	Oberlin, OH (Maine Central Institute Prep)
21***	Herb Dove	G/F	6-5	190	SR	Indianapolis, IN (Perry Meridian)
15	Alan Eldridge	G	6-1	180	FR	Fort Wayne, IN (Wayne)
20***	Todd Foster	G	6-1	195	SR	Washington, IL (Community)
55**	Paul Gilvydis	F	6-9	220	JR	Farmington Hills, MI (Harrison)
25*	Roy Hairston	F	6-8	215	SR	Jersey City, NJ (Snyder)
33***	Justin Jennings	F	6-6	210	SR	Grand Rapids, MI (Central)
31*	David Lesmond	F	6-8	210	SO	Pierrefitte, France (Robinson, IL)
52*	Brad Miller	C	6-11	235	SO	Kendallville, IN (East Noble)
23***	Porter Roberts	G	6-3	195	SR	Chattanooga, TN (School for the Arts & Sciences)
14*	Matt ten Dam	C	7-2	275	SO	Almelo, Holland (Northfield, IN)

*letters earned

RETURNING/LOST

Letterwinners Returning	YR	POS	FG%	FT%	PPG	RPG	APG
Brandon Brantley	SR	F/C	.562	.816	10.0	6.1	0.4
Roy Hairston	SR	F	.507	.489	9.6	4.5	1.3
*Brad Miller	SO	C	.582	.660	6.5	4.8	1.2
*Justin Jennings	SR	F	.600	.441	6.2	3.1	0.4
Chad Austin	SO	G	.458	.659	5.7	2.0	2.0
*Porter Roberts	SR	G	.412	.627	4.9	4.0	3.8
Herb Dove	SR	F	.569	.692	3.1	1.5	0.5
Todd Foster	SR	G	.339	.688	2.0	0.8	1.1
David Lesmond	SO	F	.273	.500	0.6	0.5	0.1
Paul Gilvydis	JR	F	.250	--	0.5	0.3	0.2
Matt ten Dam	SO	C	.333	--	0.2	0.4	0.0
Letterwinners Lost		POS	FG%	FT%	PPG	RPG	APG
*Cuonzo Martin		F	.439	.799	18.4	3.9	2.2
*Matt Waddell		G	.392	.857	9.3	2.3	3.5
Tim Ervin		G	.222	.333	0.4	0.1	0.3

*starters

Forward/center Brandon Brantley is Purdue's top returning scorer (10.0 ppg), rebounder, (6.1 rpg) and shot blocker (1.1 bpg).

1995-96 SCHEDULE

Sun., Nov. 12	Russian Select Team Aquarius (exh.) (CS) (1 EST)
Sun., Nov. 19	Athletes in Action (exh.) (CS) (1 EST)
Sat., Nov. 25	vs. Memphis (ESPN) (1:30 EST)#
Wed., Nov. 29	@ Central Michigan (CS) (7 EST)
Fri., Dec. 1	vs. Illinois-Chicago (CS) (7 EST)*
Sat., Dec. 2	vs. Murray State or Drexel (CS) (6/8 EST)*
Wed., Dec. 6	Oklahoma (ESPN) (7:30 EST)
Sat., Dec. 9	vs. Villanova (@ Anaheim) (ABC) (1 EST)
Sat., Dec. 16	vs. Texas Christian (@ Indianapolis) (CS) (7 EST)
Tue., Dec. 19	Western Michigan (CS) (8 EST)
Thu., Dec. 21	Valparaiso (CS) (8 EST)
Sat., Dec. 23	@ Seton Hall (CS) (8 EST)
Thu., Dec. 28	vs. Iowa State (6:30 EST)%
Sat., Dec. 30	vs. North Carolina-Charlotte (6:30 EST)%
Wed., Jan. 3	Iowa (ESPN) (7 EST)
Wed., Jan. 10	@ Northwestern (ESPN2) (7:30 EST)
Sat., Jan. 13	@ Minnesota (CS Regional) (2:15 EST)
Tue., Jan. 16	Indiana (ESPN) (7:30 EST)
Sat., Jan. 20	Illinois (CS) (8 EST)
Wed., Jan. 24	@ Penn State (CS) (8 EST)
Sat., Jan. 27	Ohio State (CS) (8 EST)
Wed., Jan. 31	@ Michigan (ESPN) (7 EST)
Sat., Feb. 3	Michigan State (CBS) (1 EST)
Wed., Feb. 7	@ Wisconsin (CS) (8 EST)
Sat., Feb. 10	Michigan (CS Regional) (Noon EST)
Thu., Feb. 15	@ Ohio State (ESPN) (7:30 EST)
Sat., Feb. 17	Penn State (CS) (8 EST)
Tue., Feb. 20	@ Illinois (ESPN) (7:30 EST)
Sun., Feb. 25	@ Indiana (CBS) (2 EST)
Thu., Feb. 29	Minnesota (CS) (8 EST)
Sat., Mar. 2	Northwestern (CS) (8 EST)
Sat., Mar. 9 **or**	@ Iowa (CBS) (4 EST) **or**
Sun., Mar. 10	@ Iowa (ESPN) (3 EST)

\# – The Classic, Kemper Arena, Kansas City, MO
* – Boilermaker Invitational, West Lafayette, IN
% – Puerto Rico Shootout, San Jan, PR

CS – Creative Sports Local Package
CS Regional – Creative Sports Regional Weekend Series

SUBJECT TO CHANGE

PURDUE

Boilermakers

Head Coach
GENE KEADY

Hometown: Larned, KS
Education:
Garden City (KS) Junior College... B.S. Biological Sciences/Physical Education, 1958 ... masters, Education, Kansas State, 1964.
Playing Experience:
Basketball; quarterback, football; baseball; track and field; high school... basketball; quarterback, football; baseball; track and field, Garden City (KS) JC... quarterback, football; baseball; track and field; Kansas State... Pittsburgh Steelers, 1958.
Coaching Experience:
Head coach, Beloit (KS) High School, 1957-64
Assistant coach, Hutchinson (KS) Junior College, 1964-65
Head coach, Hutchinson JC, 1965-74
Assistant coach, Arkansas, 1974-78
Head coach, Western Kentucky, 1978-80
Head coach, Purdue, 1980-present
Honors and achievements:
All-state in baseball and all-league in football in high school... all-America quarterback at Garden City JC... honorable mention all-league at Kansas State... Beloit H.S. team he coached made state tournament his last three years... in nine years at Hutchinson JC, team made national tournament six times (took second place in 1973)... regional junior college coach of the year 1971-73... took Western Kentucky to NCAA in second season... four-time national and five-time Big Ten coach of the year... five Big Ten titles at Purdue... 11 NCAA and three NIT appearances... second-winningest Purdue head men's basketball coach... 1991 U.S. Pan Am Games head coach... coached U.S. World University Games team to gold medal in 1989... has a 22-2 (.917) record as international head coach.
Personal Data:
Full name Lloyd Eugene Keady... wife Patricia... daughter, Lisa... hobby is golf... resides in Lafayette, IN.

Keady's Record:

Year	School	Overall		Big Ten	
1978-79	Western Kentucky	17-11	.607		
1979-80	Western Kentucky	21-8	.724		
1980-81	Purdue	21-11	.656	10-8	.556
1981-82	Purdue	18-14	.563	11-7	.611
1982-83	Purdue	21-9	.750	11-7	.611
1983-84	Purdue	22-7	.759	15-3	.833
1984-85	Purdue	20-9	.690	11-7	.611
1985-86	Purdue	25-10	.688	11-7	.611
1986-87	Purdue	25-5	.833	15-3	.833
1987-88	Purdue	29-4	.879	16-2	.889
1988-89	Purdue	15-16	.484	8-10	.444
1989-90	Purdue	22-8	.733	13-5	.722
1990-91	Purdue	17-12	.586	9-9	.500
1991-92	Purdue	18-15	.545	8-10	.444
1992-93	Purdue	18-10	.643	9-9	.500
1993-94	Purdue	29-5	.853	14-4	.778
1994-95	Purdue	25-7	.781	15-3	.833
School Total		322-142	.694	176-94	.652
Career Total		360-161	.691		

Big Ten Championships: (5) 1984co-87co-88-94-95
NCAA Appearances: (12) 1980-83-84-85-86-87-88-90-91-93-94-95
NIT Appearances: (3) 1981-82-92

Gene Keady

BOILERMAKERS TO WATCH

BRANDON BRANTLEY, F/C, 6-8, 205, SR, East Chicago, IN
Can play either power forward or center... Purdue's top returning scorer (10.0), rebounder (6.1) and shot blocker (1.1)... possesses a soft shooting touch in the paint and can also hit the outside jumper... extremely wiry and runs the floor well... tremendously improved post defensive player, free throw shooter and shot blocker... 19 career double-figure scoring games and seven double-digit board games... four career double-doubles.

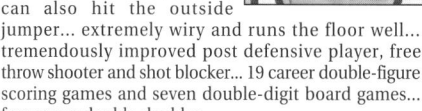

BRAD MILLER, C, 6-11, 235, SO, Kendallville, IN
Outstanding big man who plays center although his skills are probably more suited for forward... effective post moves and is a good shooter from 19 feet in... 18 career starts... averaged 6.5 points (fifth on team) and 4.8 rebounds (second on team) overall as a freshman... second on team in blocked shots (34)... recorded the second-best field goal percentage mark (.582) for a Purdue freshman.

PORTER ROBERTS, G, 6-3, 195, SR, Chattanooga, TN
Starting point guard on Purdue's last two Big Ten championship teams... top returning assist-man (3.8)... great defender who applies solid pressure on the ball... one of the top point guards in the Big Ten... Purdue's most experienced player with 62 career starts... honorable mention all-Big Ten in 1994-95 by the coaches... winner of Bob King Assist Award and Play Hard Award (a combination of steals, taking charges, grabbing loose balls, blocked shots, rebounds and assists) as a junior.

1994-95 RESULTS
(25-7/15-3)

November
25	W	71-60	Niagara**
26	W	84-71	New Orleans**
27	W	88-87	Iowa State (OT)**
30	L	66-69	Missouri (at Auburn Hills, MI)

December
3	L	87-91	James Madison
6	L	81-90	Western Michigan
9	W	81-64	AUSTIN PEAY#
10	W	79-67	RUTGERS#
17	W	76-68	New Orleans (at Indianapolis, IN)
22	W	94-77	Tennessee-Chattanooga
28	W	89-75	WEBER STATE
30	W	74-66	CENTRAL MICHIGAN

January
3	L	61-71	Michigan
7	W	68-60	MINNESOTA
10	L	58-62	ILLINOIS
14	W	84-83	Iowa
21	W	92-66	OHIO STATE
25	W	96-84	Northwestern
28	W	65-62	Penn State
31	W	76-66	INDIANA

February
7	W	78-69	Michigan State
12	L	73-82	Indiana
15	W	71-51	PENN STATE
18	W	94-57	NORTHWESTERN
22	W	64-55	Ohio State
26	W	66-56	WISCONSIN

March
1	W	92-85	IOWA
4	W	69-56	Illinois
9	W	72-59	Minnesota
12	W	73-67	MICHIGAN
17	W	49-48	Wisconsin-Green Bay*
19	L	73-75	Memphis*

* NCAA first and second round, Austin, TX
**Big Island Classic, Hilo, HI (1st)
##Boilermaker Invitational, West Lafayette, IN (1st)

1994-95 STATISTICS *(1995-96 returnees in ALL CAPS)*

Record: 25-7   Home: 12-1   Road: 8-4   Neutral: 5-2

Player	G-GS	Min-Avg	FG-FGA	Pct	3P-3PA	Pct	FT-FTA	Pct	Rebounds Off-Def	Tot-Avg	PF-FD	AT	TO	BS	ST	Pts-Avg
Cuonzo Martin	32-28	959-20.0	192-437	.439	91-194	.469	115-144	.799	53-72	125-3.9	35-0	70	47	5	21	590-18.4
BRANDON BRANTLEY	32-15	785-24.5	114-203	.562	0-1	.000	93-114	.816	68-126	194-6.1	96-4	12	61	35	6	321-10.0
ROY HAIRSTON	32-15	746-23.3	114-225	.507	13-48	.271	66-135	.489	49-96	145-4.5	56-0	42	65	27	32	307-9.6
Matt Waddell	32-23	821-25.7	96-245	.392	34-84	.405	72-84	.857	6-66	72-2.3	47-1	113	42	1	29	298-9.3
BRAD MILLER	32-18	574-17.9	71-122	.582	0-0	.000	66-100	.660	56-97	153-4.8	74-2	39	47	34	19	208-6.5
JUSTIN JENNINGS	32-16	477-14.9	84-140	.600	0-0	.000	30-68	.441	42-56	98-3.1	65-1	12	40	4	22	198-6.2
CHAD AUSTIN	32-7	456-14.3	65-142	.458	22-54	.407	29-44	.659	24-39	63-2.0	38-0	64	42	0	23	181-5.7
PORTER ROBERTS	32-31	869-27.2	54-131	.412	8-37	.216	42-67	.627	18-109	127-4.0	57-0	123	62	5	22	158-4.9
HERB DOVE	32-5	310-9.7	41-72	.569	0-0	.000	18-26	.692	20-28	48-1.5	41-0	17	27	3	9	100-3.1
TODD FOSTER	32-1	341-10.7	19-56	.339	14-46	.304	11-16	.688	3-23	26-0.8	39-1	35	27	2	11	63-2.0
DAVID LESMOND	15-0	41-2.7	3-11	.273	1-7	.143	2-4	.500	3-5	8-0.5	6-0	1	10	0	0	9-0.6
PAUL GILVYDIS	6-0	7-1.2	1-4	.250	0-0	.000	1-2	.500	2-0	2-0.3	0-0	1	0	0	2	3-0.5
Tim Ervin	15-0	23-1.5	2-0	.222	0-1	.000	2-6	.333	2-0	2-0.1	4-0	4	0	0	0	6-0.4
MATT TEN DAM	9-0	16-1.8	1-3	.333	0-0	.000	0-0	.000	1-3	4-0.4	2-0	0	1	0	0	2-0.2
Team										103						
Purdue	32	6425	857-1800	.476	183-472	.388	547-810	.675	347-720	1170-36.6	560	533	471	116	196	2444-76.4
Opponents	32	6425	831-1926	.431	172-518	.332	365-560	.652	410-671	1081-33.8	681	429	485	94	193	2199-68.7

SCHOOL RECORDS

Individual

SCORING
- Game: 61 Rick Mount vs. Iowa 2/28/70
- Season: **1,030** Glenn Robinson 1993-94
- Career: 2323 Rick Mount 1968-70

REBOUNDING
- Game: 27 Carl McNulty vs. Minnesota 2/29/51
- Season: 352 Joe Barry Carroll 1978-79
- Career: 1148 Joe Barry Carroll 1977-80

ASSISTS
- Game: **18** Bruce Parkinson vs. Minnesota 3/8/75
- Season: 207 Bruce Parkinson 1974-75
- Career: 690 Bruce Parkinson 1973-77

STEALS
- Game: 7 Bruce Parkinson vs. Indiana 2/20/77
- Season: 88 Brian Walker 1978-79
- Career: 187 Brian Walker 1978-81

BLOCKED SHOTS
- Game: 11 Joe Barry Carroll vs. Arizona 12/10/77
- Season: 105 Joe Barry Carroll 1977-78
- Career: 349 Joe Barry Carroll 1977-80

Team

SCORING
- Game: 120 2/8/69 (Indiana)
- Season: 2871 1993-94

REBOUNDING
- Game: 79 12/30/68 (Hawaii)
- Season: 1405 1973-74

ASSISTS
- Game: 35 12/22/74 (Illinois State) 12/19/72 (San Jose St.)
- Season: 680 1987-88

STEALS
- Game: 21 12/4/78 (Northern Colorado)
- Season: 280 1979-80

BLOCKED SHOTS
- Game: 15 3/2/78 (Northwestern)
- Season: 147 1978-79

Big Ten records in **bold**

TOP TEN SCORERS

1. Rick Mount (1967-70) — 2,323
2. Joe Barry Carroll (1976-80) — 2,175
3. Dave Schellhase (1963-66) — 2,074
4. Troy Lewis (1983-88) — 2,038
5. Terry Dischinger (1959-62) — 1,979
6. Walter Jordan (1974-78) — 1,813
7. Keith Edmondson (1980-82) — 1,717
8. Glenn Robinson (1992-94) — 1,706
9. Todd Mitchell (1983-88) — 1,699
10. Cuonzo Martin (1992-95) — 1,666

Senior guard Porter Roberts is Purdue's most experienced returning player with 62 career starts.

WISCONSIN

 **Badgers**

QUICK FACTS

Location: Madison, WI
Population: 200,000
Founded: 1848
Enrollment: 40,305
Nickname: Badgers
Colors: Cardinal and White
Arena: UW Field House (1930, 11,500)
Chancellor: David Ward
Faculty Representatives: James Hoyt, Barbara Wolfe
Athletic Director: Pat Richter
Head Coach: Dick Bennett (Ripon, '65), 1st year
Assistant Coaches: Brad Soderberg, Shawn Hood, Brian Hecker
Men's Sports Information Director: Steve Malchow
Basketball Contact: Justin Doherty (Assoc. SID)
SID Phone: (608) 262-1811
SID Fax Phone: (608) 262-8184
Press Row Phone: (608) 262-7869
1994-95 Record: 13-14, 7-11 Big Ten (9th)
Starters Returning/Lost: 1/4
Letterwinners Returning/Lost: 8/6
Best time to contact coach: Weekdays, mid to late mornings

Wisconsin begins the Dick Bennett era in what the first-year head coach has called a "start-over" situation. The Badgers, 13-14 overall and 7-11 (9th) in the Big Ten last season, have just one player – junior point guard Darnell Hoskins – with more than one year of Big Ten experience. Overall, the roster features six freshmen and five sophomores.

Bennett's immediate goals will be to bring the young Badgers together and focus on improving game after game. Nonetheless, he does see potential in his youthful personnel.

The Badgers are deepest at the guard positions and likely will feature a three-man backcourt consisting of Hoskins and sophomores Sean Mason and Mosezell Peterson. Hoskins (6.8 ppg., 3.4 apg), last season's starter at point guard, was the UW's leading free throw shooter (.775). Mason, who played in 25 games as a freshman, averaged 5.0 points and is the team's second-leading returning scorer. Peterson saw action in 18 games as a rookie and averaged 3.7 points, while being selected the team's Most Improved Player.

Five Wisconsin freshman – Hennssy Auriantal, Duany Duany, Jeremy Hall, Mike Kosolcharoen and D. J. Walker – also will battle for playing time on the perimeter.

Wisconsin's numbers at the forward spots will be thin – returnees senior Osita Nwachukwu, sophomores Sean Daugherty and Booker Coleman, and freshman Sam Okey – so, each player should figure into a significant role.

The 6-10 Daugherty is the most experienced of the group, having played in 26 games a year ago, including five starts. He ranked third on the team in rebounds per game with 3.8 and averaged 4.6 points per outing. Nwachukwu, at 6-8, is the UW's only senior; however, he is in just his second (and final) season with the Badgers after transferring to Wisconsin via junior college. He played in all 27 games a year ago and averaged 2.6 points and 2.8 rebounds per game. The 6-9 Coleman scored six points in a total of 10 games last season but will be looked to for increased production this year. He saw action in two foreign tours last summer.

Okey, a 6-7 product of Cassville, Wis., enters the UW as one of the school's most highly touted players ever. He is the fourth-leading scorer in state high school history and was a starter in the 1995 McDonald's High School All-America game.

DICK BENNETT
Head Coach

David Ward
Chancellor

Jim Hoyt
Faculty Representative

Barbara Wolfe
Faculty Representative

Pat Richter
Athletic Director

Steve Malchow
Men's Sports Information Director

Wisconsin Field House (1930)
Capacity 11,500

ROSTER

No.	Name	POS	HT	WT	Year	Hometown (High School)
5	Hennssy Auriantal	G	6-1	180	FR	Montreal, Quebec (Dawson College)
20*	Shawn Carlin	G	6-3	180	JR	Middleton, WI (Winona State)
41*	Booker Coleman	F	6-9	225	SO	Erie, PA (Cathedral Prep)
52*	Sean Daugherty	F	6-10	230	SO	Vincennes, IN (Lincoln)
3	Duany Duany	G	6-4	170	FR	Bloomington, IN (North)
40	Paul Grant	C	6-11	235	SR	West Bloomfield, MI (Brother Rice)
14	Jeremy Hall	G	5-10	170	FR	Garrett, KY (Allen-Central)
10**	Darnell Hoskins	G	6-0	170	JR	Dayton, OH (Chaminade-Julienne)
23	Mike Kosolcharoen	G	6-1	200	FR	Adams, WI (Adams-Friendship)
22*	Sean Mason	G	6-2	175	SO	Olympia Fields, IL (Rich Central)
0*	Osita Nwachukwu	F	6-8	230	SR	Awo-Mbieri, Owerri, Imo-State, Nigeria (Holy Ghost/Kilgore, TX)
4	Sam Okey	F	6-7	230	FR	Cassville, WI
13*	Mosezell Peterson	G	6-4	200	SO	Louisville, KY (Ballard)
33*	Brian Vraney	F	6-6	230	SO	Reedsville, WI (Valders)
32	D.J. Walker	G	6-4	185	FR	Milwaukee, WI (Marquette)

*letters earned

RETURNING/LOST

Letterwinners Returning	YR	POS	FG%	FT%	PPG	RPG	APG
*Darnell Hoskins	JR	G	.387	.775	6.8	3.1	3.4
Sean Daugherty	SO	F	.350	.588	4.6	3.8	0.5
Mosezell Peterson	SO	G	.368	.706	3.7	1.1	0.2
Sean Mason	SO	G	.336	.590	5.0	2.0	0.8
Osita Nwachukwu	SR	F	.449	.473	2.6	2.8	0.0
Booker Coleman	SO	F	.333	.333	0.6	0.8	0.0
Shawn Carlin	JR	G	.000	.000	0.0	0.9	0.3
Brian Vraney	SO	F	.000	.000	0.0	0.0	0.0
Letterwinners Lost		POS	FG%	FT%	PPG	RPG	APG
*Michael Finley		F	.379	.773	20.5	5.2	4.0
*Rashard Griffith		C	.566	.579	17.2	10.8	0.8
*Andy Kilbride		G	.375	.692	7.4	2.0	2.0
*Brian Kelley		F	.448	.405	4.5	3.4	0.6
Howard Moore		F	.541	.600	2.2	2.0	0.5
Chris Conger		G	.667	.500	0.7	0.1	0.1

*starters

1995-96 SCHEDULE

Tue., Nov. 7	Georgia Select Team (exh). (7 CST)	
Wed., Nov. 15	Marathon Oil (exh.) (7 CST)	
Mon., Nov. 20	vs. Villanova (11:30 a.m. HST)*	
Tue., Nov. 21	vs. UCLA or Santa Clara (Time TBA)*	
Wed., Nov. 22	vs. TBA*	
Tue., Nov. 28	Northeastern Illinois (7 CST)	
Sat., Dec. 2	Temple (CS) (1 CST)	
Tue., Dec. 5	@ Wright State (6:35 CST)	
Sat., Dec. 9	St. Bonaventure (7 CST)	
Mon., Dec. 11	@ Providence (CS) (7 CST)	
Thu., Dec. 14	Valparaiso (7 CST)	
Sat., Dec. 23	Wisconsin-Milwaukee (CS) (12:30 CST)	
Thu., Dec. 28	Eastern Illinois (7 CST)	
Sun., Dec. 31	Marquette (CS) (12:30 or 3:30 CST)	
Wed., Jan. 3	Michigan (CS) (7 CST)	
Sun., Jan. 7	@ Penn State (1 CST)	
Wed., Jan. 10	@ Indiana (CS) (7 CST)	
Sat., Jan. 13	Iowa (CS) (3:30 CST)	
Wed., Jan. 17	Michigan State (CS) (7 CST)	
Sat., Jan. 20	@ Northwestern (CS Regional) (1:15 CST)	
Wed., Jan. 24	Minnesota (CS) (7 CST)	
Wed., Jan. 31	@ Ohio State (ESPN2) (6:30 CST)	
Sat., Feb. 3	@ Illinois (CS) (7 CST)	
Wed., Feb. 7	Purdue (CS) (7 CST)	
Sat., Feb. 10	Ohio State (CS Regional) (1:15 CST)	
Sat., Feb. 17	@ Minnesota (CS Regional) (1:15 CST)	
Wed., Feb. 21	Northwestern (ESPN) (6 CST)	
Sat., Feb. 24	@ Michigan State (CS Regional) (11 a.m. CST)	
Wed., Feb. 28	@ Iowa (CS) (7 CST)	
Sat., Mar. 2	Indiana (CS) (4:30 CST)	
Wed., Mar. 6	Penn State (CS) (7 CST)	
Sat., Mar. 9	@ Michigan (CS) (3:30 CST)	

CS – Creative Sports Local Package
CS Regional – Creative Sports Regional Weekend Series

SUBJECT TO CHANGE

Sophomore forward Sean Daugherty is the Badgers' top returning rebounder with 3.8 rpg.

WISCONSIN

Dick Bennett

Head Coach
DICK BENNETT

Birth Date: April 20, 1943
Hometown: Pittsburg, PA
Education:
Bachelor's, physical education, Ripon, 1965; Master's, education, Wisconsin-Stevens Point
Playing Experience:
Played 4 years each of basketball, football and baseball at Ripon
Coaching Experience:
Head coach, West Bend, WI H.S., 1965-66
Head coach, Mineral Point, WI H.S. 1966-67
Head coach, Marion, WI H.S., 1967-69
Head coach, New London, WI H.S., 1969-72
Head coach, Eau Claire Memorial, WI H.S., 1972-76
Head coach, Wisconsin-Stevens Point, 1976-85
Head coach, Wisconsin-Green Bay, 1985-95
Head coach, Wisconsin, 1995-present
Honors and achievements:
Won 74 percent of his games as a high school coach... 1976 Eau Claire Memorial team was state runnerup... won 69 percent of his games at Wisconsin-Stevens Point, and appeared in NAIA national tournament three times... Pointers finished second in 1984... was named NAIA national coach of the year in '84 and *Basketball Times* Midwest coach of the year in '94... won 63 percent of his games at Wisconsin-Green Bay, 73 percent in his last six years as coach... led UW-Green Bay to five postseason appearances and three to the NCAA tournament in 1991, '94 and '95... two-time Mid-Continent Conference (1990 and '92) and Kodak/NABC District 11 (1992 and '94) coach of the year.
Personal Data:
Wife, Anne... daughter, Kathi is women's head basketball coach at Wisconsin-Oshkosh; daughter Amy is a speech therapist in Green Bay; son, Tony is a guard with the Cleveland Cavaliers... resides in Madison.

Bennett's Record:

Year	School	Overall	
1976-77	Wisconsin-Stevens Point	9-17	.346
1977-78	Wisconsin-Stevens Point	13-14	.481
1978-79	Wisconsin-Stevens Point	14-12	.538
1979-80	Wisconsin-Stevens Point	18-10	.643
1980-81	Wisconsin-Stevens Point	19-7	.731
1981-82	Wisconsin-Stevens Point	22-6	.786
1982-83	Wisconsin-Stevens Point	26-4	.867
1983-84	Wisconsin-Stevens Point	28-4	.875
1984-85	Wisconsin-Stevens Point	25-5	.833
1985-86	Wisconsin-Green Bay	5-23	.179
1986-87	Wisconsin-Green Bay	15-14	.517
1987-88	Wisconsin-Green Bay	18-9	.667
1988-89	Wisconsin-Green Bay	14-14	.500
1989-90	Wisconsin-Green Bay	24-8	.750
1990-91	Wisconsin-Green Bay	24-7	.774
1991-92	Wisconsin-Green Bay	25-5	.833
1992-93	Wisconsin-Green Bay	13-14	.481
1993-94	Wisconsin-Green Bay	27-7	.794
1994-95	Wisconsin-Green Bay	22-8	.733
Career Total		361-188	.658

NCAA Appearances: (3): 1991-94-95

BADGERS TO WATCH

**SEAN DAUGHERTY, F,
6-10, 230, SO, Vincennes, IN**

Only Badger (besides Darnell Hoskins) with starting experience... team's top returning rebounder... played in 26 of team's 27 games as a freshman... averaged 4.6 points and 3.8 rebounds per contest... rebounding average ranked third on team... scored in double figures on four occasions... made 11 of 29 (.379) three-point attempts during non-conference portion of schedule... third on team in blocked shots with eight.

**DARNELL HOSKINS, G,
6-0, 170, JR, Dayton, OH**

Only Badger with more than a year of Big Ten action under his belt... team's top returning scorer and only returning starter... fourth on team in scoring with 6.8 points per game... second on team behind Michael Finley in minutes (29.6/game), assists (3.4/game) and steals (1.2/game)... team's leading free throw shooter (55 of 71, .775)... made 40 of last 48 (.833) free throw attempts... assist-to-turnovers ratio was 64-40 in Conference games... averaged only 2.2 turnovers per game in Big Ten action.

**MOSEZELL PETERSON, G,
6-4, 200, SO, Louisville, KY**

Saw action in 18 games as a freshman... selected by teammates as Badgers' Most Improved Player... averaged 3.7 points and 1.1 rebounds per game... shot .361 from three-point range and .706 from free throw line... connected on 77 percent of free throw attempts in Conference play... scored in double figures on four occasions, including season-high 16 points in final game at Michigan State.

1994-95 RESULTS
(13-14/7-11)

November			
26	W	86-63	WRIGHT STATE
30	W	61-57	WISCONSIN-GREEN BAY
December			
3	W	70-65	TEXAS TECH
6	W	69-51	VALPARAISO
10	L	76-92	Eastern Michigan
14	W	90-64	WISCONSIN-MILWAUKEE
23	W	75-60	LOYOLA-MARYMOUNT
27	L	78-95	Stanford
31	L	65-80	Marquette
January			
4	L	64-78	MICHIGAN STATE
7	L	70-73	Indiana
11	W	81-59	Ohio State
14	W	74-67	MINNESOTA
21	L	84-96	Iowa
26	L	67-78	PENN STATE
28	W	97-73	NORTHWESTERN
February			
1	L	58-62	Michigan
4	W	73-60	ILLINOIS
11	W	70-65	MICHIGAN
15	W	70-56	Northwestern
18	L	67-74	Penn State
22	L	77-84	IOWA
26	L	56-66	Purdue
28	L	70-78	Minnesota
March			
4	W	80-69	OHIO STATE
8	L	70-72	INDIANA
11	L	72-97	Michigan State

1994-95 STATISTICS *(1995-96 returnees in ALL CAPS)*
Record: 13-14   Home: 11-4   Road: 2-10   Neutral: 0-0

Player	G-GS	Min -Avg	FG-FGA	Pct	3P-3PA	Pct	FT-FTA	Pct	Rebounds Off-Def	Tot-Avg	PF-FD	AT	TO	BS	ST	Pts-Avg
Michael Finley	27-27	1000-37.0	178-470	.379	58-204	.284	140-181	.773	39-102	141-5.2	73-1	108	80	15	52	554-20.5
Rashard Griffith	26-26	756-29.1	167-295	.566	0-0	.000	113-195	.579	76-205	281-10.8	69-3	21	76	58	11	447-17.2
Andy Kilbride	25-25	707-28.3	57-152	.375	54-134	.403	18-26	.692	10-41	51-2.0	89-3	49	43	0	19	186-7.4
DARNELL HOSKINS	27-27	798-29.6	55-142	.387	18-49	.367	55-71	.775	15-70	85-3.1	77-4	92	80	2	32	183-6.8
SEAN MASON	25-0	382-15.3	41-122	.336	21-62	.339	23-39	.590	10-39	49-2.0	53-2	20	51	6	10	126-5.0
SEAN DAUGHERTY	26-5	398-15.3	43-123	.350	13-47	.277	20-34	.588	43-56	99-3.8	61-1	13	33	8	11	119-4.6
Brian Kelley	27-15	498-18.4	52-116	.448	3-7	.429	15-37	.405	39-52	91-3.4	71-1	15	36	3	15	122-4.5
MOSEZELL PETERSON	18-0	129-7.2	21-57	.368	13-36	.361	12-17	.706	8-12	20-1.1	18-1	4	2	1	2	67-3.7
Jalil Roberts	10-2	186-18.6	12-35	.343	4-16	.250	9-12	.750	5-21	26-2.6	11-0	8	9	0	4	37-3.7
OSITA NWACHUKWU	27-0	291-10.8	22-49	.449	0-0	.000	26-55	.473	43-33	76-2.8	41-0	0	13	4	5	70-2.6
Howard Moore	21-8	178-8.5	20-37	.541	0-0	.000	6-10	.600	17-26	43-2.0	33-0	10	16	5	10	46-2.2
Chris Conger	10-0	19-1.9	2-3	.667	2-3	.667	1-2	.500	0-1	1-0.1	4-0	1	1	0	1	7-0.7
BOOKER COLEMAN	10-0	25-2.5	2-6	.333	0-0	.000	2-6	.333	2-6	8-0.8	7-0	0	4	1	0	6-0.6
BRIAN VRANEY	1-0	1-1.0	0-0	.000	0-0	.000	0-0	.000	0-0	0-0.0	0-0	0	0	0	0	0-0.0
Sean Carlin	7-0	16-2.3	0-4	.000	0-3	.000	0-2	.000	1-5	6-0.9	1-0	2	1	0	0	0-0.0
Team										85			3			
Wisconsin	27	5384	672-1611	.417	186-561	.332	440-667	.640	308-669	1062-39.3	608	343	448	103	172	1970-73.0
Opponents	27	5384	661-1612	.410	140-441	.317	472-696	.678	347-714	1061-39.3	587	328	428	86	181	1934-71.6

SCHOOL RECORDS

Individual

SCORING
- Game: 42 — Ken Barnes vs. Indiana 3/8/65
  Michael Finley at Eastern Michigan, 12/10/94
- Season: 620 — Michael Finley 1992-93
- Career: 2,147 — Michael Finley 1991-95

REBOUNDING
- Game: 30 — Paul Morrow vs. Purdue 1/3/53
- Season: 344 — Jim Clinton 1950-51
- Career: 904 — Claude Gregory 1977-81

ASSISTS
- Game: 13 — Wes Matthews vs. Army 12/30/79
  Tracy Webster vs. Michigan 2/26/92
- Season: 179 — Tracy Webster 1992-93
- Career: 501 — Tracy Webster 1991-94

STEALS
- Game: **10 — Michael Finley vs. Purdue 2/13/93**
- Season: 69 — Tracy Webster 1993-94
- Career: 183 — Tracy Webster 1991-94

BLOCKED SHOTS
- Game: 9 — Brad Sellers vs. Toledo 11/29/82
- Season: 68 — Brad Sellers 1982-83
- Career: 124 — Rashard Griffith 1993-95

Team

SCORING
- Game: 120 — 12/9/67 (Southern Methodist)
- Season: 2259 — 1993-94

REBOUNDING
- Game: 79 — 12/5/70 (Michigan Tech)
- Season: 1268 — 1970-71

ASSISTS
- Game: 33 — 3/7/53 (Northwestern)
- Season: 506 — 1986-87

STEALS
- Game: 17 — 1/7/88 (Michigan State)
- Season: 220 — 1988-89

BLOCKED SHOTS
- Game: 11 — 12/1/73 (Rollins)
  11/28/88 (Ferris State)
  11/30/91 (Portland)
  12/22/90 (Texas-Arlington)
- Season: 153 — 1991-92

Big Ten record in **bold**

TOP TEN SCORERS

1. Michael Finley (1992-95) — 2,147
2. Danny Jones (1987-90) — 1,854
3. Claude Gregory (1978-81) — 1,745
4. Rick Olson (1983-86) — 1,736
5. Trent Jackson (1986-89) — 1,545
6. Clarence Sherrod (1969-71) — 1,408
7. Cory Blackwell (1982-84) — 1,405
8. Tracy Webster (1992-94) — 1,264
9. Wes Matthews (1978-80) — 1,251
10. Joe Franklin (1965-68) — 1,215

Sophomore guard Mosezell Peterson, named Wisconsin's Most Improved Player last year, shot .361 from three-point range and .706 from the free-throw line.

BASKETBALL '96

BIG TEN ALL-STAR TOUR OF JAPAN

The Big Ten men's All-Stars completed their 1995 summer tour of Japan with a 7-0 record, marking the first time a men's All-Star squad has completed a summer tour undefeated. The Big Ten men's previous best showing was a 15-1 excursion to Australia in 1971. The 13-day sojourn through Japan was sponsored by the Noram Japan Co., LTD, the Big Ten Conference's marketing contractor in Japan. Guided by Ohio State head coach Randy Ayers, the All-Stars faced Japan's college all-star team as well as numerous club teams.

According to Ayers, a portion of the team's success was due to the amount of talent on the team. Rick Yudt, the Buckeyes' representative on the league's 1994 all-star team, and Purdue's Herb Dove manned the frontcourt and served as team leaders throughout the tour. The backcourt featured Northwestern point guard Geno Carlisle, who in his freshman year averaged 11.7 ppg and dished out 101 assists, and Penn State's Pete Lisicky, who was one of the Conference's top three-point shooters last year.

"The coaches sent us some good people," Ayers said upon the completion of the tour. "We had some of the better young talent in the Conference. The makeup was good. We had just the right amount of guards and big people. It's hard when you have 12 talented players to get everybody some playing time."

After two days of practice at the U.S. Air Force base in Yokota, the All-Stars were set for competition. The squad faced little opposition in its opening games, trouncing the Yokota Raiders, 126-79, in the tour opener on June 16, and the Japan College All-Stars, 106-66, the next day. Fatigue slowed the Big Ten in the next three contests, but the squad still managed to pull out wins in a rematch against the Japan College All-Stars (94-86) and in two games against the Yokosuka Seahawks (98-86 and 92-81).

Following two days of recuperation, the Conference wrapped up the tour by steamrolling their final two opponents, the Iwakuni Marines (99-64) and the Japan College All-Stars (103-81). The final game, played in front of 6,000 fans, benefitted the Kobe earthquake relief fund.

The All-Stars showcased an explosive offense as they outscored opponents by an average of 25 points, including a 47-point thrashing of the Yokota Raiders. Led by Dove's team-leading 14.6 ppg, the Conference had four players average more than 10 points per game. Other double-figure scorers were Indiana forward Andrae Patterson (14.4 ppg), Michigan State guard Ray Weathers (13.0 ppg) and Michigan forward/guard Willie Mitchell (10.6 ppg). Carlisle quarterbacked the All-Star offense, handing out 4.1 assists per game.

Iowa forward Ryan Bowen led all rebounders with 9.7 per game, including a team-high 18 rebounds in the second game vs. Japan's college all-stars. Frontcourt-mates Patterson and Dove chipped in 8.3 and 6.1 boards, respectively.

"Our front line people played extremely well. If you look at the stats, (Iowa's) Bowen and (Indiana's) Patterson both played extremely well," Ayers said, "Bowen rebounded the ball well. He's unbelievable on the offensive boards. Patterson is a promising star not only in our conference but on the national level."

On the defensive end, Lisicky snatched a team-high nine steals and Bowen recorded 12 blocks. According to Ayers, Minnesota's Micah Watkins was the squad's defensive stalwart despite seeing limited playing time.

"Micah Watkins was probably our best defender and it was hard to play him as much as I would have liked. But there were a couple of situations where he came in and solidified our defensive effort and helped us win the game."

Other players seeing action for the Conference were Illinois forward Brett Robisch, who averaged 6.7 ppg and 5.3 rpg, and Wisconsin forward/center Booker Coleman, who finished with 7.7 points and 6.4 rebounds per game. John Lumpkin, who is also a member of Ohio State's football team, tallied 4.0 points and 3.5 boards per game.

STATISTICS

	G-GS	FG-FGA	Pct	3P-3PA	Pct	FT-FTA	Pct	Rebounds Off-Def	Tot-Avg	PF-FD	AT	TO	BS	ST	Pts-Avg
Herb Dove	7-0	41-77	.532	0-0	.000	20-28	.714	19-24	43-6.1	7-0	15	11	3	8	102-14.6
Andrae Patterson	7-7	34-66	.515	3-8	.375	30-41	.732	28-30	58-8.3	16-0	8	17	10	5	101-14.4
Ray Weathers	7-7	32-84	.381	6-15	.400	21-31	.677	10-13	23-3.3	11-0	15	13	0	2	91-13.0
Willie Mitchell	7-6	26-66	.394	11-23	.478	11-17	.647	7-10	17-2.4	5-0	13	18	3	7	74-10.6
Ryan Bowen	7-7	30-41	.732	0-1	.000	9-11	.818	33-35	68-9.7	13-0	10	6	12	3	69-9.9
Booker Coleman	7-0	20-42	.476	0-0	.000	14-26	.538	20-25	45-6.4	7-0	1	13	9	4	54-7.7
Geno Carlisle	7-0	18-49	.367	6-21	.286	10-13	.769	13-16	29-4.1	4-0	25	13	2	7	52-7.4
Pete Lisicky	7-0	17-47	.362	10-24	.417	7-9	.778	4-9	13-1.9	8-0	12	15	0	9	51-7.3
Brett Robisch	7-7	21-46	.457	0-0	.000	5-11	.455	16-21	37-5.3	11-0	3	5	2	2	47-6.7
Rick Yudt	7-0	19-53	.358	5-20	.250	4-6	.667	9-11	20-2.9	10-0	12	13	1	5	47-6.7
John Lumpkin	7-0	8-24	.333	0-0	.000	7-16	.438	9-12	21-3.0	12-0	2	6	6	3	23-3.3
Micah Watkins	7-1	4-13	.308	0-3	.000	3-7	.429	7-10	17-2.4	10-0	10	5	1	5	11-1.6
Big Ten All-Stars	7	270-608	.444	41-115	.357	141-216	.653	175-216	391-55.9	114	126	135	49	60	722 100.3

Score by Halves	1	2	OT	Total
Big Ten All Stars:	358	364	0	7220
Opponents:	272	271	0	5430

RESULTS (7-0)

Date	Opponent	Result	Score	Site
6/16	Yokota Raiders	Won	126-79	Yokota AFB
6/17	Japan College All-Stars	Won	106-66	Tokyo
6/18	Japan College All-Stars	Won	94-86	Fukouka
6/20	Yokosuka Seahawks	Won	98-86	Yokosuka
6/21	Yokosuka Seahawks	Won	92-81	Yokosuka
6/24	Iwakuni Marines	Won	99-64	Iwakuni
6/25	Japan College All-Stars	Won	103-81	Kobe

Front Row: Micah Watkins (MINN), Rick Yudt (OSU), Geno Carlisle (ILL), Ray Weathers (MSU), Pete Lisicky (PSU), Herb Dove (PUR). Back Row: Assistant Coach Jerry Francis (OSU), Ryan Bowen (IOWA), John Lumpkin (OSU), Brett Robisch (ILL), Andrae Patterson (IND), Booker Coleman (WIS), Willie Mitchell (MICH), Head Coach Randy Ayers.

YEAR IN REVIEW

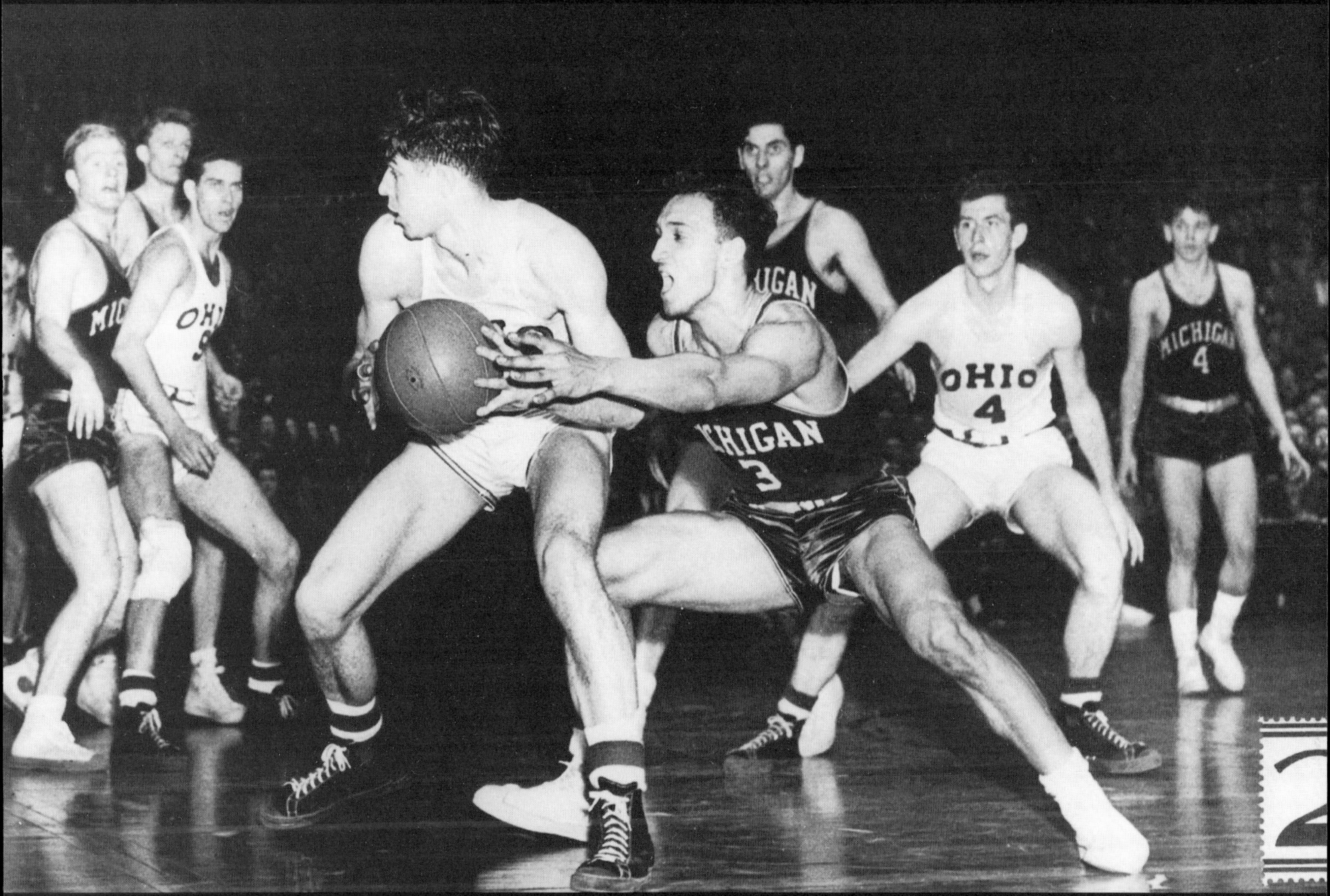

Michigan vs. Ohio State, 1948

1936-1955

- At least one Big Ten player is named all-America every year from 1936 to 1948. All told, 20 Conference players win 22 all-America awards during this era.
- No team dominates this period, although Illinois wins or shares the most Conference titles with six, including two during the "Whiz Kids" era in the early '40s, while Indiana wins its second national title in 1953.
- The Big Ten figures prominently in the first three NCAA basketball championships: Ohio State finishes runner-up in the 1939 tournament hosted by Northwestern, while Indiana in 1940 and Wisconsin in 1941 win the next two NCAA titles.
- Chicago, which hadn't won a Big Ten basketball game in six years, withdraws from the Conference in 1946. Michigan State is admitted three years later and first competes during the 1950-51 season.
- The two largest attended Big Ten games in history occur during this period. In 1946, 22,822 view Ohio State and Northwestern at Chicago Stadium and in 1955, 20,176 take in the Iowa-Minnesota game at Minnesota's Williams Arena.

1994-95 IN REVIEW
Honors

ALL-BIG TEN TEAMS
(Players names in ALL CAPS have 1995-96 eligibility)

As selected by media panel

FIRST TEAM	SECOND TEAM	THIRD TEAM
*Shawn Respert, Michigan State	Michael Finley, Wisconsin	KIWANE GARRIS, Illinois
*Alan Henderson, Indiana	Eric Snow, Michigan State	JESS SETTLES, Iowa
Cuonzo Martin, Purdue	Ray Jackson, Michigan	BRIAN EVANS, Indiana
Rashard Griffith, Wisconsin	Voshon Lenard, Minnesota	ANDRE WOOLRIDGE, Iowa
John Amaechi, Penn State	CHRIS KINGSBURY, Iowa	Townsend Orr, Minnesota

* unanimous

Honorable Mention: Shelly Clark, **Illinois;** Jimmy King, MAURICE TAYLOR, **Michigan;** JAMIE FEICK, **Michigan State;** Jayson Walton, **Minnesota;** Doug Etzler, Antonio Watson, **Ohio State;** GLENN SEKUNDA, **Penn State;** Matt Waddell, **Purdue.**

Player of the Year: Shawn Respert, Michigan State
Freshman of the Year: Maurice Taylor, Michigan
Coach of the Year: Gene Keady, Purdue

As selected by Big Ten coaches

FIRST TEAM	SECOND TEAM	THIRD TEAM
*Shawn Respert, Michigan State	Rashard Griffith, Wisconsin	JESS SETTLES, Iowa
*Alan Henderson, Indiana	Eric Snow, Michigan State	BRIAN EVANS, Indiana
Cuonzo Martin, Purdue	Ray Jackson, Michigan	Townsend Orr, Minnesota
Michael Finley, Wisconsin	Voshon Lenard, Minnesota	JAMIE FEICK, Michigan State
John Amaechi, Penn State	KIWANE GARRIS, Illinois	Jimmy King, Michigan

* unanimous

Honorable Mention: Shelly Clark, **Illinois;** ANDRE WOOLRIDGE, **Iowa;** Jayson Walton, **Minnesota;** Doug Etzler, **Ohio State;** PORTER ROBERTS, Matt Waddell, **Purdue.**

Player of the Year: Shawn Respert, Michigan State
Freshman of the Year: Maurice Taylor, Michigan
Defensive Player of the Year: Eric Snow, Michigan State

ACADEMIC ALL-BIG TEN

Name/School	YR	POS	GPA	Major	Hometown
Steve Roth/ILL	SR	C	4.50*	Sports Management	Belleville, IL
Robert Eggers/IND	SO	F	3.13	University Division	Cuyahoga Falls, OH
Todd Lindeman/IND	SR	C	3.08	Outdoor Rec./Res. Mgt.	Greenwood, IN
Nathan Koch/IOWA	SR	F	3.29	Political Science	Ames, IA
Jess Settles/IOWA	SO	F	3.72	English	Winfield, IA
Steve Nicodemus/MSU	JR	G	3.02	Food Systems Econ. & Mgt.	South Whitney, IN
Steve Polonowski/MSU	SO	F	3.25	Business Admin./Pre-Law	Rockford, MI
Mark Prylow/MSU	SR	G	3.45	Professional Accounting	Rochester Hills, MI
David Grim/MINN	JR	F	3.10	Bus. Forestry/Mktg. Prod.	Massillon, OH
Trevor Winter/MINN	SO	C	3.16	Business	Slayton, MN
Dan Kreft/NU	JR	C	3.05	Electrical Engineering	Coral Springs, FL
Doug Etzler/OSU	SR	G	3.38	Elementary Education	Convoy, OH
Nate Althouse/PSU	SR	G	3.63	Counselor Education	Lititz, PA
John Amaechi/PSU	SR	C	3.33	Psychology	Manchester, England
Greg Bartram/PSU	SR	G/F	3.66	Marketing	Chapmanville, WV
Michael Joseph/PSU	SR	C	3.07	Admin. of Justice	Oldsmar, FL
Tim Ervin/PUR	SR	G	3.59	Industrial Management	Chicago, IL

academic all-America in bold
* on a 5.00 scale

With Michigan State's Shawn Respert, Indiana's Alan Henderson was named unanimous all-Big Ten by both a media panel and Conference coaches.

STANDINGS

		Conference			Season			PTS	AVG	OPP PTS	OPP AVG
		Won	Lost	PCT	Won	Lost	PCT				
1.	Purdue	15	3	.833	25	7	.781	2444	76.4	2199	68.7
2.	Michigan State	14	4	.778	22	6	.786	2194	78.4	1926	68.8
3.	Indiana	11	7	.611	19	12	.613	2345	75.6	2158	69.6
	Michigan	11	7	.611	17	14	.548	2188	70.6	2161	69.7
5.	Illinois	10	8	.556	19	12	.613	2265	73.1	2125	68.5
	Minnesota	10	8	.556	19	12	.613	2360	76.1	2123	68.5
7.	Penn State	9	9	.500	21	11	.656	2281	71.3	2063	64.5
	Iowa	9	9	.500	21	12	.636	2757	83.5	2460	74.5
9.	Wisconsin	7	11	.389	13	14	.481	1970	73.0	1934	71.6
10.	Ohio State	2	16	.111	6	22	.214	1945	69.5	2174	77.6
11.	Northwestern	1	17	.056	5	22	.185	1766	65.4	2267	84.0

HOME ATTENDANCE

	Big Ten Games				All Games			
	Games	Total	Average	Sellouts	Games	Total	Average	Sellouts
Illinois	9	145,554	16,173	5	14	221,772	15,841	6
Indiana	9	152,806	16,978	9	13	220,382	16,952	13
Iowa	9	139,500	15,500	9	18	273,540	15,197	12
Michigan	9	122,058	13,562	9	13	175,991	13,538	12
Michigan State	9	135,426	15,047	8	15	221,127	14,742	12
Minnesota	9	129,477	14,386	6	16	224,744	14,047	7
Northwestern	9	64,951	7,217	4	13	82,965	6,382	4
Ohio State	9	101,388	11,265	1	16	177,081	11,068	1
Penn State	9	66,480	7,387	9	16	106,648	6,666	9
Purdue	9	127,107	14,123	9	13	183,599	14,123	13
Wisconsin	9	103,500	11,500	9	15	171,292	11,419	12
TOTALS	99	1,288,274	13,013	78	162	2,059,141	12,711	101

WON-LOST BREAKDOWN

	Big Ten Games						All Games							
	Home		Away		Total		Home		Away		Neutral		Total	
	W	L	W	L	W	L	W	L	W	L	W	L	W	L
Illinois	6	3	4	5	10	8	11	3	6	6	2	3	19	12
Indiana	7	2	4	5	11	7	11	2	4	6	4	4	19	12
Iowa	6	3	3	6	9	9	13	5	6	6	2	1	21	12
Michigan	8	1	3	6	11	7	10	3	4	7	3	4	17	14
Michigan State	8	1	6	3	14	4	14	1	8	4	0	1	22	6
Minnesota	7	2	3	6	10	8	12	4	4	7	3	1	19	12
Northwestern	1	8	0	9	1	17	4	9	0	13	1	0	5	22
Ohio State	2	7	0	9	2	16	6	10	0	11	0	1	6	22
Penn State	6	3	3	6	9	9	13	3	6	6	1	1	20	10
Purdue	8	1	7	2	15	3	12	1	8	4	5	2	25	7
Wisconsin	5	4	2	7	7	11	4	2	10	0	0	0	13	14
TOTALS	64	35	35	64	99	99	nonconference							
							53	9	12	16	21	18	86	43

THE BIG TEN IN THE POLLS (*Associated Press/CNN-USA Today/ *United Press International)

	ILL	IND	IOWA	MICH	MSU	MINN	PUR	WIS
Preseason	25/—/	9/7/		16/16/	20/20/			17/17/
Nov. 30		—/22/		17/16/	18/25/	15/11/		13/18/
Dec. 5		—/25/—		23/20/19	15/17/15	12/12/10		14/14/14
Dec. 12				25/22/23	18/18/20	11/11/10		20/23/19
Dec. 19	23/—/—	—/23/24			7/17/1	16/15/15		20/20/17
Dec. 26		24/20/24			15/15/16	—/25/23		19/21/15
Jan. 3		21/19/22	22/23/—		14/15/15	11/11/10		—/—/21
Jan. 9		/23/	19/19/18					
Jan. 17	20/22/22		—/25/—		12/12/12			
Jan. 23			—/24/24		10/11/9			
Jan. 30					9/10/10			
Feb. 6					7/7/7	—/24/25t	25/25/24	
Feb. 13					8/8/8	24/25/24	25/24/25	
Feb. 20					12/10/9	22/21/22	21/20/20	
Feb. 27					10/9/9		17/16/16	
Mar. 6					9/9/9		14/13/13	
Final					11/9/10		12/11/12	

MOST VALUABLE PLAYERS (Big Ten - Chicago Tribune MVP in bold)

Illinois: Shelly Clark, C	Michigan State: **Shawn Respert, G**	Ohio State: Doug Etzler, G
Indiana: Alan Henderson, F	Minnesota: Voshon Lenard, G	Penn State: John Amaechi, C
Iowa: Jess Settles, F		Townsend Orr, G	Purdue: Cuonzo Martin, F
Michigan: Ray Jackson, F	Northwestern: Cedric Neloms, F	Wisconsin: Rashard Griffith, C

PLAYER OF THE WEEK

D 5 **Jess Settles, F, IOWA** (IOWA 103, Drake 68; IOWA 99, Pepperdine 63; IOWA 91, Ohio U. 75) 22 PTS, 9 REB vs. Drake; 20 PTS, 8-13 FG vs. Pepperdine; 26 PTS, 12 REB, 9-13 FG vs. Ohio

D 12 **Alan Henderson, F, IND** (Kentucky 73, IND 70; IND 79, Morehead State 62; IND 92, Miami (OH) 77) 16 PTS, 8 REB vs. No. 7 Kentucky; 33 PTS, 7 REB vs. Morehead St.; 32 PTS, 9 REB, 7 AST vs. Miami (OH)

D 19 **Brian Evans, F, IND** (IND 80, Kansas 61) 29 PTS, 8-16 FG, 12 REB, 10 of 10 FT vs. No. 3 Kansas in 39 minutes

J 3 **Jess Settles, F, IOWA** (IOWA 81, Duke 71; IOWA 84, Hawaii 82; Arkansas 101, IOWA 92) 28 PTS, 8 REB, 10-15 FG vs. No. 7 Duke; 23 PTS, 5 REB, 9-13 FG vs. Hawaii; 15 PTS, 8-8 FT vs. No. 3 Arkansas

J 9 **Eric Snow, G, MSU** (MSU 78, WIS 64; MSU 69, IOWA 68) Career-high 22 PTS, 7-12 FG, 8-9 FT, 4 AST vs. Wisconsin; 9 PTS, 4-7 FG, game-winning shot with :01 left vs. Iowa

J 17 **Shawn Respert, G, MSU** (IND 89, MSU 82; MSU 70, Oklahoma State 69) 40 PTS, 13-21 FG, 9-13 three-pointers (Big Ten record) vs. IND; 24 PTS, 5-11 three-pointers vs. Oklahoma State

J 23 **Towsend Orr, G, MINN** (MINN 81, OSU 61; MINN 77, ILL 66) 17 PTS, 5 REB, 3 AST, 3-6 3-PT FG vs. Ohio State; 18 PTS, 9 REB, 7 AST, 6-8 3-PT FG vs Illinois

J 30 **Shawn Respert, G, MSU** (MSU 54, MINN 53; MSU 75, ILL 67) 20 PTS, 4-10 3-PT FG, 6 REB vs. Minnesota; 29 PTS, 5-9 3-PT FG, 8-8 FT, 3 AST vs. Illinois

F 6 **Alan Henderson, F, IND** (PUR 76, IND 66; IND 88, NU 67) 23 PTS, 15 REB, 9-11 FT vs. Purdue; 20 PTS, 15 REB, 3 AST vs. Northwestern

F 13 **Kiwane Garris, G, ILL** (ILL 67, PSU 58; ILL 104, IOWA 97 (OT)) 33 PTS, 10-15 FG, 10-10 FT, 8 AST vs. Penn State; 27 PTS, 11-11 FT, 6 REB, 4 STL, 3 AST vs. Iowa

F 20 **Chris Kingsbury, G, IOWA** (IOWA 74, MINN 70; IOWA 85, OSU 66) 25 PTS, 8-15 FG, 7-12 3-PT FG at Minnesota; 15 PTS, 7-7 FT, 3 AST vs. Ohio State

F 27 **Eric Snow, G, MSU** (MSU 67, MICH 64; MSU 67, NU 60) 11 PTS, 10 AST, 2 STL vs. Michigan; 13 PTS, 6-10 FG, 9 AST, 5 STL, 1 TO vs. Northwestern

M 6 **Cuonzo Martin, F, PUR** (PUR 92, IOWA 85; PUR 69, ILL 56) 29 PTS, 9-27 FG, 6-20 3-PT FG, 9 REB, 3 AST vs. Iowa; 29 PTS, 9-14 FG, 5-8 3-PT FG vs. Illinois

M 13 **Shawn Respert, G, MSU** (IOWA 79, MSU 78; MSU 97, WIS 72) 39 PTS, 15-26 FG, 7-15 3-PT FG, 4 AST vs. Iowa; 31 PTS, 8-17 3-PT FG, 7 REB, 7 AST vs. Wisconsin

1994-95 IN REVIEW

ALL GAMES

(NCAA rankings in parentheses; players with 1995-96 eligibility in ALL CAPS)

Scoring
PLAYER, TEAM	GP	FG-FGA	PCT	3PM-3PA	PCT	FT-FTA	PCT	PTS	AVG
Shawn Respert, SR, MSU (8)	28	229-484	.473	119-251	.474	139-160	.869	716	25.6
Alan Henderson, SR, IN (14)	31	284-476	.597	2- 10	.200	159-251	.633	729	23.5
Michael Finley, SR, WI	27	178-470	.379	58-204	.284	140-181	.773	554	20.5
Cuonzo Martin, SR, PUR	32	192-437	.439	91-194	.469	115-144	.799	590	18.4
BRIAN EVANS, JR, IND	31	177-383	.462	58-139	.417	126-161	.783	538	17.4
Voshon Lenard, SR, MINN	31	174-422	.412	81-244	.332	107-141	.759	536	17.3
Rashard Griffith, SO, WI	26	167-295	.566	0- 0	.000	113-195	.579	447	17.2
CHRIS KINGSBURY, SO, IA	33	169-423	.400	117-297	.394	98-122	.803	553	16.8
Doug Etzler, SR, OSU	28	163-360	.453	78-178	.438	51- 57	.895	455	16.3
John Amaechi, SR, PSU	32	168-300	.560	2- 6	.333	176-260	.677	514	16.1
KIWANE GARRIS, SO, ILL	31	150-342	.439	46-119	.387	148-178	.831	494	15.9
Ray Jackson, SR, MICH	31	177-370	.478	24- 78	.308	113-146	.774	491	15.8
JESS SETTLES, SO, IOWA	26	138-294	.469	32- 91	.352	97-121	.802	405	15.6
Antonio Watson, SR, OSU	28	166-305	.544	1- 5	.200	81-126	.643	414	14.8
Jimmy King, SR, MICH	31	168-388	.433	28-109	.257	93-137	.679	457	14.7
A. WOOLRIDGE, SO, IA	33	153-320	.478	24- 62	.387	131-171	.766	461	14.0
Cedric Neloms, SR, NU	26	113-265	.426	4- 26	.154	125-172	.727	355	13.7
Townsend Orr, SR, MINN	31	130-314	.414	67-176	.381	75-102	.735	402	13.0
GLENN SEKUNDA, JR, PSU	32	147-317	.464	26- 84	.310	91-107	.850	411	12.8
RICK YUDT, JR, OSU	25	121-271	.446	38-100	.380	39- 53	.736	319	12.8
M. TAYLOR, FR, MICH	31	161-342	.471	3- 7	.429	59- 98	.602	384	12.4

Field Goal Percentage
(minimum 5 made per game)

PLAYER, TEAM	GP	FGM	FGA	PCT
Alan Henderson, SR, IND (18)	31	284	476	.597
Rashard Griffith, SO, WIS	26	167	295	.566
John Amaechi, SR, PSU	32	168	300	.560
Antonio Watson, SR, OSU	28	166	305	.544
Ray Jackson, SR, MICH	31	177	370	.478
Shawn Respert, SR, MSU	28	229	484	.473
M. TAYLOR, FR, MICH	31	161	342	.471
JESS SETTLES, SO, IOWA	26	138	294	.469
BRIAN EVANS, JR, IND	31	177	383	.462
Doug Etzler, SR, OSU	28	163	360	.453

Three-Point Field Goals Per Game
PLAYER, TEAM	GP	3PM	3PA	AVG
Shawn Respert, SR, MSU (2)	28	119	251	4.25
C. KINGSBURY, SO, IOWA (10)	33	117	297	3.55
Cuonzo Martin, SR, PUR	32	91	194	2.84
Doug Etzler, SR, OSU	28	78	178	2.79
Voshon Lenard, SR, MINN	31	81	244	2.61
Townsend Orr, SR, MINN	31	67	176	2.16
Andy Kilbride, SR, WIS	25	54	134	2.16
Michael Finley, SR, WIS	27	58	204	2.15
PETE LISICKY, FR, PSU	32	68	173	2.13
RICHARD KEENE, JR, ILL	31	63	173	2.03

Three-Point Field Goal Pct.
(min. 1.5 made per game)

PLAYER, TEAM	GP	3PM	3PA	PCT
Shawn Respert, SR, MSU (8)	28	119	251	.474
Cuonzo Martin, SR, PUR (12)	32	91	194	.469
Doug Etzler, SR, OSU	28	78	178	.438
BRIAN EVANS, JR, IND	31	58	139	.417
Jim Bartels, SR, IOWA	33	59	143	.413
DAN EARL, SO, PSU	32	50	123	.407
Andy Kilbride, SR, WIS	25	54	134	.403
C. KINGSBURY, SO, IOWA	33	117	297	.394
PETE LISICKY, FR, PSU	32	68	173	.393
Townsend Orr, SR, MINN	31	67	176	.381

Free Throw Percentage
(minimum 2.5 made per game)

PLAYER, TEAM	GP	FTM	FTA	PCT
Shawn Respert, SR, MSU (13)	28	139	160	.869
G. SEKUNDA, JR, PSU (25)	32	91	107	.850
KIWANE GARRIS, SO, ILL	31	148	178	.831
B. BRANTLEY, JR, PUR	32	93	114	.816
C. KINGSBURY, SO, IOWA	33	98	122	.803
JESS SETTLES, SO, IOWA	26	97	121	.802
Cuonzo Martin, SR, PUR	32	115	144	.799
BRIAN EVANS, JR, IND	31	126	161	.783
Ray Jackson, SR, MICH	31	113	146	.774
Michael Finley, SR, WIS	27	140	181	.773

Rebounds
PLAYER, TEAM	GP	NO	AVG
Rashard Griffith, SO, WIS (14)	26	281	10.8
JAMIE FEICK, JR, MSU	28	281	10.0
John Amaechi, SR, PSU	32	316	9.9
Alan Henderson, SR, IND	31	302	9.7
Shelly Clark, SR, ILL	28	233	8.3
Antonio Watson, SR, OSU	28	200	7.1
Jayson Walton, SR, MINN	31	220	7.1
BRIAN EVANS, JR, IND	31	208	6.7
GLENN SEKUNDA, JR, PSU	32	202	6.3
JESS SETTLES, SO, IOWA	26	162	6.2
Jim Bartels, SR, IOWA	33	204	6.2
Robert Bennett, SR, ILL	31	191	6.2

Assists
PLAYER, TEAM	GP	NO	AVG
Eric Snow, SR, MSU (4)	28	217	7.8
A. WOOLRIDGE, SO, IOWA	33	190	5.8
DAN EARL, SO, PSU	32	181	5.7
Townsend Orr, SR, MINN	31	146	4.7
Michael Finley, SR, WIS	27	108	4.0
Doug Etzler, SR, OSU	28	109	3.9
GENO CARLISLE, FR, NU	26	101	3.9
PORTER ROBERTS, JR, PUR	32	123	3.8
KIWANE GARRIS, SO, ILL	31	117	3.8
RICHARD KEENE, JR, ILL	31	111	3.6

Wisconsin's Rashard Griffith led the Big Ten in both rebounding and blocked shots in all games played.

Steals
PLAYER, TEAM	GP	NO	AVG
Jim Bartels, SR, IOWA	33	70	2.12
Michael Finley, SR, WIS	27	52	1.93
Jimmy King, SR, MICH	31	58	1.87
Eric Snow, SR, MSU	28	52	1.86
Townsend Orr, SR, MINN	31	55	1.77
KENYON MURRAY, JR, IOWA	33	58	1.76
Shawn Respert, SR, MSU	28	38	1.36
Alan Henderson, SR, IND	31	42	1.35
A. WOOLRIDGE, SO, IOWA	33	42	1.27
Michael Hermon, FR, IND	28	35	1.25

Blocked Shots
PLAYER, TEAM	GP	NO	AVG
Rashard Griffith, SO, WIS	26	58	2.23
John Amaechi, SR, PSU	32	68	2.13
Alan Henderson, SR, IND	31	64	2.06
MAURICE TAYLOR, FR, MICH	31	34	1.10
BRANDON BRANTLEY, JR, PUR	32	35	1.09
BRAD MILLER, FR, PUR	32	34	1.06
RYAN BOWEN, FR, IOWA	33	34	1.03
TODD LINDEMAN, JR, IND	30	31	1.03
MACEO BASTON, FR, MICH	30	30	1.00
Antonio Watson, SR, OSU	28	28	1.00

Scoring
SCHOOL	GP	PTS	AVG
Iowa (23)	33	2757	83.5
Michigan State	28	2194	78.4
Purdue	32	2444	76.4
Minnesota	31	2360	76.1
Indiana	31	2345	75.6
Illinois	31	2265	73.1
Wisconsin	27	1970	73.0
Penn State	32	2281	71.3
Michigan	31	2188	70.6
Ohio State	28	1945	69.5
Northwestern	27	1766	65.4

Scoring Defense
SCHOOL	GP	PTS	AVG
Penn State (18)	32	2063	64.5
Illinois	31	2125	68.5
Minnesota	31	2123	68.5
Purdue	32	2199	68.7
Michigan State	28	1926	68.8
Indiana	31	2158	69.6
Michigan	31	2161	69.7
Wisconsin	27	1934	71.6
Iowa	33	2460	74.5
Ohio State	28	2174	77.6
Northwestern	27	2267	84.0

Scoring Margin
SCHOOL	OWN	OPP	AVG
Michigan State	78.4	68.8	9.6
Iowa	83.5	74.5	9.0
Purdue	76.4	68.7	7.7
Minnesota	76.1	68.5	7.6
Penn State	71.3	64.5	6.8
Indiana	75.6	69.6	6.0
Illinois	73.1	68.5	4.6
Wisconsin	73.0	71.6	1.4
Michigan	70.6	69.7	0.9
Ohio State	69.5	77.6	-8.1
Northwestern	65.4	84.0	-18.6

Field Goal Percentage
SCHOOL	FGM	FGA	PCT
Michigan State (8)	829	1664	.498
Indiana (13)	870	1796	.484
Purdue	857	1800	.476
Iowa	935	2034	.460
Ohio State	712	1585	.449
Illinois	823	1842	.447
Penn State	786	1761	.446
Michigan	828	1865	.444
Minnesota	841	1946	.432
Wisconsin	672	1611	.417
Northwestern	608	1525	.399

Opponents' Field Goal Percentage
SCHOOL	FGM	FGA	PCT
Penn State	785	1936	.405
Indiana	771	1881	.410
Wisconsin	661	1612	.410
Minnesota	713	1734	.411
Michigan	724	1707	.424
Purdue	831	1926	.431
Michigan State	720	1660	.434
Illinois	780	1728	.451
Northwestern	852	1816	.469
Ohio State	767	1635	.469
Iowa	936	1961	.477

Three-Point Field Goals Per Game
SCHOOL	GP	3PM	3PA	AVG
Iowa (19)	33	274	743	8.30
Wisconsin	27	186	561	6.89
Minnesota	31	202	601	6.52
Penn State	32	201	578	6.28
Purdue	32	183	472	5.72
Ohio State	28	160	404	5.71
Michigan State	28	158	387	5.64
Illinois	31	167	458	5.39
Northwestern	27	119	370	4.41
Michigan	31	114	414	3.68
Indiana	31	107	297	3.45

Three-Point Field Goal Percentage
SCHOOL	3PM	3PA	PCT
Michigan State (6)	158	387	.408
Ohio State (10)	160	404	.396
Purdue (25)	183	472	.388
Iowa	274	743	.369
Illinois	167	458	.365
Indiana	107	297	.360
Penn State	201	578	.348
Minnesota	202	601	.336
Wisconsin	186	561	.332
Northwestern	119	370	.322
Michigan	114	414	.275

Opponents' Three-Point Field Goal Pct.
SCHOOL	3PM	3PA	PCT
Penn State	165	530	.311
Wisconsin	140	441	.317
Purdue	172	518	.332
Indiana	186	555	.335
Michigan State	177	520	.340
Iowa	203	595	.341
Michigan	181	525	.345
Minnesota	195	565	.345
Illinois	190	508	.374
Northwestern	185	486	.381
Ohio State	182	468	.389

Free Throw Percentage
SCHOOL	FTM	FTA	PCT
Iowa	613	865	.709
Penn State	508	721	.705
Northwestern	431	619	.696
Minnesota	476	691	.689
Purdue	547	810	.675
Michigan State	378	562	.673
Indiana	498	748	.666
Ohio State	361	549	.658
Illinois	452	694	.651
Michigan	418	645	.648
Wisconsin	440	687	.640

Rebounds
SCHOOL	GP	RBS	AVG
Minnesota	31	1268	40.9
Wisconsin	27	1062	39.3
Michigan State	28	1074	38.4
Michigan	31	1175	37.9
Illinois	31	1173	37.8
Indiana	31	1172	37.8
Penn State	32	1188	37.1
Iowa	33	1213	36.8
Purdue	32	1170	36.6
Northwestern	27	931	34.5
Ohio State	28	931	33.3

Opponents' Rebounds
SCHOOL	GP	RBS	AVG
Michigan State	28	887	31.7
Illinois	31	988	31.9
Purdue	32	1081	33.8
Iowa	33	1148	34.8
Ohio State	28	980	35.0
Michigan	31	1087	35.1
Indiana	31	1089	35.1
Penn State	32	1156	36.1
Minnesota	31	1122	36.2
Wisconsin	27	1061	39.3
Northwestern	27	1131	41.9

Rebound Margin
SCHOOL	OWN	OPP	MAR
Michigan St. (10)	38.4	31.7	6.7
Illinois (17)	37.8	31.9	6.0
Minnesota	40.9	36.2	4.7
Michigan	37.8	34.8	3.0
Indiana	37.8	35.1	2.7
Purdue	36.4	33.8	2.7
Iowa	36.8	34.8	2.0
Penn State	36.6	35.3	1.3
Wisconsin	39.3	39.3	0.0
Ohio State	33.3	35.0	-1.8
Northwestern	34.5	41.9	-7.4

Steals
SCHOOL	GP	NO	AVG
Iowa	33	365	11.06
Minnesota	31	243	7.84
Michigan	31	235	7.58
Penn State	32	207	6.47
Michigan State	28	180	6.43
Wisconsin	27	172	6.37
Purdue	32	196	6.13
Indiana	31	184	5.94
Illinois	31	174	5.61
Ohio State	28	132	4.71
Northwestern	27	95	3.52

Blocked Shots
SCHOOL	GP	NO	AVG
Indiana	31	146	4.71
Michigan	31	130	4.19
Wisconsin	27	103	3.81
Purdue	32	116	3.63
Penn State	32	110	3.44
Iowa	33	96	2.91
Minnesota	31	86	2.77
Northwestern	27	74	2.74
Ohio State	28	51	1.82
Illinois	31	53	1.71
Michigan State	28	46	1.64

Turnover Margin
SCHOOL	OPP	OWN	MAR
Iowa	653	492	4.9
Minnesota	511	442	2.2
Illinois	447	425	0.7
Michigan	541	522	0.7
Michigan State	406	395	0.4
Purdue	485	476	0.3
Indiana	482	477	0.2
Penn State	449	468	-0.6
Wisconsin	428	448	-0.7
Ohio State	384	465	-2.9
Northwestern	328	460	-4.9

1994-95 IN REVIEW
Statistics *(players with 1995-96 eligibility in ALL CAPS)*

CONFERENCE GAMES ONLY

Scoring

PLAYER, TEAM	GP	FG-FGA	PCT	3PM-3PA	PCT	FT-FTA	PCT	PTS	AVG
Shawn Respert, SR, MSU	18	148-317	.467	80-173	.462	83- 94	.883	459	25.5
Alan Henderson, SR, IND	18	167-274	.609	0- 4	.000	82-133	.617	416	23.1
Michael Finley, SR, WIS	18	116-294	.395	35-121	.289	99-123	.805	366	20.3
Cuonzo Martin, SR, PUR	18	109-259	.421	57-121	.471	81-102	.794	356	19.8
CHRIS KINGSBURY, SO, IA	18	98-241	.407	65-163	.399	67- 81	.827	328	18.2
Rashard Griffith, SO, WI	18	115-215	.535	0- 0	.000	78-136	.574	308	17.1
Voshon Lenard, SR, MINN	18	102-238	.429	48-146	.329	53- 70	.757	305	16.9
John Amaechi, SR, PSU	18	98-175	.560	1- 5	.200	99-142	.697	296	16.4
KIWANE GARRIS, SO, ILL	18	85-192	.443	25- 66	.379	101-118	.856	296	16.4
BRIAN EVANS, JR, IND	18	99-216	.458	34- 83	.410	58- 72	.806	290	16.1
Ray Jackson, SR, MICH	18	105-229	.459	18- 50	.360	51- 68	.750	279	15.5
ANDRE WOOLRIDGE, SO, IA	18	94-193	.487	16- 41	.390	71- 97	.732	275	15.3
Doug Etzler, SR, OSU	18	98-243	.403	51-128	.398	26- 30	.867	273	15.2
Cedric Neloms, SR, NU	18	86-193	.446	2- 18	.111	84-117	.718	258	14.3
Jimmy King, SR, MICH	18	93-210	.443	14- 60	.233	47- 68	.691	247	13.7
Antonio Watson, SR, OSU	18	100-187	.535	1- 5	.200	41- 64	.641	242	13.4
Rickey Dudley, SR, OSU	18	73-162	.451	4- 12	.333	87-135	.644	237	13.2
GENO CARLISLE, FR, NU	18	77-209	.368	25- 68	.368	56- 66	.848	235	13.1
Kenneth Lee, SR, NU	17	75-195	.385	37-100	.370	35- 43	.814	222	13.1
Shelly Clark, SR, ILL	18	96-189	.508	0- 0	.000	40- 65	.615	232	12.9

Field Goal Percentage
(minimum 5 made per game)

PLAYER, TEAM	GP	FGM	FGA	PCT
Alan Henderson, SR, IND	18	167	274	.609
John Amaechi, SR, PSU	18	98	175	.560
Q. BROOKS, JR, MSU	18	90	168	.536
Rashard Griffith, SO, WIS	18	115	215	.535
Antonio Watson, SR, OSU	18	100	187	.535
Shelly Clark, SR, ILL	18	96	189	.508
A. WOOLRIDGE, SO, IOWA	18	94	193	.487
M. TAYLOR, FR, MICH	18	94	201	.468
Shawn Respert, SR, MSU	18	148	317	.467
Ray Jackson, SR, MICH	18	105	229	.459

Three-Point Field Goals Per Game

PLAYER, TEAM	GP	3PM	3PA	AVG
Shawn Respert, SR, MSU	18	*80	*173	*4.44
C. KINGSBURY, SO, IOWA	18	65	163	3.61
Cuonzo Martin, SR, PUR	18	57	121	3.17
Doug Etzler, SR, OSU	18	51	128	2.83
Voshon Lenard, SR, MINN	18	48	146	2.67
RICHARD KEENE, JR, ILL	18	43	111	2.39
Townsend Orr, SR, MINN	18	41	107	2.28
Andy Kilbride, SR, WIS	18	40	99	2.22
Kenneth Lee, SR, NU	17	37	100	2.18
Michael Finley, SR, WIS	18	35	121	1.94

Three-Point Field Goal Pct.
(min. 1.5 made per game)

PLAYER, TEAM	GP	3PM	3PA	PCT
Cuonzo Martin, SR, PUR	18	57	121	.471
Shawn Respert, SR, MSU	18	*80	*173	.462
Jim Bartels, SR, IOWA	18	34	75	.453
JERRY HESTER, SO, ILL	17	26	61	.426
BRIAN EVANS, JR, IND	18	34	83	.410
DAN EARL, SO, PSU	18	32	79	.405
Andy Kilbride, SR, WIS	18	40	99	.404
C. KINGSBURY, SO, IOWA	18	65	163	.399
Doug Etzler, SR, OSU	18	51	128	.398
RICHARD KEENE, JR, ILL	18	43	111	.387

Free Throw Percentage
(minimum 2.5 made per game)

PLAYER, TEAM	GP	FTM	FTA	PCT
Shawn Respert, SR, MSU	18	83	94	.883
Matt Waddell, SR, PUR	18	56	65	.862
KIWANE GARRIS, SO, ILL	18	101	118	.856
GENO CARLISLE, FR, NU	18	56	66	.848
B. BRANTLEY, JR, PUR	18	49	59	.831
C. KINGSBURY, SO, IOWA	18	67	81	.827
BRIAN EVANS, JR, IND	18	58	72	.806
Michael Finley, SR, WIS	18	99	123	.805
Cuonzo Martin, SR, PUR	18	81	102	.794
JESS SETTLES, SO, IOWA	14	37	48	.771

Rebounds

PLAYER, TEAM	GP	NO	AVG
Rashard Griffith, SO, WIS	18	201	11.2
JAMIE FEICK, JR, MSU	18	190	10.6
Alan Henderson, SR, IND	18	187	10.4
John Amaechi, SR, PSU	18	183	10.2
Shelly Clark, SR, ILL	18	156	8.7
Rickey Dudley, SR, OSU	18	126	7.0
Antonio Watson, SR, OSU	18	120	6.7
MACEO BASTON, FR, MICH	17	113	6.6
Robert Bennett, SR, ILL	18	111	6.2
Jayson Walton, SR, MINN	18	110	6.1
GLENN SEKUNDA, JR, PSU	18	109	6.1

Assists

PLAYER, TEAM	GP	NO	AVG
Eric Snow, SR, MSU	18	*141	*7.8
A. WOOLRIDGE, SO, IOWA	18	102	5.7
DAN EARL, SO, PSU	18	93	5.2
Townsend Orr, SR, MINN	18	86	4.8
GENO CARLISLE, FR, NU	18	75	4.2
Michael Hermon, FR, IND	18	73	4.1
Michael Finley, SR, WIS	18	71	3.9
Matt Waddell, SR, PUR	18	70	3.9
RICHARD KEENE, JR, ILL	18	66	3.7
PORTER ROBERTS, JR, PUR	18	65	3.6
DARNELL HOSKINS, SO, WIS	18	64	3.6
Doug Etzler, SR, OSU	18	64	3.6

In 1995, Michigan State guard Eric Snow set Big Ten assist records with 141 for an average of 7.8 per game in Conference games only.

Steals

PLAYER, TEAM	GP	NO	AVG
KENYON MURRAY, JR, IOWA	18	39	2.17
Michael Finley, SR, WIS	18	34	1.89
Eric Snow, SR, MSU	18	33	1.83
Townsend Orr, SR, MINN	18	31	1.72
Jimmy King, SR, MICH	18	31	1.72
Jim Bartels, SR, IOWA	18	28	1.56
Alan Henderson, SR, IND	18	25	1.39
Michael Hermon, FR, IND	18	25	1.39
ANDRE WOOLRIDGE, SO, IOWA	18	23	1.28
Ray Jackson, SR, MICH	18	22	1.22

Blocked Shots

PLAYER, TEAM	GP	NO	AVG
Rashard Griffith, SO, WIS	18	44	2.44
Alan Henderson, SR, IND	18	35	1.94
John Amaechi, SR, PSU	18	28	1.56
BRAD MILLER, FR, PUR	18	25	1.39
BRANDON BRANTLEY, JR, PUR	18	20	1.11
MAKHTAR NDIAYE, SO, MICH	18	20	1.11
MAURICE TAYLOR, FR, MICH	18	19	1.06
TODD LINDEMAN, JR, IND	18	19	1.06
MACEO BASTON, FR, MICH	17	18	1.06
ROY HAIRSTON, JR, PUR	18	17	0.94

*Big Ten record

Scoring
SCHOOL	GP	PTS	AVG
Iowa	18	1464	81.3
Purdue	18	1352	75.1
Illinois	18	1328	73.8
Michigan State	18	1327	73.7
Indiana	18	1311	72.8
Wisconsin	18	1300	72.2
Minnesota	18	1279	71.1
Michigan	18	1243	69.1
Penn State	18	1231	68.4
Northwestern	18	1172	65.1
Ohio State	18	1164	64.7

Scoring Defense
SCHOOL	GP	PTS	AVG
Michigan State	18	1179	65.5
Michigan	18	1190	66.1
Purdue	18	1191	66.2
Penn State	18	1196	66.4
Minnesota	18	1209	67.2
Indiana	18	1267	70.4
Illinois	18	1270	70.6
Wisconsin	18	1307	72.6
Ohio State	18	1383	76.8
Iowa	18	1392	77.3
Northwestern	18	1587	88.2

Scoring Margin
SCHOOL	OWN	OPP	AVG
Purdue	75.1	66.2	8.9
Michigan State	73.7	65.5	8.2
Iowa	81.3	77.3	4.0
Minnesota	71.1	67.2	3.9
Illinois	73.8	70.6	3.2
Michigan	69.1	66.1	3.0
Indiana	72.8	70.4	2.4
Penn State	68.4	66.4	2.0
Wisconsin	72.2	72.6	-0.4
Ohio State	64.7	76.8	-12.1
Northwestern	65.1	88.2	-23.1

Field Goal Percentage
SCHOOL	FGM	FGA	PCT
Indiana	502	1022	.491
Michigan State	509	1052	.484
Purdue	462	1006	.459
Iowa	489	1083	.452
Michigan	477	1059	.450
Illinois	482	1078	.447
Minnesota	464	1069	.434
Penn State	428	988	.433
Ohio State	424	980	.433
Wisconsin	441	1059	.416
Northwestern	407	1041	.390

Opponents' Field Goal Percentage
SCHOOL	FGM	FGA	PCT
Michigan	378	959	.394
Minnesota	391	967	.404
Wisconsin	444	1062	.418
Indiana	448	1063	.421
Michigan State	439	1041	.422
Purdue	444	1043	.426
Penn State	468	1089	.430
Illinois	454	966	.470
Ohio State	479	1008	.475
Northwestern	608	1210	.502
Iowa	531	1029	.516

Three-Point Field Goals Per Game
SCHOOL	GP	3PM	3PA	AVG
Iowa	18	*158	*413	8.78
Wisconsin	18	120	35	6.67
Minnesota	18	112	342	6.22
Penn State	18	109	331	6.06
Illinois	18	109	285	6.06
Michigan State	18	104	261	5.78
Purdue	18	99	257	5.50
Ohio State	18	93	258	5.17
Northwestern	18	89	274	4.94
Michigan	18	68	238	3.78
Indiana	18	61	173	3.39

Three-Point Field Goal Percentage
SCHOOL	3PM	3PA	PCT
Michigan State	104	261	.398
Purdue	99	257	.385
Iowa	158	413	.383
Illinois	109	285	.382
Ohio State	93	258	.360
Indiana	61	173	.353
Wisconsin	120	355	.338
Penn State	109	331	.329
Minnesota	112	342	.327
Northwestern	89	274	.325
Michigan	68	238	.286

Opponents' Three-Point Field Goal Pct.
SCHOOL	3PM	3PA	PCT
Penn State	86	275	.313
Purdue	86	274	.314
Michigan	97	302	.321
Wisconsin	90	276	.326
Michigan State	100	305	.328
Indiana	99	291	.340
Minnesota	114	333	.342
Iowa	109	289	.377
Ohio State	111	285	.389
Illinois	111	272	.408
Northwestern	119	286	.416

Free Throw Percentage
SCHOOL	FTM	FTA	PCT
Penn State	266	370	.719
Iowa	328	456	.719
Northwestern	271	379	.715
Minnesota	239	351	.681
Purdue	329	487	.676
Indiana	246	370	.665
Wisconsin	298	449	.664
Illinois	255	384	.664
Michigan State	205	316	.649
Michigan	221	341	.648
Ohio State	223	350	.637

Rebounds
SCHOOL	GP	RBS	AVG
Minnesota	18	684	38.0
Wisconsin	18	676	37.6
Michigan	18	676	37.6
Michigan State	18	674	37.4
Illinois	18	652	36.2
Penn State	18	646	35.9
Purdue	18	644	35.8
Indiana	18	631	35.1
Iowa	18	601	33.4
Ohio State	18	586	32.6
Northwestern	18	578	32.1

Opponents' Rebounds
SCHOOL	GP	RBS	AVG
Illinois	18	573	31.8
Michigan State	18	583	32.4
Purdue	18	612	34.0
Ohio State	18	614	34.1
Iowa	18	620	34.4
Michigan	18	629	34.9
Minnesota	18	638	35.4
Indiana	18	646	35.9
Penn State	18	650	36.1
Wisconsin	18	703	39.1
Northwestern	18	780	43.3

Rebound Margin
SCHOOL	OWN	OPP	MAR
Michigan State	37.4	32.4	5.1
Illinois	36.2	31.8	4.4
Michigan	37.2	34.6	2.7
Minnesota	38.0	35.4	2.6
Purdue	35.8	34.0	1.8
Penn State	35.6	35.6	-0.1
Indiana	35.1	35.9	-0.8
Iowa	33.4	34.4	-1.1
Wisconsin	37.6	39.1	-1.5
Ohio State	32.6	34.1	-1.6
Northwestern	32.1	43.3	-11.2

Steals
SCHOOL	GP	NO	AVG
Iowa	18	176	9.78
Minnesota	18	138	7.67
Michigan	18	130	7.22
Michigan State	18	109	6.06
Purdue	18	108	6.00
Penn State	18	108	6.00
Wisconsin	18	107	5.94
Indiana	18	98	5.44
Illinois	18	93	5.17
Ohio State	18	72	4.00
Northwestern	18	61	3.39

Blocked Shots
SCHOOL	GP	NO	AVG
Indiana	18	82	4.56
Michigan	18	77	4.28
Purdue	18	74	4.11
Wisconsin	18	73	4.06
Northwestern	18	50	2.78
Penn State	18	48	2.67
Minnesota	18	48	2.67
Iowa	18	42	2.33
Michigan State	18	33	1.83
Ohio State	18	29	1.61
Illinois	18	26	1.44

Turnover Margin
SCHOOL	OPP	OWN	MAR
Iowa	*343	253	*5.0
Purdue	278	245	1.8
Illinois	253	225	1.6
Minnesota	285	258	1.5
Michigan State	249	246	0.2
Michigan	292	288	0.2
Indiana	271	276	-0.3
Wisconsin	278	290	-0.7
Penn State	234	257	-1.3
Ohio State	243	306	-3.5
Northwestern	216	299	-4.6

* Big Ten record

1994-95 IN REVIEW
Best Performances *(NCAA rankings in parentheses)*

ALL GAMES

INDIVIDUAL

Points
42 Michael Finley, WIS vs E. Michigan - Dec 10 (14t)
40 Shawn Respert, MSU vs Indiana - Jan 11
39 Shawn Respert, MSU vs Iowa - Mar 8

Field Goals
17 Michael Finley, WIS vs E. Michigan - Dec 10
16 Alan Henderson, IND vs Iowa - Mar 12
15 Shawn Respert, MSU vs Iowa - Mar 8

Field Goal Attempts
31 Michael Finley, WIS vs E. Michigan - Dec 10
27 Michael Finley, WIS vs PENN STATE - Jan 26
26 Shawn Respert, MSU vs Wisconsin - Mar 11

Field Goal Percentage *(10 attempts minimum)*
.909 Shelly Clark, ILL vs Northwestern - Jan 7 (10-11)
.867 Rick Yudt, OSU vs MORGAN ST. - Dec 27 (13-15)
.842 Alan Henderson, IND vs Iowa - Mar 12 (16-19)

Three-Point Field Goals
10 Kenneth Lee, NU vs Minnesota - Mar 4 (3t)
9 Shawn Respert, MSU vs Indiana - Jan 11
  Chris Kingsbury, IOWA vs Long Island - Dec 17
  Chris Kingsbury, IOWA vs Drake - Nov 29

Three-Point Field Goal Attempts
19 Chris Kingsbury, IOWA vs Long Island - Dec 17
17 Shawn Respert, MSU vs Weber State - Mar 17
   Shawn Respert, MSU vs Wisconsin - Mar 11
   Kenneth Lee, NU vs Minnesota - Mar 4

Three-Point Field Goal Percentage
(6 attempts minimum)
1.000 Jim Bartels, IOWA vs Ohio State - Jan 25 (6-6)
 .875 Cuonzo Martin, PUR vs James Madison - Dec 3 (7-8)
 .833 Richard Keene, ILL vs At Iowa - Feb 1 (5-6)
      Dan Earl, PSU vs Marquette - Mar 27 (5-6)

Free Throws
15 Michael Finley, WIS vs MICHIGAN - Feb 11
   Geno Carlisle, NU vs Wisconsin - Jan 28
   Shawn Respert, MSU vs Nebraska - Dec 10

Free Throw Attempts *(10 attempts minimum)*
18 Rickey Dudley, OSU vs Minnesota - Jan 18
17 Michael Finley, WIS vs MICHIGAN - Feb 11
   Alan Henderson, IND vs BUTLER - Dec 21

Free Throw Percentage *(10 attempts minimum)*
1.000 Cuonzo Martin, PUR vs Indiana - Jan 31 (12-12)
      Kiwane Garris, ILL vs IOWA - Feb 11 (11-11)
      Brian Evans, IND vs Northwestern - Feb 4 (11-11)
      Glenn Sekunda, PSU vs CENT. CONN. ST. - Dec 10 (11-11)

Rebounds
20 Alan Henderson, IND vs MINNESOTA - Feb 8
19 Shelly Clark, ILL vs NORTHWESTERN - Mar 8
18 Rashard Griffith, WIS vs Iowa - Jan 21

Assists
13 Eric Snow, MSU vs Penn State - Feb 11
   Dan Earl, PSU vs Iowa - Mar 23
12 Eric Snow, MSU vs Iowa - Mar 8
   Eric Snow, MSU vs Illinois - Feb 15
   Eric Snow, MSU vs Illinois - Jan 28

Steals
9 Kenyon Murray, IOWA vs Ohio State - Feb 18
6 Ryan Bowen, IOWA vs Northern Iowa - Dec 7
  Roy Hairston, PUR vs Eastern Michigan - Dec 6
  Jimmy King, MICH vs UT-Chattanooga - Dec 3
  Dugan Fife, MICH vs UT-Chattanooga - Dec 3

Blocked Shots
6 Rashard Griffith, WIS vs Northwestern - Feb 15
  Rashard Griffith, WIS vs ILLINOIS - Feb 4
  John Amaechi, PSU vs Richmond (Fiesta) - Dec 30
  John Amaechi, PSU vs MARYLAND-E. SHORE - Dec 6

TEAM

Points
126 IOWA vs Morgan State - Nov 26 (18t)
121 OSU vs GEORGE MASON - Jan 8
117 MSU vs Ball State - Dec 29

Fewest Points Allowed
37 ILL vs Princeton - Dec 10
45 PSU vs AKRON - Dec 22
48 IOWA vs Northern Iowa - Dec 7

Field Goals
45 IND vs Iowa - Mar 12
   OSU vs GEORGE MASON - Jan 8
44 MSU vs Cleveland State - Dec 12

Field Goal Attempts
86 MSU vs Cleveland State - Dec 12
   IOWA vs Morgan State - Nov 26
83 WIS vs NORTHWESTERN - Jan 28

Field Goal Percentage
.672 IND vs Iowa - Mar 12 (45-67)
.643 IND vs ILLINOIS - Mar 2 (36-56)
.636 MSU vs Louisville - Dec 3 (35-55)

Lowest Field Goal Percentage Allowed
.271 WIS vs Ohio State - Jan 11 (16-59)
.295 MICH vs Illinois - Feb 26 (18-61)
.296 MICH vs Indiana - Feb 18 (16-54)

Three-Point Field Goals
15 IOWA vs Long Island - Dec 17
14 IOWA vs Michigan State - Mar 8
   IOWA vs Drake - Nov 29

Three-Point Field Goal Attempts
36 IOWA vs Long Island - Dec 17
   WIS vs Eastern Michigan - Dec 10
32 WIS vs Marquette - Dec 31

3-Pt. Field Goal Pct. *(8 attempts minimum)*
.692 PUR vs Ohio State - Jan 21 (9-13)
     IND vs Chaminade - Nov 22 (9-13)
.667 IND vs Iowa - Mar 12 (10-15)

Lowest 3-Pt. FG Pct. Allowed *(8 att. min.)*
.000 WIS vs ILLINOIS - Feb 4 (0-9)
.067 PUR vs Wisconsin - Feb 26 (1-15)
.077 IND vs Ark.-Little Rock - Dec 29 (1-13)

Free Throws
40 IOWA vs Wisconsin - Jan 21
35 MINN vs SACRAMENTO STATE - Nov 29
34 PSU vs MICHIGAN - Jan 8

Free Throw Attempts
52 IOWA vs Wisconsin - Jan 21
47 WIS vs Wright State - Nov 26
46 MINN vs SACRAMENTO STATE - Nov 29

Free Throw Percentage *(12 attempts min.)*
1.000 NU vs Penn State - Feb 22 (12-12)
 .957 IOWA vs DePaul - Mar 15 (22-23)
 .935 PUR vs Indiana - Jan 31 (29-31)

Rebounds
62 IOWA vs Drake - Nov 29
61 ILL vs NORTHWESTERN - Mar 8
60 IOWA vs Morgan State - Nov 26

Assists
33 PUR vs Tenn.-Chattanooga - Dec 22
31 IOWA vs Morgan State - Nov 26
29 IND vs Iowa - Mar 12

Steals
23 IOWA vs Northern Iowa - Dec 7
21 IOWA vs Morgan State - Nov 26
18 MICH vs UT-Chattanooga - Dec 3

Blocked Shots
10 MINN vs SACRAMENTO STATE - Nov 29
9 MICH vs Iowa - Jan 11
  PUR vs Illinois - Jan 10
  PSU vs AKRON - Dec 22

Most Turnovers Caused
29 MICH vs Portland - Dec 29
   IOWA vs Northern Iowa - Dec 7
28 IOWA vs Ohio State - Feb 18

Fewest Turnovers Made
7 MICH vs Northwestern - Jan 14
  PUR vs Penn State - Jan 28
  PSU vs Northwestern - Feb 22

RECORDS

Purdue vs. Minnesota, 1959

1956-1975

- Scoring rises steadily during this period as teams average a Big Ten-record 86 points per Conference game in 1970. The emphasis on defense returns just two years later as scoring drops to an average of 73 points a game.
- Big Ten players win four national player of the year awards from 1961 to '66 with Ohio State's Jerry Lucas (twice) and Gary Bradds, and Michigan's Cazzie Russell honored.
- Ohio State dominates the early '60s, winning or sharing a Big Ten-record five straight Conference crowns from 1960 to '64 and winning the NCAA championship in 1960 and finishing as runner-up the next two seasons.
- Ohio State center Jerry Lucas becomes the most-decorated player in Conference history as he is named national Player of the Year in 1960 and '61 and becomes the only three-time Big Ten *Chicago Tribune* Most Valuable Player from 1960 to '62.
- In 1970, Purdue's Rick Mount averages a record-39.4 points per Conference game, while league champ Iowa becomes the only team to average over 100 points a game at 102.9. Mount sets the Big Ten single game scoring record with 61 against Iowa.

RECORDS

ALL GAMES

INDIVIDUAL

Scoring

Game
61	Rick Mount, PUR vs. IOWA		2/28/70
57	Dave Schellhase, PUR vs. MICH		2/19/66
56	Jimmy Rayl, IND vs. MINN (OT)		1/27/62
	Jimmy Rayl, IND vs. MSU		2/23/63
53	Dave Downey, ILL vs. IND		2/16/63
	Rick Mount, PUR vs. IOWA		1/3/70
	Rick Mount, PUR vs. MICH		1/31/70
52	Terry Dischinger, PUR vs. MSU		2/25/61
50	Terry Dischinger, PUR vs. WIS		1/27/62
	Terry Furlow, MSU vs. IOWA		1/5/76

Season
1030	Glenn Robinson, PUR	1993-94
958	Dennis Hopson, OSU	1986-87
949	Glen Rice, MICH	1988-89
932	Rick Mount, PUR	1968-69
850	Scott Skiles, MSU	1985-86
800	Cazzie Russell, MICH	1965-66
798	Joe Barry Carroll, PUR	1978-79
793	Terry Furlow, MSU	1975-76
785	Calbert Cheaney, IND	1992-93
781	Dave Schellhase, PUR	1965-66

Career
2613	Calbert Cheaney, IND	1989-93
2531	Shawn Respert, MSU	1992-95
2442	Glen Rice, MICH	1985-89
2439	Mike McGee, MICH	1977-81
2438	Steve Alford, IND	1983-87
2323	Rick Mount, PUR	1967-70
2263	Steve Smith, MSU	1987-91
2222	Gary Grant, MICH	1986-88
2192	Don Schlundt, IND	1951-55
2175	Joe Barry Carroll, PUR	1976-80

Rebounding

Game
33	Walt Bellamy, IND vs. MICH		3/11/61
32	Frank Howard, OSU vs. BYU		1/29/56
31	Joe Ruklick, NU vs. Kansas		12/7/58
30	Charles Darling, IOWA vs. WIS		3/3/52
	Paul Morrow, WIS vs. PUR		1/3/53
	Jerry Lucas, OSU vs. Kentucky		3/18/61
	Jerry Lucas, OSU vs. UCLA		12/26/61
	Jerry Lucas, OSU vs. IND		3/10/62
	Rudy Tomjanovich, MICH vs. Loyola (IL)		
			2/1/69
29	Jim Pitts, NU vs. IND		2/13/65

Season
499	Jerry Lucas, OSU	1961-62
470	Jerry Lucas, OSU	1960-61
442	Jerry Lucas, OSU	1959-60
428	Walt Bellamy, IND	1960-61
416	Brad Sellers, OSU	1985-86
392	John Green, MSU	1957-58
389	Phil Hubbard, MICH	1976-77
387	Charles Darling, IOWA	1950-51
382	John Green, MSU	1958-59
379	M.C. Burton, MICH	1958-59

Career
1411	Jerry Lucas, OSU	1959-62
1148	Joe Barry Carroll, PUR	1976-80
1111	Herb Williams, OSU	1977-81
1092	Gregory Kelser, MSU	1975-79
1091	Alan Henderson, IND	1992-95
1088	Walt Bellamy, IND	1958-61
1039	Rudy Tomjanovich, MICH	1967-70
1037	Bill Buntin, MICH	1962-65
1036	John Green, MSU	1956-59
1031	Kent Benson, IND	1973-77
993	Loy Vaught, MICH	1986-90

Assists

Game
18	Bruce Parkinson, PUR vs. MINN		3/8/75
16	Cal Wulfsberg, IOWA vs. OSU		1/24/76
	Tony Wysinger, ILL vs. Pitt		12/6/86
	Arriel McDonald, MINN vs. WIS		1/12/94
15	Brian Walker, PUR vs. MSU		2/22/79
	Bruce Douglas, ILL vs. Hou.		12/14/83
	Keith Smart, IND vs. Auburn		1987
	B.J. Armstrong, IOWA vs. MINN		2/19/89

Season
269	Earvin Johnson, MSU	1978-79
234	Gary Grant, MICH	1987-88
233	Rumeal Robinson, MICH	1988-89
222	Earvin Johnson, MSU	1977-78
217	Eric Snow, MSU	1994-95
213	Eric Snow, MSU	1993-94
207	Bruce Parkinson, PUR	1974-75
205	Brian Walker, PUR	1980-81
203	Scott Skiles, MSU	1985-86
200	Bruce Douglas, ILL	1984-85

Career
765	Bruce Douglas, ILL	1982-86
731	Gary Grant, MICH	1984-88
690	Bruce Parkinson, PUR	1973-77
645	Scott Skiles, MSU	1982-86
599	Eric Snow, MSU	1992-95
575	Rumeal Robinson, MICH	1987-90
572	Brian Walker, PUR	1977-81
561	Mark Montgomery, MSU	1988-92
547	Arriel McDonald, MINN	1990-94
542	Quinn Buckner, IND	1972-76

Steals

Game
10	Michael Finley, WIS vs. PUR		2/13/93
9	Scott May, IND vs. MICH		1976
	Mike Heineman, WIS vs. Morgan St.		11/25/84
	Melvin Newbern, MINN vs. Rider		1/3/90
	Pat Baldwin, NU vs. Oakland		11/27/91
	Acie Earl, IOWA vs. Texas Southern		12/28/92
	Kenyon Murray, IOWA vs. OSU		2/18/95
8	Greg Kelser, MSU vs. NU		2/2/76
	Troy Taylor, OSU vs. St. Joseph's		12/29/83
	Bruce Douglas, ILL vs. PUR		2/25/84
	Darryl Johnson, MSU vs. OSU		1/10/87
	Shawn Watts, NU vs. Rollins		1987
	Bill Jones, IOWA vs. Dartmouth		1/13/88
	Melvin Newbern, MINN vs. MSU		3/8/89
	Pat Baldwin, NU vs. Vanderbilt		12/2/91

Season
101	Melvin Newbern, MINN	1988-89
90	Pat Baldwin, NU	1990-91
89	Kenny Battle, ILL	1988-89
88	Bruce Douglas, ILL	1985-86
	Brian Walker, PUR	1978-79
86	Gary Grant, MICH	1986-87
85	Bruce Douglas, ILL	1984-85
84	Gary Grant, MICH	1985-86
80	Gary Grant, MICH	1987-88
78	Bruce Douglas, ILL	1982-83

Career
324	Bruce Douglas, ILL	1982-86
300	Gary Grant, MICH	1984-88
269	Pat Baldwin, NU	1990-94
218	Kendall Gill, ILL	1986-90
215	Melvin Newbern, MINN	1987-90
204	Jay Burson, OSU	1985-89
187	Brian Walker, PUR	1979-81
183	Roy Marble, IOWA	1985-89
	Tracy Webster, WIS	1991-94
182	Steve Carfino, IOWA	1980-84

Blocked Shots

Game
12	Mychal Thompson, MINN vs. OSU		1/27/76
11	Derek Holcomb, ILL vs. So. Carolina		
			12/8/78
	Joe Barry Carroll, PUR vs. Arizona		12/10/77
10	Jim Pitts, NU vs. PUR		1/8/66
	Roy Tarpley, MICH vs. Fla. Southern		
			12/7/85
9	Herb Williams, OSU vs. IOWA		2/23/80
	Brad Sellers, WIS vs. Toledo		11/29/82
	Randy Breuer, MINN vs. MICH		3/5/83
	Brad Sellers, OSU vs. La. Tech		3/24/86
	Eric Riley, MICH vs. Utah		12/1/90
	Acie Earl, IOWA vs. WIS		1/29/92

Season
123	Jim Pitts, NU	1965-66
121	Acie Earl, IOWA	1991-92
106	Acie Earl, IOWA	1990-91
105	Joe Barry Carroll, PUR	1977-78
99	Dean Garrett, IND	1987-88
97	Roy Tarpley, MICH	1985-86
	Brad Sellers, OSU	1985-86
93	Dean Garrett, IND	1986-87
92	Joe Barry Carroll, PUR	1979-80
90	Herb Williams, OSU	1979-80
	Brad Sellers, OSU	1984-85
	Chris Webber, MICH	1992-93

Career
365	Acie Earl, IOWA	1989-93
349	Joe Barry Carroll, PUR	1977-80
328	Herb Williams, OSU	1977-81
307	Brad Sellers, WIS-OSU	1981-86
251	Roy Tarpley, MICH	1982-86
229	Greg Stokes, IOWA	1981-85
235	Kevin McHale, MINN	1976-80
228	Randy Breuer, MINN	1979-83
213	Alan Henderson, IND	1992-95
204	Uwe Blab, IND	1981-85

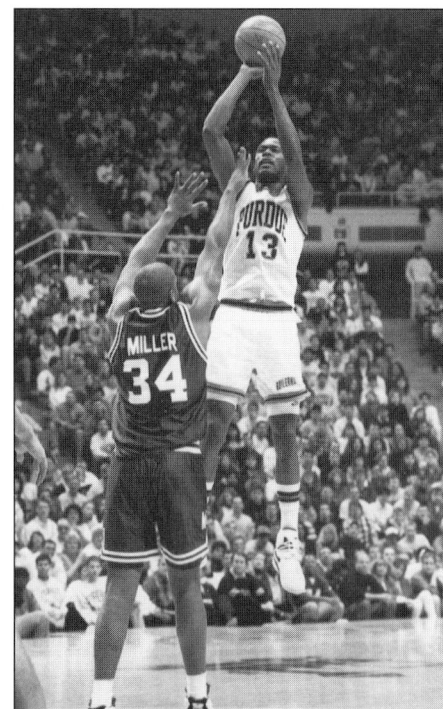

Purdue's Glenn Robinson is the only Big Ten player to ever score over 1,000 points in a season with 1,030 in 1993-94.

TEAM

Scoring

Game
128	MICH vs. PUR	2/19/66
127	MICH vs. IOWA	3/10/90
	ILL vs. Louisiana State	12/22/88
126	IOWA vs. Oral Roberts	12/30/87
	IOWA vs. Morgan State	11/26/94
125	MICH vs. Northern Michigan	12/20/88
124	IOWA vs. Cal-Irvine	12/5/87
123	MICH vs. Illinois-Chicago	12/6/86
122	IND vs. OSU	2/2/59
	IND vs. Notre Dame	1961

Season
3393	MICH	1988-89
3181	IOWA	1987-88
3110	ILL	1988-89
3055	IOWA	1986-87
3028	IND	1992-93
2973	MICH	1987-88
2957	IOWA	1988-89
2950	MICH	1992-93
2882	IND	1990-91
2837	IND	1991-92

Rebounding

Game
95	IND vs. MICH	3/11/61
89	IND vs. PUR	2/21/51
84	MSU vs. OSU	1/19/59
	MSU vs. IOWA	2/15/64
79	ILL vs. WIS	2/16/59
	PUR vs. Hawaii	12/30/68
	WIS vs. Michigan Tech	12/5/70
77	MICH vs. MSU	2/2/63
	IOWA vs. Minnesota-Duluth	12/30/72
76	IOWA vs. OSU	1/24/55
	IOWA vs. California	1960
	WIS vs. South Dakota	12/9/72

Season
1521	MICH	1964-65
1508	MSU	1958-59
	IOWA	1986-87
1493	MICH	1992-93
1476	MICH	1963-64
1443	IND	1974-75
1405	PUR	1973-74
1398	NU	1964-65
1375	MICH	1991-92
1370	IOWA	1992-93

Assists

Game
37	MICH vs. Western Michigan	12/7/87
	MICH vs. Eastern Michigan	12/12/87
36	MICH vs. IOWA	2/3/88
35	PUR vs. San Jose State	12/19/72
	PUR vs. Illinois State	12/22/74
	ILL vs. Long Island	3/10/82
	ILL vs. Utah State	12/7/85
34	IOWA vs. George Mason	1/1/84
33	WIS vs. NU	3/7/53
	MICH vs. PUR	3/7/87
	MICH vs. Chicago State	12/9/91
	ILL vs. Chicago State	12/18/93
	PUR vs. Tenn.-Chattanooga	12/22/94

Season
745	MICH	1988-89
694	MICH	1987-88
680	PUR	1987-88
655	IND	1975-76
652	MICH	1986-87
639	ILL	1988-89
630	ILL	1984-85
620	IND	1992-93
607	MINN	1993-94
600	IOWA	1984-85
	IOWA	1987-88
	MICH	1975-76

Steals

Game
23	IOWA vs. NU	2/22/86
	IOWA vs. Northern Iowa	12/7/94
22	NU vs. Chicago	12/1/92
21	MINN vs. Rider	1/3/90
	PUR vs. Northern Colorado	12/4/78
	IOWA vs. Drake	11/30/93
	IOWA vs. Morgan State	11/26/94
20	ILL vs. Texas A&M	11/24/78
	OSU vs. Siena	12/4/86
	ILL vs. PUR	2/23/87

Season
365	IOWA	1994-95
341	ILL	1988-89
329	IOWA	1987-88
310	ILL	1987-88
306	IOWA	1992-93
303	IOWA	1993-94
289	IOWA	1984-85
281	IOWA	1990-91
280	PUR	1978-79
276	MINN	1989-90
	IOWA	1991-92

Blocked Shots

Game
18	MICH vs. Florida Southern	12/7/85
15	OSU vs. IOWA	2/23/80
	PUR vs. NU	3/2/78
14	ILL vs. Denver	11/28/78
13	MINN vs. OSU	1/26/76
	OSU vs. IOWA	3/7/81
	MINN vs. MICH	3/5/83
	ILL vs. MINN	1/17/87
12	MICH vs. Chicago State	11/27/91
	MINN vs. Arizona State	11/27/91
	MICH vs. Arizona State	12/9/91
	OSU vs. West Virginia	12/19/92
	MICH vs. MINN	1/20/93

Season
191	MICH	1992-93
182	MICH	1991-92
165	IOWA	1992-93
162	ILL	1978-79
161	IOWA	1991-92
153	IOWA	1990-91
	WIS	1991-92
147	PUR	1979-80
146	MICH	1985-86
	IND	1994-95

Ohio State's Jerry Lucas owns the Big Ten career rebounding record with 1,411 and claims the league's top three season rebounding performances in 1962 (499), '61 (470) and '60 (442).

Illinois' Bruce Douglas is the Big Ten career assist leader with 765 from 1982 to '86.

On February 13, 1993, Wisconsin's Michael Finley had 10 steals against Purdue to set a Big Ten record.

RECORDS
Big Ten Men's Basketball Records

CONFERENCE GAMES ONLY

INDIVIDUAL SINGLE GAME

Most Points
61	Rick Mount, PUR vs. IOWA		2/28/70
57	Dave Schellhase, PUR vs. MICH		2/19/66
56	Jimmy Rayl, IND vs. MINN (OT)		1/27/62
	Jimmy Rayl, IND vs. MSU		2/23/63
53	Dave Downey, ILL vs. IND		2/16/63
	Rick Mount, PUR vs. IOWA		1/3/70
	Rick Mount, PUR vs. MICH		1/31/70
52	Terry Dischinger, PUR vs. MSU		2/25/61
50	Terry Dischinger, PUR vs. WIS		1/27/62
	Terry Furlow, MSU vs. IOWA		1/5/76

Most Field Goals
27	Rick Mount, PUR vs. IOWA		2/28/70
23	Jimmy Rayl, IND vs. MSU		2/23/63
	Dave Schellhase, PUR vs. MICH		2/19/66
22	Dave Downey, ILL vs. IND		2/16/63
	Rick Mount, PUR vs. IOWA		1/3/70
	and vs. MICH		1/31/70
21	Rudy Tomjanovich, MICH vs. IND (OT)		1/7/69
	Rick Mount, PUR vs. IOWA		2/4/69

Most Field Goal Attempts
52	Andy Phillip, ILL vs. Chicago		3/1/43
48	Jimmy Rayl, IND vs. MSU		2/23/63
47	Rick Mount, PUR vs. IOWA		2/28/70
43	Rick Mount, PUR vs. IOWA		1/3/70
42	Dave Schellhase, PUR vs. MICH		2/19/66
	Rick Mount, PUR vs. MICH		1/31/70
	Ollie Shannon, MINN vs. WIS		3/6/71
39	Jimmy Rayl, IND vs. MINN (OT)		1/27/62
38	Rich Falk, NU vs. IOWA		2/24/64
37	Rick Mount, PUR vs. IOWA		3/1/69
	Rick Mount, PUR vs. IOWA		2/21/70

Best Field Goal Percentage (12 or more attempts)
1.000	George Faerber, PUR vs. IOWA (12 of 12)		3/13/71
	Ron Charles, MSU vs. MICH (12 of 12)		1/24/80
.938	Tommy Davis, MINN vs. IND (15 of 16)		2/11/84
.933	Jerry Lucas, OSU vs. MINN (14 of 15)		2/10/62
	Terry Kunze, MINN vs. MICH (14 of 15)		1/14/63
.929	Quinn Buckner, IND vs. WIS (13 of 14)		1/20/75
	Terry Furlow, MSU vs. WIS (13 of 14)		1/25/75
.923	Al Henry, WIS vs. MINN (12 of 13)		1/13/70
	John Robinson, MICH vs. OSU (12 of 13)		1/4/75
	Carter Scott, OSU vs. MINN (12 of 13)		1/22/81

Most Three-Point Goals
10	Dion Lee, NU vs. MINN		3/4/95
9	Shawn Respert, MSU vs. IND		1/11/95
8	Jay Edwards, IND vs. MINN		3/10/88
	Kirk Manns, MSU vs. PUR		1/25/89
	Kirk Manns, MSU vs. IOWA		2/12/90
	Shawn Respert, MSU vs. MINN		2/23/94
	Shawn Respert, MSU vs. ILL		2/15/95
	Shawn Respert, MSU vs. WIS		3/11/95
7	Trent Jackson, WIS vs. OSU		1/15/87
	Steve Alford, IND vs. WIS		1/15/87
	Glen Rice, MICH vs. WIS		2/25/89
	Kirk Manns, MSU vs. NU		2/25/89
	Woody Austin, PUR vs. NU		1/25/92
	Todd Leslie, NU vs. IOWA		3/11/92
	Michael Finley, WIS vs. MICH		1/29/94
	Voshon Lenard, MINN vs. NU		1/11/95
	Chris Kingsbury, IOWA vs. NU		1/9/95

Most Three-Point Attempts
17	Shawn Respert, MSU vs. WIS		3/11/95
	Dion Lee, NU vs. MINN		3/4/95
15	Shawn Respert, MSU vs. IOWA		3/8/95
13	Doug Altenberger, ILL vs. WIS		2/23/87
	P.J. Bowman, ILL vs IOWA		2/6/89
	Kirk Manns, MSU vs. IOWA		1/13/90
	Kirk Manns, MSU vs. IOWA		2/12/90
	Jimmy Oliver, PUR vs. MINN		1/7/91
	Linc Darner, PUR vs. IOWA		1/31/91
	Steve Smith, MSU vs. OSU		3/3/91
	Jamie Skelton, OSU vs. PSU		2/6/93
	Michael Finley, WIS vs. MINN		2/18/93
	Chris Kingsbury, IOWA vs. MSU		1/7/95
	Shawn Respert, MSU vs. IND		1/11/95
	Chris Kingsbury, IOWA vs. NU		2/9/95
	Chris Kingsbury, IOWA vs. PUR		3/1/95

Best Three-Point Field Goal Percentage (minimum 5 made)
1.000	Glen Rice, MICH vs. WIS (7 of 7)		2/25/89
	Val Barnes, IOWA vs. PSU (6 of 6)		2/22/93
	Everette Stephens, PUR vs IOWA (5 of 5)		2/12/87
	Trent Jackson, WIS vs. NU (5 of 5)		1/30/88
	Jim Bartels, IOWA vs. OSU (6 of 6)		1/25/95
.875	Woody Austin, PUR vs. NU (7 of 8)		1/25/92
.857	Jeff Moe, IOWA vs. MINN (6 of 7)		1988
	Damon Bailey, IND vs. IOWA (6 of 7)		2/9/92
	Brian Evans, IND vs. ILL (6 of 7)		1/30/94
	Pat Graham, IND vs. OSU (6 of 7)		2/2/94

Most Free Throws
26	Greg Graham, IND vs. PUR		2/21/93
25	Don Schlundt, IND vs. OSU		3/5/55
21	Al Ferrari, MSU vs. IND		2/28/55
	Terry Dischinger, PUR vs. IOWA		2/27/61
	Don Nelson, IOWA vs. IND		2/17/62
20	Terry Furlow, MSU vs. NU		1/8/76
	Glenn Robinson, PUR vs. OSU		2/23/94
19	Kevin Smith, MSU vs. IND		1/7/82
	Deon Thomas, ILL vs. OSU		2/15/94
18	Terry Dischinger, PUR vs. MINN		2/24/62
	Gary Bradds, OSU vs. MSU		1/27/64
	Dave Schellhase, PUR vs. IOWA		2/27/65
	Ted Kitchel, IND vs. ILL		1/10/81
	Todd Jadlow, IND vs. IOWA		1/30/89

Most Free Throw Attempts
30	Don Schlundt, IND vs. OSU		3/5/55
29	Jack Runyan, PUR vs. MICH		3/2/53
28	Greg Graham, IND vs. PUR		2/21/93
26	Al Ferrari, MSU vs. IND		2/28/55
25	Don Nelson, IOWA vs. IND		2/17/62
24	Terry Dischinger, PUR vs. IOWA		2/27/62
23	Paul Morrow, WIS vs. MICH		2/21/53
	Terry Dischinger, PUR vs. MINN		2/24/62
	Dave Schellhase, PUR vs IOWA		2/27/65

Best Free Throw Percentage (14 or more attempts)
1.000	Kevin Smith, MSU vs. IND (19 of 19)		1/7/82
	Ted Kitchel, IND vs. ILL (18 of 18)		1/10/81
	Sam Vincent, MSU vs. OSU (17 of 17)		2/24/83
	Larry Siegfried, OSU vs. PUR (16 of 16)		3/7/59
	Jimmy Rayl, IND vs. MICH (15 of 15)		2/26/62
	Rick Mount, PUR vs NU (15 of 15)		2/8/69
	Don Schlundt, IND vs. MINN (14 of 14)		2/8/54
	Robin Freeman, OSU vs. MSU (14 of 14)		1/28/56
	Larry Huston, OSU vs. ILL (14 of 14)		1/3/59
	Lance Olson, MSU vs. MINN (14 of 14)		2/1/60
	C.J. Kupec, MICH vs. ILL (14 of 14)		1/2/75
	Rick Olson, WIS vs PUR (14 of 14)		2/13/86
	Damon Bailey, IND vs. OSU (14 of 14)		1/14/92
	Glenn Robinson, PUR vs. WIS (14 of 14)		2/13/93

Most Rebounds
33	Walt Bellamy, IND vs. MICH		3/11/61
30	Charles Darling, IOWA vs. WIS		3/3/52
	Paul Morrow, WIS vs. PUR		1/3/53
	Jerry Lucas, OSU vs. IND		3/10/62
29	Jim Pitts, NU vs. IND		2/13/65
28	Horace Walker, MSU vs. IOWA		1/23/60
	Walt Bellamy, IND vs. WIS		2/18/61
	Larry Mikan, MINN vs. MICH		3/3/70
27	Carl McNulty, PUR vs. MINN		2/19/51
	M.C. Burton, MICH vs. IOWA		2/16/59
	Joe Franklin, WIS vs. PUR		3/2/68
	Greg Kelser, MSU		1976

Most Assists
18	Bruce Parkinson, PUR vs. MINN		3/8/75
16	Cal Wulfsberg, IOWA vs. OSU		1/24/76
	Arriel McDonald, MINN vs. WIS		1/12/94
15	Brian Walker, PUR vs. MSU		2/22/79
	B.J. Armstrong, IOWA vs. MINN		2/19/89
14	Quinn Buckner, IND vs. ILL		2/18/74
	Bruce Parkinson, PUR vs. IND		2/10/73
	Bob Wilkerson, IND vs. MICH		1/10/76
	Ronnie Lester, IOWA vs. NU		2/16/78
	Earvin Johnson, MSU vs. WIS		1/4/79
	Curtis Wilson, OSU vs. PUR		1/7/88
	Troy Lewis, PUR vs. IND		2/21/88

Most Steals
10	Michael Finley, WIS vs. PUR		2/13/93
9	Kenyon Murray, IOWA vs. OSU		2/18/95
8	Bruce Douglas, ILL vs. PUR		2/25/84
	Darryl Johnson, MSU vs. OSU		1/10/87
	Gary Grant, MICH vs. NU		1/21/87
	Melvin Newbern, MINN vs. MSU		3/8/89
7	Kelvin Ransey, OSU vs. MINN		2/23/78
	Derek Harper, ILL vs. MICH		2/17/83
	Bruce Douglas, ILL vs. NU		2/28/84
	Scott Roth, WIS vs. NU		2/26/84
	Bruce Douglas, ILL vs. NU		2/14/85
	Gary Grant, MICH vs. PUR		2/7/85
	Bruce Douglas, ILL vs. MICH		1/8/86
	Andre Banks, IOWA vs. NU		2/22/86
	Kendall Gill, ILL vs. MSU		1/9/88
	Ken Battle, ILL vs. MICH		3/9/88
	Kendall Gill, ILL vs. IOWA		3/3/90
	Pat Baldwin, NU vs. ILL		3/2/91
	Pat Baldwin, NU vs. PUR		2/27/93

Most Blocked Shots
12	Mychal Thompson, MINN vs. OSU		1/27/76
10	Jim Pitts, NU vs. PUR		1/8/66
9	Herb Williams, OSU vs. IOWA		2/23/80
	Randy Breuer, MINN vs. MICH		3/5/83
	Acie Earl, IOWA vs. WIS		1/29/92
8	Herb Williams, OSU vs. IOWA		1/7/78
	Herb Williams, OSU vs. IOWA		3/7/81
	Dean Garrett, IND vs. IOWA		3/12/88
	Eric Riley, MICH vs. ILL		3/1/91
7	Herb Williams, OSU vs. ILL		1/24/80
	Brad Sellers, WIS vs. MINN		2/21/82
	Brad Sellers, OSU vs. NU		1/12/85
	Roy Tarpley, MICH vs. ILL		1/10/85
	Brad Sellers, OSU vs. IOWA		1/24/86
	Acie Earl, IOWA vs. MINN		2/1/92
	Acie Earl, IOWA vs. ILL		2/23/92
	Lawrence Funderburke, OSU vs. IND		2/23/92
	Deon Thomas, ILL vs. NU		2/26/92

Minnesota center Mychal Thompson blocked a Big Ten-record 12 Ohio State shots on January 27, 1976.

TEAM SINGLE GAME

Most Points
128	MICH vs. PUR	2/19/66
127	MICH vs. IOWA	3/10/90
122	IND vs. OSU	2/2/59
121	ILL vs. PUR	2/6/65
	ILL vs. MSU	3/9/65
120	MICH vs. WIS	2/12/66
	PUR vs. IND	3/8/69
	MICH vs. IOWA	2/3/88
119	IOWA vs. WIS	2/10/70
	MICH vs. IOWA	3/4/89

Most Field Goals
55	MICH vs. IOWA	3/10/90
52	MICH vs. PUR	2/19/66
50	IND vs. OSU	2/2/59
	ILL vs. PUR	2/6/65
	ILL vs. MSU	3/9/65
	IND vs. MSU	1/4/75
49	OSU vs. MSU	1/30/80
	IND vs. MSU	2/8/65
	MICH vs. WIS	2/12/66
	MICH vs. IOWA	2/3/88

Most Field Goal Attempts
114	IND vs. PUR	2/23/53
113	WIS vs. MSU	1/6/64
110	IND vs. IOWA	2/25/50
	IND vs. MSU	1/11/64
109	MICH vs. PUR	1/23/65

Most Field Goal Attempts, Two Teams
207	WIS (113) vs. MSU (94)	1/6/64
206	IND (110) vs. MSU (96)	1/11/64

Best Field Goal Percentage
.755	PUR vs. MICH (37 of 49)	1/5/81
.738	MSU vs. MINN (31 of 42)	2/28/87
.727	PUR vs. IOWA (32 of 44)	1/27/90
.723	MINN vs. IOWA (34 of 47)	1/25/60
	OSU vs. MINN (34 of 47)	1/22/81
.714	OSU vs. IOWA (25 of 35)	1/26/84
	MINN vs. IND (30 of 42)	2/11/84
.712	IND vs. MSU (42 of 59)	2/18/88
.711	IND vs. MSU (27 of 38)	2/23/89
.700	PUR vs MICH (35 of 50)	1/31/90
.697	IND vs. ILL (23 of 33)	3/5/83

Most Three-Point Field Goals
14	WIS vs. MSU	2/2/94
	WIS vs. MSU	3/8/95
13	ILL vs. IOWA	3/4/90
	ILL vs. IND	3/1/94
	IOWA vs. MINN	2/2/94
	WIS vs. MICH	1/29/94
	IOWA vs. NU	2/9/95
	NU vs. MINN	3/4/95
12	IOWA vs. MINN	2/20/88
	MSU vs. PUR	1/25/89
	MSU vs. IOWA	1/13/90
	NU vs. IOWA	3/11/92
	WIS vs. NU	3/6/93
	PUR vs. MICH	3/6/94
	MINN vs. NU	1/11/95
	IOWA vs. MINN	2/15/95
	IOWA vs. MICH	3/5/95
	ILL vs. NU	3/8/95

Most Three-Point Field Goals Attempted
32	MINN vs. ILL	2/8/90
31	WIS vs. NU	2/3/93
	IOWA vs. MINN	2/2/94
	IOWA vs. MSU	3/8/95
30	WIS vs. NU	3/6/93
	IOWA vs. PUR	3/1/95
29	NU vs. WIS	1/4/95
	IOWA vs. NU	2/9/95
28	WIS vs. PUR	2/16/94
	WIS vs. MICH	1/29/94
	WIS vs. MSU	2/2/94

Best Three-Point Field Goal Percentage (min. 5 made)
.875	MICH vs. IOWA (7 of 8)	2/3/88
	MSU vs. MINN (7 of 8)	2/6/93
.833	IND vs. MSU (5 of 6)	1/26/91
	PUR vs. MICH (10 of 12)	2/7/93
.800	PUR vs. NU (8 of 10)	1/25/92
.769	MICH vs. WIS (10 of 13)	2/25/89
.750	MICH vs. OSU (6 of 8)	1/8/87
	IOWA vs. NU (9 of 12)	3/5/87
	MSU vs. PUR (12 of 16)	1/25/89
.727	IND vs. PSU (8 of 11)	1/8/94

Most Free Throws
43	ILL vs. MSU	1/26/80
	IND vs. MICH	1/3/55
42	IND vs. PUR	1/19/53
	IND vs. MINN	2/3/91
41	WIS vs. ILL	1/1/55
	PUR vs. NU	1/1/55

Most Free Throw Attempts
65	PUR vs. MICH	1/2/53
60	IND vs. MICH	1/3/55
56	IOWA vs. IND	12/22/52
	IND vs. OSU	1/5/55
55	IND vs. PUR	1/19/53
	IOWA vs. MICH	1/11/54

Most Free Throw Attempts, Two Teams
106	PUR (65) vs. MICH (41)	3/2/53
99	PUR (51) vs. MICH (48)	12/22/52
	IND (55) vs. PUR (44)	1/19/53

Best Free Throw Percentage (min. 16 att.)
1.000	PUR vs. WIS (25 of 25)	2/7/76
	NU vs. MSU (24 of 24)	1/27/77
	ILL vs. PSU (24 of 24)	1/21/93
	NU vs. MINN (23 of 23)	2/20/86
	WIS vs. PUR (22 of 22)	2/7/76
	MINN vs. OSU (21 of 21)	1/19/74
	MSU vs. ILL (18 of 18)	1/11/86
	IND vs. OSU (18 of 18)	1/27/88
	NU vs. OSU (16 of 16)	2/2/74
	ILL vs. WIS (16 of 16)	1/17/85

Most Rebounds
95	IND vs. MICH	3/11/61
89	IND vs. PUR	2/21/51
84	MSU vs. OSU	1/19/59
79	ILL vs. WIS	2/16/59
77	MICH vs. MSU	2/2/63
76	IOWA vs. OSU	1/24/55
75	IOWA vs. PUR	1/6/51
74	IND vs. ILL	2/25/61
72	OSU vs. WIS	1/30/65
	MICH vs. IND	2/15/65

Most Assists
36	MICH vs. IOWA	2/3/88
33	WIS vs. NU	3/7/53
	MICH vs. PUR	3/7/87
32	MICH vs. PUR	2/23/74
	MINN vs. IND	2/27/94
31	OSU vs. MSU	1/6/75
	IND vs. ILL	2/24/75
30	OSU vs. IOWA	1/13/75
	ILL vs. OSU	2/22/75
	IND vs. WIS	1/31/76
	PUR vs. NU	1/16/86
	MICH vs. IOWA	1/31/87
	ILL vs. IOWA	3/8/89
	MICH vs. IOWA	3/10/90
	MINN vs. WIS	1/12/94
	WIS vs. IOWA	3/9/94

Most Steals
23	IOWA vs. NU	2/22/86
20	ILL vs. PUR	2/23/87
18	OSU vs. NU	2/25/78
	IND vs. IOWA	1/19/91
	IOWA vs. NU	3/8/93
17	NU vs. IOWA	1/12/84
	WIS vs. MSU	1/7/88
	MICH vs. NU	1/7/88
	IOWA vs. NU	2/24/88
	MINN vs. MSU	3/8/89
	IOWA vs. MICH	1/10/91

Most Blocked Shots
15	OSU vs. IOWA	2/23/80
13	OSU vs. IOWA	3/7/81
	MINN vs. MICH	3/5/83
	ILL vs. MINN	1/17/87
12	MICH vs. MINN	1/20/93
11	OSU vs. IOWA	1/7/78
	OSU vs. ILL	1/24/80
	IND vs. IOWA	3/12/88
	MICH vs. IOWA	1/20/90
	MICH vs. ILL	3/1/91
	ILL vs. NU	2/26/92

Most Personal Fouls
41	MSU vs. NU	2/2/52
40	PUR vs. ILL	3/1/52
	OSU vs. PUR	3/5/81
38	IND vs. NU	2/16/52
35	PUR vs. WIS	1/5/52
	PUR vs. MSU	1/26/52
	MICH vs. OSU	1/27/68
	OSU vs. PUR	1/10/81
	MINN vs. PUR	2/5/91
34	NU vs. IND	1952
	OSU vs. IOWA	1/7/78
	IOWA vs. ILL	3/4/91

Most Personal Fouls, Two Teams
73	PUR (40) vs. ILL (33)	3/1/52
72	IND (38) vs. NU (34)	2/16/52

Michigan forward Glen Rice, who led the Wolverines to the 1989 NCAA championship, hit all seven of his three-point field goal attempts against Wisconsin on Feb. 25, 1989 to set a Big Ten record.

RECORDS
Big Ten Men's Basketball Records

CONFERENCE GAMES ONLY

INDIVIDUAL SEASON

Most Points
560	Glenn Robinson, PUR	1994
558	Terry Furlow, MSU	1976
552	Rick Mount, PUR	1970
524	Scott Skiles, MSU	1986
510	Dennis Hopson, OSU	1987
493	Rick Mount, PUR	1969
474	Gary Bradds, OSU	1964
465	Cazzie Russell, MICH	1966
459	Don Schlundt, IND	1953
	Terry Dischinger, PUR	1962
	Glenn Robinson, PUR	1993
	Shawn Respert, MSU	1995

Most Points Per Game
39.4	Rick Mount, PUR, (552 in 14)	1970
35.2	Rick Mount, PUR (493 in 14)	1969
33.9	Gary Bradds, OSU (474 in 14)	1964
33.2	Cazzie Russell, MICH (465 in 14)	1966
32.8	Terry Dischinger, PUR (459 in 14)	1962
32.5	Robin Freeman, OSU (455 in 14)	1956
32.4	Jimmy Rayl, IND (454 in 14)	1962
32.2	Dave Schellhase, PUR (451 in 14)	1966
31.8	John Johnson, IOWA (445 in 14)	1970
31.7	Rudy Tomjanovich, MICH (444 in 14)	1970

Most Field Goals
221	Rick Mount, PUR	1970
207	Terry Furlow, MSU	1976
	Scott Skiles, MSU	1986
194	Rick Mount, PUR	1969
191	Glenn Robinson, PUR	1994
187	Mychal Thompson, MINN	1976
186	Jay Vincent, MSU	1981
182	Cazzie Russell, MICH	1966

Most Field Goals Per Game
15.8	Rick Mount, PUR (221 in 14)	1970
13.9	Rick Mount, PUR (194 in 14)	1969
13.0	Cazzie Russell, MICH (182 in 14)	1966
12.9	John Johnson, IOWA (181 in 14)	1970
12.7	Rudy Tomjanovich, MICH (178 in 14)	1970
12.4	Gary Bradds, OSU (174 in 14)	1964

Most Field Goal Attempts
456	Terry Furlow, MSU	1976
435	Rick Mount, PUR	1970
412	Glenn Robinson, PUR	1994
378	Paul Ebert, OSU	1953
375	Rick Mount, PUR	1969
373	Scott Skiles, MSU	1986
362	Rick Mount, PUR	1968
	Don Freeman, ILL	1966

Most Field Goal Attempts Per Game
31.1	Rick Mount, PUR (435 in 14)	1970
26.8	Rick Mount, PUR (375 in 14)	1969
26.2	Ralph Simpson, MSU (340 in 13)	1970
25.9	Don Freeman, ILL (362 in 14)	1966
	Rick Mount, PUR (362 in 14)	1968
25.8	Murray Wier, IOWA (309) in 12)	1948

Best Field Goal Percentage
.767	Stephen Scheffler, PUR (115 of 150)	1990
.678	Jerry Lucas, OSU (122 of 180)	1962
.677	Loy Vaught, MICH (109 of 161)	1989
.673	Ron Charles, MSU (103 of 153)	1980
.656	Jerry Lucas, OSU (143 of 218)	1960
.643	Ken Norman, ILL (133 of 207)	1986
.640	Jim Petersen, MINN (71 of 111)	1984
.638	Les Jepsen, IOWA (102 of 160)	1990
.626	Ray Tolbert, IND (107 of 171)	1981
.617	Ken Brady, MICH (74 of 120)	1970

Most Three-Point Field Goals
80	Shawn Respert, MSU	1995
65	Chris Kingsbury, IOWA	1995
58	Shawn Respert, MSU	1994
57	Cuonzo Martin, PUR	1995
55	Glen Rice, MICH	1989
54	Steve Alford, IND	1987
53	Tracy Webster, WIS	1992
52	Jay Edwards, IND	1988
	Kirk Manns, MSU	1989
51	Doug Etzler, OSU	1995

Most Three-Point Field Goals Per Game
4.44	Shawn Respert, MSU (80 in 18)	1995
3.61	Chris Kingsbury, IOWA (65 in 18)	1995

3.25	Jay Edwards, IND (52 in 16)	1988
3.22	Shawn Respert, MSU (58 in 18)	1994
3.17	Cuonzo Martin, PUR (57 in 18)	1995
3.06	Glen Rice, MICH (55 in 18)	1989
3.00	Steve Alford, IND (54 in 18)	1987
2.90	Tracy Webster, WIS (53 in 18)	1992
2.89	Kirk Manns, MSU (52 in 18)	1989
2.88	Doug Altenberger, ILL (49 in 17)	1987

Most Three-Point Attempts
173	Shawn Respert, MSU	1995
163	Chris Kingsbury, IOWA	1995
146	Voshon Leonard, MINN	1995
128	Doug Etzler, OSU	1995
126	Michael Finley, WIS	1993
125	Demetrius Calip, MICH	1991
122	Todd Leslie, NU	1994
121	Shawn Respert, MSU	1994
	Michael Finley, WIS	1995
	Cuonzo Martin, PUR	1995

Most Three-Point Field Goals Attempted Per Game
9.61	Shawn Respert, MSU	1995
9.06	Chris Kingsbury, IOWA	1995
8.11	Voshon Lenard, MINN	1995
7.11	Doug Etzler, OSU	1995
7.00	Michael Finley, WIS (126 in 18)	1993
6.94	Demetrius Calip, MICH (125 in 18)	1991
6.77	Todd Leslie, NU (122 in 18)	1994
6.72	Shawn Respert, MSU (121 in 18)	1994
	Cuonzo Martin, PUR	1995
	Michael Finley, WIS	1995

Best Three-Point Percentage (Min. 1 per game)
.656	Ted Kitchel, IND (21 of 32)	1983
.571	Jay Edwards, IND (52 of 91)	1988
.565	Woody Austin, PUR (26 of 46)	1990
.557	Tom Michael, ILL (49 of 88)	1992
.553	Kirk Manns, MSU (52 of 94)	1989
.545	Larry Huggins, OSU (18 of 33)	1983
.535	Greg Graham, IND (38 of 71)	1993
.534	Glen Rice, MICH (55 of 103)	1989
.516	Ray Gaffney, MINN (16 of 31)	1988
.511	Scott Skiles, MSU (24 of 47)	1983
	Pat Graham (23 of 45)	1994

Most Free Throws
179	Terry Dischinger, PUR	1962
175	Don Schlundt, IND	1953
157	Don Schlundt, IND	1955
153	Don Schlundt, IND	1954
150	Jimmy Rayl, IND	1962
144	Terry Furlow, MSU	1976

Most Free Throws Per Game
12.8	Terry Dischinger, PUR (179 in 14)	1962
11.2	Don Schlundt, IND (157 in 14)	1955
10.9	Don Schlundt, IND (153 in 14)	1954
10.7	Jimmy Rayl, IND (150 in 14)	1962
10.2	Terry Dischinger, PUR (143 in 14)	1961

Most Free Throw Attempts
223	Jack Runyan, PUR	1953
215	Terry Dischinger, PUR	1962
213	Don Schlundt, IND	1953
193	Paul Ebert, OSU	1953
	Don Schlundt, IND	1954
190	Don Schlundt, IND	1955

Most Free Throws Attempted Per Game
15.4	Terry Dischinger, PUR (215 in 14)	1962
13.8	Don Schlundt, IND (193 in 14)	1954
13.6	Don Schlundt, IND (190 in 14)	1955
13.1	Dick Garmaker, MINN (183 in 14)	1954
12.5	Jimmy Rayl, IND (175 in 14)	1962
12.4	Jack Runyan, PUR (223 in 18)	1953
	Don Nelson, IOWA (174 in 14)	1962
12.3	Terry Dischinger, PUR (172 in 14)	1960
11.8	Don Schlundt, IND (213 in 18)	1953
11.7	Terry Dischinger, PUR (164 in 14)	1961

Best Free Throw Shooting Percentage
.935	Steve Alford, IND (58 of 62)	1985
.927	Jerry Francis, OSU (51 of 55)	1989
.923	Jon McGlocklin, IND (36 of 39)	1965
	Rick Ford, IND (60 of 65)	1970
	Rick Olson, WIS (48 of 52)	1984
.922	Henry Ebershoff, PUR (56 of 64)	1966
.921	Dennis Graff, ILL (35 of 38)	1974
.920	Sam Gee, IND (46 of 50)	1958

.918	Larry Siegfried, OSU (56 of 61)	1961
	Bill Keller, PUR (56 of 61)	1969
	Glen Vidnovic, IOWA (78 of 85)	1970

Most Rebounds
256	Horace Walker, MSU	1960
253	Jerry Lucas, OSU	1962
249	M.C. Burton, MICH	1959
247	Walt Bellamy, IND	1961
242	John Green, MSU	1959
230	Jerry Lucas, OSU	1961
227	Rudy Tomjanovich, MICH	1970
223	Kevin Kunnert, IOWA	1972
220	Jerry Lucas, OSU	1960
216	Bill Buntin, MICH	1963

Most Rebounds Per Game
18.3	Horace Walker, MSU (256 in 14)	1960
18.1	Jerry Lucas, OSU (253 in 14)	1962
17.8	M.C. Burton, MICH (249 in 14)	1959
17.6	Walt Bellamy, IND (247 in 14)	1961
17.3	John Green, MSU (242 in 14)	1959
16.2	Rudy Tomjanovich, MICH (227 in 14)	1970

Most Assists
141	Eric Snow, MSU	1995
138	Cal Wulfsberg, IOWA	1976
133	Earvin Johnson, MSU	1979
129	Bruce Parkinson, PUR	1975
123	Eric Snow, MSU	1994
122	Earvin Johnson, MSU	1978
120	Brian Walker, PUR	1981

Most Assists, Per Game
7.8	Eric Snow, MSU (141 in 18)	1995
7.7	Cal Wulfsberg, IOWA (138 in 18)	1976
7.4	Earvin Johnson, MSU (133 in 18)	1979
7.2	Bruce Parkinson, PUR (129 in 18)	1975

Most Steals
62	Melvin Newbern, MINN	1989
52	Pat Baldwin, NU	1991
51	Bruce Douglas, ILL	1986
50	Bruce Douglas, ILL	1984
49	Bruce Douglas, ILL	1985
	Gary Grant, MICH	1988
48	Gary Grant, MICH	1987
46	Derek Harper, ILL	1983
	Tracy Webster, WIS	1993
41	Steve Carfino, IOWA	1984

Most Steals, Per Game
3.44	Melvin Newbern, MINN (62 in 18)	1989
2.89	Pat Baldwin, NU (52 in 18)	1991
2.83	Bruce Douglas, ILL (51 in 18)	1986
	Bruce Douglas, ILL (50 in 18)	1984
2.78	Bruce Douglas, ILL (48 in 18)	1985
2.72	Gary Grant, MICH (48 in 18)	1987
2.67	Gary Grant, MICH (49 in 18)	1988
2.56	Derek Harper, ILL (46 in 18)	1983
	Tracy Webster, WIS (46 in 18)	1993
2.28	Steve Carino, IOWA (41 in 18)	1984
2.25	Pat Baldwin, NU (36 in 16)	1993

Most Blocked Shots
71	Acie Earl, IOWA	1992
54	Randy Breuer, MINN	1983
	Dean Garrett, IND	1988
	Acie Earl, IOWA	1991
52	Brad Sellers, OSU	1985
51	Dean Garrett, IND	1987
50	John Amaechi, PSU	1993
49	Greg Stokes, IOWA	1983
48	Lawrence Funderburke, OSU	1992
47	Eric Riley, MICH	1991
	Acie Earl, IOWA	1993

Most Blocked Shots, Per Game
3.94	Acie Earl, IOWA (71 in 18)	1992
3.00	Randy Breuer, MINN (54 in 18)	1983
	Dean Garrett, IND (54 in 18)	1988
	Acie Earl, IOWA (54 in 18)	1991
2.89	Brad Sellers, OSU (52 in 18)	1985
2.83	Dean Garrett, IND (51 in 18)	1987
2.78	John Amaechi, PSU (50 in 18)	1993
2.72	Greg Stokes, IOWA (49 in 18)	1983
2.67	Lawrence Funderburke, OSU (48 in 18)	1992
2.61	Erie Riley, MICH (47 in 18)	1991
	Acie Earl, MICH (47 in 18)	1993

TEAM SEASON

Most Points
- 1,642 IOWA 1988
- 1,581 MICH 1989
- 1,570 IND 1975
- 1,561 MICH 1987
- 1,558 IOWA 1989
- 1,550 IND 1993
- 1,544 MICH 1976
- 1,532 MICH 1988
- 1,527 IND 1991
- 1,505 PUR 1976

Most Points, Per Game
- 102.9 IOWA (1,441 in 14) 1970
- 97.1 PUR (1,359 in 14) 1969
- 95.4 MICH (1,336 in 14) 1966
- 92.9 MICH (1,300 in 14) 1965
- 92.4 ILL (1,293 in 14) 1965
- 92.1 MSU (1,290 in 14) 1964
- 92.0 PUR (1,288 in 14) 1970
- 91.9 MICH (1,286 in 14) 1970
- 91.2 ILL (1,277 in 14) 1956
- IOWA (1,642 in 18) 1988

Most Field Goals
- 652 IND 1975
- 636 MICH 1976
- 624 MICH 1987
- 611 MICH 1988
- 606 MSU 1975
- 596 MICH 1977
- 581 MSU 1986
- 580 MICH 1986
- 576 MINN 1976
- 569 MICH 1978

Most Field Goals Per Game
- 39.9 IOWA (559 in 14) 1970
- 38.1 ILL (534 in 14) 1965
- 37.7 MICH (528 in 14) 1966
- 37.6 PUR (526 in 14) 1969
- 37.4 OSU (523 in 14) 1960

Most Field Goal Attempts
- 1,282 MINN 1952
- 1,271 IND 1975
- 1,230 MSU 1964
- 1,221 MICH 1976
- 1,212 MINN 1956
- 1,207 MICH 1987
- 1,203 NU 1952

Most Field Goal Attempts Per Game
- 87.9 MSU (1,230 in 14) 1964
- 86.6 MINN (1,212 in 14) 1956
- 85.9 NU (1,203 in 14) 1952

Best Field Goal Percentage
- .561 MICH (606 of 1,280) 1989
- .553 MSU (581 of 1,051) 1986
- .551 ILL (532 of 966) 1986
- .550 PUR (482 of 876) 1990
- .547 OSU (490 of 896) 1970
- .541 IND (490 of 906) 1981
- .540 IOWA (559 of 1,035) 1970
- .539 PUR (516 of 957) 1988
- .537 MICH (611 of 1,138) 1988
- .535 MSU (516 of 964) 1985

Most Three-Point Field Goals
- 158 IOWA 1995
- 138 WIS 1993
- 130 WIS 1994
- 127 PUR 1994
- 120 WIS 1995
- 118 MICH 1991
- IND 1993
- NU 1994
- 116 WIS 1992
- 115 WIS 1991

Most Three-Point Field Goals Attempted
- 413 IOWA 1995
- 374 WIS 1993
- 372 WIS 1994
- 355 WIS 1995
- 342 MINN 1995
- 331 PSU 1995
- 326 PUR 1994
- NU 1994
- 329 IOWA 1994
- 299 MICH 1991

Best Three-Point Field Goal Percentage
- .566 IND (30 of 53) 1983
- .500 IND (64 of 128) 1988
- .497 IND (72 of 145) 1989
- .490 ILL (75 of 153) 1987
- MICH (103 of 210) 1989
- .489 IND (68 of 139) 1987
- .470 ILL (87 of 185) 1992
- .467 ILL (14 of 30) 1983
- .465 PUR (60 of 129) 1990
- .455 MSU (96 of 211) 1990

Most Free Throws
- 442 IND 1953
- 390 IND 1991
- 376 OSU 1956
- 363 IND 1954
- 362 IOWA 1992
- 359 IOWA 1988
- IOWA 1989
- 358 IND 1992
- 356 IND 1955
- 354 IOWA 1977

Most Free Throws Per Game
- 26.9 OSU (376 in 14) 1956
- 25.9 IND (363 in 14) 1954
- 25.4 IND (356 in 14) 1955
- 25.0 MINN (350 in 14) 1954
- 24.9 IND (349 in 14) 1956
- 24.6 IND (442 in 18) 1953
- WIS (345 in 14) 1955
- 24.1 ILL (337 in 14) 1956
- 23.9 MSU (335 in 14) 1955
- 23.4 IND (328 in 14) 1963
- ILL (328 in 14) 1963

Most Free Throw Attempts
- 688 PUR 1953
- 648 IOWA 1953
- 558 MINN 1953
- 549 MINN 1954
- 542 IND 1991
- 541 IND 1954
- 517 IOWA 1954
- 515 IOWA 1988

Most Free Throws Attempted Per Game
- 39.2 MINN (549 in 14) 1954
- 38.6 IND (541 in 14) 1954
- 38.2 PUR (688 in 18) 1953
- 36.9 IOWA (517 in 14) 1954
- 36.4 OSU (509 in 14) 1956
- 36.0 IOWA (648 in 18) 1953
- 35.9 MSU (502 in 14) 1955
- 35.4 NU (638 in 18) 1953
- 35.3 NU (494 in 14) 1954
- 35.1 IND (632 in 18) 1953

Best Free Throw Percentage
- .806 PUR (307 of 381) 1969
- .798 IOWA (323 of 405) 1970
- .796 ILL (195 of 245) 1986
- .790 OSU (226 of 286) 1970
- .789 MSU (277 of 351) 1986
- .781 IND (271 of 347) 1965
- .780 IND (288 of 369) 1988
- .778 NU (228 of 293) 1976
- .777 IOWA (321 of 413) 1969
- OSU (269 of 346) 1984

Most Rebounds
- 892 MSU 1959
- 793 IND 1959
- 760 MICH 1959
- MSU 1960
- 759 IOWA 1987
- 744 IND 1961
- 737 NU 1959
- MICH 1993
- 733 IOWA 1993
- 730 MSU 1964
- IND 1959

Most Rebounds Per Game
- 63.7 MSU (892 in 14) 1959
- 56.6 IND (793 in 14) 1959
- 54.3 MICH (760 in 14) 1959
- MSU (760 in 14) 1960
- 53.1 IND (744 in 14) 1961
- 52.6 NU (737 in 14) 1959
- 52.1 MSU (730 in 14) 1964
- IND (730 in 14) 1969
- 51.7 IOWA (724 in 14) 1959
- IND (724 in 14) 1971

Highest Rebound Margin Per Game
- 12.6 IOWA 1987
- 7.9 ILL 1984
- 7.7 WIS 1974
- 7.6 IOWA 1989
- MICH 1993
- 7.2 IND 1976
- 7.0 IND 1974
- ILL 1985
- 6.5 IOWA 1993
- 6.0 MINN 1990

Most Assists
- 393 IND 1976
- 372 MICH 1987
- 368 OSU 1975
- 357 MICH 1988
- 349 PUR 1986
- MICH 1989
- 338 ILL 1987
- 337 PUR 1988
- 332 PUR 1987
- 329 MINN 1994

MISCELLANEOUS RECORDS

Most Consecutive Wins (All Games)
- 34 IND (3-1974, 31-1975)
- 33 IND (32-1976, 1-1977)
- 32 OSU (5-1960, 27-1961)

Most Consecutive Wins (Big Ten Games)
- 37 IND (1-1974, 18-1975, 18-1976)
- 27 OSU (1-1960, 14-1961, 12-1962)
- 23 WIS (12-1912, 11-1913)
- 20 IND (16-1952, 4-1953)
- 19 MICH (15-1985, 4-1986)
- 17 ILL (3-1914, 12-1915, 2-1916)
- 14 IOWA (14-1970)

Most Overtimes
- 6 MINN (59) vs. PUR (56) 1/29/55

Most Overtime Games
- 6 OSU, 1982
- MICH, 1981
- MINN, 1981

Highest Losing Score
- 111 PUR vs. IOWA (112), 1974 (3 OT)
- 110 MINN vs. PUR (111), 1976 (2 OT)

Most Consecutive Free Throws
- 46 Todd Leary, IND 1990 (4), 1991-92 (6), 1992-93 (21), 1993-94 (15)
- 45 Steve Smith, MSU 1991
- 37 Keith Smart, IND 1988
- 36 Rick Olson, WIS 1984 (28) and 1985 (8)
- 34 Glenn Vidnovic, IOWA 1969
- Jerry Sichting, PUR 1978-79 (28 in 1979)
- 33 Ben McGillmer, IOWA 1969
- 32 Jimmy Rayl, IND 1962
- 31 Gary Bradds, OSU 1961
- 30 Jody Finney, OSU 1969
- Steve Alford, IND 1985
- Sam Vincent, MSU 1985
- Kiwane Garris, ILL 1995

Most Consecutive 40-point Games
- 6 Gary Bradds, OSU 1/25 through 2/15/64
- 4 Rick Mount, PUR 3/1 through 3/8/69

Most Steals
- 184 IOWA 1994
- 176 IOWA 1995
- 167 IOWA 1991
- 162 MINN 1989
- 155 MICH 1986
- 154 OSU 1991
- IOWA 1993
- 150 ILL 1987
- 149 OSU 1987
- ILL 1988

Most Blocked Shots
- 92 IOWA 1992
- 90 MICH 1993
- 89 MINN 1983
- 85 ILL 1987
- 83 MICH 1992
- 82 IND 1995
- 79 IOWA 1991
- WIS 1994
- 78 MICH 1991
- IOWA 1993

Highest Turnover Margin Per Game
- 5.0 IOWA 1995
- 4.9 IND 1991
- 4.3 IND 1992
- 4.2 WIS 1993
- 3.7 MINN 1994
- 3.6 IOWA 1986
- OSU 1991
- OSU 1992
- 3.5 ILL 1990
- 3.3 OSU 1987

Lowest Number of Turnovers Committed Per Game
- 11.4 MINN 1986
- 11.6 IND 1993
- 11.9 MINN 1994
- ILL 1994
- 12.1 MSU 1986
- OSU 1992
- IND 1992
- 12.2 IND 1989
- ILL 1990
- 12.4 WIS 1986
- WIS 1989

Highest Number of Turnovers Forced Per Game
- 19.1 IOWA 1995
- 18.9 IOWA 1991
- 18.8 OSU 1991
- 18.1 ILL 1988
- IND 1991
- 17.6 OSU 1990
- 17.4 WIS 1993
- IOWA 1994
- 17.0 IOWA 1988
- 16.8 OSU 1987
- MICH 1991

Most Personal Fouls
- 456 MICH 1953
- 445 MINN 1991
- 442 PUR 1953
- 430 NU 1953
- 424 IND 1953
- 417 MINN 1992
- 413 MICH 1995
- 411 MINN 1995
- 410 WIS 1995
- 403 IND 1952

RECORDS

CONFERENCE GAMES ONLY

Annual Individual Statistical Champions (Big Ten records in Bold)

Scoring

Year	Name/School	G	PTS	AVG
1906	Emmett Angell, WIS		96	
1907	John Schommer, CHI		95	
1908	John Schommer, CHI		105	
1909	John Schommer, CHI		104	
1910	David Charters, PUR		112	
1911	Frank Lawler, MINN		143	
1912	Otto Stangel, WIS		177	
1913	Homer Dahringer, ILL		125	
1914	Harold Whittle, NU		109	
1915	George Levis, WIS		140	
1916	Henry Brockenbraugh, PUR		119	
1917	Harold Gillen, MINN		126	
	Ralf Woods, ILL		126	
1918	Earl Anderson, ILL		162	
1919	Gorgas, CHI		106	
1920	Charles Garney, ILL		188	
1921	Don White, PUR		154	
1922	Charles Carney, ILL		172	
1923	Jack Funk, IOWA		143	
1924	George Spradling, PUR		128	
1925	John Miner, OSU		133	
1926	Arthur Beckner, IND		108	
1927	Wilbur Cummins, PUR		128	
1928	Bennie Oosterbaan, MICH		129	
1929	Charles Murphy, PUR		145	
1930	Branch McCracken, IND		147	
1931	Joe Reif, NU		120	
1932	John Wooden, PUR		154	
1933	Joe Reif, NU		168	
1934	Norm Cottom, PUR		119	
1935	Bill Haarlow, CHI		156	
1936	Bob Kessler, PUR		160	
1937	Jewell Young, PUR		172	
1938	Jewell Young, PUR		184	
1939	Jimmy Hull, OSU	12	169	14.1
1940	Bill Hapac, ILL	12	164	13.7
1941	Joe Stampf, CHI	12	166	13.8
1942	John Kotz, WIS	14	242	17.3
1943	Andy Phillip, ILL	12	255	21.3
1944	Dick Ives, IOWA	12	208	17.3
1945	Max Morris, NU	12	189	15.8
1946	Max Morris, NU	12	198	16.5
1947	Bob Cook, WIS	12	187	15.6
1948	Murray Wier, IOWA	12	272	22.7
1949	Don Rehfeldt, WIS	12	229	19.1
1950	Don Rehfeldt, WIS	12	265	22.1
1951	Ray Ragelis, NU	14	277	19.8
1952	Carles Darling, IOWA	14	364	26.0
1953	Don Schlundt, IND	18	459	25.5
1954	Don Schlundt, IND	14	379	27.1
1955	Don Schlundt, IND	14	369	26.4
1956	Robin Freeman, OSU	14	455	32.5
1957	Archie Dees, IND	14	356	25.4
1958	Archie Dees, IND	14	362	25.9
1959	M.C. Burton, MICH	14	316	22.6
1960	Terry Dischinger, PUR	14	384	27.4
1961	Terry Dischinger, PUR	14	405	28.3
1962	Terry Dischinger, PUR	14	459	32.8
1963	Gary Bradds, OSU	14	433	30.9
1964	Gary Bradds, OSU	14	474	33.9
1965	Dave Schellhase, PUR	14	391	27.9
1966	Cazzie Russell, MICH	14	465	33.2
1967	Tom Kondla, MINN	14	396	28.3
1968	Rick Mount, PUR	14	416	29.7
1969	Rick Mount, PUR	14	493	35.2
1970	Rick Mount, PUR	14	552	**39.4**
1971	George McGinnis, IND	14	418	29.9
1972	Mike Robinson, MSU	14	381	27.2
1973	Mike Robinson, MSU	14	374	26.7
1974	Campy Russell, MICH	14	336	24.0
1975	Terry Furlow, MSU	17	363	21.4
1976	Terry Furlow, MSU	18	558	32.7
1977	Mychal Thompson, MINN	18	410	22.8
1978	Mychal Thompson, MINN	18	409	22.7
1979	Joe Barry Carroll, PUR	18	429	23.8
1980	Jay Vincent, MSU	18	397	22.1
1981	Jay Vincent, MSU	18	433	24.1
1982	Keith Edmonson, PUR	18	370	20.6
1983	Randy Breuer, MINN	18	377	20.9
1984	vacated			
1985	Sam Vincent, MSU	18	427	23.7
1986	Scott Skiles, MSU	18	524	29.1
1987	Dennis Hopson, OSU	18	510	28.3
1988	Glen Rice, MICH	18	413	22.9
1989	Glen Rice, MICH	18	447	24.8
1990	Kendall Gill, ILL	18	368	20.4
1991	Steve Smith, MSU	18	418	23.2
1992	Jim Jackson, OSU	18	396	22.0
1993	Glenn Robinson, PUR	18	459	25.5
1994	Glenn Robinson, PUR	18	**560**	31.1
1995	Shawn Respert, MSU	18	459	25.5

Most Field Goals

Year	Name/School	G	NO
1939	Jimmy Hull, OSU	12	66
1940	Bill Hapac, ILL	12	60
1941	Dick Fisher, OSU	12	62
1942	John Kotz, WIS	14	95
1943	Andy Phillip, ILL	12	111
1944	Dick Ives, IOWA	12	89
1945	Max Morris, NU	12	68
1946	Max Morris, NU	12	77

Field Goal Percentage

Year	Name/School	FG	FGA	PCT
1947	Ralph Hamilton, IND	73	195	.374
1948	Dick Schnittker, OSU	70	190	.368
1949	Jim McIntyre, MINN	68	181	.376
1950	Bob Donham, OSU	68	114	.430
1951	Ralph Gelle, MINN	43	98	.439
1952	Don Schlundt, IND	84	194	.433
1953	Dick Farley, IND	69	151	.457
1954	Don Schundt, IND	113	224	.504
1955	John Miller, OSU	93	193	.482
1956	Wally Choice, IND	93	185	.503
1957	Dick Neal, IND	84	164	.512
1958	John Green, MSU	107	199	.538
1959	Walt Bellamy, IND	95	181	.525
1960	Jerry Lucas, OSU	143	218	.656
1961	Jerry Lucas, OSU	137	224	.612
1962	Jerry Lucas, OSU	122	180	.678
1963	Gary Bradds, OSU	154	293	.526
1964	Gary Bradds, OSU	174	325	.535
1965	Skip Thoren, ILL	130	226	.575
1966	Cazzie Russell, MICH	182	336	.542
1967	Dave McClellan, MICH	67	114	.588
1968	Dave Sorenson, OSU	103	172	.599
1969	Jim Cleamons, OSU	97	155	.584
1970	John Johnson, IOWA	181	298	.607
1971	Ken Brady, MICH	74	120	.617
1972	Bill Kilgore, MSU	82	148	.554
1973	Kevin Kunnert, IOWA	131	226	.580
1974	John Garrett, PUR	121	210	.576
1975	John Robinson, MICH	76	126	.603
1976	Kent Benson, IND	140	231	.606
1977	Mychal Thompson, MINN	175	293	.597
1978	Kevin McHale, MINN	105	173	.607
1979	Marty Bodnar, MICH	76	126	.603
1980	Ron Charles, MSU	103	153	.673
1981	Ray Tolbert, IND	107	171	.626
1982	Russell Cross, PUR	73	134	.560
1983	Kevin Willis, MSU	117	195	.600
1984	Jim Peterson, MINN	71	111	.640
1985	Uwe Blab, IND	129	220	.586
1986	Ken Norman, ILL	133	207	.643
1987	Roy Marble, IOWA	93	157	.592
1988	Nick Anderson, ILL	140	231	.606
1989	Loy Vaught, MICH	109	161	.677
1990	Stephen Scheffler, PUR	115	150	**.767**
1991	Patrick Tompkins, WIS	94	159	.591
1992	Mike Peplowski, PUR	104	170	.612
1993	Greg Graham, IND	101	172	.587
1994	Deon Thomas, ILL	121	202	.599
1995	Alan Henderson, IND	167	274	.609

Most Three-Point Field Goals

Year	Name/School	G	NO
1983	Steve Carfino, IOWA	18	27
1987	Steve Alford, IND	18	54
1988	Jay Edwards, IND	18	52
1989	Glen Rice, MICH	18	55
1990	Kirk Manns, MSU	17	47
1991	Demetrius Calip, MICH	18	48
1992	Tracy Webster, WIS	18	53
1993	Michael Finley, WIS	18	44
1994	Shawn Respert, MSU	18	58
1995	Shawn Respert, MSU	18	**80**

Three-Point Field Goal Percentage

Year	Name/School	FG	FGA	PCT
1983	Ted Kitchel, IND	21	32	**.656**
1987	Jeff Moe, IOWA	32	63	.508
1988	Jay Edwards, IND	52	91	.571
1989	Kirk Manns, MSU	52	94	.553
1990	Kirk Manns, MSU	47	96	.490
1991	Tim Locum, WIS	36	73	.493
1992	Tom Michael, ILL	49	88	.557
1993	Greg Graham, IND	38	71	.535
1994	Brian Evans, IND	28	56	.500
1995	Cuonzo Martin, PUR	57	121	.471

Most Free Throws

Year	Name/School	G	NO
1939	Louis Dehner, ILL	12	43
1940	Joe Stampf, CHI	12	49
1941	Joe Stampf, CHI	12	82
1942	Otto Graham, NU	12	58
1943	Otto Graham, NU	12	41
	Ralph Hamilton, IND	12	41
1944	Walt Kirk, ILL	12	39
1945	Max Morris, NU	12	53
1946	Tony Jaros, MINN	12	79

Free Throw Percentage

Year	Name/School	FT	FTA	PCT
1947	Bob Cook, WIS	47	63	.746
1948	Ward Williams, IND	27	34	.794
1949	Howie Williams, PUR	30	35	.857
1950	Dan Page, WIS	28	32	.875
1951	Meyer Skogg, MINN	31	35	.886
1952	Gordon Stauffer, MSU	40	51	.784
	Clive Follmer, ILL	40	51	.784
1953	Don Schlundt, IND	175	213	.822
1954	W. Stoeppelwerth, NU	26	32	.813
1955	Robin Freeman, OSU	45	53	.849
1956	Hallie Bryant, IND	45	51	.882
1957	Archie Dees, IND	106	125	.848
1958	Sam Gee, IND	46	50	.920
1959	Roger Taylor, ILL	48	55	.873
1960	Govoner Vaughn, ILL	42	48	.875
1961	Larry Siegfried, OSU	56	61	.918
1962	Bill Cacciatore, NU	38	43	.884
1963	Jimmy Rayl, IND	108	122	.885
1964	Mel Garland, PUR	59	69	.855
	Jimmy Rodgers, IOWA	59	69	.855
1965	Jon McGlockin, IND	36	39	.923
1966	Henry Ebershoff, PUR	59	64	.922

Year	Name/School	G	NO	AVG
1967	Jack Johnson, IND	26	30	.867
1968	Bill Keller, PUR	50	55	.909
1969	Bill Keller, PUR	56	61	.918
1970	Rick Ford, IND	60	65	.923
1971	Larry Weatherford, PUR	71	81	.876
1972	John Ritter, IND	69	76	.906
1973	Rick Williams, IOWA	48	55	.873
1974	Dennis Graff, ILL	35	38	.921
1975	C.J. Kupec, MICH	71	80	.880
1976	Terry Furlow, MSU	144	161	.894
1977	Osborne Lockhart, MINN	43	48	.896
1978	Jerry Sichting, PUR	54	61	.885
1979	Jerry Marifke, NU	46	52	.885
1980	Wesley Matthews, WIS	82	95	.863
	Terry Donnelly, MSU	44	51	.863
1981	Jim Stack, NU	55	60	.917
1982	Ted Kitchel, IND	104	118	.881
1983	Ted Kitchel, IND	63	69	.913
1984	Rick Olson, WIS	48	52	.923
1985	Steve Alford, IND	58	62	**.935**
1986	Scott Skiles, MSU	110	124	.887
1987	Darryl Johnson, MSU	69	77	.896
1988	Jay Edwards, IND	66	72	.917
1989	Jerry Francis, OSU	51	55	.927
1990	Brian Good, WIS	46	51	.902
1991	Jimmy Oliver, PUR	75	86	.872
1992	Tracy Webster, WIS	46	53	.868
1993	Pat Baldwin, NU	53	59	.898
1994	T.J. Wheeler	40	44	.909
1995	Shawn Respert	83	94	.883

Rebounds

Year	Name/School	G	NO	AVG
1959	M.C. Burton, MICH	14	249	17.8
1960	Horace Walker, MSU	14	**256**	**18.3**
1961	Walt Bellamy, IND	14	247	17.6
1962	Jerry Lucas, OSU	14	253	18.1
1963	Bill Buntin, MICH	14	216	15.4
1964	Gary Bradds, OSU	14	194	13.9
1965	Skip Thoren, ILL	14	202	14.4
1966	Jim Pitts, NU	14	213	15.2
1967	Bill Hosket, OSU	14	193	13.8
1968	Joe Franklin, WIS	14	195	13.9
1969	Rudy Tomjanovich, MICH	14	179	12.8
1970	Rudy Tomjanovich, MICH	14	227	16.2
1971	George McGinnis, IND	14	209	14.9
1972	Kevin Kunnert, IOWA	14	223	15.9
1973	Kevin Kunnert, IOWA	14	203	14.5
1974	Lindsay Hairston, MSU	14	199	14.2
1975	Lindsay Hairston, MSU	17	192	11.3
1976	Mychal Thompson, MINN	17	209	12.3
1977	Bruce King, IOWA	16	207	12.9
1978	Mychal Thompson, MINN	18	209	11.6
1979	Herb Williams, OSU	18	189	10.5
1980	Herb Williams OSU	18	169	9.4
	Joe Barry Carroll, PUR	18	169	9.4
1981	Clark Kellogg, OSU	18	213	11.8
1982	Clark Kellogg, OSU	18	198	11.0
1983	Kevin Willis, MSU	18	184	10.2
1984	vacated			
1985	Roy Tarpley, MICH	18	178	9.9
1986	Brad Sellers, OSU	18	207	11.5
1987	Ken Norman, ILL	18	173	9.6
1988	Richard Coffey, MINN	18	161	8.9
1989	Ed Horton, IOWA	18	196	10.9
1990	Loy Vaught, MICH	18	192	10.7
1991	Chuckie White, PUR	18	155	8.6
1992	Chris Webber, MICH	18	177	9.8
1993	Chris Webber, MICH	18	175	9.7
1994	Glenn Robinson, PUR	18	177	9.8
1995	Rashard Griffith, WIS	18	201	11.2

Assists

Year	Name/School	G	NO	AVG
1975	Bruce Parkinson, PUR	18	129	7.2
1976	Cal Wulfsberg, IOWA	18	138	7.7
1977	Ray Williams, MINN	18	118	6.6
1978	Earvin Johnson, MSU	18	122	6.8
1979	Earvin Johnson, MSU	18	133	7.4
1980	Kelvin Ransey, OSU	18	115	6.3
1981	Brian Walker, PUR	18	120	6.7
1982	Derek Harper, ILL	18	100	5.6
1983	Bruce Douglas, ILL	18	103	5.7
1984	Bruce Douglas, ILL	18	100	5.6
1985	Steve Reid, PUR	18	104	5.8
1986	Bruce Douglas, ILL	18	111	6.2
1987	Tony Wysinger, ILL	18	110	6.1
1988	Gary Grant, MICH	18	117	6.5
1989	B.J. Armstrong, IOWA	18	103	5.7
1990	Tony Jones, PUR	18	107	5.9
1991	Mark Montgomery, MSU	18	103	5.7
1992	Mark Montgomery, MSU	18	112	6.2
1993	Tracy Webster, WIS	18	114	6.3
1994	Eric Snow, MSU	18	123	6.8
1995	Eric Snow, MSU	18	**141**	**7.8**

Steals

Year	Name/School	G	NO	AVG
1983	Derek Harper, ILL	18	46	2.56
1984	Bruce Douglas, ILL	18	50	2.78
1985	Bruce Douglas, ILL	18	49	2.72
1986	Bruce Douglas, ILL	18	51	2.83
1987	Gary Grant, MICH	18	48	2.67
1988	Gary Grant, MICH	18	49	2.72
1989	Melvin Newbern, MINN	18	**62**	**3.44**
1990	Kendall Gill, ILL	18	35	1.94
1991	Pat Baldwin, NU	18	52	2.89
1992	Chris Webber, MICH	18	35	1.94
1993	Tracy Webster, WIS	18	46	2.56
1994	Tracy Webster, WIS	18	40	2.22
1995	Kenyon Murray, IOWA	18	39	2.17

Blocked Shots

Year	Name/School	G	NO	AVG
1983	Randy Breuer, MINN	18	54	3.00
1984	Uwe Blab, IND	18	36	2.00
1985	Brad Sellers, OSU	18	52	2.89
1986	Roy Tarpley, MICH	18	45	2.50
1987	Dean Garrett, IND	18	51	2.83
1988	Dean Garrett, IND	18	54	3.00
1989	Terry Mills, MICH	18	22	1.22
1990	Matt Steigenga, MSU	18	21	1.17
1991	Acie Earl, IOWA	18	54	3.00
1992	Acie Earl, IOWA	18	**71**	**3.94**
1993	John Amaechi, PSU	18	50	2.78
1994	John Amaechi, PSU	18	39	2.29
1995	Rashard Griffith, WIS	18	43	2.39

Wisconsin's Emmett Angell, who would later coach the Badgers, was the Big Ten's first scoring leader with 96 points in 1906.

Center John Green, who averaged 16.6 boards a game in 1958-59, was part of a Big Ten record-setting Michigan State per game rebounding effort of 63.7 that same season.

Iowa center Acie Earl set the Big Ten Conference games only blocked shots record with 71 in 1992.

RECORDS
Annual Team Statistical Champions (Big Ten records in Bold)

CONFERENCE GAMES ONLY

Scoring

Year	School	G	PTS	AVG
1939	Indiana	12	508	42.3
1940	Indiana	12	519	43.3
1941	Wisconsin	12	536	44.7
1942	Iowa	14	721	51.5
1943	Illinois	12	755	62.9
1944	Ohio State	12	702	58.5
1945	Ohio State	12	632	52.7
1946	Michigan	12	661	55.1
1947	Wisconsin	12	677	56.4
1948	Illinois	12	692	57.7
1949	Illinois	12	783	65.3
1950	Illinois	12	798	66.5
1951	Illinois	14	989	70.6
1952	Illinois	14	1035	73.9
1953	Indiana	18	1452	80.7
1954	Ohio State	14	1087	77.6
1955	Illinois	14	1174	83.9
1956	Illinois	14	1277	91.2
1957	Illinois	14	1108	79.1
1958	Indiana	14	1170	83.6
1959	Illinois	14	1202	85.9
1960	Ohio State	14	1271	90.8
1961	Ohio State	14	1207	86.2
1962	Indiana	14	1214	86.7
1963	Indiana	14	1266	90.4
1964	Michigan State	14	1290	92.1
1965	Michigan	14	1300	92.9
1966	Michigan	14	1336	95.4
1967	Northwestern	14	1239	88.5
1968	Ohio State	15	1302	86.8
1969	Purdue	14	1359	97.1
1970	Iowa	14	1441	**102.9**
1971	Michigan	14	1238	88.4
1972	Michigan	14	1145	81.8
1973	Michigan State	14	1130	80.7
1974	Purdue	14	1206	86.1
1975	Indiana	18	1570	87.2
1976	Michigan	18	1544	85.8
1977	Michigan	18	1498	83.2
1978	Ohio State	18	1375	76.4
1979	Iowa	18	1312	72.9
1980	Illinois	18	1214	67.4
1981	Illinois	18	1335	74.2
1982	Indiana	18	1214	67.4
1983	Ohio State	18	1328	73.8
1984	Illinois	18	1196	66.4
1985	Ohio State	18	1385	76.9
1986	Michigan State	18	1439	79.9
1987	Michigan	18	1561	86.7
1988	Iowa	18	**1642**	91.4
1989	Michigan	18	1581	87.8
1990	Minnesota	18	1487	82.6
1991	Indiana	18	1527	84.8
1992	Indiana	17	1446	80.3
1993	Indiana	18	1550	86.1
1994	Purdue	18	1455	80.8
1995	Iowa	18	1464	81.3

Scoring Defense

Year	School	G	PTS	AVG
1939	Purdue	12	**339**	**28.3**
1940	Purdue	12	407	33.9
1941	Indiana	12	415	34.6
1942	Purdue	15	540	36.0
1943	Illinois	12	465	38.8
1944	Northwestern	12	487	40.1
1945	Iowa	12	486	40.5
1946	Illinois	12	499	41.6
1947	Illinois	12	536	44.7
1948	Michigan	12	556	46.3
1949	Minnesota	12	511	42.6
1950	Wisconsin	12	660	47.1
1951	Indiana	14	748	53.4
1952	Michigan	14	787	56.2
1953	Michigan State	18	1097	60.9
1954	Iowa	14	922	65.9
1955	Minnesota	14	1022	73.0
1956	Iowa	14	979	69.9
1957	Michigan State	14	947	67.6
1958	Michigan State	14	975	69.6
1959	Minnesota	14	957	68.4
1960	Northwestern	14	986	70.4
1961	Iowa	14	859	61.4
1962	Ohio State	14	951	67.9
1963	Minnesota	14	991	70.8
1964	Michigan	14	1057	75.5
1965	Iowa	14	1100	78.6
1966	Michigan State	14	1034	73.9
1967	Michigan State	14	995	71.1
1968	Illinois	14	930	66.4
1969	Illinois	14	1030	73.6
1970	Illinois	14	1053	75.2
1971	Ohio State	14	1019	72.8
1972	Minnesota	14	785	56.1
1973	Indiana	14	975	69.6
1974	Minnesota	14	887	63.4
1975	Minnesota	18	1146	63.7
1976	Indiana	18	1186	65.9
1977	Indiana	18	1243	69.1
1978	Indiana	18	1184	65.8
1979	Iowa	18	1101	61.2
1980	Indiana	18	1125	62.8
1981	Indiana	18	1077	59.8
1982	Iowa	18	1020	56.7
1983	Iowa	18	1127	62.6
1984	Illinois	18	988	54.9
1985	Illinois	18	1002	55.7
1986	Illinois	18	1145	63.3
1987	Illinois	18	1263	70.2
1988	Purdue	18	1271	70.6
1989	Wisconsin	18	1232	68.4
1990	Purdue	18	1228	68.2
1991	Michigan State	18	1192	66.2
1992	Indiana	18	1188	66.0
1993	Michigan State	18	1249	69.4
1994	Michigan State	18	1263	70.2
1995	Michigan State	18	1179	65.5

Scoring Margin

Year	School	Own	OPP	MAR/G
1940	Purdue	42.8	33.9	8.9
1941	Indiana	44.4	34.5	9.9
1942	Illinois	46.2	37.8	8.4
1943	Illinois	61.2	38.7	22.5
1944	Ohio State	58.5	45.7	12.8
1945	Ohio State	52.3	42.4	9.9
1946	Illinois	52.2	41.5	10.7
1947	Illinois	50.0	44.6	5.4
1948	Michigan	53.9	46.3	7.6
1949	Illinois	65.2	56.1	9.1
1950	Ohio State	65.5	56.6	8.9
1951	Indiana	64.1	53.4	10.7
1952	Illinois	72.2	60.7	11.5
1953	Illinois	80.1	67.9	12.2
1954	Indiana	77.3	69.9	7.4
1955	Iowa	81.5	74.7	6.8
1956	Illinois	91.2	78.0	13.2
1957	Indiana	79.7	73.8	5.9
1958	Michigan State	76.5	69.6	6.9
1959	Michigan State	85.6	78.2	7.4
1960	Ohio State	90.7	71.7	19.0
1961	Ohio State	86.2	64.7	21.5
1962	Ohio State	86.3	67.9	18.4
1963	Ohio State	80.0	73.7	6.3
1964	Michigan	85.8	75.5	10.3
1965	Michigan	92.8	80.6	12.2
1966	Michigan	95.4	85.5	9.9
1967	Iowa	84.0	79.5	4.5
1968	Ohio State	93.0	82.9	10.1
1969	Purdue	97.0	81.3	15.7
1970	Iowa	102.9	90.2	12.7
1971	Ohio State	61.6	72.7	8.9
1972	Minnesota	61.5	56.0	5.5
1973	Minnesota	79.7	71.4	8.3
1974	Indiana	80.1	66.1	14.0
1975	Indiana	87.2	64.4	**22.8**
1976	Indiana	81.5	65.8	15.7
1977	Michigan	83.2	73.8	9.4
1978	Michigan State	73.5	67.5	6.0
1979	Purdue	72.8	64.2	8.6
1980	Indiana	66.2	62.5	3.7
1981	Indiana	70.6	59.8	10.8
1982	Minnesota	64.2	58.3	5.9
1983	Indiana	70.8	63.8	7.0
1984	Illinois	66.4	54.8	11.6
1985	Michigan	76.8	68.0	8.8
1986	Michigan	78.8	68.2	10.6
1987	Iowa	83.4	72.8	10.6
1988	Michigan	85.1	74.5	10.6
1989	Michigan	87.8	78.5	9.3
	Illinois	80.4	71.1	9.3
1990	Minnesota	83.3	73.8	9.5
1991	Indiana	84.8	68.8	16.0
1992	Indiana	80.3	66.0	14.3
1993	Indiana	86.1	72.5	13.6
1994	Purdue	80.8	73.9	6.9
1995	Purdue	75.1	66.2	8.9

Most Field Goals

Year	School	G	NO
1940	Indiana	12	216
1941	Indiana	12	210
1942	Indiana	14	288
1943	Illinois	12	325
1944	Ohio State	12	294
1945	Ohio State	12	257
1946	Michigan	12	267

Field Goal Percentage

Year	School	FG	FGA	PCT
1947	Wisconsin	248	833	.298
1948	Minnesota	226	778	.290
1949	Minnesota	228	713	.320
1950	Ohio State	283	812	.349
1951	Northwestern	368	1001	.368
1952	Indiana	277	1079	.349
1953	Indiana	505	1410	.358
1954	Ohio State	381	1010	.377
1955	Iowa	418	1011	.413
1956	Iowa	415	1024	.405
1957	Ohio State	418	969	.431
1958	Northwestern	453	1115	.406
1959	Purdue	458	1066	.430
1960	Ohio State	523	1051	.497
1961	Ohio State	481	972	.495
1962	Ohio State	494	1009	.490
1963	Illinois	482	1063	.453
1964	Ohio State	484	1010	.479
1965	Illinois	534	1108	.482
1966	Michigan	528	1080	.489
1967	Iowa	434	933	.465
1968	Ohio State	512	994	.515
1969	Purdue	526	1032	.510
1970	Ohio State	490	896	.547
1971	Ohio State	437	902	.484
1972	Michigan	443	977	.453
1973	Michigan State	479	1004	.477
1974	Michigan State	462	899	.514
1975	Indiana	**652**	**1271**	.513
1976	Michigan	636	1221	.521
1977	Minnesota	575	1120	.513
1978	Minnesota	551	1150	.522
1979	Michigan State	477	946	.504
1980	Minnesota	507	990	.512
1981	Indiana	490	906	.541
1982	Indiana	459	902	.499
1983	Indiana	472	904	.522
1984	Indiana	434	819	.530
1985	Michigan State	516	964	.535

1986	Michigan State	581	1051	.553
1987	Michigan State	516	980	.527
1988	Purdue	516	957	.539
1989	Michigan	606	1080	**.561**
1990	Purdue	482	876	.550
1991	Indiana	537	1025	.524
1992	Michigan State	485	979	.495
1993	Indiana	540	1044	.517
1994	Indiana	498	1032	.483
1995	Indiana	502	1022	.491

Field Goal Defense

Year	School	FG	FGA	AVG
1974	Indiana	379	852	.445
1975	Indiana	478	1094	.437
1976	Indiana	471	1045	.451
1977	Minnesota	535	1235	.433
1978	Purdue	530	1228	.432
1979	Illinois	441	1033	.427
1980	Indiana	433	986	.439
1981	Indiana	407	962	.423
1982	Indiana	423	992	.426
1983	Indiana	454	1045	.434
1984	Illinois	402	903	.445
1985	Illinois	416	953	.437
1986	Illinois	502	1069	.470
1987	Illinois	466	1031	.452
1988	Purdue	505	1088	.464
1989	Indiana	465	1074	.433
1990	Michigan State	453	1027	.441
1991	Michigan State	428	988	.433
1992	Indiana	453	1035	.420
1993	Michigan State	454	1108	.410
1994	Wisconsin	446	1043	.428
1995	Michigan	378	959	**.394**

Most Three-Point Field Goals

Year	School	G	NO
1983	Purdue	18	52
1987	Michigan	18	89
1988	Iowa	18	107
1989	Michigan	18	103
1990	Michigan State	18	96
1991	Michigan	18	118
1992	Wisconsin	18	116
1993	Wisconsin	18	138
1994	Wisconsin	18	130
1995	Iowa	18	**158**

Three-Point Field Goal Percentage

Year	School	FG	FGA	PCT
1983	Indiana	30	53	**.566**
1987	Illinois	75	153	.490
1988	Indiana	64	128	.500
1989	Indiana	72	145	.497
1990	Purdue	60	129	.465
1991	Wisconsin	115	271	.424
1992	Illinois	87	185	.470
1993	Indiana	118	270	.437
1994	Indiana	108	242	.446
1995	Michigan State	104	261	.398

Most Free Throws

Year	School	G	NO
1940	Purdue	12	130
1941	Wisconsin	12	148
1942	Northwestern	14	161
1943	Indiana	12	139
1944	Purdue	12	118
1945	Iowa	12	146
1946	Minnesota	12	172

Free Throw Percentage

Year	School	FT	FTA	PCT
1947	Indiana	171	258	.663
1948	Wisconsin	168	253	.664
1949	Purdue	209	308	.641
1950	Wisconsin	179	265	.675
1951	Minnesota	172	234	.735
1952	Iowa	264	390	.677
1953	Minnesota	385	558	.690
1954	Wisconsin	324	457	.707
1955	Indiana	356	480	.742
1956	Illinois	337	453	.743
1957	Indiana	387	490	.734
1958	Michigan	251	342	.734
1959	Ohio State	278	390	.713
1960	Michigan State	231	318	.726
1961	Ohio State	245	330	.742
1962	Ohio State	221	297	.744
1963	Indiana	328	429	.765
1964	Indiana	257	339	.758
1965	Indiana	271	347	.781
1966	Purdue	285	371	.768
1967	Iowa	308	405	.760
1968	Purdue	277	380	.729
1969	Purdue	307	381	**.806**
1970	Iowa	323	405	.798
1971	Iowa	246	319	.771
1972	Indiana	259	354	.731
1973	Ohio State	227	304	.747
1974	Minnesota	174	225	.740
1975	Michigan	303	400	.758
1976	Michigan State	312	401	.778
1977	Purdue	312	413	.755
1978	Northwestern	313	421	.743
1979	Iowa	302	415	.728
1980	Illinois	290	375	.773
1981	Indiana	292	379	.770
1982	Indiana	314	421	.746
1983	Indiana	301	391	.770
1984	Ohio State	269	346	.777
1985	Minnesota	203	266	.763
1986	Illinois	195	245	.796
1987	Indiana	329	426	.772
1988	Indiana	288	369	.780
1989	Ohio State	301	389	.774
1990	Indiana	322	426	.756
1991	Northwestern	259	342	.757
1992	Northwestern	288	379	.760
1993	Northwestern	273	364	.750
1994	Indiana	321	421	.762
1995	Penn State	266	370	.719

Rebounds

Year	School	G	NO	AVG
1958	Indiana	14	665	47.5
1959	Michigan State	14	**892**	**63.7**
1960	Michigan State	14	760	54.3
1961	Indiana	14	744	53.1
1962	Ohio State	14	644	46.0
1963	Michigan	14	680	49.0
1964	Michigan State	14	730	52.1
1965	Michigan	14	593	49.5
1966	Northwestern	14	634	45.3
1967	Northwestern	14	660	47.1
1968	Northwestern	14	648	46.3
1969	Indiana	14	609	43.5
1970	Purdue	14	611	43.6
1971	Indiana	14	724	51.7
1972	Michigan	14	722	51.6
1973	Minnesota	14	684	49.0
1974	Purdue	14	645	46.1
1975	not available			
1976	Purdue	18	770	42.8
1977	Iowa	18	806	44.8
1978	Purdue	18	781	43.4
1979	Illinois	18	698	38.8
1980	Ohio State	18	662	36.8
1981	Ohio State	18	664	36.9
1982	Indiana	18	667	37.1
1983	Michigan	18	625	34.7
1984	Illinois	18	599	33.3
1985	Iowa	18	698	38.8
1986	Michigan	18	632	35.1
1987	Iowa	18	760	42.2
1988	Iowa	18	664	36.9
1989	Iowa	18	712	39.6
1990	Iowa	18	700	38.9
1991	Illinois	18	626	34.8
	Minnesota	18	626	34.8
1992	Michigan	18	688	38.2
1993	Michigan	18	737	40.9
1994	Iowa	18	702	39.0
1995	Minnesota	18	684	38.0

Rebound Margin

Year	School	Own	OPP	MAR/G
1974	Wisconsin	44.8	37.1	7.7
1976	Indiana	41.2	34.0	7.2
1977	Minnesota	41.0	36.3	4.7
1978	Michigan State	38.6	34.1	4.5
1979	Wisconsin	37.4	33.6	3.8
1980	Wisconsin	35.7	31.9	3.8
1981	Ohio State	36.9	32.8	4.1
1982	Indiana	37.1	32.7	4.4
1983	Illinois	32.4	29.0	3.4
1984	Illinois	33.3	25.4	7.9
1985	Iowa	38.8	31.8	7.0
1986	Michigan	35.1	29.3	5.8
1987	Iowa	42.2	29.6	**12.6**
1988	Iowa	36.9	31.5	5.4
1989	Iowa	39.6	32.0	7.6
1990	Minnesota	35.9	29.9	6.0
1991	Ohio State	34.3	29.2	5.1
1992	Michigan	38.2	32.4	5.8
1993	Michigan	40.9	33.3	7.6
1994	Illinois	34.4	31.1	3.4
1995	Michigan State	37.4	32.4	5.1

Steals

Year	School	G	NO	AVG
1986	Michigan	18	155	8.61
1987	Illinois	18	150	8.33
1988	Illinois	18	149	8.28
1989	Minnesota	18	162	9.00
1990	Minnesota	18	146	8.11
1991	Iowa	18	167	9.28
1992	Indiana	18	141	7.83
1993	Iowa	18	154	8.56
1994	Iowa	18	**184**	**10.22**
1995	Iowa	18	176	9.78

Blocked Shots

Year	School	G	NO	AVG
1982	Illinois	18	66	3.67
1983	Minnesota	18	89	4.94
1985	Ohio State	18	75	4.17
1986	Michigan	18	71	3.94
1987	Illinois	18	85	4.72
1988	Indiana	18	68	3.78
1990	Michigan	18	71	3.94
1991	Iowa	18	79	4.39
1992	Iowa	18	**92**	**5.11**
1993	Michigan	18	90	5.00
1994	Wisconsin	18	79	4.39
1995	Indiana	18	82	4.56

Turnover Margin

Year	School	OPP	Own	MAR/G
1986	Iowa	16.6	13.0	3.6
1987	Ohio State	16.8	13.5	3.3
1988	Illinois	18.1	14.9	3.2
1989	Minnesota	16.5	13.9	2.6
1990	Illinois	15.7	12.2	3.5
1991	Indiana	18.1	13.2	4.9
1992	Indiana	16.4	**12.1**	4.3
1993	Wisconsin	17.4	13.2	4.2
1994	Minnesota	15.6	11.9	3.7
1995	Iowa	**19.1**	14.1	**5.0**

RECORDS

1,000-POINT CLUB *(Conference games only)*

1,545 Shawn Respert, Michigan State 1992-278, 1993-352, 1994-456, 1995-459
1,503 Mike McGee, Michigan 1978-299, 1979-396, 1980-380, 1981-428
1,477 Mychal Thompson, Minnesota 1975-210, 1976-448, 1977-410, 1978-409
1,461 Rick Mount, Purdue 1968-416, 1969-493, 1970-552
1,451 Don Schlundt, Indiana 1952-244, 1953-459, 1954-379, 1955-369
1,406 Calbert Cheaney, Indiana 1990-294, 1991-383, 1992-343, 1993-386
1,385 Michael Finley, Wisconsin 1992-240, 1993-417, 1994-362, 1995-366
1,361 Steve Alford, Indiana 1984-304, 1985-262, 1986-404, 1987-391
1,358 Scott Skiles, Michigan State 1983-255, 1984-241, 1985-338, 1986-524
1,279 Mike Woodson, Indiana 1977-396, 1978-355, 1979-405, 1980-123
1,266 Glen Rice, Michigan 1986-99, 1987-307, 1988-413, 1989-447
1,248 Terry Dischinger, Purdue 1960-384, 1961-405, 1962-459
1,247 Herb Williams, Ohio State 1978-269, 1979-365, 1980-330, 1981-283
1,237 Gary Grant, Michigan 1985-242, 1986-229, 1987-382, 1988-384
1,232 Steve Smith, Michigan State 1988-199, 1989-292, 1990-323, 1991-418
1,230 Jay Vincent, Michigan State 1978-179, 1979-221, 1980-397, 1981-433
1,221 Dave Schellhase, Purdue 1964-379, 1965-391, 1966-451
1,212 Voshon Lenard, Minnesota 1992-219, 1993-300, 1994-388, 1995-305
1,210 Terry Furlow, Michigan State 1973-67, 1974-222, 1975-363, 1976-558
     Brad Sellers, Wisconsin/Ohio State 1982-255, 1983-217 (at Wisconsin), 1985-265, 1986-373 (at Ohio State)
1,207 Deon Thomas, Illinois 1991-220, 1992-343, 1993-317, 1994-327
1,197 Billy McKinney, Northwestern 1974-226, 1975-314, 1976-334, 1977-323
1,190 Walter Jordan, Purdue 1975-249, 1976-313, 1977-334, 1978-294
1,185 Kelvin Ransey, Ohio State 1975-209, 1978-341, 1979-363, 1980-272
1,181 Troy Lewis, Purdue 1985-185, 1986-331, 1987-359, 1988-306
1,177 Gregory Kelser, Michigan State 1976-228, 1977-362, 1978-292, 1979-295
1,171 Cazzie Russell, Michigan 1964-366, 1965-340, 1966-465
1,169 Joe Barry Carroll, Purdue 1977-140, 1978-259, 1979-429, 1980-341
1,147 Claude Gregory, Wisconsin 1978-200, 1979-264, 1980-319, 1981-364
1,134 Willie Burton, Minnesota 1987-151, 1988-283, 1989-334, 1990-366
1,122 Danny Jones, Wisconsin 1987-139, 1988-298, 1989-376, 1990-309
1,121 Dennis Hopson, Ohio State 1984-77, 1985-184, 1986-350, 1987-510
1,119 Sam Vincent, Michigan State 1982-217, 1983-301, 1984-174, 1985-427
1,113 Roy Marble, Iowa 1986-207, 1987-241, 1988-289, 1989-376
1,108 Rick Olson, Wisconsin 1983-188, 1984-260, 1985-293, 1986-367
1,093 Kevin McHale, Minnesota 1977-212, 1978-246, 1979-346, 1980-289
1,086 Shawn Respert, Michigan State 1992-278, 1993-352, 1994-456
1,077 Jim Jackson, Ohio State 1990-325, 1991-356, 1992-396
1,068 Alan Henderson, Indiana 1992-181, 1993-138, 1994-333, 1995-416
1,059 Rudy Tomjanovich, Michigan 1968-264, 1969-351, 1970-444
1,054 Randy Breuer, Minnesota 1980-117, 1981-293, 1982-267, 1983-377
1,048 Mike Robinson, Michigan State 1972-381, 1973-374, 1974-293
1,027 Paul Ebert, Ohio State 1952-300, 1953-406, 1954-321
1,026 Ronnie Lester, Iowa 1977-275, 1978-356, 1979-354, 1980-41
1,024 Calbert Cheaney, Indiana 1990-294, 1991-383, 1992-343
1,019 Jerry Lucus, Ohio State 1960-362, 1961-345, 1962-312
     Michael Finley, Wisconsin 1992-240, 1993-417, 1994-362
     Glenn Robinson, Purdue 1993-459, 1994-560
1,014 Henry Wilmore, Michigan 1971-390, 1972-328, 1973-312
1,010 Cuonzo Martin, Purdue 1992-190, 1993-333, 1994-289, 1995-356
1,009 Greg Stokes, Iowa 1982-97, 1983-302, 1984-260, 1985-350
1,004 Kent Benson, Indiana 1974-127, 1975-253, 1976-328, 1977-296
     Eugene Parker, Purdue 1975-173, 1976-307, 1077-268, 1978-256
1,000 Allan Hornyak, Ohio State 1971-329, 1972-326, 1973-345

Shawn Respert, Michigan State (1992-95)
1,000-point club leader

2,000-POINT CLUB *(all games)*

2,613 Calbert Cheaney, Indiana (1990-93)
2,531 Shawn Respert, Michigan State (1992-95)
2,442 Glen Rice, Michigan (1986-89)
2,439 Mike McGee, Michigan (1978-81)
2,438 Steve Alford, Indiana (1984-87)
2,323 Rick Mount, Purdue (1968-70)
2,263 Steve Smith, Michigan State (1988-91)
2,222 Gary Grant, Michigan (1985-88)
2,192 Don Schlundt, Indiana (1952-55)
2,175 Joe Barry Carroll, Purdue (1977-80)
2,164 Cazzie Russell, Michigan (1964-66)
2,147 Michael Finley, Wisconsin (1992-95)
2,145 Scott Skiles, Michigan State (1983-86)
2,129 Deon Thomas, Illinois (1991-94)
2,116 Roy Marble, Iowa (1986-89)
2,103 Voshon Lenard, Minnesota (1992-95)
2,096 Dennis Hopson, Ohio State (1984-87)
2,074 Dave Schellhase, Purdue (1964-66)
2,061 Mike Woodson, Indiana (1977-80)
2,028 Troy Lewis, Purdue (1985-88)
2,014 Gregory Kelser, Michigan State (1976-79)
2,011 Herb Williams, Ohio State (1976-79)

Calbert Cheaney, Indiana (1990-93)
2,000-point club leader

ALL-TIME STANDINGS
(from 1905 as Big Ten Conference member only)

School (started Big Ten play)	Won	Lost	PCT	Years	Games
Indiana (1905)	713	482	.597	88a	1195
Purdue (1905)	721	508	.587	90	1229
Illinois (1905)	715	531	.575	90	1246
Michigan (1917)	594	516	.535	78	1110
Ohio State (1912)	602	556	.520	83	1158
Iowa (1908)	582	571	.505	83b	1153
Michigan State (1950)	358	360	.499	44	718
*Minnesota (1905)	592	645	.479	88	1237
#Wisconsin (1905)	545	699	.438	90	1244
Chicago (1905)	168	296	.362	40c	464
Northwestern (1908)	395	801	.330	87	1196
Penn State (1993)	17	37	.315	3	54
Totals	6002	6002	.500	90	(6,002)

a missed 1906-07, 1907-08 seasons
b missed 1929-30 season
c missed 1944-45 season; dropped out of Conference after 1945-46 season

Playoff Games *(not included in above totals)*
1908—Chicago 18, Wisconsin 16 (played at Wisconsin-1,500 attendance)
1968—Ohio State 85, Iowa 81 (at Purdue-4,812)
1974—Michigan 75, Indiana 67 (at Illinois-15,109)

Fred Taylor coached Ohio State to a record five consecutive Big Ten titles from 1960-64, three NCAA championship finals appearances and a national title in 1960.

ALL-TIME TEAM VS. TEAM RECORDS (from 1905)
(Includes results of all games, whether or not a Big Ten member)

	vs. CHI W-L	vs. ILL W-L	vs. IND W-L	vs. IOWA W-L	vs. MICH W-L	vs. MSU W-L	vs. MINN W-L	vs. NU W-L	vs. OSU W-L	vs. PSU W-L	vs. PUR W-L	vs. WIS W-L	WON	LOST	PCT
Chicago	—	29-39	13-24	17-33	10-27	3-2	25-38	28-29	16-28	0-0	21-36	21-47	183	303	.377
Illinois	39-29	—	62-71	60-58	64-63	42-37	91-56	103-32	87-54	5-3	72-73	94-59	719	535	.573
Indiana	24-13	71-62	—	83-55	79-47	54-30	81-50	90-39	82-62	8-0	70-96	83-46	729	500	.593
Iowa	33-17	58-60	55-83	—	45-70	44-42	74-84	90-45	59-58	5-3	57-68	68-56	588	586	.501
Michigan	27-10	63-64	47-79	70-45	—	83-56	66-52	85-46	61-74	4-2	51-65	80-44	637	537	.543
Michigan State	2-3	37-42	30-54	42-44	56-83	—	38-49	55-34	45-43	7-1	29-52	51-44	392	449	.466
*Minnesota	38-25	56-91	50-81	84-74	52-66	49-38	—	80-50	43-68	5-2	64-79	92-70	613	642	.488
Northwestern	29-28	32-103	39-90	45-90	46-85	34-55	50-80	—	42-91	2-5	34-102	54-87	407	816	.336
Ohio State	28-16	54-87	62-86	58-59	74-61	43-45	68-43	91-42	—	7-4	64-72	71-51	620	566	.523
Penn State	0-0	3-5	0-8	3-5	2-4	1-7	2-5	5-2	4-7	—	2-6	3-3	24	52	.316
Purdue	36-21	73-72	96-70	68-57	65-51	52-29	79-64	102-34	72-64	6-2	—	90-51	725	511	.587
#Wisconsin	47-21	59-94	46-83	56-68	44-80	44-51	70-92	87-54	51-71	3-3	51-90	—	558	707	.441

* NCAA declared all games forfeited in 1976-77 season (included in all totals)
# forfeited all games in 1981-82, 1982-83 and 1983-84 seasons (included in all totals)

BIG TEN TEAM CHAMPIONSHIPS

20	Purdue	1911c-12c-21c-22-26c-28c-30-32-34-35c-36c-38-40-69-79c-84c-87c-88-94-95
19	Indiana	1926c-28c-36c-53-54-57c-58-67c-73-74c-75-76-80-81-83-87c-89-91c-93
15	Ohio State	1925-33c-39-44-46-50-60-61-62-63c-64c-68c-71-91c-92
14	Wisconsin	1907c-08c-12c-13-14-16-18-21c-23c-24c-29c-35c-41-47
12	Michigan	1921c-26c-27-29c-48-64c-65-66-74c-77-85-86
12	Illinois	1915-17c-24c-35c-37c-42-43-49-51-52-63c-84c
8	Minnesota	1906-07c-11c-17c-19-37c-72-82
8	Iowa	1923c-26c-45-55-56-68c-70-79c
6	Michigan State	1957c-59-67c-78-79c-90
6	Chicago	1907c-08c-09-10-20-24c
2	Northwestern	1931-33c

c-cochampionship

RECORDS

OUTSIDE THE FAMILY
Year-by-year record of Big Ten teams vs. nonconference teams (includes postseason play)

Year	Won	Lost	PCT	Accumulated Won	Accumulated Lost	Year	Won	Lost	PCT	Accumulated Won	Accumulated Lost	Year	Won	Lost	PCT	Accumulated Won	Accumulated Lost
1905-06	26	14	.650			1936-37	56	19	.747	1286	461	1966-67	60	37	.619	2910	1352
1906-07	25	6	.806	51	20	1937-38	53	22	.706	1339	483	1967-68	57	44	.564	2967	1396
1907-08	46	8	.852	97	28	1938-39	57	23	.713	1396	506	1968-69	71	32	.689	3038	1428
1908-09	23	7	.767	120	35	1939-40	60	23	.723	1456	529	1969-70	57	43	.570	3095	1471
1909-10	21	2	**.913**	141	37	1940-41	56	24	.700	1512	553	1970-71	60	42	.588	3155	1513
1910-11	29	6	.829	170	43	1941-42	35	24	.593	1547	577	1971-72	65	36	.644	3220	1549
1911-12	29	8	.784	199	51	1942-43	40	27	.597	1587	604	1972-73	71	35	.670	3291	1584
1912-13	44	14	.788	243	65	1943-44	39	46	.459	1626	650	1973-74	69	42	.622	3360	1626
1913-14	39	12	.765	282	80	1944-45	47	24	.662	1673	674	1974-75	58	33	.637	3418	1659
1914-15	41	6	.872	323	86	1945-46	63	20	.759	1736	694	1975-76	73	24	.753	3491	1683
1915-16	55	9	.859	378	95	1946-47	49	25	.662	1785	719	1976-77	60	37	.619	3551	1720
1916-17	47	12	.797	425	107	1947-48	49	24	.671	1834	743	1977-78	61	34	.642	3612	1754
1917-18	47	11	.810	472	118	1948-49	66	19	.776	1900	762	1978-79	84	28	.750	3696	1782
1918-19	48	16	.750	520	34	1949-50	74	20	.787	1974	782	1979-80	92	26	.780	3788	1808
1919-20	71	22	.763	591	156	1950-51	53	31	.631	2027	813	1980-81	84	28	.750	3872	1836
1920-21	46	14	.767	637	170	1951-52	55	29	.655	2082	842	1981-82	62	46	.574	3934	1882
1921-22	59	20	.747	696	190	1952-53	30	14	.682	2112	856	1982-83	92	26	.780	4026	1908
1922-23	19	11	.633	715	201	1953-54	60	22	.732	2172	878	1983-84	81	32	.717	4107	1940
1923-24	34	15	.694	749	216	1954-55	57	27	.679	2229	905	1984-85	94	28	.771	4201	1968
1924-25	26	17	.605	775	233	1955-56	54	30	.643	2283	935	1985-86	100	29	.775	4301	1997
1925-26	33	16	.673	808	249	1956-57	49	35	.583	2332	970	1986-87	99	31	.762	4400	2028
1926-27	31	18	.633	839	267	1957-58	48	34	.585	2380	1004	1987-88	90	38	.703	4490	2066
1927-28	33	18	.647	872	285	1958-59	49	32	.605	2429	1036	1988-89	**119**	29	.804	4609	2095
1928-29	38	11	.776	910	296	1959-60	61	36	.629	2490	1072	1989-90	96	25	.793	4705	2120
1929-30	34	20	.630	944	316	1960-61	56	44	.560	2546	1116	1990-91	90	32	.738	4795	2152
1930-31	40	10	.800	984	326	1961-62	64	36	.640	2610	1152	1991-92	98	34	.742	4893	2186
1931-32	38	17	.691	1022	343	1962-63	55	45	.550	2665	1197	1992-93	104	31	.770	4997	2217
1932-33	43	26	.623	1065	369	1963-64	58	42	.580	2723	1239	1993-94	103	29	.781	5100	2246
1933-34	49	28	.636	1114	397	1964-65	69	32	.683	2792	1271	1994-95	87	44	.664	5187	2290
1934-35	55	24	.696	1169	421	1965-66	58	44	.569	2850	1315						
1935-36	61	21	.744	1230	442												

STATISTICAL TRENDS
(Game averages–both teams, Conference games only)

	1956	1957	1958	1959	1960	1961	1962	1963	1964	1965	1966	1967	1968	1969
Points Scored	155.9	147.7	151.6	159.3	151.9	143.1	159.8	156.7	167.8	169.6	163.9	164.2	155.2	161.0
Personal Fouls	38.1	35.8	35.6	37.1	35.8	37.0	39.2	37.7	39.1	39.5	38.4	40.5	39.5	40.1
Field Goals Attempted	151.4	149.2	156.3	**158.5**	143.8	138.6	145.6	145.0	155.6	152.9	146.4	146.1	140.2	137.1
Field Goals Made	56.3	57.9	58.6	62.8	60.1	55.6	61.4	60.7	66.1	66.5	63.6	63.6	59.6	61.1
Field Goals Pct.	.372	.386	.375	.396	.418	.401	.421	.419	.425	.435	.434	.435	.426	.446
Free Throws Attempted	**63.6**	49.2	50.4	51.7	46.4	48.4	52.9	50.2	51.6	52.4	50.3	53.5	52.5	53.9
Free Throws Made	**43.4**	32.4	34.4	33.7	31.7	32.0	37.1	35.3	35.6	36.6	36.7	37.0	35.9	38.8
Free Throws Pct.	.682	.657	.683	.652	.682	.661	.701	.702	.690	.700	.729	.692	.684	.721

	1970	1971	1972	1973	1974	1975	1976	1977	1978	1979	1980	1981	1982	1983
Points Scored	**171.3**	165.0	147.6	155.0	150.6	148.1	155.3	148.1	145.3	134.8	135.0	137.9	123.1	134.8
Personal Fouls	37.7	37.7	37.6	39.8	39.0	39.3	40.8	41.1	41.2	40.4	40.7	40.8	36.8	38.3
Field Goals Attempted	143.3	144.1	131.0	141.3	133.7	131.9	132.8	127.3	123.6	115.7	112.4	111.3	103.1	109.0
Field Goals Made	**67.5**	64.2	57.1	63.4	62.6	60.6	62.8	58.7	59.9	53.9	53.1	54.6	48.4	51.8
Field Goals Pct.	.471	.445	.435	.448	.468	.459	.473	.461	.484	.466	.472	.490	.469	.475
Free Throws Attempted	49.7	52.2	42.4	41.0	36.0	38.3	40.7	42.1	42.6	38.5	39.6	39.9	37.9	39.5
Free Throws Made	36.3	37.7	27.5	28.3	25.3	27.0	29.7	30.3	30.0	26.9	28.2	28.7	26.5	27.9
Free Throws Pct.	.730	.703	.651	.690	.703	.705	.730	.719	.705	.698	.713	.718	.699	.706
3-pt. Attempts														8.7
3-pt. Made														3.4
3-pt. Pct.														.387

	1984	1985	1986	1987	1988	1989	1990	1991	1992	1993	1994	1995
Points Scored	123.9	134.7	143.3	151.9	151.5	150.4	151.8	142.3	141.2	145.7	150.4	143.1
Personal Fouls	37.1	38.8	35.1	38.4	35.8	41.4	**41.7**	39.4	37.4	37.1	38.2	39.5
Field Goals Attempted	100.4	113.8	115.5	115.0	115.5	113.8	113.7	110.3	110.7	115.7	118.4	115.5
Field Goals Made	48.7	54.7	57.9	57.5	57.3	56.0	53.4	51.6	51.1	52.9	54.2	51.4
Field Goals Pct.	.485	.481	**.503**	.491	.496	.492	.470	.468	.461	.457	.458	.445
Free Throws Attempted	36.4	34.7	37.1	40.9	42.5	42.2	45.5	44.2	43.8	43.4	42.5	43.0
Free Throws Made	26.3	27.5	25.2	29.4	30.2	29.8	31.9	30.3	30.5	30.5	29.9	29.1
Free Throws Pct.	.723	.726	**.743**	.719	.710	.708	.701	.685	.697	.702	.703	.677
3-pt. Attempts				18.0	16.5	20.9	20.7	22.9	22.4	25.9	**32.7**	32.2
3-pt. Made				7.5	6.8	8.5	8.1	8.7	8.5	9.4	**12.1**	11.3
3-pt. Pct.				**.417**	.411	.409	.391	.381	.379	.363	.369	.352

Postseason History

NCAA DIVISION I CHAMPIONSHIP RESULTS

1939–Oregon 46, **Ohio State** 33
1940–**Indiana** 60, Kansas 40
1941–**Wisconsin** 39, Washington State 34
1942–Stanford 53, Dartmouth 38
1943–Wyoming 46, Georgetown 34
1944–Utah 42, Dartmouth 40 (OT)
1945–Oklahoma State 49, New York U. 45
1946–Oklahoma State 43, North Carolina 40
1947–Holy Cross 58, Oklahoma 47
1948–Kentucky 58, Baylor 42
1949–Kentucky 46, Oklahoma State 36
1950–CCNY 71, Bradley 68
1951–Kentucky 68, Kansas State 58
1952–Kansas 80, St. John's 63
1953–**Indiana** 69, Kansas 68
1954–LaSalle 92, Bradley 76
1955–San Francisco 77, LaSalle 63
1956–San Francisco 83, **Iowa** 71
1957–North Carolina 54, Kansas 53 (OT)
1958–Kentucky 84, Seattle 72
1959–California 71, West Virginia 70
1960–**Ohio State** 75, California 55
1961–Cincinnati 70, **Ohio State** 65 (OT)
1962–Cincinnati 71, **Ohio State** 59
1963–Loyola 60, Cincinnati 58 (OT)
1964–UCLA 98, Duke 83
1965–UCLA 91, **Michigan** 80
1966–Texas Western 72, Kentucky 65
1967–UCLA 79, Dayton 64
1968–UCLA 78, North Carolina 55
1969–UCLA 92, **Purdue** 72
1970–UCLA 80, Jacksonville 69
1971–UCLA 68, Villanova 62
1972–UCLA 81, Florida State 76
1973–UCLA 87, Memphis State 66
1974–North Carolina State 76, Marquette 64
1975–UCLA 92, Kentucky 85
1976–**Indiana** 86, **Michigan** 68
1977–Marquette 67, North Carolina 59
1978–Kentucky 94, Duke 88
1979–**Michigan State** 74, Indiana State 64
1980–Louisville 59, UCLA 54
1981–**Indiana** 63, North Carolina 50
1982–North Carolina 63, Georgetown 62
1983–North Carolina State 54, Houston 52
1984–Georgetown 84, Houston 75
1985–Villanova 66, Georgetown 64
1986–Louisville 72, Duke 69
1987–**Indiana** 74, Syracuse 73
1988–Kansas 83, Oklahoma 79
1989–**Michigan** 80, Seton Hall 79 (OT)
1990–Nevada-Las Vegas 103, Duke 73
1991–Duke 72, Kansas 65
1992–Duke 71, **Michigan** 51
1993–North Carolina 77, **Michigan** 71
1994–Arkansas 76, Duke 72
1995-UCLA 89, Arkansas 78

BIG TEN IN THE NCAA CHAMPIONSHIP

	Appearances	Won	Lost	PCT	1st	2nd	3rd	4th
Indiana	24	50	19	.725	5	0	2	0
(**1940-53**-54-58-67-73-75-**76**-78-80-**81**-1982-83-84-86-**87**-88-89-90-91-92-93-94-95)								
Michigan	18	40	17	.702	1	4	1	0
(1948-64-65-66-74-75-76-77-85-86-87-88-**89**-90-92-93-94-95)								
Wisconsin	3	5	2	.714	1	0	0	0
(**1941**-47-94)								
Ohio State	18	31	17	.646	1	3	4	0
(1939-44-45-46-50-**60**-61-62-68-71-80-82-83-85-87-90-91-92)								
Michigan State	11	17	11	.607	1	0	0	1
(1957-59-78-**79**-85-86-90-91-92-94-95)								
Minnesota	5	7	5	.583	0	0	0	0
(1982-89-90-94-95)*								
Iowa	16	22	18	.550	0	1	0	2
(1955-56-70-79-80-81-82-83-85-86-87-88-89-91-92-93)								
Purdue	14	17	14	.548	0	1	1	0
(1969-77-80-83-84-85-86-87-88-90-91-93-94-95)								
Illinois	17	21	18	.538	0	0	4	0
(1942-49-51-52-63-81-83-84-85-86-87-88-89-90-93-94-95)								
TOTALS	126	210	121	.634	9	9	12	3

*1972 appearance voided; record adjusted by NCAA Committee on Infractions
NCAA champions in **bold**

BIG TEN IN THE NATIONAL INVITATION TOURNAMENT

	Appearances	Won	Lost	PCT	1st	2nd	3rd	4th
Indiana	3	8	2	.800	1	1	0	0
(1972-**79**-85)								
Purdue	6	18	5	.783	1	2	1	0
(1971-**74**-79-81-82-92)								
Penn State	1	3	1	.750	0	0	1	0
(1995)								
Michigan	5	10	4	.714	1	0	0	0
(1971-80-81-**84**-91)								
Illinois	2	5	2	.714	0	0	1	0
(1980-82)								
Minnesota	6	12	5	.706	1	1	0	0
(1973-80-81-83-92-**93**)								
Ohio State	6	13	6	.684	1	1	0	1
(1979-84-**86**-88-89-93)								
Iowa	1	2	1	.667	0	0	0	0
(1995)								
Michigan State	3	4	4	.500	0	0	1	0
(1983-89-93)								
Northwestern	2	2	2	.500	0	0	0	0
(1983-94)								
Wisconsin	3	2	3	.400	0	0	0	0
(1989-91-93)								
TOTALS	38	81	35	.698	5	5	4	1

NATIONAL INVITATION TOURNAMENT CHAMPIONS

1938–Temple
1939–Long Island
1940–Colorado
1941–Long Island
1942–West Virginia
1943–St. Johns
1944–St. Johns
1945–De Paul
1946–Kentucky
1947–Utah
1948–St. Louis
1949–San Francisco
1950–City University of New York
1951–Brigham Young
1952–La Salle
1953–Seton Hall
1954–Holy Cross
1955–Duquesne
1956–Louisville
1957–Bradley
1958–Xavier (Ohio)
1959–St. Johns
1960–Bradley
1961–Providence
1962–Dayton
1963–Providence
1964–Bradley
1965–St. Johns
1966–Brigham Young
1967–Southern Illinois
1968–Dayton
1969–Temple
1970–Marquette
1971–North Carolina
1972–Maryland
1973–Virginia Tech
1974–**Purdue**
1975–Princeton
1976–Kentucky
1977–St. Bonaventure
1978–Texas
1979–**Indiana**
1980–Virginia
1981–Tulsa
1982–Bradley
1983–Fresno State
1984–**Michigan**
1985–UCLA
1986–**Ohio State**
1987–Southern Mississippi
1988–Connecticut
1989–St. Johns
1990–Vanderbilt
1991–Stanford
1992–Virginia
1993–**Minnesota**
1994–Villanova
1995-Virginia Tech

RECORDS
NCAA Championship Results

1939 (1 team appeared; 2-1 record)
OHIO STATE 64, Wake Forest 52 (1st round)
OHIO STATE 53, Villanova 36 (semifinal)
Oregon 46, OHIO STATE 33 (championship)

1940 (1; 3-0)
INDIANA 48, Springfield 24 (1st round)
INDIANA 39, Duquesne 30 (semifinal)
INDIANA 60, Kansas State 42 (championship)

1941 (1; 3-0)
WISCONSIN 51, Dartmouth 50 (1st round)
WISCONSIN 36, Pittsburgh 30 (semifinal)
WISCONSIN 39, Washington State 34 (championship)

1942 (1; 0-2)
Kentucky 46, ILLINOIS 44 (1st round)
Penn State 41, ILLINOIS 34 (regional 3rd place)

1944 (1; 1-1)
OHIO STATE 54, Tennessee 47 (1st round)
Dartmouth 60, OHIO STATE 53 (semifinal)

1945 (1; 1-1)
OHIO STATE 45, Kentucky 37 (1st round)
New York 70, OHIO STATE 65 (OT) (semifinal)

1946 (1; 2-1)
OHIO STATE 46, Harvard 38 (1st round)
North Carolina 60, OHIO STATE 57 (semifinal)
OHIO STATE 63, California 45 (3rd place)

1947 (1; 1-1)
CCNY 70, WISCONSIN 56 (1st round)
WISCONSIN 50, Navy 49 (regional 3rd place)

1948 (1; 1-1)
Holy Cross 63, MICHIGAN 45 (1st round)
MICHIGAN 66, Colorado 49 (regional 3rd place)

1949 (1; 2-1)
ILLINOIS 71, Yale 67 (1st round)
Kentucky 76, ILLINOIS 47 (semifinal)
ILLINOIS 57, Oregon 53 (3rd place)

1950 (1; 1-1)
CCNY 56, OHIO STATE 55 (1st round)
OHIO STATE 72, Holy Cross 52 (regional 3rd place)

1951 (1; 3-1)
ILLINOIS 79, Columbia 71 (1st round)
ILLINOIS 84, North Carolina State 70 (2nd round)
Kentucky 76, ILLINOIS 74 (national semifinal)
ILLINOIS 61, Oklahoma 46 (3rd place)

1952 (1; 3-1)
ILLINOIS 80, Dayton 61 (1st round)
ILLINOIS 74, Duquesne 68 (regional championship)
St John's 61, ILLINOIS 59 (national semifinal)
ILLINOIS 67, Santa Clara 64 (3rd place)

1953 (1; 4-0)
INDIANA 82, DePaul 80 (2nd round)
INDIANA 79, Notre Dame 66 (regional championship)
INDIANA 80, Louisiana State 67 (national semifinal)
INDIANA 69, Kansas 68 (championship)

1954 (1; 1-1)
Notre Dame 65, INDIANA 64 (2nd round)
INDIANA 73, Louisiana State 62 (regional 3rd place)

1955 (1; 2-2)
IOWA 82, Penn State 53 (2nd round)
IOWA 86, Marquette 81 (regional championship)
La Salle 76, IOWA 73 (national semifinal)
Colorado 75, IOWA 54 (3rd place)

1956 (1; 3-1)
IOWA 97, Morehead 83 (2nd round)
IOWA 89, Kentucky 77 (regional championship)
IOWA 83, Temple 76 (national semifinal)
San Francisco 83, IOWA 71 (championship)

1957 (1; 2-2)
MICHIGAN STATE 85, Notre Dame 83 (2nd round)
MICHIGAN STATE 80, Kentucky 68 (regional championship)
North Carolina 74, MICHIGAN STATE 70 (3 OT) (national semifinal)
San Francisco 67, MICHIGAN STATE 60 (3rd place)

1958 (1; 1-1)
Notre Dame 94, INDIANA 87 (2nd round)
INDIANA 98, Miami (OH) 91 (regional 3rd place)

1959 (1; 1-1)
MICHIGAN STATE 74, Marquette 69 (2nd round)
Louisville 88, MICHIGAN STATE 81 (regional championship)

1960 (1; 4-0)
OHIO STATE 98, Western Kentucky 79 (2nd round)
OHIO STATE 86, Georgia Tech 69 (regional championship)
OHIO STATE 76, New York 54 (national semifinal)
OHIO STATE 75, California 55 (championship)

1961 (1; 3-1)
OHIO STATE 56, Louisville 55 (2nd round)
OHIO STATE 87, Kentucky 74 (regional championship)
OHIO STATE 95, St Joseph's (PA) 69 (national semifinal)
Cincinnati 70, OHIO STATE 65 (OT) (championship)

1962 (1; 3-1)
OHIO STATE 93, Western Kentucky 73 (2nd round)
OHIO STATE 74, Kentucky 64 (regional championship)
OHIO STATE 84, Wake Forest 68 (national semifinal)
Cincinnati 71, OHIO STATE 59 (championship)

1963 (1; 1-1)
ILLINOIS 70, Bowling Green 67 (2nd round)
Loyola, (IL) 79, ILLINOIS 64 (regional championship)

1964 (1; 3-1)
MICHIGAN 84, Loyola 80 (2nd round)
MICHIGAN 69, Ohio 57 (regional championship)
Duke 91, MICHIGAN 80 (national semifinal)
MICHIGAN 100, Kansas State 90 (3rd place)

1965 (1; 3-1)
MICHIGAN 98, Dayton 71 (2nd place)
MICHIGAN 87, Vanderbilt 85 (regional championship)
MICHIGAN 93, Princeton 76 (national semifinal)
UCLA 91, MICHIGAN 80 (championship)

1966 (1; 1-1)
MICHIGAN 80, Western Kentucky 79 (2nd round)
Kentucky 84, MICHIGAN 77 (regional championship)

1967 (1; 1-1)
Virginia Tech 79, INDIANA 70 (2nd Round)
INDIANA 51, Tennessee 44 (regional 3rd place)

1968 (1; 3-1)
OHIO STATE 79, East Tennessee 72 (2nd round)
OHIO STATE 82, Kentucky 81 (regional championship)
North Carolina 80, OHIO STATE 66 (national semifinal)
OHIO STATE 89, Houston 85 (3rd place)

1969 (1; 3-1)
PURDUE 91, Miami (OH) 71 (2nd round)
PURDUE 75, Marquette 73 (OT) (regional championship)
PURDUE 92, North Carolina 65 (national semifinal)
UCLA 92, PURDUE 72 (championship)

1970 (1; 1-1)
Jacksonville 104, IOWA 103 (2nd round)
IOWA 121, Notre Dame 108 (regional 3rd place)

1971 (1; 1-1)
OHIO STATE 60, Marquette 59 (2nd round)
Western Kentucky 81, OHIO STATE 78 (OT) (regional championship)

NCAA Championship Results *(continued)*

1972 (1; 1-1)
Florida State 70, MINNESOTA 56 (2nd place)
MINNESOTA 77, Marquette 72 (regional 3rd place)
(Note: Minnesota's participation later voided by NCAA)

1973 (1; 3-1)
INDIANA 75, Marquette 69 (2nd place)
INDIANA 72, Kentucky 65 (regional championship)
UCLA 70, INDIANA 59 (national semifinal)
INDIANA 97, Providence 79 (3rd place)

1974 (1; 1-1)
MICHIGAN 77, Notre Dame 68 (2nd round)
Marquette 72, MICHIGAN 70 (regional championship)

1975 (2; 2-2)
INDIANA 78, Texas-El Paso 53 (1st round)
INDIANA 81, Oregon State 71 (2nd round)
Kentucky 92, INDIANA 90 (regional championship)
UCLA 101, MICHIGAN 93 (OT) (1st round)

1976 (2; 9-1)
INDIANA 90, St. John's 70 (1st round)
INDIANA 74, Alabama 69 (2nd round)
INDIANA 65, Marquette 56 (regional championship)
INDIANA 65, UCLA 51 (national semifinal)
INDIANA 86, MICHIGAN 68 (championship)
MICHIGAN 74, Wichita State 73 (1st round)
MICHIGAN 80, Notre Dame 76 (2nd round)
MICHIGAN 95, Missouri 88 (regional championship)
MICHIGAN 86, Rutgers 70 (national semifinal)
INDIANA 86, MICHIGAN 68 (championship)

1977 (2; 2-2)
MICHIGAN 92, Holy Cross 81 (1st round)
MICHIGAN 86, Detroit 81 (2nd round)
North Carolina-Charlotte 75, MICHIGAN 68 (regional championship)
North Carolina 69, PURDUE 66 (1st round)

1978 (2; 3-2)
INDIANA 63, Furman 62 (1st round)
Villanova 61, INDIANA 60 (2nd round)
MICHIGAN STATE 77, Providence 63 (1st round)
MICHIGAN STATE 90, Western Kentucky 69 (2nd round)
Kentucky 52, MICHIGAN STATE 49 (regional championship)

1979 (2; 5-1)
Toledo 74, IOWA 72 (2nd round)
MICHIGAN STATE 95, Lamar 64 (2nd round)
MICHIGAN STATE 87, Louisiana State 71 (regional semifinal)
MICHIGAN STATE 80, Notre Dame 68 (regional final)
MICHIGAN STATE 101, Pennsylvania 67 (national semifinal)
MICHIGAN STATE 75, Indiana State 64 (national championship)

1980 (4; 11-5)
IOWA 86, Virginia Commonwealth 72 (1st round)
IOWA 77, North Carolina State 64 (2nd round)
IOWA 88, Syracuse 77 (regional semifinal)
IOWA 81, Georgetown 80 (regional final)
Louisville 80, IOWA 72 (national semifinal)
PURDUE 75, IOWA 58 (3rd place)
PURDUE 90, LaSalle 82 (1st round)
PURDUE 87, St. John's 72 (2nd round)
PURDUE 76, INDIANA 69 (regional semifinal)
PURDUE 68, Duke 60 (regional final)
UCLA 67, PURDUE 62 (national semifinal)
PURDUE 75, IOWA 58 (4th place)
INDIANA 69, Virginia Tech 59 (2nd round)
PURDUE 76, INDIANA 69 (regional semifinal)
OHIO STATE 89, Arizona State 75 (2nd round)
UCLA 72, OHIO STATE 68 (regional semifinal)

1981 (3; 6-2)
ILLINOIS 67, Wyoming 65 (2nd round)
Kansas State 57, ILLINOIS 52 (regional semifinal)
INDIANA 99, Maryland 64 (2nd round)
INDIANA 87, Alabama-Birmingham 72 (regional semifinal)
INDIANA 78, St. Joseph's 46 (regional final)
INDIANA 67, Louisiana State 49 (national semifinal)
INDIANA 63, North Carolina 50 (championship)
Wichita State 60, IOWA 56 (2nd round)

1982 (4; 3-4)
James Madison 55, OHIO STATE 48 (1st round)
INDIANA 94, Robert Morris 62 (1st round)
Alabama-Birmingham 80, INDIANA 70 (2nd round)
IOWA 70, Northeast Louisiana 63 (1st round)
Idaho 69, IOWA 67 (OT) (2nd round)
MINNESOTA 62, Tennessee-Chattanooga 61 (2nd round)
Louisville 67, MINNESOTA 61 (regional semifinal)

1983 (5; 5-5)
Utah 52, ILLINOIS 49 (1st round)
INDIANA 63, Oklahoma 49 (2nd round)
Kentucky 64, INDIANA 59 (regional semifinal)
IOWA 64, Utah State 59 (1st round)
IOWA 77, Missouri 63 (2nd round)
Villanova 55, IOWA 54 (regional semifinal)
OHIO STATE 79, Syracuse 74 (2nd round)
North Carolina 64, OHIO STATE 51 (regional semifinal)
PURDUE 55, Robert Morris 53 (1st round)
Arkansas 78, PURDUE 68 (2nd round)

1984 (3; 4-3)
ILLINOIS 64, Villanova 56 (2nd round)
ILLINOIS 72, Maryland 70 (regional semifinal)
Kentucky 54, ILLINOIS 51 (regional final)
INDIANA 75, Richmond 67 (2nd round)
INDIANA 72, North Carolina 68 (regional semifinal)
Virginia 50, INDIANA 48 (regional final)
Memphis State 66, PURDUE 48 (2nd round)

1985 (6; 4-6)
ILLINOIS 76, Northeastern 57 (1st round)
ILLINOIS 74, Georgia 58 (2nd round)
Georgia Tech 61, ILLINOIS 53 (regional semifinal)
Arkansas 63, IOWA 54 (1st round)
MICHIGAN 59, Farleigh Dickinson 55 (1st round)
Villanova 59, MICHIGAN 55 (2nd round)
Alabama-Birmingham 70, MICHIGAN STATE 68 (1st round)
OHIO STATE 75, Iowa State 64 (1st round)
Louisiana Tech 79, OHIO STATE 67 (2nd round)
Auburn 59, PURDUE 58 (1st round)

1986 (5; 4-6)
ILLINOIS 75, Fairfield 51 (1st round)
Alabama 58, ILLINOIS 56 (2nd round)
Cleveland State 83, INDIANA 79 (1st round)
North Carolina State 66, IOWA 64 (1st round)
MICHIGAN 70, Akron 64 (1st round)
Iowa State 72, MICHIGAN 69 (2nd round)
MICHIGAN STATE 72, Washington 70 (1st round)
MICHIGAN STATE 80, Georgetown 68 (2nd round)
Kansas 96, MICHIGAN STATE 86 (OT) (regional semifinal)
Louisiana State 94, PURDUE 87 (2 OT) (1st round)

1987 (6; 12-5)
Austin Peay 68, ILLINOIS 67 (1st round)
INDIANA 92, Fairfield 58 (1st round)
INDIANA 107, Auburn 90 (2nd round)
INDIANA 88, Duke 82 (regional semifinal)
INDIANA 77, Louisiana State 76 (regional final)
INDIANA 97, Nevada-Las Vegas 93 (national semifinal)
INDIANA 74, Syracuse 73 (championship)
IOWA 99, Santa Clara 76 (1st round)
IOWA 84, Texas-El Paso 82 (2nd round)
IOWA 93, Oklahoma 91 (OT) (regional semifinal)
Nevada-Las Vegas 84, IOWA 81 (regional final)
MICHIGAN 97, Navy 82 (1st round)
North Carolina 109, MICHIGAN 97 (2nd round)
OHIO STATE 91, Kentucky 77 (1st round)
Georgetown 82, Ohio State 79 (2nd round)
PURDUE 104, Northeastern 95 (1st round)
Florida 85, PURDUE 66 (2nd round)

RECORDS
NCAA Championship Results (continued)

1988 (5; 7-5)
ILLINOIS 81, Texas-San Antonio 72 (1st round)
Villanova 66, ILLINOIS 63 (2nd round)
Richmond 72, INDIANA 69 (1st round)
IOWA 102, Florida State 98 (1st round)
IOWA 104, Nevada-Las Vegas 86 (2nd round)
Arizona 99, IOWA 79 (regional semifinal)
MICHIGAN 63, Boise State 58 (1st round)
MICHIGAN 108, Florida 69 (2nd round)
North Carolina 78, MICHIGAN 69 (regional semifinal)
PURDUE 94, Fairleigh-Dickinson 79 (1st round)
PURDUE 100, Memphis State 73 (2nd round)
Kansas State 73, PURDUE 70 (regional semifinal)

1989 (5; 15-4)
ILLINOIS 77, McNeese State 71 (1st round)
ILLINOIS 72, Ball State 60 (2nd round)
ILLINOIS 83, Louisville 69 (regional semifinal)
ILLINOIS 89, Syracuse 86 (regional final)
MICHIGAN 83, ILLINOIS 81 (national semifinal)
INDIANA 99, George Mason 85 (1st round)
INDIANA 92, Texas-El Paso 69 (2nd round)
Seton Hall 78, INDIANA 65 (regional semifinal)
IOWA 87, Rutgers 73 (1st round)
North Carolina State 102, IOWA 96 (2 OT) (2nd round)
MICHIGAN 92, Xavier 87 (1st round)
MICHIGAN 91, South Alabama 82 (2nd round)
MICHIGAN 92, North Carolina 87 (regional semifinal)
MICHIGAN 102, Virginia 65 (regional final)
MICHIGAN 83, ILLINOIS 81 (semifinal)
MICHIGAN 80, Seton Hall 79 (OT) (championship)
MINNESOTA 86, Kansas State 75 (1st round)
MINNESOTA 80, Siena 67 (2nd round)
Duke 87, MINNESOTA 70 (regional semifinal)

1990 (7; 8-7)
Dayton 88, ILLINOIS 86 (1st round)
California 65, INDIANA 63 (1st round)
MICHIGAN 76, Illinois State 70 (1st round)
Loyola Marymount 149, MICHIGAN 115 (2nd round)
MICHIGAN STATE 75, Murray State 71 (OT) (1st round)
MICHIGAN STATE 62, UC-Santa Barbara 58 (2nd round)
Georgia Tech 81, MICHIGAN STATE 80 (OT) (regional semifinal)
MINNESOTA 64, Texas-El Paso 61 (1st round)
MINNESOTA 81, Northern Iowa 78 (2nd round)
MINNESOTA 82, Syracuse 75 (regional semifinal)
Georgia Tech 93, MINNESOTA 91 (regional final)
OHIO STATE 84, Providence 83 (OT) (1st round)
Nevada-Las Vegas 76, OHIO STATE 65 (2nd round)
PURDUE 75, Northeast Louisiana 63 (1st round)
Texas 73, PURDUE 72 (2nd round)

1991 (5; 6-5)
INDIANA 79, Coastal Carolina 69 (1st round)
INDIANA 82, Florida State 60 (2nd round)
Kansas 83, INDIANA 65 (regional semifinal)
IOWA 76, East Tennessee State 73 (1st round)
Duke 85, IOWA 70 (2nd round)
MICHIGAN STATE 60, Wisconsin-Green Bay 58 (1st round)
Utah 85, MICHIGAN STATE 84 (2 OT) (2nd round)
OHIO STATE 97, Towson State 86 (1st round)
OHIO STATE 65, Georgia Tech 61 (2nd round)
St. John's 91, OHIO STATE 74 (regional semifinal)
Temple 80, PURDUE 63 (1st round)

1992 (5; 14-5)
INDIANA 94, Eastern Illinois 55 (1st round)
INDIANA 89, Louisiana State 79 (2nd round)
INDIANA 85, Florida State 78 (regional semifinal)
INDIANA 106, UCLA 79 (regional final)
Duke 81, INDIANA 78 (national semifinal)
IOWA 98, Texas 92 (1st round)
Duke 75, IOWA 62 (2nd round)
MICHIGAN 73, Temple 66 (1st round)
MICHIGAN 102, East Tennessee State (90 (2nd round)
MICHIGAN 75, Oklahoma State 72 (regional semifinal)
MICHIGAN 75, OHIO STATE 72 (OT) (regional final)
MICHIGAN 76, Cincinnati 72 (national semifinal)
Duke 71, MICHIGAN 51 (championship)
MICHIGAN STATE 61, Southwest Missouri State 54 (1st round)
Cincinnati 77, MICHIGAN STATE 65 (2nd round)
OHIO STATE 83, Mississppi Valley State 56 (1st round)
OHIO STATE 78, Connecticut 55 (2nd round)
OHIO STATE 80, North Carolina 73 (regional semifinal)
MICHIGAN 75, OHIO STATE 72 (OT) (regional final)

1993 (5; 10-5)
ILLINOIS 75, Long Beach State 72 (first round)
Vanderbilt 85, Illinois 68 (second round)
INDIANA 97, Wright State 54 (first round)
INDIANA 73, Xavier (OH) 70 (second round)
INDIANA 82, Louisville 69 (regional semifinal)
Kansas 83, INDIANA 77 (regional final)
IOWA 82, Northeast Louisiana 69 (first round)
Wake Forest 84, IOWA 78 (second round)
MICHIGAN 84, Coastal Carolina 53 (first round)
MICHIGAN 86, UCLA 84 (OT) (second round)
MICHIGAN 72, George Washington 64 (regional semifinal)
MICHIGAN 77, Temple 72 (regional final)
MICHIGAN 81, Kentucky 78 (OT) (national semifinal)
North Carolina 77, MICHIGAN 71 (national final)
Rhode Island 74, PURDUE 68 (first round)

1994 (7; 11-7)
Georgetown 84, ILLINOIS 77 (1st round)
INDIANA 84, Ohio 72 (1st round)
INDIANA 67, Temple 58 (2nd round)
Boston College 77, INDIANA 68 (regional semifinal)
MICHIGAN 78, Pepperdine 74 (OT) (1st round)
MICHIGAN 84, Texas 79 (2nd round)
MICHIGAN 78, Maryland 71 (regional semifinal)
Arkansas 76, MICHIGAN 68 (regional final)
MICHIGAN STATE 84, Seton Hall 73 (1st round)
Duke 85, MICHIGAN STATE 74 (2nd round)
MINNESOTA 74, Southern Illinois 60 (1st round)
Louisville 60, MINNESOTA 55 (2nd round)
PURDUE 98, Central Florida 67 (1st round)
PURDUE 83, Alabama 73 (2nd round)
PURDUE 83, Kansas 78 (regional semifinal)
Duke 69, PURDUE 60 (regional final)
WISCONSIN 80, Cincinnati 70 (1st round)
Missouri 109, Wisconsin 96 (2nd round)

1995 (6; 1-6)
Western Kentucky 82, MICHIGAN 76 (OT) (first round)
PURDUE 49, Wisconsin-Green Bay 48 (first round)
Memphis 75, PURDUE 73 (second round)
Weber State 79, MICHIGAN STATE 72 (first round)
Missouri 65, INDIANA 60 (first round)
Saint Louis 64, MINNESOTA 61 (OT) (first round)
Tulsa 68, ILLINOIS 62 (first round)

Two-time consensus all-America and Big Ten MVP in 1975 and 1976, Indiana forward Scott May led the Hoosiers to a 63-1 record during that time and an NCAA title in '76.

NIT RESULTS

NIT RESULTS

1971 (2; 1-2)
MICHIGAN 82, Syracuse 76
Georgia Tech 78, MICHIGAN 70
St. Bonaventure 94, PURDUE 79

1972 (1; 0-1)
Princeton 68, INDIANA 60

1973 (1; 1-1)
MINNESOTA 68, Rutgers 59
Alabama 69, MINNESOTA 65

1974 (1; 4-0)
PURDUE 82, North Carolina 71
PURDUE 85, Hawaii 72
PURDUE 78, Jacksonville 63
PURDUE 87, Utah 81 (1st)

1979 (3; 10-3)
*PURDUE 97, Central Michigan 80
*PURDUE 84, Dayton 70
#INDIANA 78, Texas Tech 59
*OHIO STATE 80, St. Joseph's 66
*PURDUE 67, Old Dominion 59
*INDIANA 73, Alcorn State 69
#OHIO STATE 79, Maryland 72
PURDUE 87, Alabama 68
INDIANA 64, OHIO STATE 55
Alabama 96, OHIO STATE 86 (4th)
INDIANA 53, PURDUE 52 (1st)

1980 (3; 10-3)
*ILLINOIS 105, Loyola (IL) 87
*MINNESOTA 64, Bowling Green 50
*MICHIGAN 76, Nebraska 69
*ILLINOIS 75, Illinois State 65
*MINNESOTA 58, Mississippi 56
*MICHIGAN 74, Texas-El Paso 65
*ILLINOIS 65, Murray State 63
*MINNESOTA 94, S'western La. 73
#Virginia 79, MICHIGAN 68
MINNESOTA 65, ILLINOIS 63
ILLINOIS 84, UNLV 74 (3rd)
Virginia 58, MINNESOTA 55 (2nd)

1981 (3; 8-3)
*MINNESOTA 90, Drake 77
*MICHIGAN 74, Duquesne 58
*PURDUE 84, Rhode Island 58
#MINNESOTA 84, Connecticut 66
*MICHIGAN 80, Toledo 68
*PURDUE 50, Dayton 46
#West Virginia 80, MINNESOTA 69
#Syracuse 91, MICHIGAN 76
*PURDUE 81, Duke 69
Syracuse 70, PURDUE 63
PURDUE 75, West Va. 73 (3rd)

1982 (2; 5-2)
*ILLINOIS 126, Long Island 78
*PURDUE 72, Western Kentucky 65
*Dayton 61, ILLINOIS 58
*PURDUE 98, Rutgers 65
*PURDUE 86, Texas A&M 68
PURDUE 61, Georgia 60
Bradley 76, PURDUE 58 (2nd)

1983 (3; 2-3)
+NORTHWESTERN 71, Notre Dame 57
*MICH. STATE 72, Bowling Green 71
+DePaul 76, MINNESOTA 73
+DePaul 65, NORTHWESTERN 63
*Fresno State 72, MICHIGAN ST. 58

1984 (2; 5-1)
#Xavier 60, OHIO STATE 57 (OT)
*MICHIGAN 94, Wichita State 70
*MICHIGAN 83, Marquette 70
*MICHIGAN 63, Xavier 62
MICHIGAN 78, Virginia Tech 75
MICHIGAN 83, Notre Dame 63 (1st)

1985 (1; 4-1)
*INDIANA 79, Butler 57
*INDIANA 75, Richmond 53
*INDIANA 94, Marquette 82 (2 OT)
INDIANA 74, Tennessee 67
UCLA 65, INDIANA 62 (2nd)

1986 (1; 5-0)
*OHIO STATE 65, Ohio 62
*OHIO STATE 71, Texas 65
*OHIO STATE 79, Brigham Young 68
OHIO STATE 79, Louisiana Tech 66
OHIO STATE 73, Wyoming 63 (1st)

1988 (1; 4-1)
*OHIO STATE 86, Old Dominion 73
*OHIO STATE 86, Cleveland St. 80
#OHIO STATE 68, New Mexico 65
OHIO STATE 64, Colorado State 62
Conn. 72, OHIO STATE 67 (2nd)

1989 (3; 6-4)
*OHIO STATE 81, Akron 70
*WISCONSIN 63, New Orleans 61
!MICHIGAN STATE 83, Kent State 67
*OHIO STATE 85, Nebraska 74
*Saint Louis 73, WISCONSIN 68
*MICHIGAN ST. 79, Wichita St. 67
*St. John's 83, OHIO ST. 80 (OT)
#MICHIGAN STATE 70, Villanova 63
Saint Louis 74, MICHIGAN STATE 64
Ala.-Birmingham 78, MSU 76 (3rd)

1991 (2; 1-2)
*WISCONSIN 87, Bowling Green 79 (OT)
#Colorado 71, MICHIGAN 64
*Stanford 80, WISCONSIN 72

1992 (2; 2-2)
*PURDUE 82, Butler 56
#Washington State 72, MINNESOTA 70
*PURDUE 67, Texas Christian 51
%Florida 74, PURDUE 67

1993 (4; 5-3)
*MINNESOTA 74, Florida 65
*MINNESOTA 86, Oklahoma 72
*MINNESOTA 76, Southern California 58
MINNESOTA 76, Providence 70
MINNESOTA 62, Georgetown 61 (1st)
#Oklahoma 88, MICHIGAN STATE 86
*Miami (OH) 56, OHIO STATE 53
*Rice 77, WISCONSIN 73

1994 (1; 1-1)
*NORTHWESTERN 69, DePaul 68
*Xavier 83, NORTHWESTERN 79 (OT)

1995 (2; 6-2)
@IOWA 96, DePaul 87
* IOWA 66, Ohio 62
* PENN STATE 62, Miami (FL) 56
# PENN STATE 65, Nebraska 59
** PENN STATE 67, IOWA 64
Marquette 87, PENN STATE 79
PENN STATE 66, Canisius 62 (3rd)

* home game
\# away game
+ at Rosemont, IL
! at Detroit, MI
% at Indianapolis, IN
@ at Moline, IL
** at Iowa City, IA
all other games at Madison Square Garden, New York, NY

As tournament MVP, Voshon Lenard led Minnesota to the NIT Championship in 1993.

RECORDS
National Basketball Rankings

Selected by the nation's sportswriters (AP-Associated Press) and a panel of coaches (UPI-United Press International or CNN-USA Today starting in 1991-92).

1949
AP
1. Kentucky
2. Oklahoma A&M
3. St. Louis
4. Illinois
5. Western Kentucky
6. Minnesota
7. Bradley
8. San Francisco
9. Tulane
10. Bowling Green

1950
AP
1. Bradley
2. Ohio State
3. Kentucky
4. Holy Cross
5. North Carolina State
6. Duquesne
7. UCLA
8. Western Kentucky
9. St. John's (NY)
10. LaSalle

1951
AP	UPI	
1	1	Kentucky
2	2	Oklahoma State
3	5	Columbia
4	3	Kansas State
5	4	Illinois
6	6	Bradley
7	8	Indiana
8	7	North Carolina State
9	9	St. John's (NY)
10		St. Louis
10		Brigham Young

1952
AP	UPI	
1	1	Kentucky
2	2	Illinois
3	6	Kansas State
4	4	Duquesne
5	7	St. Louis
6	5	Washington
7	8	Iowa
8	3	Kansas
9		West Virginia
10	9	St. John's (NY)

1953
AP	UPI	
1	1	Indiana
2	2	Seton Hall
3	5	Kansas
4	3	Washington
5	6	Louisiana State
6	4	LaSalle
7		St. John's (NY)
8	7	Oklahoma State
	8	North Carolina State
9		Duquesne
	9	Kansas State
10		Notre Dame
	10	Illinois

1954
AP	UPI	
1	2	Kentucky
2		LaSalle
3	9	Holy Cross
4	1	Indiana
5	3	Duquesne
6	5	Notre Dame
7		Bradley
8	6	Western Kentucky
9		Penn State
10		Oklahoma State
	10	Iowa

1955
AP	UPI	
1	1	San Francisco
2	2	Kentucky
3	3	LaSalle
4	6	North Carolina State
5	5	Iowa
6	7	Duquesne
7	4	Utah
8	9	Marquette
9	10	Dayton
10	8	Oregon St

1956
AP	UPI	
1	1	San Francisco
2	2	North Carolina State
3	3	Dayton
4	4	Iowa
5	5	Alabama
6	7	Louisville
7	6	Southern Methodist
8	9	UCLA
9		Kentucky
10	8	Illinois
	10	Vanderbilt

1957
AP	UPI	
1	1	North Carolina
2	2	Kansas
3	3	Kentucky
4	4	Southern Methodist
5	5	Seattle
6	8	Louisville
7		West Virginia
8		Vanderbilt
9		Oklahoma State
	9	UCLA
10	9	St. Louis

1958
AP	UPI	
1	1	West Virginia
2	2	Cincinnati
3	4	Kansas State
4	3	San Francisco
5	5	Temple
6	6	Maryland
7	8	Kansas
8	7	Notre Dame
9		Kentucky
	9	Dayton
10		Duke
	10	Indiana

1959
AP	UPI	
1	1	Kansas State
2	2	Kentucky
3	6	Mississippi State
4	8	Bradley
5	4	Cincinnati
6	5	North Carolina State
7	3	Michigan State
8	10	Auburn
9	6	North Carolina
	9	California
10		West Virginia

1960
AP	UPI	
1	2	Cincinnati
2	1	California
3	3	Ohio State
4	4	Bradley
5	6	West Virginia
6	5	Utah
7	10	Indiana
8	7	Utah State
9		St. Bonaventure
10		Miami (FL)
	9	Villanova

1961
AP	UPI	
1	1	Ohio State
2	2	Cincinnati
3	3	St. Bonaventure
4	4	Kansas State
5	6	North Carolina
6	7	Bradley
7	5	Southern Cal
8	10	Iowa
9		West Virginia
10	9	Duke
	10	Wake Forest

1962
AP	UPI	
1	1	Ohio State
2	2	Cincinnati
3	3	Kentucky
4	4	Mississippi State
5	6	Bradley
6	5	Kansas St.
7	10	Utah
8	9	Bowling Green
9	8	Colorado
10		Duke
	7	Wake Forest

1963
AP	UPI	
1	1	Cincinnati
2	2	Duke
3	4	Loyola (IL)
4	3	Arizona State
5	6	Wichita State
6	7	Mississippi State
7	8	Ohio State
8	5	Illinois
9		New York University
10	9	Colorado
10		Stanford

1964
AP	UPI	
1	1	UCLA
2	2	Michigan
3	4	Duke
4	3	Kentucky
5	6	Wichita State
6	5	Oregon State
7	7	Villanova
8	8	Loyola (IL)
9		DePaul
	9	UTEP
10	10	Davidson

1965
AP	UPI	
1	1	Michigan
2	2	UCLA
3	3	St. Joseph's (PA)
4	4	Providence
5	5	Vanderbilt
6	7	Davidson
7	8	Minnesota
8		Villanova
9	6	Brigham Young
10	9	Duke
	10	San Francisco

1966
AP	UPI	
1	1	Kentucky
2	2	Duke
3	3	UTEP
4	4	Kansas
5	6	St. Joseph's (PA)
6	5	Loyola (IL)
7	9	Cincinnati
8	8	Vanderbilt
9	7	Michigan
10		Western Kentucky
	10	Providence

1967
AP	UPI	
1	1	UCLA
2	2	Louisville
3	4	Kansas
4	3	North Carolina
5	5	Princeton
6	7	Western Kentucky
7	6	Houston
8	9	Tennessee
9	10	Boston College
10	8	UTEP

1968
AP	UPI	
1	1	Houston
2	2	UCLA
3	3	St. Bonaventure
4	4	North Carolina
5	5	Kentucky
6	7	New Mexico
7	6	Columbia
8	9	Davidson
9	8	Louisville
10		Duke
10		Marquette

1969
AP	UPI	
1	1	UCLA
2	6	LaSalle
3	4	Santa Clara
4	2	North Carolina
5	3	Davidson
6	7	Purdue
7	5	Kentucky
8	8	St. John's (NY)
9	10	Duquesne
10		Villanova

1970
AP	UPI	
1	1	Kentucky
2	2	UCLA
3	3	St. Bonaventure
4	5	Jacksonville
5	4	New Mexico State
6	6	South Carolina
7	7	Iowa
8	10	Marquette
9	8	Notre Dame
	9	Drake
10		North Carolina State

1971
AP	UPI	
1	1	UCLA
2	2	Marquette
3	3	Pennsylvania
4	4	Kansas
5	5	Southern Cal
6	6	South Carolina
7	7	Western Kentucky
8	8	Kentucky
9	9	Fordham
10	10	Ohio State

1972
AP	UPI	
1	1	UCLA
2	2	North Carolina
3	3	Pennsylvania
4	4	Louisville
5	6	Long Beach State
6	5	South Carolina
7	7	Marquette
8	8	Southwestern Louisiana
9	9	Brigham Young
10	10	Florida State

1973
AP	UPI	
1	1	UCLA
2	2	North Carolina State
3	3	Long Beach State
4	5	Providence
5	4	Marquette
6	6	Indiana
7	7	Southwestern Louisiana
8		Maryland
9	7	Kansas State
10		Minnesota
10		Maryland

1974
AP	UPI	
1	1	North Carolina State
2	2	UCLA
3	5	Marquette
4	4	Maryland
5	3	Notre Dame
6		**Michigan**
7	10	Kansas
8	6	Providence
9	9	**Indiana**
10		Long Beach State

1975
AP	UPI	
1	2	UCLA
2	4	Kentucky
3	1	**Indiana**
4	3	Louisville
5	5	Maryland
6		Syracuse
7	9	North Carolina State
8	7	Arizona State
9	10	North Carolina
10	8	Alabama

1976
AP	UPI	
1	1	**Indiana**
2	2	Marquette
3	4	UNLV
4	3	Rutgers
5	5	UCLA
6	7	Alabama
7	8	Notre Dame
8	6	North Carolina
9	9	**Michigan**
10		Western Michigan
	10	Washington

1977
AP	UPI	
1	1	**Michigan**
2	4	UCLA
3	5	Kentucky
4	6	UNLV
5	3	North Carolina
6	9	Syracuse
7		Marquette
8	2	San Francisco
9		Wake Forest
10		Notre Dame
	10	Utah

1978
AP	UPI	
1	1	Kentucky
2	2	UCLA
3	7	DePaul
4	5	**Michigan State**
5	6	Arkansas
6		Notre Dame
7	9	Duke
8	3	Marquette
9		Louisville
10		Kansas
10		North Carolina

1979
AP	UPI	
1	1	Indiana State
2	2	UCLA
3	4	**Michigan State**
4	5	Notre Dame
5	6	Arkansas
6	8	DePaul
7	9	Louisiana State
	7	Duke
8	10	Syracuse
9	3	North Carolina
10		Marquette

1980
AP	UPI	
1	1	DePaul
2	4	Louisville
3	2	Louisiana State
4	3	Kentucky
5	5	Oregon State
6	6	Syracuse
7	7	**Indiana**
8	8	Maryland
9		Notre Dame
10	9	**Ohio State**
	10	Georgetown

1981
AP	UPI	
1	1	DePaul
2	2	Oregon State
3	5	Arizona State
4	4	Louisiana State
5	3	Virginia
6	6	North Carolina
7	9	Notre Dame
8	8	Kentucky
9	7	**Indiana**
10		UCLA
	10	Utah

1982
AP	UPI	
1	1	North Carolina
2	2	DePaul
3	3	Virginia
4	4	Oregon State
5	5	Missouri
6	7	Georgetown
7	6	**Minnesota**
8	8	Idaho
9	9	Memphis State
10		Tulsa
	10	Fresno State

1983
AP	UPI	
1	1	Houston
2	2	Louisville
3	3	St. John's (NY)
4	4	Virginia
5	5	**Indiana**
6	6	UNLV
7	7	UCLA
8	8	North Carolina
9	9	Arkansas
10		Missouri
	10	Kentucky

1984
AP	UPI	
1	1	North Carolina
2	2	Georgetown
3	3	Kentucky
4	4	DePaul
5	5	Houston
6	6	**Illinois**
7	8	Oklahoma
8	7	Arkansas
9	9	UTEP
10		**Purdue**
	10	Maryland

1985
AP	UPI	
1	1	Georgetown
2	2	**Michigan**
3	3	St. John's (NY)
4	5	Oklahoma
5	4	Memphis State
6	6	Georgia Tech
7	7	North Carolina
8	8	Louisiana Tech
9	9	UNLV
10		Duke
	10	Illinois

1986
AP	UPI	
1	1	Duke
2	2	Kansas
3	4	Kentucky
4	3	St. John's (NY)
5	5	**Michigan**
6	6	Georgia Tech
7	7	Louisville
8	8	North Carolina
9	9	Syracuse
10		Notre Dame
	10	UNLV

1987
AP	UPI	
1	1	UNLV
2	3	North Carolina
3	2	**Indiana**
4	4	Georgetown
5	5	DePaul
6	7	**Iowa**
7	6	**Purdue**
8	8	Temple
9	9	Alabama
10	10	Syracuse

1988
AP	UPI	
1	1	Temple
2	2	Arizona
3	3	**Purdue**
4	4	Oklahoma
5	5	Duke
6	6	Kentucky
7	8	North Carolina
8	7	Pittsburgh
9	9	Syracuse
10	10	**Michigan**

1989
AP	UPI	
1	1	Arizona
2	2	Georgetown
3	3	**Illinois**
4	5	Oklahoma
5	4	North Carolina
6	8	Missouri
7	9	Syracuse
8	6	**Indiana**
9	7	Duke
10	10	**Michigan**

1990
AP	UPI	
1	1	Oklahoma
2	2	Kansas
3	3	UNLV
4	4	Syracuse
5	6	Georgetown
6	5	Missouri
7	8	**Michigan State**
8	7	Connecticut
9	10	Arkansas
10	9	**Purdue**

1991
AP	UPI	
1	1	UNLV
2	2	Arkansas
3	3	**Indiana**
4	4	North Carolina
5	5	**Ohio State**
6	6	Duke
7	8	Syracuse
8	7	Arizona
9		Kentucky
	9	Nebraska
10	10	Utah

1992
| | CNN/ | |
AP	USA	
1	1	Duke
2	7	Kansas
3	4	**Ohio State**
4	8	UCLA
5	2	**Indiana**
6	6	Kentucky
7		Nevada-Las Vegas
8		Southern California
9	10	Arkansas
	10	Arizona
	3	**Michigan**
	5	Cincinnati
	9	Oklahoma State

1993
| | CNN/ | |
AP	USA	
1	5	**Indiana**
2	3	Kentucky
3	2	**Michigan**
4	1	North Carolina
5		Arizona
6		Seton Hall
7	6	Cincinnati
8	8	Vanderbilt
9	4	Kansas
10	9	Duke
	7	Florida State
	10	Arkansas

1994
| | CNN/ | |
AP	USA	
1	9	North Carolina
2	1	Arkansas
3	5	**Purdue**
4	7	Connecticut
5	6	Missouri
6	2	Duke
7		Kentucky
8		Massachusetts
9	3	Arizona
10	10	Louisville
	4	Florida
	8	**Michigan**

1995
| | CNN/ | |
AP	USA	
1	1	UCLA
2	5	Kentucky
3	9	Wake Forest
4	3	North Carolina
5	10	Kansas
6	2	Arkansas
7	7	Massachusetts
8	6	Connecticut
9		Villanova
10		Maryland
	4	Oklahoma State
	8	Virginia

Michigan guard Cazzie Russell, a three-time all-Big Ten pick, led the Wolverines to a national No. 1 ranking in 1965 and No. 2 in '64.

RECORDS

BIG TEN "10-YEAR" MEN'S BASKETBALL COACHES
(Ranked by overall winning percentage)

		All Games			Big Ten Games		
	Years	Won	Lost	PCT	Won	Lost	PCT
Bob Knight, IND (1972-)	24	659	235	.737	304	116	.724
Walter Meanwell, WIS (1912-17, '21-34)	20	246	99	.712	158	80	.660
Ward Lambert, PUR (1917, '19-45)	28	371	152	.709	228	105	.685
Doug Mills, ILL (1937-47)	11	151	66	.696	88	47	.652
Gene Keady, PUR (1981-)	15	360	161	.691	176	94	.652
Harry Combes, ILL (1948-67)	20	316	150	.678	174	104	.619
Branch McCraken, IND (1935-43, '47-65)	24	364	174	.677	210	116	.644
Lou Henson, ILL (1976-)	20	645	318	.670	207	153	.575
Burke M. Herman, PSU (1916-17, 1920-32)	15	148	74	.667	--	--	--
L.J. Cooke, MINN (1897-1924)	27	238	122	.660	112	96	.538
John Orr, MICH (1969-80)	12	209	111	.653	120	72	.625
Fred Taylor, OSU (1959-76)	18	297	158	.653	158	102	.608
Everett Dean, IND (1925-38)	14	162	93	.635	96	72	.571
John Lawther, PSU (1937-49)	13	150	93	.617	--	--	--
O.B. Cowles, MINN (1948-59)	11	147	93	.612	96	68	.585
Jud Heathcote, MSU (1976- 95)	19	420	273	.606	182	160	.532
J. Craig Ruby, ILL (1923-36)	14	148	97	.604	93	74	.557
Eldon Miller, OSU (1977-86)	10	176	118	.599	98	82	.544
John Egli, PSU (1955-68)	14	187	135	.581	--	--	--
Harold Olsen, OSU (1923-46)	24	255	192	.570	154	135	.533
Dave MacMillan, MINN (1927-42, '48)	18	196	157	.555	103	116	.470
Jim Dutcher, MINN (1975-86)	11	166	136	.550	83	103	.446
Arthur Lonborg, NU (1928-50)	23	236	230	.536	138	141	.495
Ray Eddy, PUR (1951-65)	15	176	164	.518	92	122	.430
Bruce Parkhill, PSU (1984- 95)	12	181	169	.517	17	37	.315
Rollie Williams, IOWA (1930-43, '51)	15	146	141	.509	72	101	.416
Forrest Anderson, MSU (1954-65)	11	125	124	.502	69	85	.448
John Bach, PSU (1969-1978)	10	122	121	.501	--	--	--
Harold "Bud" Foster, WIS (1935-59)	25	265	267	.498	143	182	.440
Steve Yoder, WIS (1982-92)	10	205	227	.475	50	134	.272

HOME ATTENDANCE RECORDS

School Season

Season	School	Games	Total	Average
1973	Minnesota	13	232,491	17,883
1994	Indiana	13	221,622	17,048
1976	Indiana	12	202,700	16,892
1975	Minnesota	13	219.047	16,841
1980	Indiana	14	234,667	16,762
1991	Indiana	13	217,610	16,739
1987	Indiana	16	248,946	16,596
1992	Indiana	14	231,503	16,536
1990	Indiana	15	246,865	16,458
1975	Indiana	14	230,218	16,444

Conference Games Only

Season	Games	Total	Average
1963	70	597,625	8,538
1964	70	641,139	9,159
1965	70	596,771	8,525
1966	70	596,296	8,519
1967	70	580,752	8,296
1968	71	671,897	9,463
1969	70	722,563	10,322
1970	70	691,382	9,877
1971	70	723,163	10,330
1972	70	795,072	11,358
1973	70	799,289	11,418
1974	70	713,045	10,186
1975	90	911,897	10,132
1976	90	879,078	9,768
1977	90	923,686	10,263
1978	90	1,032,743	11,474
1979	90	1,083,751	12,042
1980	90	1,121,206	12,458
1981	90	1,119,011	12,433
1982	90	1,093,223	12,147
1983	90	1,111,208	12,347
1984	90	1,150,078	12,779
1985	90	1,414,298	12,681
1986	89	1,129,020	12,628
1987	90	1,136,539	12,686
1988	90	1,129,415	12,686
1989	90	1,174,889	13,054
1990	90	1,253,160	*13,924
1991	90	1,213,330	13,481
1992	90	1,218,104	13,534
1993	99	1,295,768	13,089
1994	99	*1,301,079	13,142
1995	99	1,288,274	13,013

* all-time Big Ten and NCAA record

All Games

Season	Games	Total	Average
1972	110	1,214,039	11,036
1973	116	1,312,048	11,310
1974	121	1,138,406	9,408
1975	129	1,264,204	9,801
1976	134	1,213,874	9,059
1977	133	1,329,121	9,993
1978	136	1,529,946	11,243
1979	135	1,607,346	11,906
1980	154	1,877,048	12,189
1981	148	1,779,345	12,022
1982	141	1,660,970	11,780
1983	151	1,715,701	11,362
1984	144	1,727,938	12,000
1985	156	1,877,817	12,037
1986	153	1,809,773	11,829
1987	151	1,799,716	11,919
1988	154	1,876,325	11,829
1989	156	1,947,280	12,482
1990	148	1,991,396	*13,455
1991	152	1,988,446	13,082
1992	155	1,994,144	12,866
1993	169	*2,145,677	12,696
1994	165	2,112,126	12,801
1995	162	2,059,141	12,711

Single Game

22,822 Ohio State vs. Northwestern, Chicago Stadium, Chicago, IL, Feb. 23, 1946
20,176 Iowa at Minnesota, Williams Arena, Feb. 28, 1955
17,970 Indiana at Minnesota, Williams Arena, 1973
17,912 Michigan State at Indiana, Assembly Hall, March 8, 1975

MOST BIG TEN VICTORIES
(50 or more) (Conference Games Only)

1. Bob Knight, IND (1972-)	304
2. Ward Lambert, PUR (1917, '19-45)	228
3. Branch McCracken, IND (1935-43, '47-65)	210
4. Lou Henson, ILL (1976-)	207
5. Jud Heathcote, MSU (1976-95)	182
6. Gene Keady, PUR (1981-)	176
7. Harry Combes, ILL (1948-67)	174
8. Fred Taylor, OSU (1959-76)	158
Walter Meanwell, WIS (1912-17, '21-34)	158
10. Harold Olsen, OSU (1923-46)	154
11. Harold "Bud" Foster, WIS (1935-59)	143
12. Arthur Lonborg, NU (1928-50)	138
13. John Orr, MICH (1969-80)	120
14. L.J. Cooke, MINN (1897-1924)	112
15. Dave MacMillan, MINN (1927-42, '45-48)	103
16. Eldon Miller, OSU (1977-86)	98
Bill Frieder, MICH (1981-89)	98
18. Everett Dean, IND (1925-38)	96
O.B. Cowles, MINN (1948-59)	96
20. J. Craig Ruby, ILL (1923-36)	93
21. Ray Eddy, PUR (1951-65)	92
Lute Olson, IOWA (1975-83)	92
23. Tom Davis, IOWA (1986-)	90
24. Doug Mills, ILL (1937-47)	88
25. Jim Dutcher, MINN (1975-86)	83
26. Rollie Williams, IOWA (1930-43, '51)	72
Bucky O'Connor, IOWA (1952-58)	72
28. Forrest Anderson, MSU (1954-65)	69
Steve Fisher, MICH (1989-)	69
30. Clem Haskins, MINN (1987-)	68
31. John Kundla, MINN (1959-68)	67
32. E.J. Mather, MICH (1920-28)	64
Ralph Jones, ILL (1913-20)	64
Fred Schaus, PUR (1973-78)	64
35. George King, PUR (1966-72)	61
36. Dave Strack, MICH (1961-68)	58
37. Ralph Miller, IOWA (1965-70)	54
38. John Erickson, WIS (1960-68)	52
39. Steve Yoder, WIS (1982-92)	50

Ward "Piggy" Lambert led Purdue to six Big Ten championships and five co-championships and holds the Conference record for longevity. He was the Boilermakers' coach for 28 years.

All-Time Standings *(Standings based on percentage basis)*

BIG TEN CONFERENCE

	Conference			Season		
	W	L	PCT	W	L	PCT
1905-1906						
Minnesota	6	1	.857	13	2	.867
Wisconsin	6	2	.750	12	2	.857
Indiana	2	2	.500	7	9	.438
Chicago	3	5	.375	5	5	.500
Illinois	3	7	.250	6	8	.429
Purdue	3	6	.250	4	8	.333
Iowa	-	-	-	5	6	.455
1906-1907						
Chicago	6	2	.750	22	2	.917
Minnesota	6	2	.750	13	2	.867
Wisconsin	6	2	.750	11	3	.786
Purdue	2	6	.250	7	9	.438
Illinois	0	8	.000	1	10	.091
Iowa	-	-	-	10	6	.625
Indiana	-	-	-	9	4	.692
Northwestern	-	-	-	1	5	.167
1907-1908						
Chicago	7	1	.875	21	2	.913
Wisconsin	7	1	.875	10	2	.833
Illinois	4	4	.500	20	6	.769
Minnesota	2	6	.250	11	7	.611
Purdue	0	8	.000	5	10	.333
Indiana	-	-	-	7	3	.700
Iowa	-	-	-	7	6	.538
Northwestern	-	-	-	2	7	.222
1908-1909						
Chicago	12	0	1.000	12	0	1.000
Purdue	6	4	.600	8	4	.667
Wisconsin	5	4	.556	8	4	.667
Illinois	5	6	.455	8	6	.571
Minnesota	3	6	.333	8	6	.571
Indiana	2	6	.250	5	8	.385
Northwestern	1	4	.200	1	7	.125
Iowa	1	5	.167	8	7	.533
1909-1910						
Chicago	9	3	.750	9	3	.750
Minnesota	7	3	.700	10	3	.769
Wisconsin	7	5	.583	9	5	.643
Illinois	5	4	.556	5	4	.566
Iowa	2	2	.500	11	3	.786
Purdue	5	5	.500	8	5	.615
Indiana	3	7	.300	5	8	.385
Northwestern	0	9	.000	0	9	.000
1910-1911						
Purdue	8	4	.667	11	4	.733
Minnesota	8	4	.667	10	4	.714
Chicago	7	5	.583	13	6	.684
Illinois	6	5	.545	6	6	.500
Iowa	2	2	.500	9	4	.692
Indiana	5	5	.500	10	5	.667
Wisconsin	6	6	.500	9	6	.600
Northwestern	1	12	.083	1	12	.077
1911-1912						
Wisconsin	12	0	1.000	15	0	1.000
Purdue	10	0	1.000	12	0	1.000
Chicago	7	5	.583	8	5	.615
Minnesota	6	6	.500	7	6	.538
Illinois	4	8	.333	8	8	.500
Indiana	1	9	.100	6	11	.353
Iowa	0	4	.000	1	7	.125
Northwestern	0	8	.000	3	9	.250
1912-1913						
Wisconsin	11	1	.917	14	1	.933
Northwestern	7	2	.778	9	3	.750
Chicago	8	4	.667	11	4	.733
Purdue	6	5	.545	7	5	.583
Illinois	7	6	.538	10	6	.625
Ohio State	4	5	.444	13	7	.632
Minnesota	2	8	.200	3	8	.273
Iowa	1	5	.167	9	13	.409
Indiana	0	10	.000	5	11	.313
1913-1914						
Wisconsin	12	0	1.000	15	0	1.000
Ohio State	5	1	.833	10	4	.714
Chicago	8	4	.667	10	6	.625
Illinois	7	4	.636	9	5	.643
Northwestern	6	5	.545	6	5	.545
Minnesota	4	8	.333	9	11	.450
Purdue	3	9	.250	5	9	.357
Iowa	1	5	.167	11	7	.611
Indiana	1	11	.083	2	12	.143

	Conference			Season		
	W	L	PCT	W	L	PCT
1914-1915						
Illinois	12	0	1.000	16	0	1.000
Chicago	9	3	.750	15	5	.737
Wisconsin	8	4	.667	13	4	.765
Minnesota	6	6	.500	12	6	.667
Northwestern	5	5	.500	5	5	.500
Purdue	4	8	.333	5	8	.385
Iowa	2	6	.250	9	8	.529
Ohio State	3	9	.250	6	10	.375
Indiana	1	9	.100	4	9	.308
1915-1916						
Wisconsin	11	1	.917	20	1	.952
Illinois	9	3	.750	13	3	.813
Northwestern	9	3	.750	9	3	.750
Minnesota	6	6	.500	8	6	.571
Indiana	3	5	.375	4	6	.400
Iowa	2	4	.333	12	4	.750
Chicago	4	8	.333	9	9	.500
Ohio State	2	8	.200	10	12	.455
Purdue	2	10	.167	4	10	.286
1916-1917						
Minnesota	10	2	.833	12	2	.857
Illinois	10	2	.833	13	3	.813
Purdue	7	2	.778	11	3	.786
Wisconsin	9	3	.750	15	3	.833
Indiana	3	5	.375	3	5	.375
Chicago	4	8	.333	9	12	.429
Ohio State	3	9	.250	15	11	.577
Northwestern	2	10	.167	3	10	.231
Iowa	1	8	.111	7	9	.438
1917-1918						
Wisconsin	9	3	.750	14	3	.824
Minnesota	7	3	.700	9	3	.750
Northwestern	5	3	.625	5	3	.625
Indiana	3	3	.500	10	4	.714
Purdue	5	5	.500	11	5	.688
Ohio State	5	5	.500	12	7	.632
Illinois	6	6	.500	9	6	.600
Chicago	6	6	.500	11	8	.579
Iowa	4	6	.400	6	8	.429
Michigan	0	10	.000	6	12	.333
1918-1919						
Minnesota	10	0	1.000	13	0	1.000
Chicago	10	2	.833	12	3	.800
Northwestern	6	4	.600	6	4	.600
Michigan	5	5	.500	18	6	.750
Illinois	5	7	.417	6	8	.429
Indiana	4	6	.400	9	7	.563
Iowa	4	7	.364	8	7	.533
Purdue	4	7	.364	6	8	.429
Ohio State	2	6	.250	7	12	.368
Wisconsin	3	9	.250	5	11	.313
1919-1920						
Chicago	10	2	.833	14	4	.778
Purdue	8	2	.800	16	4	.800
Illinois	8	4	.667	9	4	.692
Indiana	6	4	.600	13	8	.619
Wisconsin	7	5	.583	15	5	.750
Iowa	6	6	.500	9	10	.474
Ohio State	3	9	.250	17	10	.630
Minnesota	3	9	.250	7	9	.438
Michigan	3	9	.250	10	13	.435
Northwestern	2	6	.250	2	6	.250
1920-1921						
Michigan	8	4	.667	16	4	.800
Wisconsin	8	4	.667	13	4	.765
Purdue	8	4	.667	13	7	.650
Minnesota	7	5	.583	10	5	.667
Illinois	7	5	.583	11	7	.611
Indiana	6	5	.545	14	6	.700
Iowa	6	5	.545	8	8	.500
Chicago	6	6	.500	12	6	.667
Ohio State	2	10	.167	4	13	.235
Northwestern	1	11	.083	1	11	.083
1921-1922						
Purdue	8	1	.889	15	3	.833
Michigan	8	4	.667	15	4	.789
Wisconsin	8	4	.667	14	5	.737
Illinois	7	5	.583	14	5	.737
Iowa	5	6	.455	12	7	.632
Minnesota	5	7	.417	6	7	.462
Ohio State	5	7	.417	8	10	.445
Chicago	5	7	.417	8	1	.421
Indiana	3	7	.300	10	10	.500
Northwestern	3	9	.250	7	11	.389

	Conference			Season		
	W	L	PCT	W	L	PCT
1922-1923						
Iowa	11	1	.917	12	2	.857
Wisconsin	11	1	.917	12	3	.800
Michigan	8	4	.667	11	4	.733
Illinois	7	5	.583	9	6	.600
Purdue	7	5	.583	9	6	.600
Chicago	6	6	.500	7	7	.500
Indiana	5	7	.417	8	7	.533
Northwestern	3	9	.250	5	10	.333
Ohio State	1	11	.083	4	11	.267
Minnesota	1	11	.083	2	13	.133
1923-1924						
Wisconsin	8	4	.667	11	5	.688
Illinois	8	4	.667	11	6	.647
Chicago	8	4	.667	9	7	.563
Ohio State	7	5	.583	12	5	.706
Purdue	7	5	.583	12	5	.706
Indiana	7	5	.583	11	6	.647
Michigan	6	6	.500	10	7	.588
Minnesota	5	7	.417	9	8	.529
Iowa	4	8	.333	7	10	.412
Northwestern	0	12	.000	0	16	.000
1924-1925						
Ohio State	11	1	.917	14	2	.875
Indiana	8	4	.667	12	5	.706
Illinois	8	4	.667	11	6	.647
Purdue	7	4	.636	9	5	.643
Michigan	6	5	.545	8	6	.571
Minnesota	6	6	.500	10	7	.588
Iowa	5	7	.417	6	10	.375
Northwestern	4	8	.333	6	10	.375
Wisconsin	3	9	.250	6	11	.353
Chicago	1	11	.083	1	13	.071
1925-1926						
Purdue	8	4	.667	13	4	.765
Indiana	8	4	.667	12	5	.706
Michigan	8	4	.667	12	5	.706
Iowa	8	4	.667	12	5	.706
Ohio State	6	6	.500	10	7	.588
Illinois	6	6	.500	9	8	.529
Minnesota	5	7	.417	7	10	.412
Wisconsin	4	8	.333	8	9	.471
Chicago	4	8	.333	5	11	.313
Northwestern	3	9	.250	5	12	.294
1926-1927						
Michigan	10	2	.833	14	3	.824
Indiana	9	3	.750	13	4	.765
Purdue	9	3	.750	12	5	.706
Wisconsin	7	5	.583	10	7	.588
Illinois	7	5	.583	10	7	.588
Iowa	7	5	.583	9	8	.529
Ohio State	6	6	.500	11	6	.647
Chicago	3	9	.250	4	11	.267
Minnesota	1	11	.083	3	13	.188
Northwestern	1	11	.083	3	14	.176

	Conference			Season		
	W	L	PCT	W	L	PCT
1927-1928						
Indiana	10	2	.833	15	2	.882
Purdue	10	2	.833	15	2	.882
Wisconsin	9	3	.750	13	4	.765
Northwestern	9	3	.750	12	5	.706
Michigan	7	5	.583	10	7	.588
Chicago	5	7	.417	7	8	.467
Iowa	3	9	.250	6	11	.353
Ohio State	3	9	.250	5	12	.294
Illinois	2	10	.167	5	14	.263
Minnesota	2	10	.167	4	12	.250
1928-1929						
Wisconsin	10	2	.833	15	2	.882
Michigan	10	2	.833	14	2	.875
Purdue	9	3	.750	13	4	.765
Northwestern	7	5	.583	12	5	.706
Illinois	6	6	.500	10	7	.588
Ohio State	6	6	.500	9	8	.529
Iowa	5	7	.417	9	8	.529
Indiana	4	8	.333	7	10	.412
Chicago	2	10	.167	3	12	.200
Minnesota	1	11	.083	3	13	.188
1929-1930						
Purdue	10	0	1.000	13	2	.867
Wisconsin	8	2	.800	15	2	.822
Michigan	6	4	.600	9	5	.643
Illinois	7	5	.583	8	8	.500
Indiana	7	5	.583	8	9	.471
Northwestern	6	6	.500	9	8	.529
Minnesota	3	9	.250	8	9	.471
Chicago	2	10	.167	3	11	.214
Ohio State	1	9	.100	4	11	.267
Iowa	-	-	-	4	13	.235
1930-1931						
Northwestern	11	1	.917	16	1	.941
Michigan	8	4	.667	13	4	.765
Minnesota	8	4	.667	13	4	.765
Purdue	8	4	.667	12	5	.706
Illinois	7	5	.583	12	5	.706
Indiana	5	7	.417	9	8	.519
Wisconsin	4	8	.333	8	9	.471
Chicago	4	8	.333	6	8	.429
Ohio State	3	9	.250	4	13	.235
Iowa	2	10	.167	5	12	.294
1931-1932						
Purdue	11	1	.917	17	1	.944
Minnesota	9	3	.750	15	3	.833
Northwestern	9	3	.750	12	5	.706
Michigan	8	4	.667	11	6	.647
Illinois	7	5	.583	11	6	.647
Ohio State	5	7	.417	7	9	.500
Indiana	4	8	.333	8	10	.444
Wisconsin	3	9	.250	8	10	.444
Iowa	3	9	.250	5	12	.294
Chicago	1	11	.083	1	13	.071

Doug Mills, here as an Illinois player in 1929, coached the Illini "Whiz Kids" in 1942 and '43.

RECORDS

All-Time Standings *(continued)*

1932-1933	Conference W	L	PCT	Season W	L	PCT
Ohio State	10	2	.833	17	3	.850
Northwestern	10	2	.833	15	4	.789
Iowa	8	4	.667	15	5	.750
Michigan	8	4	.667	10	8	.556
Illinois	6	6	.500	11	7	.611
Purdue	6	6	.500	11	7	.611
Indiana	6	6	.500	10	8	.556
Wisconsin	4	8	.333	7	13	.350
Minnesota	1	11	.083	5	15	.250
Chicago	1	11	.083	1	14	.067

1933-1934	W	L	PCT	W	L	PCT
Purdue	10	2	.833	17	3	.850
Wisconsin	8	4	.667	14	6	.700
Northwestern	8	4	.667	11	8	.579
Illinois	7	5	.583	13	6	.684
Iowa	6	6	.500	13	6	.684
Indiana	6	6	.500	13	7	.650
Minnesota	5	7	.417	9	11	.450
Ohio State	4	8	.333	8	12	.400
Michigan	4	8	.333	6	14	.300
Chicago	2	10	.167	4	14	.222

1934-1935	W	L	PCT	W	L	PCT
Purdue	9	3	.750	17	3	.850
Illinois	9	3	.750	15	5	.750
Wisconsin	9	3	.750	15	5	.750
Indiana	8	4	.667	14	6	.700
Ohio State	8	4	.667	14	6	.700
Iowa	6	6	.500	10	9	.526
Minnesota	5	7	.417	11	9	.550
Northwestern	3	9	.250	10	10	.500
Michigan	2	10	.167	8	12	.400
Chicago	1	11	.083	1	15	.063

1935-1936	W	L	PCT	W	L	PCT
Indiana	11	1	.917	18	2	.900
Purdue	11	1	.917	16	4	.800
Michigan	7	5	.583	15	5	.750
Illinois	7	5	.583	13	6	.684
Northwestern	7	5	.583	13	6	.684
Ohio State	5	7	.417	12	8	.600
Iowa	5	7	.417	9	10	.474
Wisconsin	4	8	.333	11	9	.550
Minnesota	3	9	.250	5	15	.250
Chicago	0	12	.000	4	12	.250

1936-1937	W	L	PCT	W	L	PCT
Minnesota	10	2	.833	14	6	.700
Illinois	10	2	.833	14	6	.700
Michigan	9	3	.750	16	4	.800
Purdue	8	4	.667	15	5	.750
Ohio State	7	5	.583	13	7	.650
Indiana	6	6	.500	13	7	.650
Northwestern	4	8	.333	11	9	.550
Iowa	3	9	.250	11	9	.550
Wisconsin	3	9	.250	8	12	.400
Chicago	0	12	.000	1	15	.063

1937-1938	Conference W	L	PCT	Season W	L	PCT
Purdue	10	2	.883	18	2	.900
Minnesota	9	3	.750	18	2	.900
Ohio State	7	5	.583	12	8	.600
Northwestern	7	5	.583	10	10	.500
Michigan	6	6	.500	12	8	.600
Iowa	6	6	.500	9	10	.475
Wisconsin	5	7	.417	10	10	.500
Indiana	4	8	.333	10	10	.500
Illinois	4	8	.333	9	9	.500
Chicago	2	10	.167	3	10	.231

1938-1939	W	L	PCT	W	L	PCT
Ohio State	10	2	.833	16	7	.696
Indiana	9	3	.750	17	3	.850
Illinois	8	4	.667	14	5	.737
Minnesota	7	5	.583	14	6	.700
Purdue	6	6	.500	12	7	.632
Northwestern	5	7	.417	7	13	.350
Michigan	4	8	.333	11	9	.550
Wisconsin	4	8	.333	10	10	.500
Chicago	4	8	.333	9	11	.450
Iowa	3	9	.250	8	11	.421

1939-1940	W	L	PCT	W	L	PCT
Purdue	10	2	.833	16	4	.800
Indiana	9	3	.750	20	3	.869
Ohio State	8	4	.667	13	7	.650
Illinois	7	5	.583	14	6	.700
Northwestern	7	5	.583	13	7	.650
Michigan	6	6	.500	13	7	.650
Minnesota	5	7	.417	12	8	.600
Iowa	4	8	.333	9	12	.529
Wisconsin	3	9	.250	5	15	.250
Chicago	1	11	.083	5	14	.263

1940-1941	W	L	PCT	W	L	PCT
Wisconsin	11	1	.917	20	3	.870
Indiana	10	2	.833	17	3	.850
Illinois	7	5	.583	13	7	.650
Minnesota	7	5	.583	11	9	.550
Ohio State	7	5	.583	10	10	.500
Purdue	6	6	.500	13	7	.650
Michigan	5	7	.417	9	10	.474
Iowa	4	8	.333	12	8	.600
Northwestern	3	9	.250	7	11	.389
Chicago	0	12	.000	4	16	.200

1941-1942	W	L	PCT	W	L	PCT
Illinois	13	2	.867	18	5	.783
Indiana	10	5	.667	15	6	.714
Wisconsin	10	5	.667	14	7	.667
Iowa	10	5	.667	12	8	.600
Minnesota	9	6	.600	15	6	.714
Purdue	9	6	.600	14	7	.667
Northwestern	5	10	.333	8	13	.381
Michigan	5	10	.333	6	14	.300
Ohio state	4	11	.267	6	14	.300
Chicago	0	15	.000	2	19	.095

Bill Seaberg, Bill Logan and Carl Cain (with coach Bucky O'Connor) formed the nucleus of Iowa teams that won Big Ten titles in 1955 and 1956 and finished third nationally in '55 and second in '56.

1942-1943	Conference W	L	PCT	Season W	L	PCT
Illinois	12	0	1.000	17	1	.944
Indiana	11	2	.846	18	2	.900
Northwestern	7	5	.583	8	9	.471
Wisconsin	6	6	.500	12	9	.571
Purdue	6	6	.500	9	11	.450
Minnesota	5	7	.417	10	9	.526
Ohio State	5	7	.417	8	9	.471
Michigan	4	8	.333	10	8	.556
Iowa	3	9	.250	7	10	.412
Chicago	0	9	.000	0	18	.000

1943-1944	W	L	PCT	W	L	PCT
Ohio State	10	2	.833	14	7	.667
Iowa	9	3	.750	14	4	.778
Wisconsin	9	3	.750	12	9	.571
Northwestern	8	4	.667	12	7	.632
Purdue	8	4	.667	11	10	.524
Illinois	5	7	.417	11	9	.550
Michigan	5	7	.417	8	10	.444
Minnesota	2	10	.167	7	14	.333
Indiana	2	10	.167	7	15	.318
Chicago	0	8	.000	1	19	.050

1944-1945	W	L	PCT	W	L	PCT
Iowa	11	1	.917	17	1	.944
Ohio State	10	2	.833	15	5	.750
Illinois	7	5	.583	13	7	.650
Purdue	6	6	.500	9	11	.450
Michigan	5	7	.417	12	7	.632
Wisconsin	4	8	.333	10	11	.476
Minnesota	4	8	.333	8	13	.381
Northwestern	4	8	.333	7	12	.368
Indiana	3	9	.250	10	11	.476
Chicago	-	-	---	7	8	.467

1945-1946	W	L	PCT	W	L	PCT
Ohio State	10	2	.833	16	5	.762
Indiana	9	3	.750	18	3	.857
Iowa	8	4	.667	14	4	.778
Northwestern	8	4	.667	15	5	.750
Illinois	7	5	.583	14	7	.667
Minnesota	7	5	.583	14	7	.667
Michigan	6	6	.500	12	7	.632
Purdue	4	8	.333	10	11	.476
Wisconsin	1	11	.083	4	17	.190
Chicago	0	12	.000	6	14	.300

1946-1947	W	L	PCT	W	L	PCT
Wisconsin	9	3	.750	16	6	.727
Illinois	8	4	.667	14	6	.700
Indiana	8	4	.667	12	8	.600
Minnesota	7	5	.583	14	7	.667
Michigan	6	6	.500	12	8	.600
Iowa	5	7	.417	12	7	.632
Ohio State	5	7	.417	7	13	.350
Purdue	4	8	.333	9	11	.450
Northwestern	2	10	.167	7	13	.350

1947-1948	W	L	PCT	W	L	PCT
Michigan	10	2	.833	15	5	.750
Iowa	8	4	.667	15	4	.789
Illinois	7	5	.583	15	5	.750
Wisconsin	7	5	.583	12	8	.600
Purdue	6	6	.500	11	9	.550
Ohio State	5	7	.417	10	10	.500
Minnesota	5	7	.417	10	10	.500
Indiana	3	9	.250	8	12	.400
Northwestern	3	9	.250	6	14	.300

1948-1949	W	L	PCT	W	L	PCT
Illinois	10	2	.833	21	4	.840
Minnesota	9	3	.750	18	3	.857
Michigan	7	5	.583	15	6	.714
Ohio State	6	6	.500	14	7	.667
Indiana	6	6	.500	14	8	.636
Purdue	6	6	.500	13	9	.591
Wisconsin	5	7	.417	12	10	.545
Iowa	3	9	.250	10	10	.500
Northwestern	2	10	.167	5	16	.455

1949-1950	W	L	PCT	W	L	PCT
Ohio State	11	1	.917	22	4	.846
Wisconsin	9	3	.750	17	5	.773
Indiana	7	5	.583	17	5	.773
Illinois	7	5	.583	14	8	.636
Iowa	6	6	.500	15	7	.682
Minnesota	4	8	.333	13	9	.591
Michigan	4	8	.333	11	11	.500
Northwestern	3	9	.250	10	12	.455
Purdue	3	9	.250	9	13	.410

1950-1951	Conference W	L	PCT	Season W	L	PCT
Illinois	13	1	.929	22	5	.815
Indiana	12	2	.857	19	3	.864
Iowa	9	5	.643	15	7	.682
Minnesota	7	7	.500	13	9	.591
Northwestern	7	7	.500	12	10	.545
Wisconsin	7	7	.500	10	12	.455
Michigan St.	5	9	.357	10	11	.476
Purdue	4	10	.286	8	14	.364
Michigan	3	11	.214	7	15	.318
Ohio State	3	11	.214	6	16	.273

1951-1952	W	L	PCT	W	L	PCT
Illinois	12	2	.857	22	4	.846
Iowa	11	3	.786	19	3	.863
Minnesota	10	4	.714	15	7	.682
Indiana	9	5	.643	16	6	.727
Michigan St.	6	8	.429	13	9	.591
Ohio State	6	8	.429	8	14	.364
Wisconsin	5	9	.357	10	12	.455
Michigan	4	10	.286	7	15	.318
Northwestern	4	10	.286	7	15	.318
Purdue	3	11	.214	8	14	.367

1952-1953	W	L	PCT	W	L	PCT
Indiana	17	1	.944	23	3	.885
Illinois	14	4	.778	18	4	.818
Minnesota	11	7	.611	14	8	.636
Michigan St.	11	7	.611	13	9	.591
Wisconsin	10	8	.556	13	9	.591
Iowa	9	9	.500	12	10	.545
Ohio State	7	11	.389	10	12	.455
Northwestern	5	13	.278	6	16	.273
Michigan	3	15	.167	6	16	.273
Purdue	3	15	.167	4	18	.182

1953-1954	W	L	PCT	W	L	PCT
Indiana	12	2	.857	20	4	.833
Iowa	11	3	.786	17	5	.773
Illinois	10	4	.714	17	5	.773
Minnesota	10	4	.714	17	5	.773
Wisconsin	6	8	.429	12	10	.545
Northwestern	6	8	.429	9	13	.410
Ohio State	5	9	.357	11	11	.500
Michigan St.	4	10	.286	9	13	.410
Michigan	3	11	.214	9	13	.410
Purdue	3	11	.214	9	13	.410

1954-1955	W	L	PCT	W	L	PCT
Iowa	11	3	.786	19	7	.731
Illinois	10	4	.714	17	5	.773
Minnesota	10	4	.714	15	7	.682
Michigan St.	8	6	.571	13	9	.591
Northwestern	7	7	.500	12	10	.545
Purdue	5	9	.357	12	10	.545
Michigan	5	9	.357	11	11	.500
Wisconsin	5	9	.357	10	12	.455
Indiana	5	9	.357	8	14	.636
Ohio State	4	10	.286	10	12	.455

1955-1956	W	L	PCT	W	L	PCT
Iowa	13	1	.929	20	6	.769
Illinois	11	3	.786	18	4	.818
Ohio State	9	5	.643	16	6	.727
Purdue	9	5	.643	16	6	.727
Michigan St.	7	7	.500	13	9	.591
Indiana	6	8	.429	13	9	.591
Minnesota	6	8	.429	11	11	.500
Michigan	4	10	.286	9	13	.409
Wisconsin	4	10	.286	6	16	.273
Northwestern	1	13	.071	2	20	.091

1956-1957	W	L	PCT	W	L	PCT
Indiana	10	4	.714	14	8	.636
Michigan St.	10	4	.714	16	10	.615
Minnesota	9	5	.643	14	8	.636
Ohio State	9	5	.643	14	8	.636
Purdue	8	6	.571	15	7	.682
Michigan	8	6	.571	13	9	.591
Illinois	7	7	.500	14	8	.636
Iowa	4	10	.286	8	14	.364
Wisconsin	3	11	.214	5	17	.227
Northwestern	2	12	.143	6	16	.273

	Conference			Season		
1957-1958	**W**	**L**	**PCT**	**W**	**L**	**PCT**
Indiana	10	4	.714	13	11	.542
Michigan St.	9	5	.643	16	6	.727
Purdue	9	5	.643	14	8	.636
Northwestern	8	6	.571	13	9	.591
Ohio State	8	6	.571	9	13	.409
Iowa	7	7	.500	13	9	.591
Michigan	6	8	.429	11	11	.500
Illinois	5	9	.357	11	11	.500
Minnesota	5	9	.357	10	12	.455
Wisconsin	3	11	.214	8	14	.364
1958-1959						
Michigan St.	12	2	.857	19	4	.826
Michigan	8	6	.571	15	7	.682
Northwestern	8	6	.571	15	7	.682
Purdue	8	6	.571	15	7	.682
Illinois	7	7	.500	12	10	.545
Indiana	7	7	.500	11	11	.500
Ohio State	7	7	.500	11	11	.500
Iowa	7	7	.500	10	12	.455
Minnesota	5	9	.357	8	14	.364
Wisconsin	1	13	.071	3	19	.136
1959-1960						
Ohio State	13	1	.929	25	3	.893
Indiana	11	3	.786	20	4	.833
Illinois	8	6	.571	16	7	.696
Minnesota	8	6	.571	12	12	.500
Northwestern	8	6	.571	11	12	.478
Iowa	6	8	.429	14	10	.583
Purdue	6	8	.429	11	12	.478
Michigan St.	5	9	.357	10	11	.476
Wisconsin	4	10	.286	8	16	.333
Michigan	1	13	.071	4	20	.167
1960-1961						
Ohio State	14	0	1.000	27	1	.964
Iowa	10	4	.714	18	6	.750
Purdue	10	4	.714	16	7	.696
Indiana	8	6	.571	15	9	.625
Minnesota	8	6	.571	10	13	.435
Northwestern	6	8	.429	10	12	.455
Illinois	5	9	.357	9	15	.375
Wisconsin	4	10	.286	7	17	.292
Michigan St.	3	11	.214	7	17	.292
Michigan	2	12	.143	6	18	.250

Patrick Baldwin is Northwestern's all-time steals leader with 272 and the school's No. 10 career scorer with 1,189 points.

	Conference			Season		
1961-1962	**W**	**L**	**PCT**	**W**	**L**	**PCT**
Ohio State	13	1	.929	26	2	.929
Wisconsin	10	4	.714	17	7	.708
Purdue	9	5	.643	17	7	.708
Illinois	7	7	.500	15	8	.652
Indiana	7	7	.500	13	11	.542
Iowa	7	7	.500	13	11	.542
Minnesota	6	8	.429	10	14	.417
Michigan	5	9	.357	7	17	.292
Michigan St.	3	11	.214	8	14	.364
Northwestern	3	11	.214	8	15	.348
1962-1963						
Ohio State	11	3	.786	20	4	.833
Illinois	11	3	.786	20	6	.769
Indiana	9	5	.643	13	11	.542
Michigan	8	6	.571	16	8	.667
Minnesota	8	6	.571	12	12	.500
Wisconsin	7	7	.500	14	10	.583
Northwestern	6	8	.429	9	15	.375
Iowa	5	9	.357	9	15	.375
Michigan St.	3	11	.214	6	17	.261
Purdue	2	12	.143	7	17	.292
1963-1964						
Michigan	11	3	.786	23	5	.821
Ohio State	11	3	.786	16	8	.667
Minnesota	10	4	.714	17	7	.708
Michigan St.	8	6	.571	14	10	.583
Purdue	8	6	.571	12	12	.500
Illinois	6	8	.429	13	11	.542
Northwestern	6	8	.429	8	13	.381
Indiana	5	9	.357	9	15	.375
Iowa	3	11	.214	8	15	.348
Wisconsin	2	12	.143	8	16	.333
1964-1965						
Michigan	13	1	.929	24	4	.857
Minnesota	11	3	.786	19	5	.792
Illinois	10	4	.714	18	6	.750
Indiana	9	5	.643	19	5	.792
Iowa	8	6	.571	14	10	.583
Ohio State	6	8	.429	12	12	.500
Purdue	5	9	.357	12	12	.500
Wisconsin	4	10	.286	10	14	.417
Northwestern	3	11	.214	7	17	.292
Michigan St.	1	13	.071	5	18	.217
1965-1966						
Michigan	11	3	.786	18	8	.692
Michigan St.	10	4	.714	17	7	.708
Iowa	8	6	.571	17	7	.708
Illinois	8	6	.571	12	12	.500
Minnesota	7	7	.500	14	10	.583
Northwestern	7	7	.500	12	12	.500
Wisconsin	6	8	.429	11	13	.458
Ohio State	5	9	.357	11	13	.458
Indiana	4	10	.286	8	16	.333
Purdue	4	10	.286	8	16	.333
1966-1967						
Indiana	10	4	.714	18	8	.692
Michigan St.	10	4	.714	16	7	.696
Iowa	9	5	.643	16	8	.667
Wisconsin	8	6	.571	13	11	.542
Purdue	7	7	.500	15	9	.625
Northwestern	7	7	.500	11	11	.500
Ohio State	6	8	.429	13	11	.542
Illinois	6	8	.429	12	12	.500
Minnesota	5	9	.357	9	15	.375
Michigan	2	12	.143	8	16	.333
1967-1968						
Ohio State	10	4	.714	21	8	.724
Iowa	10	4	.714	16	9	.640
Purdue	9	5	.643	15	9	.625
Northwestern	8	6	.571	13	10	.565
Wisconsin	7	7	.500	13	11	.542
Michigan St.	6	8	.429	12	12	.500
Illinois	6	8	.429	11	13	.458
Michigan	6	8	.429	11	13	.458
Indiana	4	10	.286	10	14	.417
Minnesota	4	10	.286	7	17	.292

	Conference			Season		
1968-1969	**W**	**L**	**PCT**	**W**	**L**	**PCT**
Purdue	13	1	.929	23	5	.821
Illinois	9	5	.643	19	5	.792
Ohio State	9	5	.643	17	7	.708
Michigan	7	7	.500	13	11	.542
Northwestern	6	8	.429	14	10	.583
Minnesota	6	8	.429	12	12	.500
Michigan St.	6	8	.429	11	12	.478
Iowa	5	9	.357	12	12	.500
Wisconsin	5	9	.357	11	13	.458
Indiana	4	10	.286	9	15	.375
1969-1970						
Iowa	14	0	1.000	20	6	.769
Purdue	11	3	.786	18	6	.750
Ohio State	8	6	.571	17	7	.708
Illinois	8	6	.571	15	9	.625
Minnesota	7	7	.500	13	11	.542
Michigan	5	9	.357	10	14	.417
Wisconsin	5	9	.357	10	14	.417
Michigan St.	5	9	.357	9	15	.375
Northwestern	4	10	.286	9	15	.375
Indiana	3	11	.214	7	17	.292
1970-1971						
Ohio State	13	1	.929	20	6	.769
Michigan	12	2	.857	19	7	.731
Purdue	11	3	.786	18	7	.720
Indiana	9	5	.643	17	7	.708
Illinois	5	9	.357	11	12	.478
Minnesota	5	9	.357	11	13	.458
Michigan St.	4	10	.286	10	14	.417
Iowa	4	10	.286	9	15	.375
Wisconsin	4	10	.286	9	15	.375
Northwestern	3	11	.214	7	17	.292
1971-1972						
Minnesota	11	3	.786	18	7	.720
Ohio State	10	4	.714	18	6	.750
Indiana	9	5	.643	17	8	.680
Michigan	9	5	.643	14	10	.583
Wisconsin	6	8	.428	13	11	.542
Michigan St.	6	8	.428	13	11	.542
Purdue	6	8	.428	12	12	.500
Illinois	5	9	.357	14	10	.583
Iowa	5	9	.357	11	13	.458
Northwestern	3	11	.214	5	18	.217
1972-1973						
Indiana	11	3	.786	22	6	.786
Minnesota	10	4	.714	21	5	.808
Purdue	8	6	.571	15	9	.625
Ohio State	8	6	.571	14	10	.583
Illinois	8	6	.571	14	10	.583
Michigan St.	6	8	.429	13	11	.542
Iowa	6	8	.429	13	11	.542
Michigan	6	8	.429	13	11	.542
Wisconsin	5	9	.357	11	13	.458
Northwestern	2	12	.143	5	19	.208
1973-1974						
Indiana	12	2	.857	23	5	.821
Michigan	12	2	.857	22	5	.814
Purdue	10	4	.714	21	9	.700
Wisconsin	8	6	.571	16	8	.667
Michigan St.	8	6	.571	13	11	.542
Minnesota	6	8	.429	12	12	.500
Iowa	5	9	.357	8	16	.333
Ohio State	4	10	.286	9	15	.375
Northwestern	3	11	.214	9	15	.375
Illinois	2	12	.143	5	18	.217
1974-1975						
Indiana	18	0	1.000	31	1	.969
Michigan	12	6	.667	19	8	.704
Minnesota	11	7	.611	18	8	.692
Purdue	11	7	.611	17	11	.607
Michigan St.	10	8	.555	17	9	.654
Ohio State	8	10	.444	14	14	.500
Iowa	7	11	.389	10	16	.385
Wisconsin	5	13	.278	8	18	.308
Illinois	4	14	.222	8	18	.308
Northwestern	4	14	.222	6	20	.231

	Conference			Season		
1975-1976	**W**	**L**	**PCT**	**W**	**L**	**PCT**
Indiana	18	0	1.000	32	0	1.000
Michigan	14	4	.778	25	7	.781
Purdue	11	7	.661	16	11	.592
Michigan St.	10	8	.556	13	13	.518
Iowa	9	9	.500	19	10	.655
Minnesota	8	10	.444	16	10	.616
Illinois	7	11	.389	14	13	.518
Northwestern	7	11	.389	12	14	.444
Wisconsin	4	14	.222	10	16	.384
Ohio State	2	16	.111	6	20	.231
1976-1977						
Michigan	16	2	.889	26	4	.867
Purdue	14	4	.778	20	8	.714
Iowa	12	6	.667	20	7	.741
Indiana	11	7	.611	16	11	.593
Michigan St.	9	9	.500	12	15	.444
Illinois	8	10	.444	16	14	.533
Wisconsin	7	11	.389	11	16	.407
Northwestern	7	11	.389	9	18	.333
Ohio State	6	12	.333	11	16	.407
Minnesota*	0	18	.000	0	27	.000
*NCAA declares all games forfeited						
1977-1978						
Michigan St.	15	3	.833	25	5	.833
Indiana	12	6	.667	21	8	.724
Minnesota	12	6	.667	17	10	.630
Michigan	11	7	.611	16	11	.593
Purdue	11	7	.611	16	11	.593
Ohio State	9	9	.500	16	11	.593
Illinois	7	11	.389	13	14	.481
Iowa	5	13	.278	12	15	.444
Northwestern	4	14	.222	8	19	.296
Wisconsin	4	14	.222	8	19	.296
1978-1979						
Michigan St.	13	5	.722	26	6	.813
Purdue	13	5	.722	27	8	.771
Iowa	13	5	.722	20	8	.714
Ohio State	12	6	.667	19	12	.613
Indiana	10	8	.556	22	12	.647
Michigan	8	10	.444	15	12	.556
Illinois	7	11	.389	19	11	.633
Wisconsin	6	12	.333	12	15	.444
Minnesota	6	12	.333	11	16	.408
Northwestern	2	16	.111	6	21	.222
1979-1980						
Indiana	13	5	.722	21	8	.724
Ohio State	12	6	.667	21	8	.724
Purdue	11	7	.611	23	10	.687
Iowa	10	8	.556	23	10	.687
Minnesota	10	8	.556	21	11	.656
Illinois	8	10	.444	22	13	.629
Michigan	8	10	.444	17	13	.567
Wisconsin	7	11	.389	15	14	.517
Michigan St.	6	12	.333	12	15	.444
Northwestern	5	13	.278	10	17	.370
1980-1981						
Indiana	14	4	.778	26	9	.743
Iowa	13	5	.722	21	7	.750
Illinois	12	6	.667	21	8	.724
Purdue	10	8	.556	21	11	.656
Minnesota	9	9	.500	19	11	.633
Ohio State	9	9	.500	14	13	.519
Michigan	8	10	.444	19	11	.633
Michigan St.	7	11	.389	13	14	.481
Wisconsin	5	13	.278	11	16	.423
Northwestern	3	15	.167	9	18	.333
1981-1982						
Minnesota	14	4	.778	23	6	.793
Iowa	12	6	.667	21	8	.724
Ohio State	12	6	.667	21	10	.677
Indiana	12	6	.667	19	10	.655
Purdue	11	7	.611	18	14	.563
Illinois	10	8	.556	18	11	.621
Michigan St.	7	11	.389	12	16	.429
Michigan	7	11	.389	8	19	.296
Northwestern	5	13	.278	9	18	.333
#Wisconsin	0	18	.000	0	27	.000

RECORDS
All-Time Standings (continued)

1982-1983	Conference W L PCT	Season W L PCT
Indiana	13 5 .722	24 6 .800
Iowa	11 7 .611	22 9 .710
Purdue	11 7 .611	21 9 .700
Ohio State	11 7 .611	20 10 .667
Illinois	11 7 .611	21 11 .656
Minnesota	9 9 .500	18 11 .621
Michigan St.	9 9 .500	17 13 .567
Northwestern	8 10 .444	18 12 .600
Michigan	7 11 .389	16 12 .571
#Wisconsin	0 18 .000	0 28 .000

1983-1984	Conference W L PCT	Season W L PCT
Illinois	15 3 .833	26 5 .839
Purdue	15 3 .833	22 7 .759
Indiana	13 5 .722	22 9 .710
Michigan	11 7 .611	24 9 .727
Michigan St.	9 9 .500	16 12 .571
Ohio State	8 10 .444	15 14 .517
Northwestern	7 11 .389	14 14 .500
Minnesota	6 12 .333	15 13 .536
Iowa	6 12 .333	13 15 .464
#Wisconsin	0 18 .000	0 28 .000

#Wisconsin forfeits all games from 1981-82 to 1983-84

1984-1985	Conference W L PCT	Season W L PCT
Michigan	16 2 .889	26 4 .867
Illinois	12 6 .667	26 9 .743
Purdue	11 7 .611	20 9 .690
Ohio State	11 7 .611	20 10 .667
Iowa	10 8 .556	21 11 .656
Michigan St.	10 8 .556	19 10 .655
Indiana	7 11 .389	19 14 .576
Minnesota	6 12 .333	13 15 .464
Wisconsin	5 13 .278	14 14 .500
Northwestern	2 16 .111	6 22 .214

1985-1986	Conference W L PCT	Season W L PCT
Michigan	14 4 .778	28 5 .848
Indiana	13 5 .722	21 8 .724
Michigan St.	12 6 .667	23 8 .742
Purdue	11 7 .611	22 10 .688
Illinois	11 7 .611	22 10 .688
Iowa	10 8 .556	20 12 .625
Ohio State	8 10 .444	19 14 .576
Minnesota	5 13 .278	15 16 .484
Wisconsin	4 14 .222	12 16 .429
Northwestern	2 16 .111	8 20 .286

1986-1987	Conference W L PCT	Season W L PCT
Indiana	15 3 .833	30 4 .882
Purdue	15 3 .833	25 5 .833
Iowa	14 4 .778	30 5 .857
Illinois	13 5 .722	23 8 .742
Michigan	10 8 .556	20 12 .625
Ohio State	9 9 .500	20 13 .606
Michigan St.	6 12 .333	11 17 .393
Wisconsin	4 14 .222	14 17 .452
Minnesota	2 16 .111	9 19 .321
Northwestern	2 16 .111	7 21 .250

1987-1988	Conference W L PCT	Season W L PCT
Purdue	16 2 .889	29 4 .879
Michigan	13 5 .722	26 8 .765
Iowa	12 6 .667	24 10 .706
Illinois	12 6 .667	23 10 .697
Indiana	11 7 .611	19 10 .655
Ohio State	9 9 .500	20 13 .606
Wisconsin	6 12 .333	12 16 .429
Michigan St.	5 13 .278	10 18 .357
Minnesota	4 14 .222	10 18 .357
Northwestern	2 16 .111	7 21 .250

1988-1989	Conference W L PCT	Season W L PCT
Indiana	15 3 .833	27 8 .771
Illinois	14 4 .778	31 5 .861
Michigan	12 6 .667	30 7 .811
Iowa	10 8 .556	23 10 .697
Minnesota	9 9 .500	19 12 .613
Wisconsin	8 10 .444	18 12 .600
Purdue	8 10 .444	15 16 .484
Ohio State	6 12 .333	19 15 .559
Michigan St.	6 12 .333	18 15 .546
Northwestern	2 16 .111	9 19 .321

1989-1990	Conference W L PCT	Season W L PCT
Michigan St.	15 3 .833	28 6 .824
Purdue	13 5 .722	22 8 .733
Michigan	12 6 .667	23 8 .742
Illinois	11 7 .611	21 8 .724
Minnesota	11 7 .611	23 9 .719
Ohio State	10 8 .556	17 13 .567
Indiana	8 10 .444	18 11 .621
Wisconsin	4 14 .222	14 17 .452
Iowa	4 14 .222	12 16 .429
Northwestern	2 16 .111	9 19 .321

1990-1991	Conference W L PCT	Season W L PCT
Ohio State	15 3 .833	27 4 .871
Indiana	15 3 .833	29 5 .853
Illinois	11 7 .611	21 10 .677
Michigan St.	11 7 .511	19 11 .633
Iowa	9 9 .500	21 11 .656
Purdue	9 9 .500	17 12 .586
Wisconsin	8 10 .444	15 15 .500
Michigan	7 11 .389	14 15 .483
Minnesota	5 13 .278	12 16 .429
Northwestern	0 18 .000	5 23 .179
Penn State	- - ---	21 11 .656

1991-1992	Conference W L PCT	Season W L PCT
Ohio State	15 3 .833	26 6 .813
Indiana	14 4 .778	27 7 .794
Michigan	11 7 .611	25 9 .735
Michigan St.	11 7 .611	22 8 .733
Iowa	10 8 .556	19 11 .633
Purdue	8 10 .444	18 15 .545
Minnesota	8 10 .444	16 16 .500
Illinois	7 11 .389	13 15 .464
Wisconsin	4 14 .222	13 18 .419
Northwestern	2 16 .111	9 19 .321
Penn State	- - ---	21 8 .724

1992-1993	Conference W L PCT	Season W L PCT
Indiana	17 1 .944	31 4 .886
Michigan	15 3 .833	31 5 .861
Iowa	11 7 .611	23 9 .719
Illinois	11 7 .611	19 13 .594
Minnesota	9 9 .500	22 10 .688
Purdue	9 9 .500	18 10 .643
Ohio State	8 10 .444	15 13 .536
Michigan State	7 11 .389	15 13 .536
Wisconsin	7 11 .389	14 14 .500
Northwestern	3 15 .167	8 19 .296
Penn State	2 16 .111	7 20 .259

1993-1994	Conference W L PCT	Season W L PCT
Purdue	14 4 .778	29 5 .853
Michigan	13 5 .722	24 8 .750
Indiana	12 6 .667	21 9 .700
Minnesota	10 8 .556	21 12 .636
Michigan St.	10 8 .556	20 12 .625
Illinois	10 8 .556	17 11 .607
Wisconsin	8 10 .444	18 11 .621
Penn State	6 12 .333	13 14 .481
Ohio State	6 12 .333	13 16 .448
Northwestern	5 13 .278	15 14 .517
Iowa	5 13 .278	11 16 .407

1995-95	Conference W L PCT	Season W L PCT
Purdue	15 3 .833	25 7 .781
Michigan St.	14 4 .778	22 6 .786
Indiana	11 7 .611	19 12 .613
Michigan	11 7 .611	17 14 .548
Illinois	10 8 .556	19 12 .613
Minnesota	10 8 .556	19 12 .613
Penn State	9 9 .500	21 11 .656
Iowa	9 9 .500	21 12 .636
Wisconsin	7 11 .389	13 14 .481
Ohio State	2 16 .111	6 22 .214
Northwestern	1 17 .056	5 22 .185

Ohio State won the 1960 NCAA championship and finished second in 1961 and '62 with such stars as Jerry Lucas (11), John Havlicek (5), Larry Siegfried (21), Mel Nowell (14) and Bob Knight (24)

HONORS

Indiana vs. Penn State, 1994

1976-1995

- Conference attendance totals soar as the Big Ten leads the nation in attendance every year beginning in 1977. Boosted by Penn State's addition in 1992, the league sets an NCAA attendance record with 1,301,079 during the 1993-94 season.
- As the NCAA Championship bracket expands, more Big Ten teams are invited to the tournament. In 1976, '80, '89 and '92, two Big Ten teams make it to the Final Four, with championships to league teams coming in 1976, '79, '81, '87 and '89.
- Fourteen players win 17 consensus all-America honors with Indiana having three two-time winners. IU's Scott May in 1976 and Calbert Cheaney in 1993 and Purdue's Glenn Robinson in 1994 are named national Division I players of the year.
- Of the top six coaches ranked according to number of Big Ten victories, four are active in this period. Indiana's Bob Knight becomes the all-time league leader in Conference wins and overall winning percentage.
- Indiana reasserts itself as a national power, winning three NCAA championships (1976, '81 and '87). The '76 Hoosiers rank as one of the greatest college teams ever. They are the only undefeated (32-0) Big Ten team in the modern era.

HONORS
Individual Big Ten Honors

Chicago Tribune BIG TEN MOST VALUABLE PLAYER

1946 - Max Morris, F, NU
1947 - Glen Selbo, G, WIS
1948 - Murray Wier, F, IOWA
1949 - Dwight Eddleman, F, ILL
1950 - Don Rehfeldt, W, WIS
1951 - Don Sunderlage, G, ILL
1952 - Chuck Darling, C, IOWA
1953 - Don Schlundt, C, IND
1954 - John (Red) Kerr, C, ILL
1955 - Chuck Mencel, G, MINN
1956 - Robin Freeman, G, OSU
1957 - Archie Dees, C, IND
1958 - Archie Dees, C, IND
1959 - John Green, C, MSU
1960 - Jerry Lucas, C, OSU
1961 - Jerry Lucas, C, OSU
1962 - Jerry Lucas, C, OSU
1963 - Gary Bradds, C, OSU
1964 - Gary Bradds, C, OSU
1965 - Cazzie Russell, G, MICH
1966 - Cazzie Russell, G, MICH
1967 - Jim Dawson, G, ILL
1968 - Sam Williams, F, IOWA
1969 - Rick Mount, G, PUR
1970 - Rick Mount, G, PUR
1971 - Jim Cleamons, G, OSU
1972 - Jim Brewer, C, MINN
1973 - Steve Downing, C, IND
1974 - Campy Russell, F, MICH
1975 - Scott May, F, IND
1976 - Scott May, F, IND
1977 - Kent Benson, C, IND
1978 - Mychal Thompson, C, MINN
1979 - Earvin Johnson, G, MSU
1980 - Mike Woodson, F, IND
1981 - Ray Tolbert, C, IND
1982 - Clark Kellogg, F, OSU
1983 - Randy Whittman, G-F, IND
1984 - Jim Rowinski, C, PUR
1985 - Roy Tarpley, C, MICH
1986 - Scott Skiles, G, MSU
1987 - Steve Alford, G, IND
1988 - Gary Grant, G, MICH
1989 - Glen Rice, F, MICH
1990 - Steve Smith, G, MSU
1991 - Jim Jackson, G-F, OSU
1992 - Jim Jackson, G-F, OSU
1993 - Calbert Cheaney, F, IND
1994 - Glenn Robinson, F, PUR
1995 - Shawn Respert, G, MSU

AS SELECTED BY MEDIA PANEL (M) AND COACHES (C)

Player of the Year
1985 Roy Tarpley, C, MICH
1986 Scott Skiles, G, MSU
1987 Dennis Hopson, G, OSU
1988 Gary Grant, G, MICH
1989 Jay Edwards, G, IND (M)
        Glen Rice, F, MICH (C)
1990 Stephen Scheffler, C, PUR
1991 Jim Jackson, G-F, OSU
1992 Jim Jackson, G-F, OSU
1993 Calbert Cheaney, F, IND
1994 Glenn Robinson, F, PUR
1995 Shawn Respert, G, MSU

Freshman of the Year
1986 Gary Grant, G, MICH (M only)
1987 Dean Garrett, C, IND* (C only)
1988 Jay Edwards, G, IND (M only)
1989 Eric Anderson, C, IND
1990 Jim Jackson, G, OSU
1991 Damon Bailey, G, IND
1992 Chris Webber, F, MICH
1993 Greg Simpson, G, OSU
1994 Jess Settles, F, IOWA
1995 Maurice Taylor, C-F, MICH

* selected as "Newcomer of the Year"

Coach of the Year
(selected by media and coaches since 1987; media only since 1992)
1973 Bob Knight, IND
1974 Johnny Orr, MICH
1975 Bob Knight, IND*
1976 Bob Knight, IND*
1977 Johnny Orr, MICH
1978 Jud Heathcote, MSU
1979 Lute Olson, IOWA
1980 Bob Knight, IND
1981 Bob Knight, IND
1982 Jim Dutcher, MINN
1983 Eldon Miller, OSU
1984 Gene Keady, PUR*
1985 Bill Frieder, MICH
1986 Jud Heathcote, MSU
1987 Tom Davis, IOWA*
1988 Gene Keady, PUR
1989 Bob Knight, IND
1990 Gene Keady, PUR*
1991 Randy Ayres, OSU
1992 Randy Ayers, OSU
1993 Lou Henson, ILL
1994 Gene Keady, PUR
1995 Gene Keady, PUR

*national Coach of the Year

Defensive Player of the Year
(selected by Big Ten radio broadcasters; by coaches only since 1992)
1984 Ricky Hall, G, PUR
1985 Bruce Douglas, G, ILL
1986 Bruce Douglas, G, ILL
1987 Gary Grant, G, MICH
1988 Gary Grant, G, MICH
1989 Stephen Bardo, G, ILL
1990 Ken Redfield, F, MSU
1992 Acie Earl, C, IOWA
1993 Greg Graham, G, IND
1994 Patrick Baldwin, G, NU
1995 Eric Snow, G, MSU

Note: Player, Freshman and Coach of the Year selected under auspices of Associated Press and United Press International from 1986 to 1989.

NCAA Division I Player of the Year
1961 Jerry Lucas, C, OSU (AP, UPI, USBWA)
1962 Jerry Lucas, C, OSU (AP, UPI, USBWA)
1964 Gary Bradds, C, OSU (AP, UPI)
1966 Cazzie Russell, G, MICH (AP, UPI, USBWA)
1976 Scott May, F, IND (AP, UPI, NABC, N)
1993 Calbert Cheaney, F, IND (AP, UPI, UWBWA, NABC, N)
1994 Glenn Robinson, F, PUR (AP, UPI, UWBWA, NABC, N)

AP–Associated Press   UPI–United Press International
UWBWA–U.S. Basketball Writers Association
NABC–National Association of Basketball Coaches
N–Naismith

CONSENSUS ALL-AMERICAS

Illinois
Bill Hapac, F, 1940
*Andy Phillip, F, 1942-43
Walton Kirk, G, 1945
Rod Fletcher, G, 1952

Indiana
*Branch McCracken, F, 1930
Vern Huffman, G, 1936
Ernie Andres, G, 1939
Ralph Hamilton, 1947
Don Schlundt, C, 1954
Scott May, F, 1975-76
Kent Benson, C, 1976-77
Isiah Thomas, G, 1981
Steve Alford, G, 1986-87
Calbert Cheaney, F, 1993

Iowa
Murray Wier, F, 1948
Chuck Darling, C, 1952

Michigan
Cazzie Russell, G, 1965-66
Rickey Green, G, 1977
Gary Grant, G, 1988
Chris Webber, F, 1993

Michigan State
Earvin Johnson, F, 1979
Shawn Respert, G, 1995

Minnesota
Jim McIntyre, C, 1948
Dick Garmaker, G, 1955
Mychal Thompson, C, 1978

Northwestern
Joe Reiff, C, 1931-33
Otto Graham, F, 1944
Max Morris, F, 1946

Ohio State
Wes Fesler, G, 1931
Jimmy Hull, F, 1939
Dick Schnittker, F, 1950
Robin Freeman, G, 1956
Jerry Lucas, C, 1960-61-62
Gary Bradds, C, 1964
Jim Jackson, G-F, 1991-92

Purdue
Charles Murphy, C, 1929-30
*John Wooden, G, 1930-31-32
Norman Cottom, F, 1934
Robert Kessler, F, 1936
Jewell Young, F, 1937-38
Terry Dischinger, C, 1961-62
Dave Schellhase, F, 1966
Rick Mount, G, 1969-70
Joe Barry Carroll, C, 1980
Glenn Robinson, F, 1994

Wisconsin
Gene Englund, F, 1941
John Kotz, F, 1942

*Hall of Fame selection

All-Big Ten

FIRST TEAM FROM 1948

Illinois
Dwight Eddleman, F, 1948-49
Don Sunderlage, G, 1951
Rod Fletcher, G, 1952
Irv Bemoras, G, 1953
John Kerr, C, 1954
Paul Judson, G, 1955-56
George Bon Salle, C, 1956
Bill Ridley, G, 1956
Don Ohl, G, 1957-58
Dave Downey, F, 1963
Skip Thoren, C, 1965
Tal Brody, G, 1965
Don Freeman, F, 1966
Jim Dawson, G, 1967
Dave Scholz, C, 1968-69
Nick Weatherspoon, F, 1973
Eddie Johnson, F, 1981
Derek Harper, G, 1983
Bruce Douglas, G, 1984
Ken Norman, F, 1986-87
Nick Anderson, F, 1989
Kendall Gill, G, 1990

Indiana
Lou Watson, G, 1950
Bill Garrett, C, 1951
Don Schlundt, C, 1953-54-55
Bob Leonard, G, 1953-54
Archie Dees, C, 1957-58
Walt Bellamy, C, 1960-61
Jimmy Rayl, G, 1962-63
Tom Bolyard, F, 1963
Dick Van Arsdale, F, 1964
Harry Joyner, F, 1967
George McGinnis, F, 1971
Joby Wright, F, 1972
Steve Downing, C, 1973
Steve Green, F, 1974-75
Quinn Buckner, G, 1974-75
Scott May, F, 1975-76
Kent Benson, C, 1975-76-77
Mike Woodson, F, 1979
Isiah Thomas, G, 1980-81
Ted Kitchel, F, 1982-83
Randy Wittman, G-F, 1983
Steve Alford, G, 1984-86-87
Uwe Blab, C, 1985
Dean Garrett, C, 1988
Jay Edwards, G, 1989
Calbert Cheaney, G-F, 1991-92
Eric Anderson, F, 1991
Calbert Cheaney, F, 1993
Greg Graham, G, 1993
Damon Bailey, G, 1994
Alan Henderson, F, 1995

Iowa
Murray Wier, F, 1948
Chuck Darling, C, 1952
Bill Logan, C, 1955-56
Carl Cain, F, 1956
Dave Gunther, F, 1959
Don Nelson, C-F, 1961-62
Sam Williams, F, 1967-68
John Johnson, F, 1970
Fred Brown, G, 1971
Ronnie Lester, G, 1978-79
Kevin Boyle, F, 1981
Greg Stokes, C, 1985
Ed Horton, F, 1989
Acie Earl, C, 1992

Dwight "Dike" Eddleman, Illinois, All-Big Ten, 1948-49

Kent Benson, Indiana All-Big Ten, 1975-76-77

Sam Williams, Iowa All-Big Ten, 1967-68

Rudy Tomjanovich, Michigan All-Big Ten, 1969-70

Michigan
Pete Elliott, G, 1948
Bob Harrison, G, 1948-49
M.C. Burton, F, 1959
Bill Buntin, C, 1963-65
Cazzie Russell, G, 1964-65-66
Rudy Tomjanovich, F, 1969-70
Henry Wilmore, F, 1971-72
Campy Russell, F, 1974
Rickey Green, G, 1976-77
Phil Hubbard, F, 1977
Mike McGee, F, 1978-81
Roy Tarpley, C, 1985-86
Gary Grant, G, 1987-88
Glen Rice, F, 1988-89
Rumeal Robinson, G, 1990
Chris Webber, F, 1993
Juwan Howard, C, 1994
Jalen Rose, G, 1994

Michigan State
Julius McCoy, F, 1956
Jack Quiggle, G, 1957
Johnny Green, C, 1958-59
Horace Walker, F, 1960
Stan Washington, F, 1966
Lee Lafayette, C, 1969
Ralph Simpson, F, 1970
Mike Robinson, G, 1972-73-74
Lindsay Hairston, C, 1974-75
Terry Furlow, F, 1975-76
Earvin Johnson, G, 1978-79
Gregory Kelser, F, 1979
Jay Vincent, C, 1980-81
Kevin Smith, G, 1982
Sam Vincent, G, 1985
Scott Skiles, G, 1986
Steve Smith, G, 1990-91
Mike Peplowski, C, 1992
Shawn Respert, G, 1994-95

Minnesota
Jim McIntyre, C, 1948
Whitney Skoog, G, 1950-51
Charles Mencel, G, 1953-55
Dick Garmaker, G, 1954-55
George Kline, F, 1957-58
Ron Johnson, C, 1959-60
Lou Hudson, F, 1965
Archie Clark, G, 1966
Tom Kondla, C, 1967
Clyde Turner, F, 1972
Ron Behagen, F, 1973
Jim Brewer, C, 1973
Mychal Thompson, C 1976-77-78
Kevin McHale, C, 1980
Randy Breuer, C, 1982-83
Darryl Mitchell, G, 1982
Tommy Davis, F, 1985
Willie Burton, F, 1990

Northwestern
Ray Ragelis, C, 1951
Frank Ehmann, F, 1955
Joe Ruklick, C, 1959
Rick Lopossa, F, 1964
Jim Burns, G, 1967
Billy McKinney, G, 1977

Randy Breuer, Minnesota All-Big Ten, 1992-93

Dave Sorenson, Ohio State All-Big Ten, 1969-70

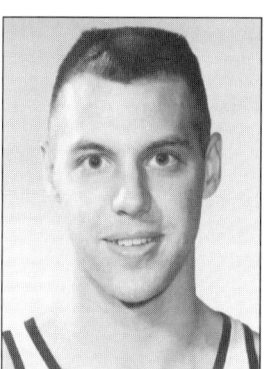
Terry Dischinger, Purdue All-Big Ten, 1960-61-62

Don Rehfeldt, Wisconsin All-Big Ten, 1949-50

Ohio State
Dick Schnittker, F, 1949-50
Bob Donham, F, 1950
Paul Ebert, C, 1952-54
Robin Freeman, G, 1955-56
Frank Howard, F, 1957-58
Jerry Lucas, C, 1960-61-62
John Havlicek, F, 1961-62
Larry Siegfried, G, 1961
Gary Bradds, C, 1963-64
Bill Hosket, F, 1967-68
Dave Sorenson, C, 1969-70
Jim Cleamons, G, 1971
Luke Witte, C, 1971
Allan Hornyak, G, 1971-72-73
Kelvin Ransey, G, 1978-79-80
Herb Williams, C, 1980
Clark Kellogg, F, 1982
Tony Campbell, F, 1983-84
Brad Sellers, C, 1986
Dennis Hopson, F, 1987
Jay Burson, G, 1989
Jim Jackson, G-F, 1991-92

Purdue
Howard Williams, G, 1949
Carl McNulty, C, 1952
Willie Merriweather, G, 1959
Terry Dischinger, C, 1960-61-62
Mel Garland, G, 1963
Dave Schellhase, F, 1964-66
Rick Mount, G, 1968-70
Herman Gilliam, F, 1969
Bob Ford, F, 1972
Frank Kendrick, F, 1974
Bruce Parkinson, G, 1975
John Garrett, C, 1975
Walter Jordan, F, 1977-78
Joe Barry Carroll, C, 1979-80
Keith Edmondson, G, 1982
Russell Cross, C, 1983
Jim Rowinski, C, 1984
James Bullock, F-C, 1985
Troy Lewis, G, 1987-88
Todd Mitchell, F, 1988
Stephen Scheffler, C, 1990
Jimmy Oliver, F, 1991
Woody Austin, G, 1992
Glenn Robinson, F, 1993-94
Cuonzo Martin, F, 1995

Wisconsin
Don Rehfeldt, C, 1949-50
Ab Nicholas, G, 1951-52
Joe Franklin, F, 1968
Patrick Tompkins, C, 1991
Michael Finley, F-G, 1993-95
Rashard Griffith, C, 1995

HONORS
Most Valuable Players *(Big Ten Chicago Tribune Most Valuable Player in bold)*

1946
George Raby, C, CHI
Bob Doster, F, ILL
John Wallace, F, IND
Herb Wilkinson, G, IOWA
Dave Strack, F-G, MICH
Tony Jaros, F, MINN
Max Morris, F, NU
Paul Huston, G, OSU
Rudy Lawson, G, PUR
Bob Cook, F, WIS

1947
Jack Smiley, G, ILL
Ralph Hamilton, F, IND
Murray Wier, F, IOWA
Mack Suprunowicz, F, MICH
Jim McIntyre, C, MINN
Bernard Schadler, G, NU
Jack Underman, C, OSU
Paul Hoffman, G, PUR
Glen Selbo, G, WIS

1948
Jack Burmaster, G, ILL
Ward Wiliams, F, IND
Murry Wier, F, IOWA
Pete Elliott, G, MICH
Harry (Bud) Grant, F, MINN
Charles Tourek, G, NU
Dick Schnittker, F, OSU
Bob Berberian, G, PUR
Bob Cook, F, WIS

1949
Dwight Eddleman, F, Ill
Lou Watson, G, IND
Charlie Mason, F, IOWA
Bob Harrison, G, MICH
Harold Olson, F, MINN
Bill Stricklen, NU
Dick Schnittker, F, OSU
Howie Williams, G, PUR
Ron Rehfeldt, C, WIS

1950
Wally Osterkorn, C, ILL
Lou Watson, G, IND
Franklin Calsbeek, F, IOWA
Mack Suprunowicz, F, MICH
Meyer (Whitney) Skoog, G, MINN
Ray Ragelis, C, NU
Bob Donham, F, OSU
Howie Williams, G, PUR
Don Rehfeldt, C, WIS

1951
Don Sunderlage, G, ILL
Bill Garrett, C, IND
Franklin Calsbeek, F, IOWA
Leo VanderKuy, C, MICH
Jim Snodgrass, F, MSU
Meyer (Whitney) Skoog, G, MINN
Ray Ragelis, C, NU
Jim Remington, F, OSU
Carl McNulty, C, PUR
Ab Nicholas, G, WIS

1952
Rod Fletcher, G, ILL
Bob Leonard, F, IND
Chuck Darling, C, IOWA
Jim Skala, F, MICH
Bill Bower, F, MSU
Dick Means, F, MINN
Frank Petranceck, C, NU
Paul Ebert, C, OSU
Carl McNulty, C, PUR
Ab Nicholas, G, WIS

1953
Irv Bemoras, G, ILL
Don Schlundt, C, IND
Herb Thompson, F, IOWA
Paul Groffsky, C, MICH
Al Farari, F, MSU
Bob Gelle, F, MINN
John Biever, G, NU
Paul Ebert, C, OSU
Jack Runyan, F, PUR
Chuck Siefert, G, WIS

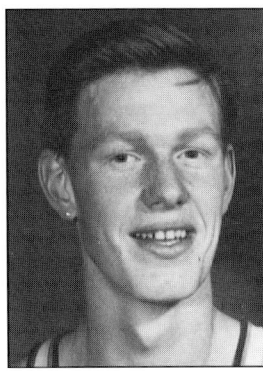
Johnny "Red" Kerr, Illinois

1954
John (Red) Kerr, C, ILL
Don Schlundt, C, IND
Carl Cain, F, IOWA
Jim Barron, G, MICH
Al Ferrari, F, MSU
Ed Kalafat, C, MINN
Fran Ehmann, F, NU
Paul Ebert, C, OSU
Dennis Blind, G, PUR
Paul Morrow, C, WIS

1955
Paul Judson, G, ILL
Don Schlundt, C, IND
Bill Seaburg, G, IOWA
Ron Kramer, C, MICH
Al Ferrari, F, MSU
Chuck Mencel, G, MINN
Frank Ehmann, F, NU
John Miller, F, OSU
Don Beck, F, PUR
Dick Cable, F, WIS

1956
Bruce Brothers, F, ILL
Wally Choice, F, IND
Carl Cain, F, IOWA
Ron Kramer, C, MICH
Julius McCoy, F, MSU
Dave Tucker, F, MINN
Dick Mast, C, NU
Robin Freeman, G, OSU
Joe Sexson, F, PUR
Dick Miller, G, WIS

1957
Harv Schmidt, F, ILL
Archie Dees, C, IND
Dave Gunther, F, IOWA
Ron Kramer, C, MICH
George Ferguson, F, MSU
Jed Dommeyer, C, MINN
Joe Ruklick, C, NU
Gene Millard, G, OSU
Lamar Lundy, C, PUR
Bob Litzow, F, WIS

1958
Don Ohl, G, ILL
Archie Dees, C, IND
Dave Gunther, F, IOWA
Pete Tillotson, C-F, MICH
John Green, C, MSU
George Kline, F, MINN
Joe Ruklick, C, NU
Ken Sidle, F, OSU
Wilson Elson, C, PUR
Walter Holt, G, WIS

1959
Roger Taylor, G, ILL
Walt Bellamy, C, IND
Dave Gunther, F, IOWA
M.C. Burton, F, MICH
John Green, C, MSU
Rogert Johnson, G, MINN
Willie Jones, F, NU
Larry Siegfried, G, OSU
Willie Merriweather, G, PUR
Bob Barneson, F, WIS

1960
Govoner Vaughn, F, ILL
Walt Bellamy, C, IND
Don Nelson, C, IOWA
Lovell Farris, F-C, MICH
Horace Walker, F, MSU
Ron Johnson, C, MINN
Willie Jones, F, NU
Jerry Lucas, C, OSU
Terry Dischinger, C, PUR
Fred Clow, C, WIS

1961
Dave Downey, F, ILL
Walt Bellamy, C, IND
Don Nelson, C-F, IOWA
John Tidwell, G, MICH
Art Schwarm, G, MSU
Dick Erickson, F, MINN
Ralph Wells, F, NU (co)
Brad Snyder, F, NU (co)
Jerry Lucas, C, OSU
Terry Dischinger, G, PUR
Ken Siebel, F, WIS

1962
Dave Downey, F, ILL
Jimmy Rayl, G, IND
Don Nelson, F, IOWA
John Harris, C, MICH
Pete Gent, F, MSU
Ray Cronk, F, MINN
Ralph Wells, G, NU
Jerry Lucas, C, OSU
Terry Dischinger, C, PUR
Ken Siebel, F, WIS

1963
Dave Downey, F, ILL
Tom Bolyard, F, IND
Jerry Messick, C, IOWA
Bill Buntin, C, MICH
Ted Williams, C, MSU
Eric Magdanz, F, MINN
Rich Falk, G, NU
Gary Bradds, C, OSU
Mel Garland, G, PUR
Ken Siebel, F, WIS

1964
Skip Thoren, F, ILL
Tom Van Arsdale, F (co)
Dick Van Arsdale, F, IND (co)
Jimmy Rodgers, G, IOWA
Cazzie Russell, G, MICH
Fred Thomann, C, MSU
Bill Davis, F, MINN
Rich Falk, G, NU (co)
Rick Lopossa, F, NU (co)
Garry Bradds, C, OSU
Dave Schellhase, F, PUR
Ken Gustafson, F, WIS

1965
Skip Thoren, C, ILL
Dick Van Arsdale, F, IND (co)
Tom Van Arsdale, F, IND (co)
Jimmy Rodgers, G, IOWA
Bill Buntin, C, MICH (co)
Cazzie Russell, G, MICH (co)
Stan Washington, G, MSU
Lou Hudson, F, MINN
Jim Pitts, C, NU
Dick Ricketts, G, OSU
Dave Schellhase, F, PUR
Jim Bohen, G, WIS

1966
Don Freeman, F, ILL
Max Walker, G, IND
Denny Pauling, G, IOWA
Cazzie Russell, G, MICH
Stan Washington, F, MSU
Archie Clark, G, MINN
Jim Pitts, C, NU
Bob Dove, C, OSU
Dave Schellhase, F, PUR
Paul Morenz, G, WIS

1967
Jim Dawson, G, ILL
Harry Joyner, F, IND
Gerry Jones, F, IOWA
Dennis Bankey, F, MICH
Matthew Aitch, C, MSU
Tom Kondla, C, MINN
Jim Burns, G, NU (co)
Mike Weaver, F, NU (co)
Bill Hoskett, C, OSU
Herman Gilliam, F, PUR
Joe Franklin, F, WIS

1968
Dave Scholz, C, ILL
Vern Payne, G, IND
Sam Williams, F, IOWA
Jim Pitts, G, MICH
Lee Lafayette, C, MSU
Tom Kondla, C, MINN
Mike Weaver, F, NU
Bill Hosket, C, OSU
Herman Gilliam, F, PUR (co)
Bill Keller, G, PUR (co)
Joe Franklin, F, WIS

1969
Dave Scholz, F, ILL
Ken Johnson, F, IND
John Johnson, F, IOWA
Rudy Tomjanovich, C, MICH
Lee Lafayette, C, MSU
Al Nuness, G, MINN
Don Adams, F, NU
Dave Sorenson, C, OSU
Rick Mount, G, PUR
Jim Johnson, F, WIS

1970
Mike Price, G, ILL
Jim Harris, G, IND
John Johnson, F, IOWA
Rudy Tomjanovich, C, MICH
Ralph Simpson, F, MSU
Larry Mikan, C, MINN
Dale Kelley, G, NU (co)
Don Adams, F, NU (co)
Dave Sorenson, C, OSU
Rick Mount, G, PUR
Al Henry, C, WIS

1971
Rick Howat, G, ILL
George McGinnis, F, IND
Fred Brown, G, IOWA
Dan Fife, G, MICH (co)
Henry Wilmore, F, MICH (co)
Bill Kilgore, C, MSU
Jim Brewer, F, MINN
Rick Sund, G, NU
Jim Cleamons, G, OSU
Larry Weatherford, G, PUR
Glenn Richgels, C, WIS

1972
Nick Weatherspoon, F, ILL
Joby Wright, F, IND
Rick Williams, G, IOWA (co)
Kevin Kunnert, C, IOWA (co)
Henry Wilmore, F, G, MICH
Bill Kilgore, C, MSU
Jim Brewer, C, MINN
Paul Douglass, G, NU
Mark Minor, F, OSU
Bob Ford, F, PUR
Leon Howard, F, WIS

1973
Nick Weatherspoon, F, ILL
Steve Downing, C, IND
Kevin Kunnert, C, IOWA
Ken Brady, C, MICH
Bill Kilgore, C, MSU
Jim Brewer, C, MINN
Mark Sibley, G, NU
Allan Hornyak, G, OSU
Frank Kendrick, F, PUR
Leon Howard, F, WIS (co)
Kim Hughes, C, WIS (co)

1974
Rick Schmidt, F, ILL
Steve Green, F, IND
Candy LaPrince, G, IOWA
Campy Russell, F, MICH
Mike Robinson, G, MSU
Peter Gilcud, C, MINN
Bryan Ashbaugh, F, NU
Bill Andreas, F, OSU
Frank Kendrick, F, PUR
Gary Anderson, G, WIS (co)
Kim Hughes, C, WIS (co)

Rick Mount, Purdue

Most Valuable Players (continued)

1975
Rick Schmidt, F, ILL
Quinn Buckner, G, IND (co)
Steve Green, F, IND (co)
Scott May, F, IND (co)
Dan Frost, F, IOWA
C.J. Kupec, C, MICH (co)
Joe Johnson, G, MICH (co)
Lindsay Hairston, C, MSU
Mark Olberding, F, MINN
Bill McKinney, G, NU
Bill Andreas, F, OSU
John Garrett, C, PUR
Dale Koehler, F, WIS

1976
Nate Williams, G, ILL
Scott May, F, IND
Scott Thompson, G, IOWA
Rickey Green, G, MICH
Terry Furlow, F, MSU
Mychal Thompson, C, MINN (co)
Ray Williams, G, MINN (co)
Bill McKinney, G, NU
Craig Taylor, C, OSU
Eugene Parker, G, PUR
Dale Koehler, F, WIS

1977
Audie Matthews, F, ILL
Kent Benson, C, IND
Bruce King, C, IOWA
Phil Hubbard, C, MICH
Bob Chapman, G, MSU
Mychal Thompson, C, MINN
Bill McKinney, G, NU
Larry Bolden, G, OSU
Walter Jordan, F, PUR
Bob Falk, G, WIS

1978
Audie Matthews, F, ILL
Wayne Radford, F, IND
Ronnie Lester, G, IOWA
Joel Thompson, C, MICH
Greg Kelser, F, MSU
Mychal Thompson, C, MINN
Tony Allen, F, NU
Kelvin Ransey, G, OSU
Walter Jordan, F, PUR
Arnold Gaines, G, WIS

1979
Mark Smith, F, ILL
Mike Woodson, F, IND
Ronnie Lester, G, IOWA
Phil Hubbard, C, MICH
Earvin Johnson, G, MSU
Kevin McHale, F, MINN
Bob Klaas, C, NU
Herb Williams, C, OSU
Joe Barry Carroll, C, PUR
Wes Matthews, G, WIS

1980
Eddie Johnson, F, ILL
Mike Woodson, F, IND
Ronnie Lester, G, IOWA
Mike McGee, F, MICH
Jay Vincent, C, MSU
Kevin McHale, C, MINN
Mike Campbell, F, NU
Kelvin Ransey, G, OSU
Joe Barry Carroll, C, PUR
Joe Chrnelich, F, WIS

1981
Eddie Johnson, F, ILL
Ray Tolbert, C, IND
Vince Brookins, G, IOWA
Mike McGee, F, MICH
Jay Vincent, C, MSU
Mark Hall, G, MINN (co)
Trent Tucker, F, MINN (co)
Rod Roberson, G, NU
Herb Williams, C, OSU
Brian Walker, G, PUR
Claude Gregory, F, WIS

1982
Perry Range, G, ILL
Ted Kitchel, F, IND
Kevin Boyle, F, IOWA
Thad Garner, F, MICH
Kevin Smith, G, MSU
Darryl Mitchell, G, MINN
Jim Stack, F, NU
Clark Kellogg, F, OSU
Keith Edmonson, G, PUR
John Bailey, G, WIS

1983
Derek Harper, G, ILL
Randy Wittman, G-F, IND
Bob Hansen, G, IOWA
Eric Turner, G, MICH
Sam Vincent, G, MSU
Randy Breuer, C, MINN
Jim Stack, F, NU
Tony Campbell, F, OSU
Russell Cross, C, PUR
Cory Blackwell, F, WIS

1984
Bruce Douglas, G, ILL (co)
Quinn Richardson, G, ILL (co)
Steve Alford, G, IND
Steve Carfino, G, IOWA
Roy Tarpley, C, MICH
Sam Vincent, G, MSU
Tommy Davis, G, MINN
Art Aaron, F, NU
Tony Campbell, F, OSU
Jim Rowinski, C, PUR (co)
Ricky Hall, G, PUR (co)
Cory Blackwell, F, WIS

1985
Doug Altenberger, G, ILL
Uwe Blab, C, IND (co)
Steve Alford, G, IND (co)
Greg Stokes, C, IOWA
Roy Tarpley, C, MICH
Sam Vincent, G, MSU
Tommy Davis, F, MINN
Andre Goode, F, NU
Ron Stokes, G, OSU
James Bullock, F-C, PUR
Scott Roth, F, WIS

1986
Ken Norman, C, ILL
Steve Alford, G, IND
Andre Banks, G, IOWA
Roy Tarpley, C, MICH
Scott Skiles, G, MSU
John Shasky, C, MINN (co)
Marc Wilson, G, MINN (co)
Shon Morris, C, NU
Brad Sellers, C, OSU
Mack Gadis, G, PUR
Rick Olson, G, WIS

1987
Ken Norman, F, ILL
Steve Alford, G, IND
Kevin Gamble, G, IOWA (co)
Roy Marble, F, IOWA (co)
Gary Grant, G, MICH
Darryl Johnson, G, MSU
Terrence Woods, G, MINN
Shon Morris, F, NU
Dennis Hopson, F, OSU
Doug Lee, F, PUR
J. J. Weber, F, WIS

1988
Kenny Battle, F, ILL (co)
Nick Anderson, F, ILL (co)
Dean Garrett, C IND (co)
Keith Smart, G, IND (co)
Bill Jones, F-G, IOWA (co)
Roy Marble, F, IOWA (co)
B.J. Armstrong, F, IOWA (co)
Gary Grant, G, MICH (co)
Glen Rice, F, MICH (co)
Carlton Valentine, F, MSU (co)
Ken Redfield, F, MSU (co)
Richard Coffey, F, MINN (co)
Willie Burton, F, MINN (co)
Shon Morris, F, NU
Jay Burson, G, OSU
Everette Stephens, G, PUR (co)
Troy Lewis, G, PUR (co)
Trent Jackson, G, WIS

1989
Nick Anderson, F, ILL
Joe Hillman, G, IND
Roy Marble, F, IOWA
B.J. Armstrong, G, IOWA (co)
Ed Horton, F, IOWA (co)
Glen Rice, F, MICH
Steve Smith, G, MSU
Willie Burton, F, MINN
Walker Lambiotte, F, NU
Jay Burson, G, OSU
Tony Jones, G, PUR
Trent Jackson, G, WIS

1990
Kendall Gill, G, ILL
Calbert Cheaney, F, IND
Les Jepsen, C, IOWA
Rumeal Robinson, G, MICH (co)
Terry Mills, C, MICH (co)
Steve Smith, G, MSU
Willie Burton, F, MINN
Walker Lambiotte, F, NU
Perry Carter, C, OSU (co)
Jim Jackson, G, OSU (co)
Stephen Scheffler, C, PUR
Ryan Berning, F, PUR
Tony Jones, G, PUR
Danny Jones, F, WIS

1991
Andy Kpedi, C, ILL (co)
Larry Smith, G, ILL (co)
Calbert Cheaney, G-F, IND
Acie Earl, C, IOWA (co)
James Moses, G, IOWA (co)
Demetrius Calip, G, MICH
Steve Smith, G, MSU
Kevin Lynch, G, MINN
Pat Baldwin, G, NU
Jim Jackson, G-F, OSU
Jimmy Oliver, F, PUR
Patrick Tompkins, F, WIS

1992
Deon Thomas, F-C, ILL
Calbert Cheaney, F, IND
Acie Earl, C, IOWA
Chris Webber, F, MICH (co)
Jalen Rose, G, MICH (co)
Mike Peplowski, C, MSU
Arriel McDonald, G, MINN
Cedric Neloms, F, NU (co)
Kevin Rankin, C-F, NU (co)
Todd Leslie, G, NU (co)
Jim Jackson, G-F, OSU
Woody Austin, G, PUR
Tracy Webster, G, WIS

1993
Deon Thomas, C-F, ILL
Calbert Cheaney, F, IND
Acie Earl, C, IOWA
Chris Webber, F, MICH
Mike Peplowski, C, MSU
Voshon Lenard, G, MINN
Pat Baldwin, G, NU (co)
Cedric Neloms, F, NU (co)
Laurence Funderburke, F, OSU (co)
Jamie Skelton, G, OSU (co)
John Amaechi, C, PSU (co)
DeRon Hayes, F, PSU (co)
Glenn Robinson, F, PUR
Michael Finley, G-F, WIS

1994
Deon Thomas, F-C, ILL
Damon Bailey, G, IND (co)
Alan Henderson, F, IND (co)
James Winters, F, IOWA
Juwan Howard, C, MICH (co)
Jalen Rose, G, MICH (co)
Shawn Respert, G, MSU
Voshon Lenard, G, MINN
Kevin Rankin, C, NU
Lawrence Funderburke, C-F, OSU
John Amaechi, C, PSU
Glenn Robinson, F, PUR
Michael Finley, F, WIS

1995
Shelly Clark, C, ILL
Alan Henderson, F, IND
Jess Settles, F, IOWA
Ray Jackson, G, MICH
Shawn Respert, G, MSU
Voshon Lenard, G, MINN (co)
Townsend Orr, G, MINN (co)
Cedric Neloms, F, NU
Doug Etzler, G, OSU
John Amaechi, C, PSU
Cuonzo Martin, F, PUR
Rashard Griffith, C, WIS

Michigan State's Steve Smith was a three-time Spartan most valuable player and 1990 Big Ten MVP.

HONORS
Academic all-Big Ten *(academic all-America in bold)*

1964
Dick Van Arsdale, INDIANA; Mel Northway, MINNESOTA; Rich Falk, NORTHWESTERN; Mel Garland, Dave Schellhase, PURDUE.

1965
Tal Body, ILLINOIS; **Dick Van Arsdale, Tom Van Arsdale,** INDIANA; Jim Pitts, NORTHWESTERN; **Dave Schellhase,** PURDUE.

1966
Bill Curtis, MICHIGAN STATE; Jim Burns, Jim Pitts, NORTHWESTERN; **Bill Hosket,** OHIO STATE; **Dave Schellhase,** PURDUE.

1967
Jim Dawson, Dave Scholz, ILLINOIS; **Jim Burns,** NORTHWESTERN; Bill Hosket, OHIO STATE; Chuck Nagle, WISCONSIN.

1968
Dave Scholz, ILLINOIS; Rolly McGrath, IOWA; Steve Rymal, MICHIGAN STATE; Dan Davis, NORTHWESTERN; **Bill Hoskett,** OHIO STATE.

1969
Denny Pace, **Dave Scholz,** ILLINOIS; Chad Calabria, IOWA; Larry Overskei, MINNESOTA; Craig Barclay, OHIO STATE.

1970
Rick Howat, ILLINOIS; **Ralph Simpson,** MICHIGAN STATE; Jim Cleamons, OHIO STATE; George Faerber, PURDUE; Clarence Sherrod, WISCONSIN.

1971
Rick Howat, ILLINOIS; John Ritter, INDIANA; Ken Grabinski, Gary Lusk, IOWA; George Faerber, PURDUE.

1972
John Ritter, Frank Wilson, INDIANA; Rick Sund, NORTHWESTERN; **Bob Ford,** PURDUE; Lee Oler, WISCONSIN.

1973
Jeff Dawson, Otho Tucker, ILLINOIS; John Laskowski, **John Ritter,** INDIANA; Rick Sund, NORTHWESTERN.

1974
Rick Schmidt, ILLINOIS; **Steve Green,** John Laskowski, INDIANA; Bryan Ashbaugh, NORTHWESTERN; Gary Anderson, WISCONSIN.

1975
Rick Schmidt, ILLINOIS; **Steve Green,** INDIANA; **Steve Grote,** MICHIGAN; Dan Weston, OHIO STATE; Dick Satterfield, PURDUE.

1976
Otho Tucker, ILLINOIS; **Kent Benson,** INDIANA; Scott Thompson, Cal Wulfsberg, IOWA; **Steve Grote,** MICHIGAN.

1977
Kent Benson, INDIANA; Cal Wulfsberg, IOWA; Steve Grote, Tom Staton, MICHIGAN; Bruce Parkinson, PURDUE.

1978
Wayne Radford, INDIANA; Dave Baxter, MICHIGAN; Terry Donnelly, MICHIGAN STATE; Mike Campbell, NORTHWESTERN; Bill Pearson, WISCONSIN.

1979
Rob Judson, ILLINOIS; Steve Waite, IOWA; Marty Bodnar, MICHIGAN; **Gregory Kelser,** MICHIGAN STATE; Brian Walker, PURDUE.

1980
Rob Judson, ILLINOIS; Steve Waite, IOWA; Marty Bodnar, Paul Heuerman, MICHIGAN; **Mike Campbell,** NORTHWESTERN.

1981
Randy Wittman, INDIANA; Steve Waite, IOWA; Marty Bodnar, Paul Heuerman, MICHIGAN; **Brian Walker,** PURDUE.

1982
Bryan Leonard, ILLINOIS; **Randy Wittman,** INDIANA; Dan Pelekoudas, MICHIGAN; **Keith Edmonson,** PURDUE; Steve Jacobson, WISCONSIN.

1983
Bryan Leonard, ILLINOIS; Uwe Blab, **Randy Wittman,** INDIANA; Dan Pelekoudas, MICHIGAN; Curt Clawson, Steve Reid, PURDUE.

1984
Uwe Blab, INDIANA; Tim McCormick, Dan Pelekoudas, MICHIGAN; Curt Clawson, Steve Reid, Jim Rowinski, PURDUE.

1985
Uwe Blab, INDIANA; Elliot Fullen, John Peterson, NORTHWESTERN; Troy Taylor, OHIO STATE; Steve Reid, PURDUE; Rod Ripley, WISCONSIN.

1986
Butch Wade, MICHIGAN; Joe Flanagan, Elliot Fullen, **Shon Morris,** NORTHWESTERN; Troy Lewis, PURDUE; Rod Ripley, WISCONSIN.

1987
Jens Kujawa, ILLINOIS; Elliot Fullen, **Shon Morris,** NORTHWESTERN; Doug Lee, PURDUE; Rod Ripley, WISCONSIN.

1988
Jens Kujawa, ILLINOIS; Joe Hillman, Magnus Pelkowski, INDIANA; Mike Griffin, MICHIGAN; Kim Zurcher, MINNESOTA; **Shon Morris,** Brian Schwabe, NORTHWESTERN; Anthony White, OHIO STATE; Rob Willey, WISCONSIN.

1989
Joe Hillman, Magnus Pelkowski, INDIANA; Brian Schwabe, NORTHWESTERN; Anthony White, OHIO STATE; Dave Barrett, John Brugos, PURDUE.

1990
P.J. Bowman, ILLINOIS; Brigham Tubbs, IOWA; Mike Griffin, MICHIGAN; Mark Montgomery, Matt Steigenga, MICHIGAN STATE; Walker Lambiotte, Don Polite, Brian Schwabe, NORTHWESTERN; Steven Hall, OHIO STATE; Dave Barrett, Craig Riley, PURDUE; Billy Douglas, WISCONSIN.

1991
Brig Tubbs, IOWA; Sean Dobbins, Rob Pelinka, James Voskuil, MICHIGAN; Mark Montgomery, Mike Peplowski, Matt Steigenga, MICHIGAN STATE; Jake Haunty, Tom Heise, NORTHWESTERN; Steve Hall, OHIO STATE UNIVERSITY; Dave Barrett, Craig Riley, Todd Schoettelkotte, PURDUE; Damon Harrell, Grant Johnson, Jay Peters, WISCONSIN.

1992
James O'Connor, IOWA; Rob Pelinka, James Voskuil, MICHIGAN; Matt Steigenga, MICHIGAN STATE; Aaric Queen, Kevin Rankin, NORTHWESTERN; Steve Hall, OHIO STATE; **Craig Riley,** PURDUE; Damon Harrell, Grant Johnson, Jay Peters, Jeffrey Peterson, WISCONSIN.

1993
Tom Michael, ILLINOIS; Alan Henderson, Chris Reynolds, INDIANA; Sean Dobbins, Rob Pelinka, James Voskuil, MICHIGAN; David Grim, Ernest Nzigamasabo, MINNESOTA; Kevin Rankin, NORTHWESTERN; Douglas Ray Etzler, OHIO STATE; John Amaechi, Greg Bartram, Jon Dietz, PENN STATE; Damon Harrell, Jason Johnsen, Grant Johnson, Jeff Petersen, WISCONSIN.

1994
Tom Michael, ILLINOIS; Todd Lindeman, INDIANA; Nahtan Koch, IOWA; Steve Polnowski, Erik Qualman, MICHIGAN STATE; **Kevin Rankin,** NORTHWESTERN; Douglas Ray Etzler, Nathan Wilbourne, OHIO STATE; Nate Althouse, John Amaechi, Greg Bartram, Steven Wydman, PENN STATE; Tim Ervin, PURDUE; Chris Conger, Grant Johnson, Jeff Petersen, WISCONSIN.

1995
Steve Roth, ILLINOIS; Robert Eggers, Todd Lindeman, INDIANA; Nathan Koch, Jess Settles, IOWA; Steve Nicodemus, Steve Polonowski, Mark Prylow, MICHIGAN STATE; David Grim, Trevor Winter, MINNESOTA; Dan Kreft, NORTHWESTERN; Doug Etzler, OHIO STATE; Nate Althouse, **John Amaechi,** Greg Bartram, Michael Joseph, PENN STATE; Tim Ervin, PURDUE.

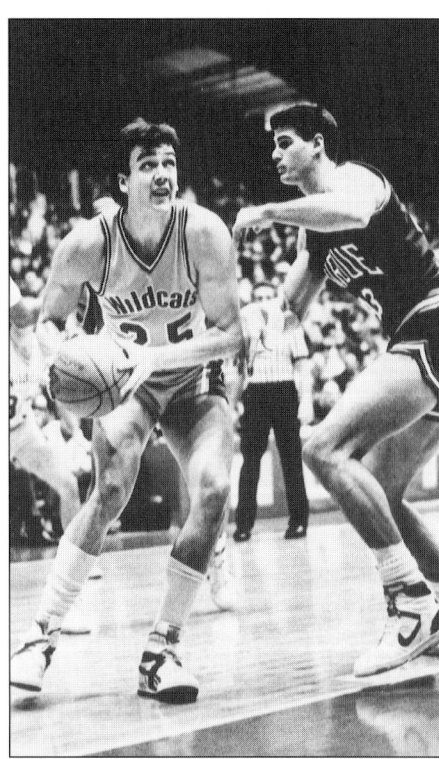

Northwestern forward-center Shon Morris, who was a three-time Wildcat MVP, was also named academic all-America in 1987 and '88.